THE CHARTER
OF RIGHTS
AND FREEDOMS

THE CHARTER OF RIGHTS AND FREEDOMS

30+ YEARS OF DECISIONS THAT SHAPE CANADIAN LIFE

IAN GREENE

James Lorimer & Compay Ltd., Publishers
Toronto

Notice to educators

This book is available for purchase in print and ebook form. Copies can be purchased from our website at www.lorimer.ca. Copies of individual chapters or portions of the full text in print or digital form are also available for sale at reasonable prices. Contact us for details at rights@lorimer.ca.

The publisher and the author of this work expect that portions of this work will be useful for education, and expect reasonable compensation for this use. This can be readily achieved by arranging to purchase these portions from the publisher. Contrary to the view of university administrators and their legal advisors, it is unlikely that use of a chapter or 10% of this work for educational purposes with no payment to the publisher or author would be found to be fair dealing under the Canadian Copyright Act.

James Lorimer & Company Ltd., Publishers acknowledges the support of the Ontario Arts Council. We acknowledge the financial support of the Government of Canada through the Canada Book Fund for our publishing activities. We acknowledge the support of the Canada Council for the Arts which last year invested $24.3 million in writing and publishing throughout Canada. We acknowledge the Government of Ontario through the Ontario Media Development Corporation's Ontario Book Initiative.

Cover image: The Canadian Press/Sean Kilpatrick

Library and Archives Canada Cataloguing in Publication

Greene, Ian, author
    The Charter of Rights and Freedoms : 30+ years of decisions that shape Canadian life / Ian Greene.

Includes bibliographical references and index.
Issued in print and electronic formats.
ISBN 978-1-4594-0661-2 (pbk.).--ISBN 978-1-4594-0662-9 (epub)

    1. Canada. Canadian Charter of Rights and Freedoms. 2. Canada. Canadian Charter of Rights and Freedoms--Cases. 3. Civil rights--Canada--Cases. I. Title.

KE4381.5.G745 2014   342.7108'5   C2014-904331-7
KF4483.C519G745 2014   C2014-904332-5

James Lorimer & Company Ltd., Publishers
317 Adelaide Street West, Suite 1002
Toronto, ON, Canada
M5V 1P9
www.lorimer.ca

Printed and bound in Canada.

To Mom and Dad, and Helen and John,
from whom I have learned that mutual respect is the basis of rights.

CONTENTS

PREFACE

*"The protection of human rights is the final end of govern-
ment and . . . the degree to which human rights are
safeguarded is the final test by which any polity should be
judged."*

— *Donald Smiley*[1]

Most Canadians would likely agree with the above quote from one of
Canada's foremost political scientists of the twentieth century. According
to public opinion polls, however, the great majority of Canadians would
disagree with the main argument in the essay in which the quote appears:
that a constitutional charter of rights is *not* the best way to protect human
rights in Canada.[2]

We have had the *Charter* since 1982. While the question of whether we
should have had a constitutional bill of rights is now irrelevant, other questions have replaced it: Has the *Charter* been a success? What has its impact
been? How might it affect our lives in the future? This book is intended
to provide readers with the raw materials to reach their own conclusions
about these questions.

My first book on the Charter was published in 1989, when I was a relatively young professor at York University being considered for tenure. Now,
in 2014, I am officially retired, which means I have time, once again, to

write about the *Charter*. Like Donald Smiley, I was initially skeptical about whether the *Charter* would do any good. That is because of the unenlightened decisions made by some Canadian judges based on the *Canadian Bill of Rights*, which was enacted in 1960. But unlike the *Bill of Rights*, the *Charter* became part of our constitution in 1982, and therefore the judiciary has interpreted the *Charter* with a focus on truly safeguarding human rights. A second change between the pre-Charter and post-Charter eras is that beginning in the 1980s, a new generation of better-educated lawyers and judges has been respectively arguing cases and deciding cases.[3] My current view is that the *Charter* has so far contributed positively to safeguarding human rights in Canada. Nevertheless, I have tried to provide readers with balanced summaries of the majority and minority opinions in leading Supreme Court of Canada decisions on the *Charter* so that they can decide for themselves, although I have not shied away from presenting my opinion when a decision appears to be particularly helpful or unhelpful.

After more than thirty years of university teaching, I have learned that it is useful to provide my students with information on the backgrounds of the authors I have them read, because these backgrounds provide a platform for students to judge the usefulness of the readings. Therefore, a word about my own background. I grew up in a small Alberta town where I was motivated more by extracurricular activities such as music and politics than by my classes. Nevertheless, I managed to get into the University of Alberta to study political science, and during the summer after my second year was the campaign manager for the winning candidate in Red Deer in the 1968 federal election. That experience was invaluable in learning about the nitty-gritty of practical politics, and it resulted in my interest in promoting higher ethical standards in politics. I got accepted into graduate school and law school, but opted for graduate studies at the University of Toronto instead, where Peter Russell kindled my interest in constitutional law and court management. Between my masters and PhD programs, I worked as assistant to a cabinet minister in the Peter Lougheed government in Alberta during a time of significant human rights reforms. My PhD dissertation research centred on the causes of unnecessary delay in courts. After completing my dissertation in the early 1980s, I spent three years working for Alberta Social Services as a middle manager, as well as teaching part-time at the University of Lethbridge.

At York University since 1985, I have focused on public policy and administration, and specifically public law, ethics in the public sector, and court administration. Since becoming a professor, I have shied away from partisan politics, and my voting preferences depend on candidates and party platforms. My practical experience, both in politics and in public service, has impacted my thinking about human rights and the *Charter*. I see democracy as a continuous work in progress. Public policy is impacted by elected politicians, public opinion, public servants, and court decisions. The optimal mix of all these depends on what contributes most to mutual respect, which I consider the basic principle behind democracy.

A few words about the layout of the book are in order. The original concept of this book was as a second edition of my 1989 book on the Charter;[4] however, because of the vast additions to Charter jurisprudence since 1989, the end product is a new book. Some parts of this book have still incorporated relevant parts of the 1989 book. Chapters 1 and 2 provide a background to understanding Charter decisions. Chapter 1 considers the nature of human rights and civil liberties. It also recounts some human rights issues in Canada prior to the Charter era, including some leading Canadian Bill of Rights decisions. In chapter 2, the events leading to the creation of the *Charter* are summarized, and the links between the *Charter* and other human rights legislation (such as the *Bill of Rights*) are pointed out. Chapter 2 also summarizes the hopes of the *Charter*'s supporters, and the fears of its opponents.

Chapters 3 to 8 comment on specific cases and controversies arising from the *Charter*. Chapter 3 focuses on the section of the *Charter* that encompasses the "fundamental freedoms": freedom of religion, expression, assembly, and association. The Supreme Court's decisions regarding Sunday-closing legislation, the wearing of religious symbols, and the right to strike are discussed, along with decisions on French-only signs laws in Quebec, hate-speech cases, and pornography decisions.

Chapter 4 deals with judicial decisions regarding the "democratic rights" — for example, whether prisoners can vote, whether the *Charter* might force a more equitable distribution of voters between urban and rural ridings, and what constitutes fair regulation election campaigns. The chapter also considers some significant non-Charter democratic rights decisions, such as the *Quebec Secession Reference.*

The Supreme Court's controversial decision to strike down Canada's abortion law is reviewed in chapter 5, which centres on the "legal rights" sections of the *Charter*. Also considered in this chapter are Supreme Court decisions concerning the right to an independent judge, the right to counsel (especially with regard to drunk drivers), police powers of search and seizure, the presumption of innocence, and whether cruise-missile testing violates security of the person. Supreme Court decisions concerning the treatment of terrorist suspects are analyzed. Finally, the application of the right to "security of the person" is considered with regard to prostitutes and those in harm-reduction programs.

Chapter 6 deals with the *Charter*'s "equality rights," perhaps the most challenging section of the document. Beginning in 1989, the Supreme Court set out a test for the application of section 15, modified it in 1999, and revised it once again in 2008. The equality tests have been applied in cases dealing with the question of fetal rights, denominational school rights, social services, women's rights, fathers' rights, retirees' rights, sexual orientation, the rights of the physically challenged, and affirmative action programs.

Chapter 7 reviews the *Charter*'s effect on the status of the official languages of Canada and minority-language education rights. The chapter focuses on Supreme Court decisions that interpret language rights inside and outside of the *Charter*. These cases deal with language rights in Quebec, New Brunswick, Alberta, Manitoba, Saskatchewan, and Nova Scotia, and have had an important impact on minority-language communities across Canada.

Chapter 8 is on Aboriginal rights. Section 35 of the *Constitution Act, 1982* — the section affirming Aboriginal rights — is the first section after the *Charter of Rights*. Although not officially part of the *Charter*, it is as important as the *Charter* itself when considering the "degree to which human rights are safeguarded" in Canada. The Supreme Court has made a number of decisions that have recognized Aboriginal land claims and protected, to some extent, Aboriginal traditional rights. Canadians need to know about these decisions in order to advance the reconciliation process with Aboriginal peoples.

In total, more than seventy about forty Supreme Court of Canada decisions are considered in detail, and mention is made of other significant decisions. The cases chosen are those that seem to best illustrate how the Supreme Court is interpreting the *Charter* and Aboriginal rights. A number of lower-court decisions are also referred to. What the book tries to explain is the reasoning process the judges followed, and the human stories leading to the litigation, so that readers can enter into the debate about the interpretation of rights and freedoms. From this perspective, a fair amount of attention is given to dissenting opinions, since they represent alternative viewpoints. Readers are encouraged to read the judicial decisions for themselves. All of the Supreme Court decisions referred to in this book can be downloaded from the Supreme Court of Canada website.[5]

The concluding chapter assesses the effect of the *Charter* and s. 35 on the general respect for human rights in Canada. It argues that while the *Charter* itself may have had only limited success in promoting mutual respect across the board — which is what rights are all about — its impact has been felt in other ways. It has given hope and respect to some groups of disadvantaged Canadians. It has provided politicians with new challenges in dealing with the rule of law and facing perplexing human rights issues. It has provided new interdisciplinary challenges for lawyers, judges, and expert witnesses in preparing for cases. The *Charter* continues to have a positive potential for helping to promote human rights. I suggest some strategies that may help to nurture this potential and, at the same time, strengthen our democratic institutions.

— Ian Greene, Toronto, September 2014

CHAPTER 1

CIVIL RIGHTS IN CANADA DURING THE PRE-CHARTER ERA

Ronald Dworkin, a well-known legal theorist of the late twentieth and early twenty-first centuries, has described the basis of rights in a liberal society as follows: "We might say that individuals have a right to equal concern and respect in the design and administration of the political institutions that govern them . . . [T]hey possess [this right] not by virtue of birth or characteristic or merit or excellence but simply as human beings with the capacity to make plans and give justice."[1] Four Canadian scholars who conducted research into the thinking of Canadians about human rights concluded that those who are committed to civil liberties show "a generalized commitment to tolerance."[2] As well, these authors argued that a commitment to *individual* rights can coexist with a commitment to the larger community.

Further to these approaches, at the basis of the concept of human rights or civil liberties is the belief that every human being deserves — and owes to others — respect and fair treatment.[3] Human beings deserve these things simply because they are human beings.

This definition of rights consciousness emphasizes that rights are not simply claims individuals can demand with no responsibilities attached.

In order to have rights, rights-bearers themselves have a coincidental responsibility toward others to respect their rights. Some, like Canadian political philosopher C. B. Macpherson, would go further and argue that rights-bearers also have a responsibility to take action to ensure others have the opportunity to exercise their rights; that is, to pursue self-realization.[4]

Controversies about rights often involve the question of whether individuals' personal claims should be given priority over their responsibilities to others. Such issues can rarely be resolved through applying "correct" legal reasoning. Rather, what is involved is human rights policy-making.

CIVIL RIGHTS
RIGHTS AND FREEDOMS

The phrases "human rights" and "civil liberties" are often used interchangeably, as they are in this book. However, a distinction can be made between rights and liberties that helps to shed some light on the content of the more general concept of civil rights.[5]

A "liberty" can be thought of as the ability to do something without constraints imposed or permitted by the state. For example, freedom of expression and freedom of religion can be considered liberties in this sense.

A "right" can be regarded as the consequence of a duty that is placed on an individual or on the state either by law or some higher authority. For example, some of the legal and language rights in the *Charter* can be viewed in this way. They are rights owed to individuals because of duties imposed by law on the state. Section 10(a) of the *Charter* gives the state the duty of informing "promptly" persons who are arrested or detained of "the reasons therefor." As a result of the state's legal duty, everyone has that particular right. Similarly, section 18(1) of the *Charter* provides that Parliament shall print and publish in English and French all "statutes, records, and journals." Because of this duty, Canadians have a right to certain bilingual documents. However, if the legal duty were ever repealed, the right would cease to exist.

According to those who adhere to one of the schools of natural law (for example, Plato, Aristotle, St. Thomas Aquinas, John Locke, and Jean-Jacques Rousseau), a law of nature can impose certain duties on the state regardless of whether these duties are enshrined in a government's laws. The laws of nature that give rise to natural rights may derive from correct reasoning or from a deity. However, according to judicial positivists (like Jeremy Bentham, John Austin, and H. L. A. Hart), only laws made by legislatures can impose duties on governments. The positivists take this position because, among other reasons, the natural law theorists themselves do not agree about the content of the supposed laws of nature.

Approaches to rights based on natural law theories have been more influential among jurists in the United States and the continent of Europe than among jurists in the Anglo-Canadian tradition. Even so, Supreme Court of Canada judges have drawn on the works of natural law theorists such as Dworkin and John Rawls when interpreting the general phrases in the *Charter*.[6]

Whether a person adheres to a positivist or natural law conception of rights may depend to some extent on whether government is viewed as friend or enemy. For some, government in a democracy represents community interests. From this perspective, a government's role in the human rights field is primarily to ensure that optimum conditions exist for citizens to use their rights and freedoms. These people are likely to view rights from a positivist standpoint because government, as an instrument of the people, can generally be trusted to take appropriate action. For others, those who control government — even in a democracy — tend to run it in their own self-interest or for the wrong interests. Thus, government itself is the major threat to human rights, and a legal fence is needed to keep governments within bounds. These people may tend to believe in natural rights.

The fact that the *Charter* refers to both rights and liberties is reflected in its full title — the *Charter of Rights and Freedoms*. Yet it is not always possible to easily distinguish between a right and a liberty. For example, it is not clear whether the right to retain counsel in section 10(b) means a *right* that is a result of a duty imposed on the state to ensure the provision of counsel, or that people who are arrested or detained are at *liberty* to choose a lawyer, or both. As a result, I have not attempted to distinguish in any systematic way between rights and freedoms when describing the *Charter*. Supreme Court judges have, on occasion, referred to this distinction when interpreting the *Charter*, as noted in chapter 7.

The terms "human rights" and "civil liberties" are emotionally charged. Some people feel strongly that they are entitled to certain natural rights, and they become very zealous about protecting them. In addition, there has been a tendency in recent years to frame what were formerly called political demands as human rights claims.[7] For example, we now hear about a student's right to a student loan, non-smokers' rights, or the right of autistic children to expensive government-funded therapy.[8] Donald V. Smiley, one of Canada's foremost political scientists in the late 1900s, has suggested translating the term "right" into "claim upon the state" in order to promote clearer thinking about the appropriateness of such claims without the emotional overtones.[9]

RIGHTS IN LIBERAL DEMOCRACIES

In societies in which mutual respect, self-worth, and fairness are considered important either for religious or secular reasons, these values have been promoted in culturally specific ways. In Western liberal societies, civil rights claims have traditionally involved one or more of three elements:

- Individual citizens should have a wide range of freedom to think and do as they please, subject to some limits intended to prevent harm to others or to promote particular social goals. This element has two implications: first, that governments must refrain from acting so as to restrict freedom unnecessarily, and second, that governments must sometimes act to ensure the protection of freedom. For example, governments must refrain from interfering with religious ceremonies but should act to protect worshippers who are physically or psychologically threatened by their opponents.[10]
- In situations in which it is acceptable either for the state or another citizen to restrict an individual's freedom, certain principles of fairness that are intended to ensure that freedom is not restrained unnecessarily must be followed. For example, those accused of criminal activity are presumed innocent until proven guilty before an independent and impartial judge.
- The same standards of freedom and acceptable restraints should apply equally to everyone unless there is a valid reason why they should not. This is because all people are considered as equally deserving of respect.

A recent example will help to illustrate these elements. Following the dreadful attack on the World Trade Center in New York on September 11, 2001, the federal government enacted legislation which allowed two federal cabinet ministers to issue certificates of inadmissibility that would result in the detention of foreign nationals whom the ministers considered to be a threat to Canadian security.[11] Although these certificates were subject to review by a judge, the subject of a certificate was not entitled to review all of the evidence against him/her and could be deported, possibly to face torture. Between 2003 and 2005, Adil Charkaoui, a permanent resident of Canada, was detained pursuant to a security certificate. Charkaoui and others subject to security certificates challenged the constitutional validity of the legislation, and the challenges reached the Supreme Court in 2007. The Supreme Court held that the security certificate legislation violated the *Charter of Rights* because of all three of the elements listed above.[12] Charkauoi's freedom was unnecessarily restricted, his freedom was restricted in a way that prevented the right to due process, and the legislation singled out foreign nationals and denied them equality before the law.

Another early Charter decision is also instructive. In 1988 the Supreme Court struck down section 251 of the *Criminal Code*, the law that prohibited abortions unless they endangered a woman's life or health and unless they had been approved in advance by a hospital abortion committee.[13] What the Supreme Court decided was that Parliament had restricted abortions in an unjust manner. For example, Chief Justice Brian Dickson noted that a woman who wanted an abortion had to prove that continuing the pregnancy would endanger her life or health, but no definition of health was given in the legislation. This introduced an element of unfairness, as the woman wanting an abortion could not know what standards of proof she would have to meet. Furthermore, five judges criticized section 251 because it condoned unequal access to abortions. As a result of the procedural barriers the law had erected, only 20 per cent of Canadian hospitals could or would perform abortions. Therefore, in many parts of Canada abortions could not be obtained at all. The Supreme Court decision meant that if Parliament wanted to regulate abortions, it would have to do so in a way that respected the guarantees of procedural fairness, or "fundamental justice," in section 7 of the *Charter*.

The Supreme Court's decision about the abortion law illustrates two of the three elements included in the liberal-democratic concept of civil liberties or human rights. With respect to the second element — procedural fairness — the court decided that the limits to a pregnant woman's liberty and security of person must meet specific standards of procedural fairness. In relation to the third element — equality — the court held that the same freedoms, restraints, and standards of procedural fairness should apply to all women in Canada who are contemplating an abortion. (The court did not rely on section 15, the equality rights section of the *Charter*, but on the general notion that rights apply equally to everyone.) The Supreme Court did not consider the issue related to the first civil liberties element — optimal freedom — specifically, whether the Charter rights to liberty and security of the person include a right for pregnant women to decide whether to have abortions. This is because judges usually prefer to decide cases on the narrowest and simplest grounds, and in this case, the procedural question was the easiest to decide. This important decision is discussed in more detail in chapter 5.

In many countries, a controversy over whether women have a right to obtain abortions would not arise. Canada is currently among a minority of countries that proclaim an important place for civil rights in their systems of government. We share this viewpoint with the citizens of other countries that adhere to the liberal-democratic tradition. The liberal democracies tend to place a higher value on civil rights because of the heritage of their religious, ideological, economic, and political traditions, which stress the importance of individual initiative and which regard most people as capable of making prudent decisions about how to use their freedom.

The belief in individualism, which is so much a part of our political culture, is not shared by a great many of the world's governments, even though it may be sought after by many of their citizens. Some governments with a Marxist ideology, for example, claim that the logic of capitalism prevents the owners of capital from making economic decisions that will benefit the entire community. From this perspective, the capitalist economic system compels the owners of capital to exploit labour. Economic freedom for capitalists necessarily results in economic servitude for labour.

In authoritarian states like China or Saudi Arabia, civil liberties are viewed by the government as an impediment to stability and economic growth, just as they were in western European countries prior to the long struggle for rights and freedoms that started during the Enlightenment and progressed into the latter half of the twentieth century.[14] It would appear that a society that protects and promotes rights and freedoms needs to be a mature, well-educated society in which mutual respect is an important value both in theory and practice. Moreover, the long and bloody struggle for rights and freedoms indicates that our thinking about the nature of rights and freedoms evolves as society matures; an example is the legislative and judicial recognition of same-sex marriage in Canada in the early 2000s. As well, it should be noted that without vigilance, rights and freedoms can suffer erosion either through ignorance or fear, as happened to the civil liberties of some Muslim Canadians after the horrific attack on the World Trade Center in 2001.[15]

LIMITS TO RIGHTS

Even in the liberal democracies, there are good reasons why individual freedom is far from absolute, and inequality in treatment is often acceptable. The following are several examples of generally accepted restrictions on liberty, procedural fairness, or equality in Canada:

- Inequality of treatment is practised in numerous cases of relevant differences in ability. For example, it makes sense that only those with excellent grades in relevant subjects should be admitted to medical school. We also tolerate an unequal distribution of wealth, which can contribute to social inequality.[16]
- Freedom of expression does not include the right to disseminate false information. Thus, it is possible to sue for libel, and there are laws against misleading advertising and perjury. In 1990 Alberta high school teacher James Keegstra was convicted of the *Criminal Code* offense of willfully promoting hatred against a recognizable group.[17] Keegstra, a Holocaust denier, taught his students that a Jewish conspiracy was planning to control much of the western world. The court

considered that the prohibition of the promotion of hatred was a reasonable limit to freedom of expression. The government's desire to promote public order gives rise to another set of restrictions. Individuals cannot carry a handgun unless they are police officers or otherwise licensed to do so. Furthermore, civil liberties can be suspended, within limits, to punish or rehabilitate criminal offenders or to keep them from creating additional disorder.

- Emergencies, such as wars, epidemics, or forest fires, sometimes cannot be dealt with effectively unless certain human rights are temporarily curtailed. Canada's federal *Emergencies Act*, which received unanimous consent from the House of Commons in 1988 and replaced the old *War Measures Act*, outlines the situations in which the federal government would consider itself justified in assuming emergency powers.

- The unrestricted practise of some rights results in a violation of other rights. There is perhaps no clearer example of this conflict than the question of national security: To what extent is it justifiable to limit the right to a fair hearing of someone suspected by security intelligence officials of being a terrorist, versus the right of all Canadians to reasonable security? Another example consists of the gag orders judges sometimes place on the publication of information pertinent to a controversial trial. There is a conflict between the accused person's right to a fair trial and the freedom of the media. In such cases of conflict between two incompatible rights, one or both will have to be limited in order for the conflict to be resolved.

- There are numerous restrictions on our freedom so that important public policy goals can be promoted. For example, Canadians are forced to contribute toward the cost of health-care services, whether or not they use them, and doctors are not allowed to extra bill.[18] Our federal and provincial govern-ments claim to support free enterprise but intervene regularly in the marketplace in the name of fair competition, consumer protection, labour peace, and the mitigation of serious financial crises such as the economic meltdown of 2008–09.

- Although we are a relatively tolerant society, accepting a diversity of moral standards, there are nevertheless certain moral prohibitions that restrict our liberty. According to public opinion polls, the majority of Canadians support the laws that restrict exploitative prostitution, hard-core pornographic films and videos, and child pornography.

It is obvious, then, that our commitment to freedom and equality in Canada is not absolute. We value these principles but within what we consider to be reasonable limits. Our beliefs about the balance between rights and limits are the product of our religious, philosophic, economic, and political convictions. If there are diverse opinions about these matters — as there obviously are in Canada — there is bound to be disagreement about the appropriate border between rights and limits.

John Stuart Mill, the nineteenth-century English philosopher, claimed that restrictions on our liberties were justifiable to prevent harm to others. Many of the restrictions noted above could be considered as measures to prevent individuals from harming others.[19] With regard to limits designed to promote public policy goals, however, the harm principle is not always clearly evident. Concerning the legislation on so-called victimless morality issues, the harm principle is the least evident. Nevertheless, it is possible that indulgence in pornography is associated with the tendency to commit various crimes; the scientific evidence is inconclusive. It is also arguable that prostitution encourages relationships of exploitation and subservience, but it is not clear to what extent this harm has a ripple effect beyond the willing participants. Plainly, there is no easy solution to the problem of where to draw the line between rights and limits.

The thinking of Canadians about rights and limits depends on the nature of their rights-consciousness. There are four major sources of rights-consciousness in our society: the liberal political ideology, the emergence of democratic values, the impact of the American *Bill of Rights* on our thinking, and Canada's bilingual and bireligious heritage.

THE ORIGINS OF RIGHTS-CONSCIOUSNESS LIBERALISM

The political philosophy of liberalism, which stresses individual self-determination and equality, developed in the context of a number of events that occurred in Europe several centuries ago. First, the Renaissance, which spread across Europe in the fifteenth century, celebrated with new vigour the dignity of man. Second, the Protestant Reformation of the sixteenth century led to rebellion against the rigidly hierarchical structure of church and state. Luther's theology — that human beings could establish individual relationships with God and that church authorities were not necessary as intermediaries — set the stage for the further development of individualist ideals, especially in an England beset by civil wars in the seventeenth century.

In these wars, the traditional order was pitted against the new ideals of individualism: the traditional hierarchical church against the individualist reformers; the absolute authority of the monarch against the supremacy of Parliament; judicial subservience to the Crown against judicial independence; the economic privilege of the nobility against the rising merchant class. In the Glorious Revolution of 1688, the new order triumphed. The revolution resulted in the supremacy of Parliament, the ideal of the impartial application of the law, new economic freedom for the merchant class, and somewhat greater religious toleration. John Locke, who wrote his *Second Treatise on Government* in 1659, became the chief defender of the new order.

Locke attempted to convince his readers of the inherent rationality of the new political system. He began with the premise that human beings are basically reasonable. If they could wipe the slate of history clean and negotiate a new social contract, they would agree on the need for creating a government. This government would provide the necessary social order so that people could pursue their own individual goals in life. It follows that government must exist only by the consent and for the benefit of the governed.

To give all people an equal chance to pursue their goals, an elected legislature should enact laws that would be equally applicable to all citizens. As Locke put it, the laws are "not to be varied in particular Cases, but [there should be] one Rule for the Rich and Poor, for the Favourite at Court, and the Country Man at Plough." So that the laws could be administered without favouritism, administrative officials and judges should act impartially. In other words, the state would be ruled by equally applicable, impartially administered laws, not by the arbitrary whims of government officials. This principle became known as the rule of law. The preamble to the *Canadian Charter of Rights and Freedoms* proclaims that Canada is founded on "principles that recognize . . . the rule of law."[20]

Locke's political philosophy became known as liberalism. During the eighteenth century, the ideals of liberalism took a firm hold on the property-owning classes in the United Kingdom. Judicial independence — an essential precondition for the rule of law — was guaranteed by an act of Parliament in 1701. Certain human rights, such as freedom of speech, religion, assembly, and association, became accepted as constitutional principles. These principles were respected to the extent that politicians and public servants had the knowledge and integrity to observe them, and to the extent that voters would not re-elect governments that violated them.

The ideals of liberalism had an important influence on the courts in England. Since the twelfth century, if Parliament had not provided a law defining how a dispute should be settled, the courts would settle the dispute according to what the judges believed to be the community standards. The decisions of the higher courts became precedents for the deciding of future cases. The whole body of this judge-made law became known as the common law. With the advent of the ideology of liberalism, the judiciary expanded the common law to reflect liberal ideals.

The most important method the courts developed to protect individual freedom was to pay strict attention to the principle of the rule of law. Pursuant to the rule of law, government officials may act only if authorized to do so by a law enacted by the legislature, and the law is presumed to apply equally to all. A good example of the application of this principle is the case of *Entick v. Carrington*[21] in 1765. A British cabinet minister had signed a search warrant that no law had given him the power to sign. The person who had been searched illegally was successful in suing the Crown for trespass.

Another principle developed through the common law to prevent unnecessary restrictions of a person's liberty when confronted with the power of the state in court was *mens rea* (guilty mind). Pursuant to this doctrine, a court will refuse to convict unless it can be shown that an accused person *intended* to commit the act of which he or she is accused or that the person acted recklessly. Other safeguards developed through the common law include the principle that the Crown must prove its case beyond a reasonable doubt in a criminal prosecution, that confessions will not be accepted by judges unless they are given freely, that an accused person cannot be compelled to testify, and that no one can be forced to incriminate him- or herself. In addition, the courts developed procedures known as prerogative writs, which are court orders intended to help remedy unlawful violations of public liberties by government officials. The best known of these is the writ of *habeas corpus*, which is intended to determine whether a person who has been imprisoned has been dealt with according to law.[22]

These common-law principles and procedures are all reflected in the *Canadian Bill of Rights* and the *Charter of Rights and Freedoms*.

It should be noted that the liberal ideology has a number of variants. There is the rationalist approach characteristic of the Enlightenment and American liberalism, which claims that correct reasoning can accurately describe natural rights. In contrast, there is Burkean liberalism (also known as conservatism), which is skeptical about the ability of human beings to devise correct solutions through the reasoning process and is more inclined to trust the lessons of history. Peter Russell, the founder of the political science study of the law in Canada, claims that Canadian liberalism has more in common with the Burkean tradition.[23] Liberals like Ronald Dworkin stress the respect that each individual is *owed*[24] — and this is particularly true of American liberalism — while Burkean liberals place more weight on the respect that is owed to others and the community as a whole. Patrick Monahan, a former Dean of Osgoode Hall Law School, maintains that Canadian liberalism has a more communitarian flavour than the highly individualistic American liberalism.[25]

THE DEVELOPMENT OF DEMOCRATIC VALUES

After the Glorious Revolution in England, the people who could elect members of the House of Commons were those with newly established economic power — property owners. The franchise remained extremely limited; because of property qualifications, only the wealthiest 5 per cent of the population could vote. As C. B. Macpherson[26] has pointed out, the United Kingdom became liberal long before it became democratic.

Adam Smith became the philosopher of economic liberalism during the eighteenth century, emphasizing the overall benefits that would accrue to society if individuals had as much freedom as possible to pursue their economic goals.[27] The emphasis that liberalism placed on equality — equal access to the marketplace, equal application of the law — eventually caused the disenfranchised propertyless classes to demand equality in the right to vote. Thomas Paine became their spokesperson, and his famous book, *The Rights of Man*, became their rallying cry.[28] Yet the extension of the franchise was slow to be accepted, first in the United Kingdom and then in Canada. This was because of the fear that the poor might use democracy to destroy the upper classes, an apprehension generated by the excesses of both the American and French revolutions.[29]

In Canada, because property qualifications limited the franchise in 1867, and because women, Aboriginal people, and some Asians were disenfranchised, the country at that time could not be considered democratic. But the logic of the liberal ethic of equality proved too strong for the privileged classes to resist, and by 1920 the franchise had been extended to most non-Aboriginal adults in federal and provincial elections, except in Quebec, where women were not granted the right to vote until 1940. Aboriginal Canadians who lived on reserves were not enfranchised until 1960. Some groups were excluded from voting until Charter litigation — or the fear of it — resulted in their enfranchisement: prisoners, the mentally incompetent, and judges. (Judges had previously been prohibited from voting as a mechanism to ensure their impartiality and independence.) It was not until the *Charter* came into effect that the right to vote received recognition in the written constitution. Charter challenges to restrictions on the right to vote are discussed in chapter 4.

Thus, while the right of all adults to vote and to participate in the political life of the country is recognized today as an important human right, it was slow to be accepted.

THE US BILL OF RIGHTS

The American *Declaration of Independence* of 1776 reflected the liberal ideals of individual freedom and equality.

> *We hold these truths to be self-evident, that all men are*
> *created equal, that they are endowed by their Creator with*
> *certain unalienable Rights, that among these are Life, Liberty,*
> *and the pursuit of Happiness. That to secure these rights,*
> *Governments are instituted among Men, deriving their just*
> *powers from the consent of the governed.*

Much of the impetus behind the American Revolution was the idea that an independent America could protect human rights more effectively than had the British colonial administration. The more influential framers of the US Constitution, such as James Madison and Alexander Hamilton, thought that the checks and balances built into the 1787 Constitution, and the fact that many states had their own bills of rights, would be sufficient to protect civil liberties, especially with regard to Congress, which was granted a limited list of powers. However, some state leaders were not as trusting. In order to secure the states' ratification of the Constitution, a bill of rights was added in 1789 consisting of the first ten amendments to the Constitution.[30]

The bill enumerated the civil rights the newly independent Americans were most worried about losing based on the experience of their colonial heritage. It prohibited the US Congress from restricting freedom of speech, of the press, and of assembly, and from adopting an official state religion. It protected certain procedural rights: not to be subjected to unreasonable searches or seizures; not to have to testify against oneself; not to be punished twice for the same offence; not to be deprived of life, liberty, or property except through the due process of law; and not to be subjected to cruel and unusual punishment. It also contained some positive legal rights: to a speedy trial, to a jury in more serious cases, and to reasonable bail. There were rights that might seem odd to us today but were of particular concern to Americans because of abuse suffered at the hands of British soldiers: the right not to provide accommodation to soldiers and the right to bear arms.

Three amendments added after the civil war abolished slavery, extended the guarantee of due process and equal protection to the state jurisdictions, and prohibited racial discrimination concerning the right to vote. Three more amendments added in the twentieth century gave women the right to vote, abolished the poll taxes that some states had been using to disenfranchise blacks, and set a uniform voting age of eighteen years. The history of the American *Bill of Rights* indicates that a society's approach to rights evolves over time.

Most of the human rights the Americans placed in their Constitution had been recognized as unwritten constitutional principles in the United Kingdom during the eighteenth century or had developed as principles of common law to protect the rule of law and individual freedom. Yet the British authorities had been far more careful to ensure that these principles were observed at home than in the colonies. The Americans were therefore not impressed with simply entrusting their rights to unwritten constitutional principles or the common law. Converting these human rights tenets into prose, and then placing them in a written constitution that could not easily be amended, was an experiment in devising a more effective means of protecting rights and liberties. It is a procedure Canada initially rejected but eventually adopted — keeping in mind lessons learned from the US experience with a written bill of rights.

CANADA'S BILINGUAL AND BIRELIGIOUS HERITAGE

The two most important cleavages in the colonies that were to become Canada were language and religion. An agreement to create a new federation could be secured only if there were minimal constitutional guarantees for the linguistic and religious minorities in each of the new provinces and for the francophone minority in federal institutions. The minorities in the provinces overlapped each other, but not perfectly. Although francophones tended to be Roman Catholic and anglophones Protestant, there were also anglophone Catholics in each colony. Thus, the Canadian constitution contains separate guarantees of minority-language rights and minority-religious education rights.

Section 133 of the *British North America Act* (*BNA Act*) — renamed the *Constitution Act, 1867* — states that either English or French may be spoken by anyone in Parliament or the Quebec legislature and that both languages must be used in the records, journals, and enactments of both legislatures. Further, either language may be used in the courts of Quebec or in any courts established by Parliament (today, these are the Supreme Court of Canada, the Federal Court, and the Tax Court). Section 133 was thus intended to protect the anglophone minority in Quebec and the francophone minority in federal institutions. When Manitoba gained provincehood in 1870, after Louis Riel's failed rebellion, Franco-Manitobans were granted similar language guarantees in the *Manitoba Act*. The francophone minority in the Northwestern Territory[31] was provided with similar language rights in a federal statute. These provisions continued in Alberta and Saskatchewan when these provinces were created in 1905, subject to change by the provincial legislatures.

The denominational-school rights are contained in the somewhat complex section 93 of the *BNA Act*. Section 93 gives the provincial legislatures the power to make laws in relation to education, except that no law can "prejudicially affect any Right or Privilege with respect to Denominational Schools which any Class of Persons" had in a province when it was admitted to Canada. If a province attempts to reduce the denominational-school rights of a religious minority, those affected can appeal to the federal government, not only to request protection of rights granted at the time of entry into Canada, but also to request the protection of rights granted since that time. If the government decides that the grievance is legitimate, then the federal Parliament may enact legislation to remedy the situation. Parliament's power to enact remedial legislation has never been used, although in 1896 the federal Conservative government drafted remedial legislation to protect Roman Catholic schools in Manitoba. An election intervened, however, and it was won by the Liberals. The new prime minister, Wilfrid Laurier, negotiated a settlement with the Manitoba government instead of amending the legislation.

The language- and denominational-school rights in the *BNA Act* have been called a "small bill of rights" by Peter Hogg.[32] They were so important to the creation of Canada that they were the only substantive rights written into our original constitution. The Fathers of Confederation did not regard this small bill of rights as a bill of rights in the American sense, but simply as a practical necessity to bring about the union of the British North American colonies. The constitutional rights in Canada resulted more from duties owed by governments as a result of political compromises than from the idea that there are natural liberties with which governments cannot interfere. The US *Bill of Rights* concentrated more on rights in the latter sense.

In fact, Canada's political elite was very much opposed to the concept of an American-style bill of rights. The Fathers of Confederation preferred the parliamentary form of government that had evolved in the United Kingdom. One of the working principles behind the parliamentary system is legislative supremacy, and this principle has overshadowed the entire debate about how civil liberties should be protected in Canada. Fears about losing legislative supremacy hampered judicial enforcement of the civil liberties principles before 1960. With one exception, the Supreme Court's view of legislative supremacy also prevented the judiciary from striking down statutes that conflicted with the *Canadian Bill of Rights*. The same principle continues to trouble the Supreme Court in its search for an acceptable interpretation of the *Charter*. For these reasons, it is necessary to take a closer look at the concept.

LEGISLATIVE SUPREMACY

At first glance, legislative supremacy may seem like a straightforward legal concept that has no obvious connection with civil liberties. After the Glorious Revolution of 1688, it was accepted that the legislative branch of government could determine the powers of the other two branches: the executive (which became known as the cabinet and the public service) and the judiciary. Canada inherited the principle of legislative supremacy pursuant to the preamble of the *BNA Act*, which stated that Canada would have a constitution "similar in principle to that of the United Kingdom."

Legislative supremacy could not apply to Canada in exactly the same way as it applied to the UK for three reasons. First, because Canada was a federal country, there was no single legislature that was "supreme." Instead, each legislature, federal or provincial, was supreme within its own jurisdiction. Second, because Canada was, until 1931, subservient to the British government with regard to external relations, no legislature in Canada was supreme in this field.[33] Third, because the *British North America Act* did not contain a constitutional amending formula, the British Parliament, until 1982, had legal responsibility for amending Canada's constitution. (After 1867, however, the British Parliament amended it only according to the wishes of the relevant Canadian authorities.) In sum, legislative supremacy in Canada meant simply that the federal and provincial legislatures, within the bounds of their jurisdictions, could determine the powers of the other two branches and of subordinate administrative bodies.

The usefulness of the principle of legislative supremacy in a legal sense is that it provides judges with a guide for ranking legal rules. If a judge encounters a conflict between a statute and a cabinet order, or between a statute and the common law, the statute takes precedence in both cases because legislatures, which create statutes, are superior to cabinets and the judiciary. If there is a conflict between two statutes, the more recent one takes precedence because a current legislature is legally supreme at any given time. Clearly, judges need rules to assist them in distinguishing between valid and invalid laws, and legislative supremacy is helpful in this regard.

The principle of legislative supremacy, however, took on an aura far in excess of these straightforward implications. From the late eighteenth century until the advent of the *Charter*, legislative supremacy was thought to have almost sacrosanct properties. Canadian judges between 1960 and 1982 were reluctant to give priority to the *Canadian Bill of Rights* over other statutes because they feared that in doing so they would negate legislative supremacy. In large measure, this expansion of the principle was the result of the writings of the late-nineteenth-century British constitutional lawyer A. V. Dicey. In 1885 Dicey published a comprehensive analysis of the British constitution entitled *Introduction to the Study of the Law of the Constitution*.[34] The book has had an enormous impact on the thinking of British and Canadian lawyers and judges. Dicey declared that legislative supremacy was "the dominant characteristic of [British] political institutions."

Dicey wrote at a time when notions of British political and cultural superiority were in the ascendant, and a major purpose of his analysis seems to have been to prove the excellence of British constitutional principles compared to those of other world powers such as France, Germany, and the United States. Dicey praised legislative supremacy for its promotion of popular sovereignty — the legislative branch, controlled by the (property-owning) people, is supreme — for enabling governments to react quickly to crises, and for facilitating flexible constitutional adaptation to changing circumstances. Contrasting the virtues of legislative supremacy with some of the problems that he identified with the US Constitution, he pointed out that the US Constitution was so difficult to amend that it could be considered practically unamendable. (Amendments require the assent of three-quarters of the state legislatures — all of which, with one exception, are bicameral — and two-thirds of each house of Congress.) Thus, instead of having popular sovereignty in any real sense, Americans lived under a regime of constitutional supremacy. Because judges decide the meaning of the Constitution, constitutional supremacy really meant judicial supremacy. Dicey also claimed that the US Constitution limits the ability of governments to respond to crises and prevents adaptation to changing times.

The process judges follow when they compare lower-status laws with higher-status ones (laws with constitutional status), with a view to striking down lower-status laws that are incompatible with higher ones, is known as "judicial review on constitutional grounds." Dicey considered that judicial review of legislative enactments on constitutional grounds cannot coexist with legislative supremacy. He thought that one of the legal implications of legislative supremacy — that a legislature must be considered free to change previous legislation — should be broadened to become a *political* principle of the constitution — that a legislature cannot set limits on itself, even limits it can amend. This Diceyan thinking had a predominant impact on the way in which Canadian courts approached the *Canadian Bill of Rights*. But even before the *Bill of Rights*, Canadian judges were often reluctant to tamper with government decisions affecting human rights.

CIVIL LIBERTIES CASES PRIOR TO THE *CANADIAN BILL OF RIGHTS*

The record of the courts in protecting civil liberties during the first nine decades after Confederation is mixed. As a rule, judges felt that because of legislative supremacy, they had no power to stop violations of human rights unless the law that caused the violation offended the federal division of powers. In 1899 the Judicial Committee of the Privy Council in London (which served as Canada's highest appeal court until 1949) struck down a British Columbia law that prohibited anyone of Chinese origin from working in mines.[35] The committee found that this provincial law interfered with federal jurisdiction over "naturalization and aliens." In 1902, however, the Judicial Committee upheld British Columbia legislation that denied the vote to Canadians of Asiatic origin as being within the proper bounds of provincial jurisdiction.[36] This legislation remained in effect until after the Second World War. The Judicial Committee commented, in accord with the principle of legislative supremacy, that the judges could not consider "the policy or impolicy of such enactment."

Some judges believed that the liberal ideal of equality applied to all private facilities that had a government licence. As an illustration, in 1899 a black man successfully sued a Montreal theatre in the Quebec Superior Court for refusing to allow him and his female companion to occupy the better seats in the house.[37] This approach did not win many fans among the judges, however. In 1921 the Quebec Court of Appeal found that racial segregation in theatres was acceptable as an exercise of the private rights of theatre owners.[38] In 1924, the Supreme Court of Ontario dismissed a suit by a black man against a restaurant owner who would not serve blacks.[39] Similarly, in 1939 the Supreme Court of Canada dismissed a suit by a black man who was refused service in the tavern at the Montreal Forum. The majority on the court stated that "[a]ny merchant is free to deal as he may choose with any individual member of the public," unless a specific law creates restrictions.[40]

In 1914 the Supreme Court upheld Saskatchewan legislation that forbade those of Chinese origin to employ white women. The chief justice actually applauded the legislation for protecting the "bodily health [and] morals" of white women.[41] During this era, federal immigration laws made it almost impossible for Chinese women to enter Canada; these laws remained in place until the 1950s.[42]

It was not until 1930 that women were recognized as legal persons. In 1928 the Supreme Court was asked whether the word "persons" in section 24 of the *BNA Act* — the section that defined eligibility for Senate appointments — included women. The Supreme Court gave the standard legal answer up to that time: no. The appeal to the Judicial Committee produced a different result.[43] The Judicial Committee likened the Canadian constitution, the *BNA Act*, to a "living tree" that should be interpreted in the light of changing social circumstances. The committee noted that attitudes toward the position of women had changed, and that the Constitution should take this into account. It declared that women should now be included in the term "persons" in section 24.

Beginning in the 1930s, some judges attempted to establish a new route to protect civil liberties claims, over and above the established rules of common law. This approach was rooted in the preamble to the *BNA Act*. The preamble to the 1867 constitution states that the provinces forming the new country "[d]esire to be federally united . . . with a Constitution similar in Principle to that of the United Kingdom." These words imply that the civil liberties principles that had developed in the UK before 1867 (being part of that country's unwritten constitution) became an essential feature of our constitution. The question arises, however, whether legislative enactments that violate the human rights principles developed in the UK are subject to judicial review in this country.

The Supreme Court of Canada was faced with this question in 1938. The previous year, the Social Credit legislature in Alberta enacted a package of legislation that was intended to put Social Credit theory into effect to bring the province out of the Depression. The federal government referred the legislation to the Supreme Court of Canada. (The *Supreme Court Act* permits the federal government to send "references," which are often questions about the constitutionality of legislation, directly to the Supreme Court.)

The package of legislation referred to the court included the *Accurate News and Information Act*,[44] better known as the *Alberta Press Bill*. This legislation gave a board composed of five Social Credit backbenchers (the Social Credit Board) the power to prohibit the publication of a newspaper, force a newspaper to print corrections of articles the board considered inaccurate, and prohibit newspapers from publishing articles written by certain blacklisted individuals. The reason that the bill was included with the Social Credit legislation was that the government thought that the monetary reforms would work only if the people *believed* in them. Leading Alberta newspapers had ridiculed Social Credit theory, thus diminishing the theory's credibility.

The court unanimously found the *Alberta Press Bill ultra vires* (beyond the powers of the legislature).[45] It viewed the bill as closely connected to other Social Credit bills it had declared *ultra vires* because they invaded the central government's jurisdiction over banking, interest, and legal tender. Three judges, led by Chief Justice Lyman Duff, saw the *Alberta Press Bill* as so contrary to the constitutional principle of freedom of the press that they felt compelled to give additional reasons.

Duff based his civil liberties argument on two points. First, as noted earlier, the preamble to the *BNA Act* has the effect of implanting in Canada the civil liberties principles of the UK, which included freedom of the press and freedom of speech. Although Duff did not explicitly refer to the preamble, he did so implicitly by stating that "Under the British system which is ours, no political party can erect a prohibitory barrier to prevent the electors from getting information concerning the policy of the government." Second, because the *BNA Act* stipulates that the House of Commons must be elected and that its members must represent the provinces proportionately according to their populations, the House is a "representative" body. Both of these features mean that the constitution "contemplates a parliament working under the influence of public opinion and public discussion . . . [I]t is axiomatic that the practice of this right of free public discussion of public affairs, notwithstanding its incidental mischiefs, is the breath of life for parliamentary institutions." In other words, freedom of the press is essential to democracy. (The almost-universal adult franchise achieved by 1937 gave somewhat more weight to Duff's argument than it would have had in 1867.)

I will refer to this reasoning as the Duff Doctrine. Had it ever been adopted by the majority of the Supreme Court, it is possible there might have been less public demand for a charter of rights and freedoms because the Duff Doctrine would have been there to protect rights. Duff's approach raised issues the court was never able to resolve, and thus a majority never endorsed it until the Charter era. The most important of these issues is the question of whether Duff's approach can be squared with legislative supremacy.

If Canada did have a legally enforceable implied bill of rights, then what had been constitutional principle in the UK, as enforced through the political process, would become part of a rigid constitution in Canada, as enforced by judges. This judicial enforcement of civil liberties could limit the powers of legislatures and would call legislative supremacy into question. Moreover, because the implied bill of rights would consist of abstract principles and judicial decisions about these abstractions, it would be even less clear than a written bill of rights. As a result, legislative powers would not only be limited, but limited in a very imprecise fashion. Judges understandably were reluctant to impose such a major change on the Canadian political system.

Neither the implied bill of rights nor any of the other procedures the courts had developed to protect civil liberties were of much use to Japanese Canadians during and immediately after the Second World War. In one case, a 1945 deportation order issued against British subjects of Japanese origin was upheld by the Judicial Committee.[46] (In the United States, the judiciary allowed the detention of Japanese Americans in spite of the *Bill of Rights*.) The total suspension of human rights for Canadians of Japanese origin, the confiscation of their property, and their forced internment during the war marked one of the low points for civil liberties in Canada. Although Prime Minister Mackenzie King had personal doubts about the necessity for this treatment of Canada's Japanese citizens, he realized that the majority of Canadians were suspicious and distrustful of the Japanese Canadians and wanted tough action.[47] The measures taken may have been carried out more to boost the morale of the average Canadian for the war effort than for security reasons.

Another major civil liberties issue prominent around the same time concerned the Gouzenko affair. In September of 1945, Igor Gouzenko, a Soviet cipher clerk, defected and provided Canadian authorities with a list of Soviet spies in Canada. As a result, at least sixteen people were arrested and held incommunicado. The usual procedural rights were suspended under the authority of the *War Measures Act*, and in-camera hearings were held before a royal commission headed by two Supreme Court justices, Roy Lindsay Kellock and Robert Taschereau, in 1946.[48] Detainees and many witnesses were not allowed to consult counsel and were not informed that their testimony might be used as evidence against them. When these abuses became public knowledge in 1946, many concluded that the government had unnecessarily restricted basic legal rights. The civil liberties section of the Canadian Bar Association viewed such measures as "totally unacceptable in peacetime and a threat to Canadian democracy and the rule of law."[49] Nevertheless, following the Royal Commission's 1946 reports, a number of suspects were prosecuted either for violating the *Official Secrets Act* or conspiracy to do so, and eleven were convicted and sentenced to jail terms of between two to six years. Evidence from the notorious Royal Commission was used to secure their convictions.[50]

The Supreme Court did succeed to some extent in protecting civil liberties in Quebec during the infamous and repressive era of Premier Maurice Duplessis. During the 1950s, the court was challenged by seven cases in which individuals claimed their civil rights had been unfairly restricted. In all of these cases, the Supreme Court decided in favour of the civil liberties claim and against the submissions of the Quebec government.

Three cases are particularly interesting. The *Saumur* case involved a Jehovah's Witness who had been distributing literature on the streets of Quebec City.[51] Both provincial and municipal authorities had been active in restricting the activities of the Jehovah's Witnesses, whose doctrine was highly insulting to the Roman Catholic Church. The Quebec City council had enacted a bylaw, ostensibly to keep the streets free of litter, which prohibited the distribution of literature on sidewalks without a permit from the chief of police. The chief, of course, would give permits to people other than Jehovah's Witnesses. Saumur appealed his conviction under the bylaw all the way to the Supreme Court. He claimed that his freedom of religion and of speech, as protected by Canada's implied bill of rights pursuant to the Duff Doctrine, had been violated. The Supreme Court struck down the Quebec City bylaw in a five to four decision, but the majority could not agree on their reasons. Two judges cited the Duff Doctrine, interpreting it to include freedom of religion as well as freedom of speech and the press, while two others claimed that only the federal Parliament could restrict freedom of religion under its criminal-law power. A fifth judge found that the bylaw conflicted with a provincial statute that protected freedom of worship.

In 1937 the Quebec legislature enacted a law, commonly known as the padlock law, which allowed the police to lock up any premises that were used to distribute information on communism. A tenant named John Switzman had been distributing Communist literature from his apartment in 1949, and he was duly locked out of his home as a result. His landlady, Freda Elbling, sued for cancellation of the lease. Switzman claimed that the padlock law was *ultra vires*, both because of the Duff Doctrine and because it trenched on the federal criminal power. Eight years after Switzman was locked out of his home, the Supreme Court struck down the padlock law on the grounds that it violated the federal Parliament's criminal jurisdiction. Five of the eight judges in the majority relied on the criminal power argument. Only three judges invoked the Duff Doctrine in their reasoning.[52]

Because of the many instances of harassment of Jehovah's Witnesses by Quebec authorities in the 1940s, the Witnesses were frequently in court and often had to post bail to stay out of jail until their trials. A wealthy Montreal restaurateur by the name of Frank Roncarelli frequently posted bail for the Witnesses, much to the annoyance of the authorities. Premier Duplessis tried to bring Roncarelli to heel by ordering the cancellation of his liquor licence. Frank Scott, a well-known civil liberties lawyer and professor, represented Roncarelli in his suit to regain the licence. Scott argued that Duplessis had violated the rule of law in that the premier had no statutory authority to order the cancellation of Roncarelli's licence. Moreover, by singling out Roncarelli, the premier had acted in an arbitrary fashion, thus violating the principle of the equal application of the law. The Supreme Court agreed, but the case was not decided until 1959, too late for Roncarelli to regain his licence.[53]

The Duplessis era, along with the early Social Credit period in Alberta, the early civil liberties abuses in BC and Saskatchewan, legalized discrimination against blacks, and the treatment of Japanese Canadians during the Second World War had taught important lessons about civil liberties. Legislatures, cabinets, and the majority of voters, it was clear, could not always be trusted to enforce human rights. As well, the mechanisms developed by the common-law courts to protect civil liberties, while spectacularly effective in a case like *Roncarelli*, were not as effective as might have been hoped. Finally, the Duff Doctrine of an implied bill of rights seemed incapable of winning the support of the majority of the Supreme Court.

THE *CANADIAN BILL OF RIGHTS* ERA

John Diefenbaker (Progressive Conservative prime minister of Canada from 1957 to 1963) was a prairie populist who was concerned about the potential that the rapidly expanding federal and provincial bureaucracies had for limiting individual freedoms and procedural safeguards. That concern, coupled with an abhorrence of racial discrimination, convinced him that Canada needed a bill of rights. He also realized the potential that a Canadian bill of rights could have for promoting the concept of "one Canada." According to Diefenbaker, the bill could become a symbol that would transcend regional identities and apply to "all, including the poor, the dispossessed, the ignored, and the shut-out."

Diefenbaker was familiar with the *Saskatchewan Bill of Rights*, which had been enacted by the provincial CCF (Co-operative Commonwealth Federation) government in 1947. The Saskatchewan bill was the first written bill of rights to be enacted in any Canadian jurisdiction. It applied only within the province, and it contained no enforcement mechanism. There was very little litigation concerning the Saskatchewan bill, in part because lawyers were not used to a bill of rights and were therefore uncomfortable with pursuing claims under its authority. However, the bill was popular with voters and did have educational value.

The *Saskatchewan Bill of Rights* was enacted during CCF Premier Tommy Douglas's first term in office. As a teenager, Douglas had witnessed police brutality during the 1919 Winnipeg General Strike and against protesters in Saskatchewan in the 1930s, and so he was not content with the traditional common-law safeguards for human rights that Canada relied on.[54] During the Second World War, a consensus developed among the Allied powers that in order to prevent future gross violations of human rights, a new international organization was needed, one of whose purposes would be the promotion and protection of human rights. Douglas not only agreed with this strategy but was able to secure the passage of the *Saskatchewan Bill of Rights* eighteen months before the United Nations adopted the *Universal Declaration of Human Rights* in 1948.[55] It is noteworthy that the primary drafter of the *Universal Declaration of Human Rights* was a Canadian, John Peters Humphrey,[56] who later advised Pierre Trudeau regarding the wording of the *Canadian Charter of Rights and Freedoms*.[57]

There is evidence from Diefenbaker's own writing that he preferred a Canadian bill of rights that would have a superior status over other laws. In other words, the bill would be entrenched into the constitution through an amendment to the *BNA Act*. The *BNA Act*, as a British imperial statute, took priority over the enactments of federal and provincial legislatures.

Diefenbaker was unable to obtain the broad consent of the provincial governments that was needed for such an amendment. He therefore settled for a bill of rights that was just an ordinary enactment of Parliament. As such, it lacked the constitutional authority of the *BNA Act*. Moreover, it could apply only to matters under the jurisdiction of the federal government.[58] Nevertheless, Diefenbaker and his party thought they had created a bill of rights the courts could use to nullify federal legislation that conflicted with it.

The *Bill of Rights* is relatively simple in its format. Its central provisions cover only one and a half pages. This compares with seven equivalent pages for the *Canadian Charter of Rights and Freedoms*.

Section 1 of the *Bill* declares that several rights and freedoms "have existed and shall continue to exist." They include the following: the right to life, liberty, security of the person and enjoyment of property, unless deprived thereof "by due process of law"; the right to "equality before the law and the protection of the law"; and the freedoms of religion, speech, assembly, association, and the press. These rights and freedoms are "to exist without discrimination by reason of race, national origin, colour, religion, or sex."

Section 2 protects a number of rights that Canadians have when confronted with the legal-judicial system. These rights are based on the procedures developed by judges through the common law to protect civil liberties. They include the right not to be arbitrarily detained, imprisoned, or subjected to cruel and unusual treatment or punishment. Moreover, no one can be arrested or detained without knowing the reason, and detainees have a right to retain a lawyer "without delay." Section 2 affirms the *habeas corpus* remedy. Furthermore, it states that individuals cannot be forced to give evidence without their lawyer being present or to give evidence that would incriminate them.

Section 2 also confirms the right to "a fair hearing in accordance with the principles of fundamental justice for the determination of . . . rights and obligations, the right to be presumed innocent until proven guilty in a fair and public hearing by an independent and impartial tribunal, the right to reasonable bail, and the right to an interpreter."

Section 2 of the *Bill* contains a controversial notwithstanding clause, which reads as follows: "Every law of Canada shall, unless it is expressly declared . . . that it shall operate notwithstanding the *Canadian Bill of Rights*, be so construed and applied as not to abrogate . . . any of the rights or freedoms herein recognized." Some may wonder what use a bill of rights is if Parliament can override it through a notwithstanding clause. Yet, upon closer examination, the clause provides some benefits. For one thing, it clearly indicates that the *Bill* was intended to take priority over other ordinary statutes. If the *Bill* was not intended to be superior to other statutes that contradicted it, there would be no need for the notwithstanding clause. It must also be kept in mind that if Parliament utilizes the notwithstanding clause, it is not necessarily overriding a right in the abstract but rather the Supreme Court's *interpretation* of a right. As the court decisions discussed below will show, since judicial reasoning about rights can sometimes leave much to be desired, an escape clause for legislatures can be more than justified on this ground alone.

The major legal hurdle involving the new *Bill of Rights* was how, in a system with legislative supremacy, an ordinary statute like the *Bill* could take precedence over other ordinary statutes, particularly those enacted after it. According to legislative supremacy, a current legislature is always supreme and cannot be prevented from amending laws by the enactments of a previous legislature. Diefenbaker and his supporters were never clear on how this difficulty could be overcome. They seemed simply to have faith that judges would somehow find a solution.

Canadian judges did not find the solution to the apparent constraints of legislative supremacy. In a 1985 Charter case, Mr. Justice Gerald Le Dain commented on the reason the Supreme Court had failed to give the *Bill of Rights* the broad and liberal interpretation it gave to the *Charter*.

> [A] court cannot, in my respectful opinion, avoid bearing
> in mind an evident fact of Canadian judicial history, which

> *must be squarely and frankly faced: that on the whole, with*
> *some notable exceptions, the courts have felt some uncertainty*
> *or ambivalence in the application of the Canadian Bill of*
> *Rights because it did not reflect a clear constitutional mandate*
> *to make judicial decisions having the effect of limiting or*
> *qualifying the traditional sovereignty of Parliament.*[59]

The Supreme Court's first major decision on the *Canadian Bill of Rights, Robertson and Rosetanni v. The Queen,*[60] was one of those decisions in which the court demonstrated the uncertainty or ambivalence referred to by Le Dain. The issue was whether the federal *Lord's Day Act* violated the guarantee of freedom of religion in the *Bill*. Robertson and Rosetanni operated a bowling alley in Hamilton and kept it open on Sundays in violation of the *Act*. They argued that the guarantee of freedom of religion in the *Bill of Rights* should take priority over the *Lord's Day Act*. Their position was that the *Act* violated freedom of religion because it forced them to comply with a religious practice — the observance of a religious holy day — against their will.

A panel of five judges heard the case, and Mr. Justice Roland Ritchie wrote the opinion for the majority of four. Ritchie contended that the *Bill* was not intended to protect rights and freedoms in the abstract but rather rights and freedoms as they existed in 1960. He referred to section 1 of the *Bill*, which states that the rights in the *Bill* "have existed and shall continue to exist." (This phrase had been added to allay the perception that the *Bill* was giving Canadians *new* rights that had not previously existed in convention or the common law.) He argued that the *Bill* therefore referred to freedom of religion as it existed in Canada in 1960.

Ritchie concluded that freedom of religion in 1960 implied an absence of disabilities. In other words, governments should not *prevent* people from participating in their preferred religious practices, but they are free to *promote* certain religious practices. The *Lord's Day Act*, he claimed, merely promoted the observance of the Christian holy day. It did not prevent members of other religions from practising their own religions — it simply resulted in a minor inconvenience for them. According to Ritchie, "the practical result of this law on those whose religion requires them to observe a day of rest other than Sunday is a purely secular and financial one in that they are required to refrain from carrying on or conducting their business on Sunday as well as on their own day of rest."

Ritchie acknowledged that the *Lord's Day Act* had a clearly religious purpose. He claimed, however, that in determining an infringement of freedom of religion, it was the effect rather than the purpose of the legislation that counted. For Ritchie, the effect of the act was purely secular. It merely established a weekly holiday. (In a 1985 Charter case known as *Big M*[61] the Supreme Court rejected Ritchie's interpretation of freedom of religion. This case is reviewed in chapter 3.)

This narrow interpretation of the *Bill of Rights* allowed the court's majority to avoid the appearance of interfering with legislative supremacy. Mr. Justice John Cartwright dissented, however, claiming that the *Lord's Day Act* plainly violated the *Bill*. He disagreed with Ritchie that the purpose of legislation is irrelevant in determining an infraction of freedom of religion. "[T]he purpose and the effect of the *Lord's Day Act* are to compel under the penal sanctions of the criminal law, the observance of Sunday as a religious holy day by all the inhabitants of Canada . . . In my opinion a law which compels a course of conduct, whether positive or negative, for a purely religious purpose infringes the freedom of religion."

Cartwright was also of the opinion that the *Bill of Rights* authorized judges to strike down laws that violated rights. Some lower-court judges and academics had argued that the *Bill* should be treated as a mere aid to interpretation in order to protect legislative supremacy. If the *Bill* were treated as an aid to interpretation, or a "rule of construction," it would mean that judges would apply the *Bill* only in cases where it was unclear whether Parliament had intended a particular law to violate a right. In cases where a law clearly violated a right, the *Bill* would be of no use. Cartwright disagreed with this rule-of-construction approach. He pointed to the notwithstanding clause in the *Bill* and contended that if Parliament had intended it to be simply a rule of construction, the notwithstanding clause would have been unnecessary.

The only case prior to 1982 in which the Supreme Court applied the *Bill* in such a way that a discriminatory statute became inoperative — the most famous of the notable exceptions referred to by Le Dain — was the *Drybones* decision.[62] During the seven years between *Robertson and Rosetanni* and *Drybones*, the Supreme Court had been subjected to a great deal of criticism from civil libertarians, who saw the judges as slaves to the theory of legislative supremacy. Whether because of sensitivity to this criticism or for some other reason, the majority in the *Drybones* decision applied the *Bill* so as to render inoperative a section of the *Indian Act*. The section in question created a liquor offence that applied specifically to Indians and created harsher penalties than the equivalent offence for the general public.

Ritchie, who wrote the majority decision, found that the *Indian Act* resulted in racial discrimination, since it denied Drybones equality before the law as guaranteed by the *Bill of Rights*. In explaining why the *Bill* gave the court the power to declare the discriminatory section of the *Indian Act* inoperative, he followed the same line of reasoning that Cartwright had used in *Robertson and Rosetanni* to hold that the *Bill* was more than a rule of construction. Ritchie summarized his judgment with the following words: "[In] a nation in which, under the laws of Canada, it is made an offence punishable at law on account of race for a person to do something which all Canadians who are not members of that race, may do with impunity," that person has been denied equality before the law. It is ironic that in the *Drybones* decision, Mr. Justice Cartwright dissented. He declared that his decision in *Robertson and Rosetanni* had been wrong. He now concluded that it would be dangerous for the courts to usurp the legislature's role by striking down statutes that conflict with the *Bill of Rights*.

Within a few years, the majority on the court came around to an approach approximating that of Cartwright's dissent in *Drybones*. In the *Lavell* and *Bédard* decisions of 1974, the court again adopted the *Robertson and Rosetanni* style of interpreting the *Bill* so as to avoid declaring statutes inoperative.[63] The issue was whether section 12 of the *Indian Act*, which defines a status Indian and at that time treated Indian men more favourably than Indian women, violated the *Bill*. Section 12 declared that if an Indian woman married a non-Indian, she automatically forfeited her Indian status. However, if an Indian man married a non-Indian, he not only retained his Indian status, but his wife gained Indian status as well.

The cases were brought forward by two Indian women who had married non-Indians, thereby losing their Indian status. They claimed section 12 discriminated against them on the basis of sex and that therefore they had been denied equality before the law.

This time the judges were split five to four, with the majority finding no violation of sexual equality. Once again, Mr. Justice Ritchie wrote opinion for the majority. Ritchie identified the central issue in the case as the meaning of the phrase "equality before the law" in the *Bill of Rights*. The influence of Dicey in deciding this issue is evident.

> [E]quality before the law as recognized by Dicey as a segment
> of the rule of law, carries the meaning of equal subjection
> of all classes to the ordinary law of the land . . . and in my
> opinion the phrase "equality before the law" as employed in
> section 1(b) of the Bill of Rights is to be treated as meaning
> equality in the administration or application of the law by the
> law enforcement authorities and the ordinary courts of the
> land . . . The fundamental distinction between the present
> case and that of Drybones, however, appears to me to be that
> the impugned section in [Drybones] could not be enforced
> without denying equality of treatment in the administration
> and enforcement of the law before the ordinary courts of the
> land to a racial group, whereas no such inequality of treatment
> between Indian men and women flows as a necessary result of
> the application of s.12 (1)(b) of the Indian Act.

Legal experts have been puzzling over this passage since it was written. Perhaps Ritchie was drawing attention to the fact that nothing *compels* Indian women to marry non-Indians, let alone to marry at all, so discrimination based on sex is not a necessary result of section 12. However, the general consensus among legal commentators is that Ritchie did not convincingly distinguish between the discrimination in *Drybones* and that in *Lavell* and *Bédard*. Mr. Justice Bora Laskin, who had been appointed to the Supreme Court in 1971, wrote in his dissenting opinion that "unless we are to depart from what was said in *Drybones*," Lavell and Bédard were discriminated against contrary to the *Bill*. It seems likely that the court had buckled under the strain of continued worry over the possible abandonment of legislative supremacy.

After *Lavell* and *Bédard,* the Supreme Court continued to find no inconsistency between the *Bill of Rights* and discriminatory provisions in federal legislation. A good example of this is the *Bliss* case, in which the court considered whether the provisions of the *Unemployment Insurance Act* that related to pregnant women violated the *Bill of Rights.*[64] In the 1970s the *Unemployment Insurance Act* stipulated a longer qualifying period for unemployment insurance benefits for pregnant women than for others to ensure that no pregnant woman could claim unemployment insurance benefits unless she was already working when she became pregnant. The majority on the Supreme Court could find no discrimination based on sex in these provisions; rather, the discrimination was based on pregnancy (notwithstanding that, barring new developments in medical science, only women can be pregnant).

OTHER CIVIL LIBERTIES CASES

Not only did the Supreme Court interpret the *Canadian Bill of Rights* narrowly during this period, it also tended to dismiss civil liberties claims that arose outside of the *Bill.* It should be noted that the *Bill* applied only to federal laws and administrative activities. Therefore, civil liberties claims that did not challenge a federal law or administrative action tended to rely on the twin claims of the Duff Doctrine: that Canada inherited the conventional civil liberties of the United Kingdom in a judicially enforceable form and that freedom of expression is the "life and breath" of a democracy.

One such case arose in British Columbia in the early 1960s. In 1960 the Social Credit government of Premier W. A. C. Bennett was seriously threatened by the New Democratic Party (NDP) in a provincial election. Alarmed at gains made by the NDP, the right-wing Social Credit party determined to weaken the position of the NDP. The government realized that the NDP received most of its financial support from contributions by unions and that most unions received their funds from compulsory deductions from workers' paychecks (known as the union check-off). In 1961 the Social Credit legislature enacted a law forbidding unions to donate money to any political party — federal or provincial — if that money had been collected through the union check-off procedure.

However, no similar ban was placed on business donations to political parties. This move effectively cut off the NDP's funding, while the Social Credit party's funding was left intact.

The issue of the validity of the BC labour legislation came to the Supreme Court of Canada in 1963 in the *Oil, Chemical and Atomic Workers Union* case.[65] The unions argued that the legislation violated the Duff Doctrine, since it prevented freedom of expression. In other words, funds were needed to fight an election campaign, and unless unions could spend their funds in the same way that businesses could during an election, they would be effectively muzzled.

The majority on the Supreme Court panel, four of seven judges, not only upheld the BC legislation, but praised it for protecting the right of workers not to have to contribute indirectly to a political campaign. The three dissenting judges, however, applied the Duff Doctrine. One of these judges, Mr. Justice Cartwright, noted that since unions in BC received 99.8 per cent of their funds from the union check-off, the new labour legislation had the practical effect of preventing unions from participating in political campaigns. (The issue of whether unions may contribute funds to political parties has led to several Charter cases. Most notable is the *Lavigne* case, in which Merv Lavigne, a college teacher, sought a declaration that union political contributions financed through the check-off violate freedom of association as protected by the *Charter*.[66] Lavigne lost in the Ontario Court of Appeal and also in the Supreme Court of Canada — an outcome quite different from the Oil, Chemical and Atomic Workers Union decision of 1963.)

Another civil liberties case involved the Hutterites. During the Second World War, there was a great deal of resentment against the communities of Hutterites in Alberta. The Hutterites (a Christian sect formed during the Reformation), being pacifist, refused to join the Canadian armed forces. They believe in communal living and operate a number of communal farms in Alberta. In response to public pressure, Alberta's Social Credit legislature enacted the *Communal Property Act*, which restricted the growth of the Hutterite communities. This discriminatory legislation was upheld by the Supreme Court in 1969 as a valid exercise of provincial jurisdiction over property.[67] The legislation was eventually repealed by the Progressive

Conservative legislature in 1972 because it violated the spirit of the *Alberta Bill of Rights*, enacted in 1971.

Then there was the case of the journalist who in the 1970s challenged the constitutional validity of Nova Scotia's film censorship law.[68] The provincial censorship board had banned *Last Tango in Paris*, which the journalist wanted to see. When the case reached the Supreme Court of Canada in 1978, the court's majority upheld the censorship laws as coming within provincial jurisdiction over "matters of a merely local or private nature" (section 92[16] of the *Constitution Act, 1867*). (Under the *Charter*, provincial film censorship laws will survive a court challenge only if the government can demonstrate that they are reasonable limits to freedom of expression.)

The last major case in which the Supreme Court considered the Duff Doctrine before the Charter era was a case involving the right to hold a demonstration. In November 1969 the Montreal City council passed a bylaw permitting the executive committee of the city to ban all public demonstrations for thirty-day periods. Shortly after the bylaw was passed, the executive committee issued an ordinance prohibiting demonstrations for a month. This was a time of frequent demonstrations in Montreal — by students for changes in the universities, by supporters of Quebec independence, and by protesters against the war in Vietnam. There had been about one hundred demonstrations in the first nine months of the year. The police were seriously concerned about terrorists taking advantage of police preoccupation with demonstrations. With the police busy watching the crowds, it would be easier for a terrorist to slip a bomb into a mailbox or a public building.

The validity of the bylaw was challenged in court by Claire Dupond, and the case eventually made its way to the Supreme Court of Canada in 1978.[69] Dupond argued that the bylaw offended the Duff Doctrine because it restricted freedom of speech. Demonstrations were considered to be "speech in action." Civil rights promoters throughout the Western world had learned that in order to increase public awareness of human rights, it was important to get media attention, and demonstrations were a very effective way of doing this. Demonstrations could also provide a rough indication of the level of public support for the demonstrators' ideas.

Mr. Justice Jean Beetz wrote the opinion for the majority. He not only rejected all of Dupond's arguments but dismissed the claim based on the Duff Doctrine with a vigour that disturbed many civil liberties advocates in Canada. He wrote that "none of the freedoms referred to is so enshrined in the constitution as to be above the reach of competent legislation." As Peter Russell has commented, this decision appeared "to be virtually the final nail in the coffin of [the Duff Doctrine's contention that there are] constitutional limits on provincial laws affecting fundamental rights and freedoms."[70]

Furthermore, Beetz scoffed at the idea that demonstrations could be considered speech in action.

> *Freedoms of speech, of assembly and association, of the press,*
> *and of religion are distinct and independent of the faculty of*
> *holding assemblies, parades, gatherings, demonstrations, or*
> *processions on the public domain of a city . . . Demonstrations*
> *are not a form of speech but of collective action.*

Mr. Justice Laskin wrote a strongly worded dissent, which was concurred with by Justices Spence and Dickson.

> *Here [in the Montreal bylaw], persons who might seek to*
> *associate or gather for innocent purposes are to be barred . . .*
> *because of a desire to forestall the violent or the likely violent.*
> *This is the invocation of a doctrine which should alarm*
> *free citizens even if it were invoked and applied under the*
> *authority of the Parliament of Canada.*

Surprisingly, the reasonable presumption that the Duff Doctrine died in the *Dupond* decision has turned out to be highly exaggerated. In the case of *OPSEU v. A.-G. for Ontario*[71] (a 1987 case discussed in chapter 4), the Duff Doctrine was resurrected — by Mr. Justice Beetz. But in 1978 few would have predicted such an event.

JUDICIAL PROTECTION OF CIVIL LIBERTIES TO 1982

It is clear that by the late 1970s the Supreme Court had adopted the view that if a particular law violated a human right, it was the responsibility of the appropriate legislature, not the courts, to amend that law. Most of the judges of our highest court did not wish to become involved in the determination of difficult civil liberties issues — issues they considered as more fittingly resolved by legislatures. As a result, the judges were reluctant to take steps that might weaken the political principle of legislative supremacy. As well as these practical considerations, they may also have considered that legislative supremacy was such a basic principle of our constitution that it ought not to be tampered with except through constitutional amendment.

So faithful was the Supreme Court to the Diceyan view of legislative supremacy that a widely accepted alternative to Dicey's view was never mentioned by the judges. This is the "manner and form" approach to the interpretation of bills of rights. According to proponents of this view,[72] a bill of rights represents a change in the procedure legislatures follow in creating laws. Such procedures are known as manner and form requirements — for example, subjecting proposed legislation to three votes, or readings, in the legislature. Considered as a change to manner and form requirements, a bill of rights indicates that in addition to voting on a proposal three times, legislators will have to decide whether each statute they enact should be subjected to judicial review under the bill of rights. If they decide that the bill of rights *should* apply to a particular piece of legislation, then they merely enact the legislation. If they decide that the bill of rights *should not* apply, then they indicate this decision by declaring that the new legislation will operate notwithstanding the bill of rights.

If the court had adopted the manner and form approach, it could have given effect to the *Bill* without abandoning allegiance to legislative supremacy. And the long-term consequences may well have been significant. A major impetus for a constitutional charter of rights came from those who were disappointed with how the Supreme Court had interpreted the *Bill of Rights*. For them, the only solution was the replacement of the legislative supremacy of the era of the *Bill of Rights* with a constitutional-supremacy approach under an entrenched charter of rights. Had the Supreme Court given effect to the *Bill*, the pressure for a constitutional charter of rights would have been considerably less and the 1982 constitutional reforms might have taken an a different form.

In spite of the approaches the judges were taking to the *Canadian Bill of Rights*, statutory human rights legislation proliferated. This is because bills of rights tend to be popular with the voters, most of whom have little idea of how the bills are interpreted by the courts. In 1971 Peter Lougheed, then leader of the Opposition in Alberta, promised voters during the provincial election campaign that, if he became premier, the first task of the new Alberta legislature would be the enactment of an Alberta bill of rights. Lougheed won an upset victory, and the *Alberta Bill of Rights* became law in 1972.

In the early 1970s the image of the government of Quebec premier Robert Bourassa was tarnished by the human rights violations that occurred during the October Crisis. To counter its negative image, the government introduced the Quebec *Charter of Human Rights and Freedoms* into the legislature. The *Charter* was enacted in 1975. But the strategy of appealing to the electorate with human rights legislation did not succeed for Bourassa, whose government was defeated by the Parti Québécois (PQ) in 1976.

By 1975, there were four statutory bills of rights in Canada — three provincial bills (in Saskatchewan, Alberta, and Quebec) and the *Canadian Bill of Rights*. However, these bills were generally not taken very seriously by the legal community and little litigation arose from them.

The four bills of rights applied to relations between governments and citizens. They were meant to protect private citizens from potential human rights violations by a government. They had no effect on human rights abuses in the private sector — for example, discrimination in employment, housing, or restaurants. In order to combat such private discrimination, the Ontario legislature enacted a human rights code in 1962. Unlike the four bills of rights discussed above, the Ontario *Human Rights Code* was administered by a human rights commission. The commission would investigate complaints of discrimination, and where complaints were well-founded, it would attempt to negotiate a settlement. Because the commission would take a violation of the *Human Rights Code* to court only as a last resort, very little reliance was placed on the judiciary for enforcement of the code.

All of the other provinces eventually followed Ontario's example, and in 1977 the federal Parliament enacted the *Canadian Human Rights Act* to control private discrimination within federally regulated workplaces. The human rights commissions have successfully dealt with numerous examples of unjust discrimination, and from this perspective they have been successful. On the other hand, they can act only if they receive complaints, and consequently a great many cases of private discrimination are left unresolved.

The creation of the *Canadian Charter of Rights and Freedoms* has not diminished the importance of the human rights codes in combatting private discrimination, because like the four statutory bills of rights, the *Charter* applies only to violations of civil liberties by governments. The *Charter* duplicates most of the provisions of the statutory bills of rights. Those parts of the statutory bills that have not been duplicated by the *Charter*, however, are still in effect. There are two sections in the *Canadian Bill of Rights* not duplicated by the *Charter*: the right to the enjoyment of property (section 1[a]) and the right to a fair hearing in accordance with the principles of fundamental justice for the determination of rights and obligations (section 2[e]).

It is ironic that since 1982 the Supreme Court seems to have overcome its reluctance to enforce the statutory bills of rights. In fact, the statutory bills of rights, and also the human rights codes, have been labelled "quasi-constitutional" by the Supreme Court. In conjunction with the *Charter*, they have become important mechanisms for promoting human rights in Canada.

OVERVIEW

Human rights are about mutual respect. How a political system can best protect human rights depends on variables specific to the time and the culture. The liberal democracies have attempted to promote rights through emphasizing individual liberty, procedural safeguards, and equality of treatment. Canada's particular approach has been moulded by a somewhat greater stress on the responsibility aspect of rights than is the case in countries that put a higher value on the individualistic aspect of rights, and by the heritage of political compromises that created language rights and minority-language education rights.

Canada's record of promoting human rights has been mixed. The history of human rights in Canada can be divided into three periods, each reflecting the different sets of mechanisms used to protect rights. During the first period, from Confederation to 1960, legislatures had primary responsibility for safeguarding the human rights principles inherited from the United Kingdom. The judiciary also played a role through its responsibility for upholding the common-law principles that had developed to protect rights. Neither the judiciary nor the legislatures had an unblemished record during this time, but neither did they have an exceptionally bad record compared with other liberal democracies. The second period began with the advent of the *Canadian Bill of Rights*. Courts were invited by legislatures to take on more responsibility for settling controversial human rights issues, but the invitation was rejected. The third period began in 1982 with the *Charter of Rights and Freedoms*, the topic of the next chapter.

CHAPTER 2

THE *CHARTER*

The circumstances that led to the adoption of the *Charter of Rights and Freedoms* in 1982 help explain the form the document finally took. These events have also provided the setting for some of the more recent controversies about the *Charter*, such as whether the provision allowing legislatures to override parts of the *Charter* should be removed, or whether the *Charter* has given judges power to decide policy issues in a counter-democratic fashion.

Someone who knew little of Canada's most pressing political issues in the early 1980s might be forgiven for assuming that the *Charter* was a reaction to human rights abuses, or the imminent threat of such abuses. Although the Supreme Court's narrow interpretation of the *Bill of Rights* encouraged some pro–civil liberties activists to campaign for an entrenched charter of rights, human rights violations — or the fear of them — did not constitute a major issue in Canada during the ten or fifteen years before 1982. A possible exception was the October Crisis of 1970, when the arbitrary powers provided by the *War Measures Act* were abused by some authorities. Most Canadians, however, supported the government's tough stance against terrorists. Moreover, the man who decided to invoke the *War Measures Act,*

Pierre Trudeau, was the same person who championed the cause of the *Charter*. Public pressure to protect civil liberties can therefore explain only part of the drive for an entrenched bill of rights.

Rainer Knopff and F. L. Morton, prominent Charter analysts at the University of Calgary, have argued that the goal of entrenching a charter of rights was a key ingredient in the federal government's nation-building strategy from 1967 to 1982. That strategy had three major elements:

- to create the conditions that would encourage a stronger national identity to counteract the forces of provincialism;
- to patriate the constitution (end the role of the UK Parliament in the constitutional amendment process and provide for an entirely Canadian amending procedure); and
- to extend language rights and to create new mobility rights so that Canadians would feel at home in any province and would not be deterred from moving within the country.[1]

From this perspective, it was hoped that the proposed charter would become an instrument of national unity. An entrenched bill of rights that applied across the country would lead, it was expected, to a national discourse about human rights. New national coalitions and identities would be created that would transcend and weaken the forces of regionalism and provincialism.

A major problem faced by the government was that Canadians were not very concerned about the patriation issue. As well, the subject of language rights was divisive. Neither the patriation nor the language rights goals were likely to succeed if they were promoted on their own. The federal strategy was to join the proposed charter and patriation in an inseparable package and to include language rights in the broader list of rights and freedoms. Alan Cairns, a prominent Canadian political scientist, has argued that the strategy not only worked, but an unexpected side effect was that the advent of the *Charter* energized and mobilized a number of groups that had not previously been as deeply involved in Canadian politics, such as new Canadians, Aboriginal Canadians, seniors, visible minorities, and women.[2]

THE ROAD TO THE *CHARTER*

This strategy, however ingenious, could not have worked without the perseverance of someone as determined as Pierre Trudeau. In addition to realizing the strategic value of the proposed charter, Trudeau believed in it for its own sake. This may be because he had first-hand experience with the civil liberties abuses of the Duplessis regime. He had been a vocal critic of the Union Nationale government, and as a result, government supporters had pressured universities not to hire him as a law professor.[3] By the late 1950s, Trudeau became convinced that a constitutional bill of rights was needed to supplement the protection of human rights through constitutional conventions, the common law, and ordinary statutory bills of rights.[4]

As the federal minister of justice, Trudeau had promoted a constitutional charter of rights in a 1968 policy paper, "A Canadian Charter of Human Rights." In the same year, Prime Minister Lester B. Pearson called the first of what became a series of federal-provincial conferences to consider a constitutional bill of rights and a method of patriating the constitution. The 1968 conference failed to produce an agreement, and in 1970 the federal government established a special committee of Parliament (the Molgat-MacGuigan Committee) to consider constitutional reform. The committee received 1,700 briefs or representations, many of them recommending that the proposed charter of rights include protection for groups, with particular grievances, that were often ignored by politicians — groups such as persons with disabilities, women, seniors, and the poor. This marked the beginning of a new trend in thinking about human rights in Canada: once the public became formally involved in the Charter project, many claims previously thought of as political demands — such as the abolition of compulsory retirement, adequate welfare payments, access to public buildings for persons with disabilities, and affirmative action programs for women — were transformed into human rights claims.[5] The committee rejected most of the demands of these traditionally marginalized groups, but the hearings gave these groups experience in navigating the political process that would prove valuable a decade later.

In 1971 the first ministers reached an agreement, known as the Victoria Charter, to patriate the constitution and at the same time entrench a charter of rights. The agreement failed to take effect, however, because of objections from Quebec and Alberta. The Quebec cabinet would not endorse the agreement without additional guarantees of cultural sovereignty. In Alberta a provincial election produced a change in government. The new premier, Peter Lougheed, was opposed to the proposed constitutional amending formula in the Victoria Charter because by giving a *de facto* veto power only to Ontario, Quebec, and British Columbia, it made Alberta and the other six provinces "second class."[6]

After this setback, the momentum for constitutional change slowed down considerably. The success of the Parti Québécois in winning the Quebec election of 1976 became a further obstacle to constitutional reform. Although there were several constitutional reform initiatives during the next few years, it was not until the defeat of the sovereignty-association concept in the 1980 Quebec referendum that there was again a serious opportunity for constitutional reform. In the meantime, Canada's accession to the *International Covenant on Civil and Political Rights* and the *International Covenant on Economic, Social, and Cultural Rights* in 1976 helped supporters of a constitutional bill of rights keep the idea alive.

During the Quebec referendum campaign, Trudeau promised Quebeckers that if they voted "non" to sovereignty-association, they could look forward to a renewed federalism. After the 60 to 40 per cent victory of the "non" to separation side, he set out to fulfill this promise by reviving his government's nation-building strategy: the patriation of the constitution and the creation of a constitutional charter of rights and freedoms.

A First Ministers' Conference was called for September 1980. The constitutional conference ended with no agreement, and the federal government announced a plan for unilateral patriation of the constitution. The plan was that the Canadian Parliament would request the UK Parliament place an amending formula in the constitution (the 1971 Victoria Charter formula would be used), as well as the *Charter of Rights,* and then abdicate all future responsibilities for changing the Canadian constitution. The federal government claimed that it could accomplish this feat without provincial support because of the conventions that had developed governing constitutional amendment. The federal argument was that when a constitutional change had been required in the past, the federal Parliament alone would request the amendment, and the amendment would automatically be enacted by the London Parliament. The *BNA Act* had been amended twenty-two times since 1867, and no provincial legislature had ever officially participated in the process.[7]

This claim was only part of the truth. Of the twenty-two amendments, only five had affected provincial powers. In each of these five cases, provincial premiers or cabinets in the provinces affected had approved the amendments. Thus, there was a well-founded claim that a convention of provincial consent existed regarding constitutional amendments that affected the provinces.

Trudeau nevertheless denied that provincial consent was a convention, and he determined to push on with unilateral patriation. The patriation resolution, including the proposed charter, was sent to a special committee of Parliament for consideration. The committee held televised public hearings and received almost one thousand submissions. The hearings, as expected, demonstrated widespread public support for the proposed *Charter*. Prominent among the witnesses before the committee were representatives of many of the traditionally marginalized groups whose representations had failed to produce the desired results during the Molgat-MacGuigan hearings in 1971. But this time, circumstances favoured these groups.

The government needed all the support it could muster to counteract the eight premiers (all except those of Ontario and New Brunswick) who opposed unilateral patriation. Early in 1981 the government accepted a series of proposals to expand the provisions of the *Charter*. The equality rights section (section 15) was broadened according to the recommendations of feminist groups and a special guarantee of gender equality (section 28) was added. The equality rights section was also expanded to prohibit discrimination based on mental or physical disability. And two sections were added, one inside the *Charter* (section 25), and one outside, a provision affirming existing Aboriginal rights (section 35). Public response to these proposals was very positive, thus strengthening the government's drive for unilateral patriation.

Meanwhile, the eight provincial governments opposed to unilateral patriation and the *Charter* launched a counteroffensive. These governments had a variety of reasons for opposing the package, including reservations about the Victoria Charter amending formula (which gave a *de facto* veto to Ontario, Quebec, and BC but not to other provinces), and doubts about the proposed charter of rights. In April 1981 the eight premiers, including René Lévesque, agreed to support an alternative amending formula. The so-called Vancouver Consensus formula would require the agreement of Parliament and of seven out of ten provincial legislatures representing 50 per cent of the population of the provinces for most future constitutional changes. The inspiration behind this proposal was Peter Meekison, the former chair of the department of political science at the University of Alberta, who became deputy minister of Alberta's intergovernmental affairs department. Alberta had opposed the Victoria Charter amending formula because it privileged Ontario and Quebec in a federation in which Peter Lougheed believed that all provinces were equal. Meekison had been charged with finding an alternative amending formula that respected the principle of the equality of provinces. Meekison's proposal, first unveiled in Vancouver, became known as the Vancouver Consensus.

One may well ask why Quebec supported the Vancouver Consensus, given that this formula abandoned Quebec's traditional demand for a veto over constitutional amendments. The answer may be that René Lévesque, having known Trudeau for many years, concluded that he was not likely to compromise about his insistence on the Victoria Charter formula, and so Quebec's loss of the veto was a remote possibility. In the post-referendum climate, Lévesque was no doubt trying to present himself as someone trying his best to work within the federalist structure, flawed though he believed it to be, and he quite likely expected that the obstinacy of Trudeau over the amending formula debate would prove once and for all that federalism was doomed to failure. For Lévesque, there was no harm in supporting the Vancouver Consensus and possibly some political capital to be gained.

Other premiers feared that an entrenched charter would not have the positive impact its supporters cheerfully assumed. For example, Saskatchewan's NDP premier, Allan Blakeney, feared that wealthy corporations would pursue litigation under an entrenched charter to limit government social programs and the powers of labour unions. Because judges tend to come from backgrounds sympathetic to business interests, he predicted that such litigation would have a reasonable chance of succeeding.

Three of the eight provinces opposed to unilateral patriation, Newfoundland, Quebec, and Manitoba, launched legal challenges by sending reference questions to their provincial courts of appeal. The "gang of eight" that opposed Trudeau's package carefully chose these courts based on the premiers' perceptions about which courts were most likely to rule in their favour.[8] The courts were asked whether a convention of provincial consent existed and whether such a convention could prevent the Canadian Parliament from proceeding.

The results of the constitutional reference in the three provincial courts of appeal were inconclusive. The courts in Manitoba and Quebec held that provincial consent was not a legal requirement, but the Newfoundland court held that it was, although there were dissenting opinions in all three courts. These decisions were appealed to the Supreme Court of Canada, which announced its decision in late September 1981. The decision was so important that, for the first time in Canadian history, television cameras were allowed in the courtroom to record the historic verdict. Unfortunately, one of the judges tripped over a cable and disconnected the main microphone so that the chief justice's announcement was barely audible. Hearing the announcement, however, would probably not have improved the understanding of the decision for a great many people. The court decided that a convention of "substantial provincial consent" did exist, but it added that conventions cannot be enforced by the courts because constitutional conventions represent unwritten laws that are enforced by the political process, not by courts. In other words, while no court-recognized legal rules could stop Parliament from proceeding with the unilateral patriation project, this action would nevertheless break a constitutional convention.[9] By tradition, voters are expected to defeat governments that operate counter to important constitutional conventions, where such action appears to erode democracy.

The Supreme Court's decision, which produced no clear winners in the dispute between eight provinces and the federal government, forced the two sides back to the bargaining table. The first ministers met again on November 2, 1981. On the morning of November 5 an agreement was announced to patriate the constitution with the Vancouver Consensus amending formula and with a constitutional charter of rights.[10] All of the first ministers agreed to the package except for René Lévesque. Politically, it would probably have been impossible for a separatist premier to agree to such a renewal of the Canadian constitution. Technically, however, the agreement was close to what Lévesque had already endorsed when he was convinced that Trudeau would never accept the position of the eight provinces that supported the Vancouver Consensus.

The agreement of November 5 included compromises on both sides. Although Trudeau preferred the Victoria Charter amending formula, he agreed to a modified version of the Vancouver Consensus formula. (The Vancouver Consensus formula would be used to amend the *Charter of Rights* and the division of powers, but up to three provinces could opt out of some kinds of amendments. If an amendment transferred provincial powers to Ottawa, provinces that opted out would be compensated financially to continue to offer services for the area they'd opted out of. As well, there would be three less onerous procedures for amending parts of the constitution not needing wide agreement. A few very controversial subjects — such as the amending formula itself — would need unanimous consent for amendment.) In return, the eight provinces agreed to a constitutional charter of rights, but only if the *Charter* contained a clause permitting federal and provincial legislatures to enact specific statutes that would override the *Charter*. (It was thought that this override procedure would provide a counterbalance to unacceptable or unworkable judicial interpretations about the meaning of the *Charter*.) Trudeau agreed to the override clause on the condition that every specific use of it would expire automatically after five years and that the clause would not apply to democratic rights, mobility rights, language rights, and minority-language education rights. This solution, which enabled legislatures temporarily to exclude judicial review based on sections 2 and 7–15 of the *Charter*, became that document's infamous legislative override clause, or section 33.

As noted earlier, the federal-provincial compromise of November 5 appeared to satisfy most of the points in Lévesque's bargaining position. One of Quebec's demands which was not met, however, concerned the section of the *Charter* dealing with minority-language education rights (section 23). One of the effects of this provision was that anglophones who had been educated in English anywhere in Canada would have the right to have their children educated in English in Quebec (this was known as the "Canada clause"). Lévesque had wanted the rights of an English education in Quebec restricted to children of parents who had been educated in English in Quebec. (This provision was already contained in Quebec's *Charter of the French Language* [Bill 101] and was known as the "Quebec clause.") Furthermore, the *Charter* would extend the right to English education in Quebec to children whose parents' mother tongue was English, even if they did not qualify under the Canada clause (the "mother tongue clause"). Lévesque was opposed to this provision as well. In order to try to weaken Quebec opposition to the patriation/Charter project, a provision was added so that the mother tongue clause would not apply to Quebec until approved by the Quebec National Assembly.

After the November 5 agreement, final preparations were made for the patriation of the Canadian constitution. With the consent of nine provinces, the federal Parliament passed a resolution with all-party support that requested the UK Parliament to amend the Canadian constitution one last time. The Westminster Parliament's *Canada Act, 1982* added the *Constitution Act, 1982* to Canada's constitution and changed the name of the *BNA Act* (which remains an integral part of the constitution) to the *Constitution Act, 1867*. The *Constitution Act, 1982* contains the *Charter of Rights and Freedoms* and the Vancouver Consensus amending formula. The Quebec government sent a reference question to its court of appeal asking whether the "substantial provincial consent" convention that the Canadian Supreme Court had declared was the old amending convention meant that the consent of Quebec was mandatory. Before the Quebec Court of Appeal could decide the case, the Westminster Parliament had enacted the *Canada Act*. On April 17, 1982, the queen signed the *Canada Act* in a ceremony on Parliament Hill. The era of the *Charter of Rights and Freedoms* had begun.

Later, both the Quebec Court of Appeal and the Supreme Court of Canada ruled that substantial provincial consent did not make Quebec's consent mandatory. Although this interpretation of the convention is questionable, from a political perspective the courts probably had no choice. Legally, the UK Parliament had already changed Canada's constitution for the final time. Future change would have to occur entirely in Canada.[11] Thus, the *Charter* and the new amending formula applied in law to Quebec, although many Quebeckers felt that the new constitution lacked moral legitimacy because of Quebec's failure to ratify it.

The election of a federal Conservative government in 1984, and of a Liberal government in Quebec in 1985, opened the door to obtaining, belatedly, the consent of the Quebec legislature to the 1982 constitutional accord. The new prime minister, Brian Mulroney, was anxious to obtain Quebec's official endorsement of the 1982 changes. He recognized that no constitution, however legally binding, can keep a country together unless the people consider it to be legitimate. Premier Bourassa produced a list of five conditions that would have to be met before Quebec would agree to the constitutional accord: recognition of Quebec as a distinct society, more provincial power over immigration, constitutional recognition that three of the nine Supreme Court of Canada judges must be from Quebec, limits to federal spending power in provincial jurisdiction, and a Quebec veto over future constitutional changes. All of these demands were accommodated in the Meech Lake Accord announced on April 30, 1987. Instead of providing Quebec with a veto over all constitutional changes, however, financial compensation would be provided to provinces that opted out of a constitutional amendment with regard to any matter, rather than the more restrictive provisions for financial compensation included in the *Constitution Act, 1982*. For Quebec and other provinces that might opt out of a constitutional amendment, opting out with financial compensation would be tantamount to a veto with regard to the impact of the amendment in that province.[12]

The Meech Lake Accord required unanimous consent of Parliament and all provinces within three years to become law, and because of electoral changes in provincial governments, Manitoba and Newfoundland did not approve it within that time frame. The failure of Meech Lake was blamed by many observers on the process — negotiations were restricted primarily to the first ministers and their key advisors. A new round of constitutional negotiations that included broad consultation of the Canadian public was begun, and the result was the Charlottetown Accord of August 1992. This was a complex agreement that included the substantive provisions of the Meech Lake Accord and other constitutional changes that included accommodation of some of the interests of Aboriginal Canadians, and Senate reform. The Charlottetown Accord was subjected to a referendum within two months, and as might be expected when voters had only a short time to evaluate a complex proposal, was rejected by 54 per cent of Canadians in a 72 per cent turnout. This debacle was seized on by Quebec nationalists as an indication of the inevitable failure of federalism, and in 1995, a Quebec referendum on separation from Canada came within a hair of succeeding.[13] Throughout this tumultuous post-1982 period, it is significant that none of the contentious issues engaged the *Charter of Rights*. Over the years, the *Charter* became one of the icons of Canadian identity that a large majority identified with.

THE SUBSTANTIVE PROVISIONS IN THE *CHARTER*

The substantive provisions in the *Charter* appear in seven parts separated by headings: (1) fundamental freedoms, (2) democratic rights, (3) mobility rights, (4) legal rights, (5) equality rights, (6) language rights, and (7) minority-language educational rights.

FUNDAMENTAL FREEDOMS (SECTION 2)

These are the familiar civil liberties that grew into constitutional conventions in the United Kingdom as a result of the adoption of the ideology of liberalism — the same ones that the Duff Doctrine sought to protect. They include freedom of conscience and religion; freedom of thought, belief, opinion, and expression (including freedom of the communications media); freedom of peaceful assembly; and freedom of association. The fundamental freedoms in the *Charter* are also listed in the *Bill of Rights*, but the wording of most of them has been slightly changed with the hope of providing greater clarity and comprehensiveness.

DEMOCRATIC RIGHTS (SECTIONS 3-5)

The *Canadian Bill of Rights* made no mention of democratic rights, and Trudeau's first proposal for an entrenched charter of rights in 1968 did not suggest entrenching democratic rights — a shortcoming emphasized in Donald Smiley's 1969 commentary on the Trudeau proposals.[14] This kind of criticism had some effect, because in 1971 the bill of rights in the Victoria Charter included references to the right to vote, universal suffrage, and free elections at least every five years. These principles now appear in the *Charter*.

Section 3 states that every citizen has the right to vote in federal and provincial elections, as well as the right to be qualified for membership in the House of Commons and provincial legislatures. Section 4(1) stipulates that no more than five years may elapse between general elections for the House of Commons or provincial legislatures. Section 4(2) provides that "in time of real or apprehended war, invasion, or insurrection," a two-thirds vote in the House of Commons can continue the life of the House beyond five years. There is no limit on how long elections may be delayed; this is left to the development of future conventions. A similar provision is made for provincial legislatures to continue beyond five years in equivalent emergency circumstances. Section 5 declares that both Parliament and provincial legislatures must have a sitting at least once in every twelve-month period.

The guarantee of the rights to vote and to be qualified for elected office in section 3 apply to all citizens. There are no restrictions listed pertaining to age, mental competence, or imprisonment, for example. However, legislatures expect to be able to justify some of these restrictions as reasonable limits to the *Charter* pursuant to section 1, the limitations clause, which is discussed later in this chapter.

MOBILITY RIGHTS (SECTION 6)

One of the federal government's overall policy objectives during the Trudeau era was to promote national unity by making it easier for Canadians to move from province to province to find work. Provincial governments had created a number of restrictions to interprovincial mobility, such as residency requirements for certain provincial benefits and hiring practices favouring current residents of the province. Section 6 was an attempt to limit such restrictions. Section 6(2) declares that every citizen and "permanent resident has the right a) to move and take up residence in any province, and b) to pursue the gaining of a livelihood in any province."

It proved impossible to obtain provincial agreement to such an unqualified guarantee of freedom of movement. Newfoundland wanted to be able to give priority in jobs to local residents in the expected offshore oil fields. Quebec wanted to encourage the use of French by individuals and companies moving to that province. The richer provinces were concerned that people from poorer provinces might move in simply to take advantage of more-generous social welfare or health benefits. To obtain provincial agreement for mobility rights, a number of exceptions were specified in sections 6(3) and 6(4). Social service recipients may be subjected to reasonable residency requirements. Mobility is also subject to "any [existing] laws or practices of general application in force in a province," except those that blatantly discriminate on the basis of province of residence. Furthermore, provinces with high unemployment can discriminate against residents from other provinces until their unemployment rate reaches the Canadian average. These exceptions have watered down the potential impact of mobility rights considerably.

In addition to internal mobility rights, section 6(1) also guarantees every citizen of Canada "the right to enter, remain in, and leave" the country. The right to enter Canada means that citizens travelling abroad cannot be prevented from returning home, for example, for political reasons. The right to remain in Canada means that Canada's extradition laws have been subjected to challenges under the *Charter*. The right to leave is meant to preclude situations developing in Canada analogous to those faced by Soviet Jews who wished to emigrate but were denied permission. The right to leave may also affect the federal government's ability to place restrictions on the amount of currency Canadian travellers or emigrants may take with them, should the federal authorities ever wish to exercise this power.

The most publicized decision under section 6 is the Abdelrazik decision of the Federal Court in 2009.[15] Abousfian Abdelrazik came to Canada as a refugee from Sudan in 1990 and became a Canadian citizen in 1995. In 2003, along with his wife and three children, he returned to Sudan to visit his ailing mother. When his wife and children returned to Canada several months later, he remained in Sudan and was "arrested without charge, imprisoned for several years, and tortured."[16] In 2006 he was released from prison but was unable to return to Canada both because his passport had expired and because he was on a United Nations no-fly list. The Harper government refused to issue him a new passport and, after some time, claimed that this was because of national security concerns. Meanwhile, Abdelrazik took refuge in the Canadian embassy in Khartoum, fearing further abuse by Sudanese authorities. He slept on a cot in the embassy's lobby for fourteen months and from there instructed his Canadian lawyers to apply to the Federal Court for an order requiring the Canadian government to issue him a passport under section 6(1) of the *Charter* — the right of Canadian citizens to enter Canada. In early June of 2009, Justice Russel Zinn of the Federal Court declared that because the government presented no evidence to show that Abdelrazik was a security risk, he had the right to return to Canada. Zinn ordered the minister of foreign affairs to provide Abdelrazik with an emergency passport and an escort on the flight back to Canada to ensure his safety. As well, he ordered Abdelrazik to appear before him upon his return so that the court could be satisfied that he had actually returned. After some hesitation, the government complied with the order, and Abdelrazik was back in Canada before the end of June. In September of 2009, he launched a lawsuit against the government for $27 million.[17]

Other than the Abdelrazik case, mobility rights in the *Charter* have had little impact on the Canadian political system. A number of section 6 cases have involved litigants who tried to avoid extradition by claiming the right to remain in Canada. The Supreme Court has held that extradition to a foreign country for the purpose of standing trial there is a reasonable limit to section 6. However, if the person being extradited might face the death penalty if found guilty, the court required that prior to extradition, the minister of justice must first obtain an assurance from the foreign jurisdiction that the death penalty will not be imposed.[18] In a 1989 case, *Black v. Law Society of Alberta*, the Supreme Court of Canada struck down a Law Society of Alberta rule that prohibited lawyers from entering into a partnership with another member of the law society not ordinarily resident in the province. The court declared that the rule was inconsistent with section 6(2) of the *Charter*.[19] With regard to professional qualifications, however, the fact that the requirements for becoming a chartered accountant in Saskatchewan are more stringent than those in Ontario was found not to be a violation of section 6(2) because the requirements applied both to Saskatchewan residents and non-residents.[20] In a British Columbia Supreme Court case, a medical doctor succeeded in invoking section 6 to obtain a billing number from the province's health insurance agency. The doctor had previously been denied the number simply because she had moved from out of the province.[21] And the Federal Court has ruled that section 6(1) implies that Canadian citizens have a right to a passport, subject to reasonable limits such as proven national security issues.[22] Because there are so few high court decisions under section 6 and it is not yet clear what impact it will have on government policies, section 6 cases are not discussed in a separate chapter.

It is somewhat ironic that the Supreme Court's first Charter case arose under section 6. This was the case of Joel Skapinker, a South African citizen who had taken a law degree in Canada. The Law Society of Upper Canada, the regulatory body for lawyers in Ontario, had denied Skapinker permission to practise law because he was not a citizen. Skapinker took the law society to court under the *Charter*, claiming that section 6 guaranteed permanent residents, like himself, the right to gain a livelihood in any province. Skapinker lost because the Supreme Court decided that section 6 applied only to persons moving from one province to another or to persons living in one province and working in another.[23]

LEGAL RIGHTS (SECTIONS 7–14)

The legal rights section of the *Charter* includes a number of procedural safeguards designed to protect those subjected to governmental intervention under the law, such as those accused of federal criminal offences or provincial highway traffic violations, as well as visitors to Canada who are ordered deported by federal immigration authorities. As the legal rights apply to "every person" or "everyone," they apply to any person subjected to federal or provincial authorities — not simply to citizens or permanent residents. According to Supreme Court decisions, "legal persons," such as corporations, are also covered.[24]

The legal rights are a reflection of the second aspect of civil liberties claims mentioned in chapter 1: that when it is acceptable for governments to restrict freedoms, certain procedures must be followed to ensure that freedoms are not unnecessarily restricted.

The legal rights sections of the *Charter* repeats most of the legal rights listed in the *Canadian Bill of Rights*, except for the right to a fair hearing in accordance with the principles of fundamental justice to determine rights and obligations (section 2[e] of the *Bill*) and the right not to be deprived of the enjoyment of property except through the due process of law (section 1[a] of the *Bill*). These particular rights will continue to be covered by the *Bill of Rights* rather than the *Charter*, but they apply only to the federal government.

The *Charter* lists a number of legal rights not covered by the *Bill of Rights*. For example, the *Charter* prohibits unreasonable search and seizure, the retroactive criminalization of actions other than war crimes,[25] and double jeopardy, that is, being tried and possibly punished more than once for the same offence.[26] In addition, the *Charter* provides the right to be tried within a reasonable time, the right to a jury trial if the offence carries a penalty of five years in jail or more, and the right to the least punishment if the punishment for an offence varied between the time the offence was committed and the time of sentencing. As well, the *Charter* goes further than the *Bill* in protecting the right to counsel by stipulating the right to be informed of the right to counsel upon arrest or detention.

The *Charter*'s various legal rights sections are arranged in order from the general to the specific, and from the early stages of the criminal process to the later stages. Section 7 is a general guarantee of procedural rights. It states that everyone has the right to life, liberty, and security of person unless deprived thereof pursuant to "fundamental justice." Fundamental justice refers to recognized procedural safeguards to ensure fairness of treatment to those who have been detained or put on trial. Many of these procedural safeguards are included in sections 8–14, but section 7 implies even broader protection than the safeguards specifically spelled out in sections 8–14. We will see examples of the scope of section 7 in the decisions discussed in chapter 5. However, the Supreme Court has determined that section 7 may not be interpreted so liberally as to nullify the *Criminal Code* provision that allows dangerous offenders to be given indeterminate sentences[27] or to preclude the fingerprinting of accused persons.[28]

Section 8 prohibits unreasonable search or seizure. Section 9 forbids arbitrary (meaning unlawful) detention or imprisonment. Section 10 includes a list of rights that apply when a person is arrested or detained, such as the right to counsel and the right to be informed of the reasons for being detained. Section 11 contains rights that come into effect upon being charged with an offence, such as the right to be presumed innocent until proven guilty and the right to a trial within a reasonable time. (The Supreme Court has decided that the issue of unreasonable delay must be raised at a trial and not a preliminary hearing).[29] Section 12 prohibits cruel and unusual treatment or punishment. Section 13 stipulates that witnesses in trials be protected from having self-incriminating evidence used against them in future trials. This allows witnesses to concentrate on giving accurate evidence for the trial they are participating in, without having to worry that they might accidentally, or through the urging of the Crown, give evidence that could be used against them personally in a future trial. Section 13 also means that accused persons who are tried for particular offences and who testify on their own behalf need not worry that their testimony at the trial may be used against them in another trial.[30] Finally, section 14 provides the right to an interpreter for any party in a trial (civil or criminal) or any witness who does not speak the language of the trial, or for any deaf person.

EQUALITY RIGHTS (SECTION 15)

Section 15(1) states that every individual (meaning that only human beings are covered, and not legal persons such as corporations) "is equal before and under the law and has the right to the equal protection and equal benefit of the law without discrimination." Before examining the remainder of this section, it is worthwhile noting that whereas the *Bill of Rights* protects equality before the law, the *Charter* safeguards equality "before *and under*" (emphasis added) the law. The phrase "and under" was added to counteract the narrow interpretation by the Supreme Court of the phrase "equality" in the *Bill of Rights*, especially in cases such as *Lavell* and *Bédard*.[31] In other words, it is not good enough for the courts to ensure that all Indian women are treated equally by judges. It is also necessary for judges to strike down a law that applies unequally without sufficient reason.

Similarly, whereas the *Bill* mentions the right to protection of the law, the equivalent Charter right is to "the equal protection and equal benefit of the law." The reference to "benefit" is there to encourage judges to apply the equality principle not only to laws that protect citizens from unjustified government encroachment, but also to laws that provide a positive benefit, like employment insurance. Section 15 guarantees equality without discrimination, which means any type of discrimination. The section, however, continues by listing specific forms of discrimination that are prohibited: "discrimination based on race, national or ethnic origin, colour, religion, sex, age, or mental or physical disability." Apparently, the framers of the *Charter* (those who participated in drafting it) wished to signal to the judiciary that particular forms of discrimination are especially unacceptable. This list of particularly repugnant forms of discrimination is similar to the list in the *Bill of Rights*, except that ethnic origin has been added to national origin to broaden the scope of this category, and age as well as mental or physical disability have been added. These latter two additions came about as a result of recommendations from groups representing seniors and the mentally and physically disabled during the parliamentary committee hearings on the proposed charter in 1981. They represented part of the federal government's strategy for increasing the public demand for a charter in the face of provincial opposition to unilateral patriation.

A prominent American *Bill of Rights* issue in recent years has been to what extent governments can institute affirmative action programs without violating equality rights. An affirmative action program is a government initiative that discriminates in favour of groups that have been the victims of unjustified discrimination in the past so that these groups may achieve equality sooner than they otherwise might. A specified minimum number of places for blacks in universities and pay equity programs for women are two examples. As Laurence Tribe has noted, while the US Supreme Court is clearly committed to overcoming racial and gender discrimination, affirmative action programs have not always survived the court's test for equality.[32] To ensure the constitutionality of Canadian affirmative action programs, section 15(2) of the *Charter* specifically protects affirmative action programs from being limited by the equality guarantee section 15(1).

The equality rights in the *Charter* could potentially have the greatest impact on existing federal and provincial legislation as procedures. This is because almost every law discriminates among individuals or groups in some way. Whenever a law is challenged in court as discriminatory, the Crown will have the option of defending the law as a reasonable limit to equality, a defense allowed by section 1 of the *Charter*, the limitations clause. Because of the potentially enormous impact section 15 could have on government programs, it did not come into force until April 17, 1985. The delay allowed the federal and provincial governments time to review their laws and change those that discriminated unnecessarily. Although all the governments went through this exercise, the resulting changes were not very far-reaching because the reviewers were unable to guess how section 15 would be interpreted by the Supreme Court.

LANGUAGE RIGHTS (SECTIONS 16–22)

Some of the language rights provisions contained in sections 16–22 already existed in section 133 of the *BNA Act*. For example, sections 17–19 of the *Charter* duplicate the *BNA Act* by guaranteeing that either English or French may be used in parliamentary debates or the proceedings of the courts created by Parliament (the Supreme Court of Canada, the Federal Court, and the Tax Court) and requiring the use of English and French in the statutes of Canada, the Hansard, and other official records. One purpose of this section is to create the impression that language rights are an important part of the Canadian concept of rights. In addition, sections 17–19 extend the language guarantees of section 133 to New Brunswick.

By 1982 New Brunswick had become an officially bilingual province in all but a constitutional sense. It was the hope of federal officials that other provinces with a significant francophone minority such as Ontario, Manitoba, and Newfoundland would also assent to be included in the language rights sections of the *Charter*, but only New Brunswick agreed. Other provinces, however, may opt in to these sections in the future. Quebec did not opt in because it would have been incongruous for the Parti Québécois government to promote a document that purported to strengthen the bilingual and bicultural nature of Canada. In any case, the language rights contained in section 133 of the *Constitution Act, 1867* still apply to Quebec.

Section 16 declares that French and English are the official languages of Canada (meaning the jurisdiction of the central government) and of New Brunswick, and that they have equal status and "equal rights and privileges as to their use in all institutions." Although this declaration has a potentially powerful symbolic value, Peter Hogg is doubtful whether it will have much impact on judicial decisions.[33]

Section 20 provides language rights that go well beyond those in section 133. With regard to government services provided by the central government, section 20(1) states that "[a]ny member of the public . . . has the right to communicate with, and to receive available services" in French or English in three circumstances: in the central offices of a government department or other federal institution; in other federal government offices where there is a significant demand for bilingual services; and where "due to the nature of the office, it is reasonable" to provide such services. These categories are extremely vague, and it is up to the Canadian judiciary to define them as cases develop. Section 20(2) provides New Brunswickers with the same right to communicate with government and to receive services in the official language of choice, but the right is not limited to any particular set of circumstances.

Sections 21 and 22 state that the language rights in the *Charter* should not be interpreted as "abrogating or derogating" from the language rights in section 133 and that other "legal or customary" rights concerning the use of languages other than English or French will continue, unaffected by the *Charter*.

MINORITY-LANGUAGE EDUCATION RIGHTS (SECTION 23)

Section 23 is difficult to comprehend at first reading because it is the result of numerous compromises between federal and provincial officials with regard to the contentious language-of-education issue. The first two subsections of section 23 guarantee to Canadian citizens the right to have their children receive primary and secondary school instruction in either English or French in any province, if one or more of the following conditions are met:

- the preferred language of education for the children is the mother tongue of one of the parents (the mother tongue clause);
- the preferred language of education for the children is the language in which one of the parents received his or her primary school education somewhere in Canada (the Canada clause); or
- the preferred language of education for one of the children is the language in which one of the child's siblings received, or is receiving, primary school education in order to accommodate family unity (the sibling clause).[34]

In 1981 and 1982 Quebec objected both to the Canada clause and the mother tongue clause, as noted above. Although Quebec had no objections to providing an English education to children of anglophone Quebeckers who had received their education in Quebec, it was determined to educate the children of new immigrants, whether from Canada or from abroad, in French. It feared that with increased immigration into the province and declining birth rates, Quebec might eventually become an anglophone province unless the children of new immigrants became francophones.

Because the *Charter* was put into effect without the consent of Quebec, a provision was inserted into the final version of the *Constitution Act, 1982* that delayed the application of the mother tongue clause to Quebec until such time as the Quebec National Assembly ratified it. However, the Canada clause was imposed on Quebec in spite of Quebec's objections. When the issue eventually went to court after 1982, Quebec attempted — unsuccessfully — to justify the Quebec clause as a reasonable limit to the Canada clause. This important case, known as the *Quebec Protestant School Board* case,[35] is discussed in chapter 7.

THE APPLICATION CLAUSES (SECTIONS 1, 24, 32, AND 33)

There are four clauses in the *Charter* that define its application: section 32, which deals with the laws and activities covered by the *Charter*; section 1, which suggests the kinds of reasonable limits to the *Charter* that are acceptable; section 33, the legislative override clause; and section 24, which describes how the *Charter* may be enforced.

WHAT THE *CHARTER* COVERS (SECTION 32)

The *Charter* applies only to the relations between governments and persons (including corporations with regard to some clauses). Section 32 states that the *Charter* applies to Parliament, provincial legislatures, and federal and provincial governments (meaning cabinets and the public service, but not the courts; see the *Dolphin Delivery* case,[36] chapter 3.) Thus, all statutes created by Parliament and the legislatures are covered by the *Charter*, as well as all cabinet regulations and the actions of administrative officials who are responsible to a cabinet minister, Parliament, or a legislature. The bylaws and administrative actions of municipal authorities are also included, because municipalities are created by provincial legislation. Furthermore, the regulations created by agencies that exercise power on behalf of government fall within the *Charter*'s purview. Thus, Skapinker was able to sue the Law Society of Upper Canada under the *Charter* because the regulation of the law profession has been delegated by the Ontario legislature to the law society.

The *Charter* does not cover private relations between persons. To the extent that human rights are to be enforced in the private sphere, this is accomplished through the provincial and federal human rights codes and the common law. However, the human rights codes, and other legislation regulating private relations, must conform to the *Charter*. Justine Blainey was able to win the right to play hockey in what was previously a boys-only league because she successfully challenged a provision of the Ontario *Human Rights Code* that exempted sports associations from provisions that prohibited discrimination based on sex.[37] Similarly, gays and lesbians won protection from discrimination in the human rights codes through the Supreme Court's decision in *Vriend* in 1998.[38]

THE LIMITATIONS CLAUSE (SECTION 1)

Section 1 was intended to provide judges with some direction in determining limits to Charter rights. It declares that the *Charter* "guarantees the rights and freedoms set out in it subject only to such reasonable limits prescribed by law as can be demonstrably justified in a free and democratic society."

There are three important features of section 1 that have emerged from judicial decisions on the *Charter*. First, the phrase "demonstrably justified" places the onus on the party wanting to limit a right (usually a government) to prove that the limitation is reasonable. In the absence of evidence to the contrary, judges will presume that a limit placed on a right is *not* reasonable.[39]

Second, the phrase "prescribed by law" means that a limit must be expressly provided for by statute or regulation, or results by necessary implication from the terms of a statute or regulation or from operating requirements. The limit may also result from the application of a common-law rule.[40] In other words, under the principle of the rule of law, government may not take action, including action to limit rights, except through law. For example, the law that created the Ontario Censor Board in 1911 was struck down as a violation of the *Charter* by the Supreme Court of Ontario in 1984 because it was too open-ended: it gave the board a broad discretion to censor films and videos as it saw fit.[41] The replacement legislation, which created the Ontario Film Review Board, focused more on classification than censorship, and the regulation permitting some censorship is very specific.[42] However, limits may occasionally be *implied* by a law. For example, the Supreme Court of Canada has held that the section of the *Ontario Highway Traffic Act* that allows police officers to stop motor vehicles at random contains an implied limit to the section 9 Charter right not to be arbitrarily detained, as well as an implied limit on the right to counsel.[43]

Third, the Supreme Court of Canada has defined a test for what constitutes a reasonable limit that can be demonstrably justified in a free and democratic society. This test is known as the Oakes test because it was developed in the case of *The Queen v. Oakes*.[44] (The Oakes case itself is an example of the presumption of innocence for a person charged with drug trafficking, and the case is considered further in chapter 5.) The Oakes test has two key components. First, the objective of the government in limiting a right must be of sufficient importance to society to justify encroachment on a right. Second, the limit must be reasonable and demonstrably justified in terms of not being out of proportion to the government objective, and must therefore satisfy three criteria: (a) it must be rationally connected to the government objective, and not arbitrary or capricious; (b) it should impair the right as little as is necessary to achieve the government objective; and (c) even if the previous points are satisfied, the effects of the limit cannot be out of proportion to what is accomplished by the government objective — in other words, the cure cannot be allowed to be more harmful than the disease.

Whenever a Charter decision turns on limits to rights in particular situations, legal arguments focus on section 1. It is worth noting that in the United States, where there is a bill of rights with no limitations clause, the United States Supreme Court created the notion of an implied limitations clause. The American judges assumed that the framers of the *Bill of Rights* realized that no right is absolute. The fact that Canada's *Charter* contains an explicit limitations clause is a reflection of the desire to provide guidance to the judiciary, but it is obvious that the judges are still left with a tremendous amount of discretion in setting limits on rights.

THE LEGISLATIVE OVERRIDE (SECTION 33)

Section 33 allows the federal Parliament or a provincial legislature to insert a clause into any specific statute declaring that the statute will operate notwithstanding sections 2 and 7–15 of the *Charter*. Any application of the override will automatically expire at the end of five years but may be renewed. This clause does not release legislatures and Parliament from their obligations under the *Charter*, but it permits them to put off particular cases of judicial review under the *Charter* so that they themselves can determine their obligations for five-year intervals. The override is a reflection of the skepticism felt by some Canadian politicians about the potential quality or impact of judicial review under the *Charter*.

A consensus seems to be emerging among our political leaders that the override will normally be used in extraordinary circumstances, such as emergency situations or to advance important social policy goals that could be or are being blocked by judicial review. Under most circumstances, however, a government wishing to limit a right would have to justify its action under section 1. Significantly, even the federal *Emergencies Act* does not invoke section 33. Although the *Emergencies Act*, like the old *War Measures Act*, which it replaced in 1988, does infringe civil liberties, the government expects to be able to justify such restrictions under section 1 of the *Charter*.

Section 33 has been used in four major circumstances to date. The Quebec National Assembly, when controlled by the Parti Québécois, amended all pre-1982 Quebec statutes to include an override clause and also included an override clause in all new legislation as a form of protest over being left out of the constitutional accord.[45] Second, the government of Saskatchewan used the override clause in legislation that settled a public service strike in 1986. The government feared that if the Supreme Court found a right to strike in section 2 of the *Charter*, the back-to-work legislation would be ineffective. As it turned out, the Supreme Court had, for twenty years, denied that a right to strike existed in the *Charter*[46] (see chapter 3), and Saskatchewan's use of the override was unnecessary. The third instance was the Quebec government's decision to use the override to protect the commercial signs provisions of the province's *Charter of the French Language* following a Supreme Court decision of December 1988[47] that struck down some of these provisions (see chapter 3). Fourth, the

Alberta government used s. 33 in 2000 to attempt to protect a provincial law stipulating that marriage could involve only opposite-sex couples.[48] There have been several trivial uses of s. 33, none of which are currently in effect.[49]

ENFORCEMENT (SECTION 24)

Section 24(1) gives anyone the right to apply to a court "of competent jurisdiction" for a remedy if that person thinks that his or her rights under the *Charter* have been infringed or denied. This section gives the judiciary a very broad scope to enforce the provisions of the *Charter* and to invent creative remedies for violations. Superior courts (whose judges are federally appointed) are always considered courts of competent jurisdiction. Inferior courts and administrative tribunals may declare a Charter remedy if the law creating the inferior court or tribunal grants such jurisdiction. However, section 24 does not empower persons whose rights have not been directly affected to apply to a court, nor does it allow for applications from those concerned about possible future violations of rights (unless these violations are imminent).[50]

Three decisions concerning remedies illustrate the latitude that judges have to impose what they consider to be appropriate remedies for a violation of the *Charter*. The first involves the case of French-speaking parents in Nova Scotia who were upset at what they considered to be the unnecessary delay by the provincial government in building French-language schools for their children, further to Section 23 of the *Charter*. They brought an application to a superior court judge in 1999 to order the provincial government to use its "best efforts" to complete the building of the schools in a timely fashion. Justice Arthur LeBlanc granted the order. By way of a remedy, he ordered the Nova Scotia government to complete the building of several French-language schools by specific dates, and also ordered government officials to report to the court at specified periods on its progress in meeting the deadlines. The government appealed this decision, and it ended up at the Supreme Court of Canada in 2003. By this time, the schools had been built. The Supreme Court heard the appeal anyway, and in a five to four decision upheld the original decision of the superior court judge to impose this kind of remedy.[51]

The second case is the Abdelrazik decision of 2009, discussed above in relation to the jurisprudence of section 6 of the *Charter*. As a remedy to the government's Charter violations of Abdelrazik's rights, a Federal Court judge ordered the government to provide Abdelrazik with an emergency passport and an escort so that he could return to Canada within a month. The judge also ordered that Abdelrazik be brought to his court upon returning so that he could be ensured the government had complied with his order. The government did not appeal, but did comply.[52]

The third decision concerns the sad case of a Canadian, Omar Khadr, who was a fifteen-year-old child soldier in Afghanistan. He had been coerced by his family to leave Canada and fight for al Qaeda.[53] In July of 2002, he was captured by US forces after a firefight and was later accused of killing an American soldier. After recovering from his wounds, Khadr was transferred to the US detention centre at Guantanamo Bay in Cuba. At Guantanamo Bay, he was repeatedly tortured, and after one torture session was questioned by representatives of the Canadian Security Intelligence Service and the RCMP. The George W. Bush administration had set up special military tribunals to try prisoners held at Guantanamo Bay. These tribunals were ruled illegal by the US Supreme Court and outside the rules of international law[54] and were established because so many detainees at Guantanamo Bay were tortured to give evidence, contrary to international law.[55] Neither legitimate military tribunals nor the internal courts of any democratic country will admit evidence obtained under torture. Nor will they allow the prosecution, as an adult, of a child soldier. For these reasons, in early 2010, the Supreme Court of Canada unanimously found that Khadr's Charter rights as a Canadian had been grievously violated. The court left it up to the Canadian government to determine an appropriate remedy.[56] The government — rather than requesting Khadr be returned to Canada to be dealt with under Canadian law[57] — asked US authorities not to use evidence gathered by the Canadian public servants — members of CSIS and the RCMP — in the prosecution of Khadr. The request was refused by the US. As a result, Khadr was advised by his lawyers to plead guilty to some of the charges against him in return for a plea bargain that would allow him to return to Canada to serve an eight-year sentence. Khadr was transferred to a Canadian penitentiary in Ontario in September of 2012 and in 2013 to a federal prison in Alberta. (Because this case also relates to the violation of Khadr's section 7 rights, the Khadr case is reviewed in more detail in chapter 5).

Section 24(2) gives judges the option to exclude evidence from trials if in the collecting of the evidence a Charter right was violated. Judges may exclude evidence if its admission "would bring the administration of justice into disrepute." Chapter 5 reviews several decisions in which evidence was excluded pursuant to section 24(2). Some of these decisions had a huge impact on the justice system, resulting in the dropping of thousands of criminal charges.

THE INTERPRETIVE CLAUSES OF THE *CHARTER* (SECTIONS 25–31)

The interpretive clauses are intended to provide guidance to judges in their attempts to interpret the *Charter*.

ABORIGINAL RIGHTS (SECTION 25)

Section 25 directs judges not to interpret the *Charter* "so as to abrogate or derogate from any aboriginal, treaty or other rights or freedoms that pertain to the aboriginal peoples of Canada including (a) any rights or freedoms that have been recognized by the Royal Proclamation of October 7, 1763; and (b) any rights or freedoms that now exist by way of land claims agreements or may be so acquired." To the extent that the *Indian Act* is seen by judges as promoting treaty rights or land claims, it will be upheld. This is in spite of the fact that the *Indian Act* singles out a particular racial group, and so might be considered discriminatory contrary to section 15 were it not for section 25.

The Royal Proclamation of 1763, during the British era, was the first constitution of what is now Canada. In this document, the British authorities agreed to protect the aboriginal peoples of British North America from unfair treatment at the hands of the British settlers, and to recognize aboriginal title. For that reason, many native leaders regard the Royal Proclamation as a guarantee of their sovereignty. It is unlikely, however, that the courts will very often interpret section 25 broadly so as to advance aboriginal rights. Aboriginals brought nineteen claims to court under section 25 between 1982 and 1985 and lost all nineteen.[58]

It is much more likely that Aboriginal rights will be upheld or advanced under section 35 of the Constitution Act, 1982, which is the focus of chapter 8. Section 35 recognizes and affirms "existing aboriginal and treaty rights." Section 35, the first section of the Constitution Act, 1982 outside the Charter, is meant to protect Aboriginal rights from erosion by Parliament or provincial legislatures, while section 25 of the Charter is merely an interpretive clause that puts Aboriginal rights on an equal footing with other rights in the Charter. The native peoples had wanted a declaration in the *Constitution Act, 1982* that their original rights under the treaties and the Royal Proclamation would be reinstated and protected. Such a declaration could have resulted in very significant costs to the federal and provincial governments, and the first ministers were not willing to yield on this point. As a result, there was strong opposition by native groups to the 1982 constitutional amendment.

MULTICULTURALISM (SECTION 27)

Section 27 instructs judges to interpret the *Charter* "in a manner consistent with the preservation and enhancement of the multicultural heritage of Canadians." There is mixed opinion as to whether this clause serves a merely symbolic function or whether it might actually have an important impact on Charter interpretation.

In the 1985 case in which the Supreme Court struck down the federal *Lord's Day Act*,[59] the multiculturalism clause was mentioned as one reason why a law favouring the Christian religion could not stand against the *Charter's* equality guarantee. The multiculturalism clause, however, was not critical to the outcome of the case.

GENDER EQUALITY (SECTION 28)

Section 28 declares that "[n]otwithstanding anything in this *Charter*, the rights and freedoms referred to in it are guaranteed equally to male and female persons." This section came about as a result of the urging of several women's organizations, whose members were concerned that equality rights for women might be overridden through section 33 and that judges, who are predominantly male, might consider limits to gender equality as reasonable under section 1.

Although section 28 in many respects duplicates the prohibition of discrimination based on sex in section 15, section 28 cannot be overridden under section 33. Furthermore, the very forceful opening words of section 28 might encourage judges not to subject gender equality to reasonable limits, or at least to demand higher standards for limits to gender equality.

DENOMINATIONAL SCHOOL RIGHTS (SECTION 29)

There is no doubt that the special rights granted to denominational schools under section 93 of the *Constitution Act, 1867* violate in principle the equality rights provisions in section 15, since they result in special privileges to some, but not all, religious denominations. However, in creating the *Charter*, Canadian legislators had no intention of abolishing denominational school rights; after all, these rights had been considered an essential part of the Confederation bargain for the original four provinces. (As well, denominational school rights were created in each of the provinces that joined Canada after 1867.)

Section 29 states the clear intention of the *Charter's* framers that the denominational school rights in Canada's original constitution be continued: "Nothing in this *Charter* abrogates or derogates from any rights or privileges guaranteed by or under the Constitution of Canada in respect of denominational, separate or dissentient schools." Chapter 6 considers the Supreme Court decision that resulted from the extension of funding to Roman Catholic high schools in Ontario in 1985, as well as other more recent decisions concerning section 29.

MISCELLANEOUS (SECTIONS 26, 30-31)

There are three remaining interpretive clauses. Section 26 instructs judges not to interpret the *Charter* so as to deny the existence of any other rights or freedoms that exist in Canada. This means that the *Charter* does not take precedence over rights (such as the original language rights) found in other constitutional documents. Further, section 26 seems to suggest that judges should not hesitate to apply the statutory bills of rights and the human rights codes merely because of the existence of the *Charter*.

Section 30 states that whenever the word "province" appears in the *Charter*, it is understood to include the Yukon, Northwest Territories, and

Nunavut. Section 31 indicates that the purpose of the *Charter* is to limit the powers of government and that therefore the *Charter* may not be interpreted so as to extend existing powers.

THE *CHARTER* AND ITS CRITICS

There are three major reasons why the *Canadian Charter of Rights and Freedoms* became reality: Pierre Trudeau, the nation-building strategy of the federal government, and the legacy of the Supreme Court's narrow interpretation of the *Bill of Rights*. Had any one of these ingredients been missing, it is unlikely that the *Charter* would have materialized during the 1980s.

Certainly, public concern about protecting and promoting rights and liberties played an important role in generating popular support for the concept of a charter of rights, but as already noted, public pressure was not the primary reason for the *Charter*'s creation. Trudeau was determined to succeed in his charter project, and his overriding goal was to give Canadians a national code of values promoting national unity. He hoped that the document would encourage a continuing national dialogue about Charter questions that would cut across the preoccupation with provincial issues. From the perspective of this nation-building strategy, the language rights were a central feature of the document. To entrench the *Charter* in the constitution seemed to be the only way of getting the judiciary to take it seriously, based on experience with the *Bill of Rights*. As Allan Blakeney is said to have remarked, "They convulsed the nation to convince the judges."

In the early years of the *Charter*, a good deal was written about its potential as a nation-building tool by authors like Russell,[60] Williams,[61] and Knopff and Morton.[62] There is evidence that this nation-building strategy has worked, at least at a symbolic level. For example, according to a 2014 survey conducted by Leger Marketing for the Association of Canadian Studies, the Charter of Rights is the top item that unites Canadians, reflecting the results of similar surveys since 1982.[63]

Further, while the *Charter* was not created primarily to promote human rights, many of its supporters were optimistic that it would be a valuable tool in furthering that cause. In an evaluation of leading *Charter of Rights* decisions published in 2006, I concluded that "a number of decisions have opened the door to higher levels of inclusiveness and participation in the

Canadian political system, although it will be up to individual Canadians to utilize the possibilities opened by the courts."[64] I cautioned, however, that "it is disturbing in a democratic policy that so many citizens would prefer to have issues related to [democracy] decided by the courts rather than by elected legislatures, because they perceive the courts as more likely to give them a fair hearing."[65] This is a reference to research which has consistently shown that Canadians trust the courts far more than their elected representatives to make decisions about human rights issues.[66]

Charter critics have based their reasoning on several premises: the *Charter* undermines legislative supremacy; it will work in the interests of the powerful in society who can afford the cost of litigation; it facilitates the "capture" of the courts by special interest groups, especially those on the left; it diverts attention from the most serious threats to social well-being; and that courts are inappropriate institutions for human rights policy-making.

Contemporary political commentators who are concerned about the erosion of legislative supremacy are not worried, as A. V. Dicey was, about the *theory* of legislative supremacy. Instead, they are worried, first, about the erosion of democratic reasoning skills in society. As John Stuart Mill argued, democracy means far more than holding elections. A democratic society will lose its ability to promote human excellence if its citizens have not learned to participate intelligently in making decisions about important public policy issues, such as human rights.[67] The *Charter* may transfer an important part of this responsibility from the democratic process to the (unelected) judiciary. In the United States, where the judiciary has played the predominant role in human rights policy-making for more than two centuries, some political theorists are concerned that the ability of average citizens to think carefully about civil rights issues has atrophied to some extent.[68] Second, they are concerned that judicial decisions that contradict government policy sabotage the will of the people, as expressed through their elected legislatures.[69]

The second argument is that because litigation is expensive, the determination of human rights issues through the courts will tend to work in favour of those who can afford the costs. For example, the National Citizens' Coalition, a well-financed right-wing lobby group, spent an estimated $500,000 to support Merv Lavigne's attempt to curtail union contributions to political parties through a Charter challenge even before the case reached the Supreme Court of Canada.[70] Charter litigation also forces less-advantaged groups to spend large sums on legal defence for themselves. Ontario unions allegedly spent $400,000 defending themselves in the *Lavigne* case prior to the Supreme Court stage.[71]

The third argument is that special interest groups, especially those on the left, have often captured the courts, and especially the Supreme Court, in order to tilt outcomes to their preferences. These groups, such as the Women's Legal Education and Action Fund (LEAF) and the Canadian Civil Liberties Association, it is argued by critics like Ted Morton and Rainer Knopff, are more likely to win a court challenge to a public policy they oppose than to win by working through the democratic process. This "court capture," they argue, is anti-democratic.[72]

The fourth argument is that the *Charter* diverts attention from the more serious threats to social well-being. According to critics like Michael Mandel and Allan Hutchinson,[73] the *Charter* is resulting in a significant reduction in the ability of governments in Canada to assist and protect society's disadvantaged. This is because the *Charter* focuses on preventing state infringements on individual liberty, but such infringements are often necessary in order for the state to intervene on behalf of those in need. For example, in the *BC Motor Vehicle Act* case (see chapter 5),[74] the Supreme Court interpreted the right to liberty broadly so that it would be more difficult for provincial governments to enforce the suspension of licenses of poor drivers. The result is that while poor drivers will enjoy fewer restrictions on their liberty, more innocent people may be injured in traffic accidents.

The fifth argument — that courts are inappropriate institutions for policy-making regarding human rights — is the most complex. This argument sets out three factors that make courts poorly suited to resolving human rights policy issues: the doctrine of *stare decisis*, the adversary system, and the backgrounds of the judges. We will return to the arguments of the critics after reviewing these three factors.

STARE DECISIS

In common-law jurisdictions, precedents are applied to current cases according to a set of principles known as *stare decisis*. According to *stare decisis,* every court must follow the precedents established by a higher court in the same court system, and the precedents of the highest court trump those of any lower courts. In the absence of conflicting precedents established by a higher court, a court usually follows its own precedents. The precedents of higher or equal-status courts in another common-law jurisdiction are influential but not binding. (American *Bill of Rights* precedents are often cited in Charter cases [because US courts retained their membership in the common-law system after the American revolution], but they are only sometimes followed.) Precedents must be followed only when the facts in the current case and the precedent case are substantially the same. If a judge considers the facts in a current case to be significantly different, the judge may "distinguish" the precedent and depart from it.

Thus, all courts in Canada must follow precedents established by the Supreme Court. The Supreme Court itself almost always follows its own precedents. In the mid-1970s, the court announced that it might occasionally overrule its own precedents (or those established by the Judicial Committee of the Privy Council) if it considered them to be clearly wrong or inappropriate. Since that time, the Supreme Court has overruled fewer than twenty precedents;[75] such overruling does not occur frequently because it would destroy the predictability of the decision-making process in courts.

Stare decisis makes the courts' decision-making process fundamentally different from the policy-making process that takes place in the policy development sections of government departments, cabinets, and legislatures. In courts, established principles must stand, errors can very rarely be admitted, and changes in approach are few. In the executive and legislative branches, established principles can more easily evolve, errors can more easily be admitted, and changes in policy are to be expected as values and priorities change and as more is learned from research.

The decision-making process in courts, called adjudication, works best when judges can apply relatively clear rules (statutes or the common law) to factual situations. The training of judges and lawyers is fitted to that process. With regard to policy development, the policy branches of government departments, cabinets, and legislatures have different resources that have been honed to that particular process. These include skilled policy research staff, facilities conducting pilot studies and evaluations, links with other social science research institutions, access to experts connected with various interest groups, and the ability to conduct public hearings. These resources are not available in the same way to courts. Judges must rely primarily on the factums and oral presentations of counsel for both sides, the factums and presentations of intervenors (when present), and court research staff.[76] The factums may refer to social scientific, historic, or scientific evidence, whether in published form, or commissioned by counsel as expert evidence reports. There is no need, however, for the policy-making process in government — which emphasizes research and evaluation — and the adjudicative process in courts — which emphasizes fairness — to behave as if one approach was completely independent of the other. On the one hand, proposed government legislation is scrutinized by government lawyers who try to ensure that it will withstand Charter challenges, based on the most recent court decisions.[77] On the other hand, Peter Hogg and others have suggested that when a government re-enacts legislation that has been struck down by the Supreme Court on Charter grounds, after changing the legislation based both on Charter prerequisites and research, the Supreme Court carefully examines the government's reasoning and more often than not, accepts it. This process is part of the so-called dialogue between courts and legislatures, to be discussed further in the concluding chapter.[78]

When judges are asked to give meaning to unclear law or to speculate on the meaning of law in the absence of a factual situation, they move from the adjudicative into the policy-making realm. Policy-making means the development of programs that will meet specific goals effectively and at the least cost. Of course, it is impossible to establish a precise dividing line between adjudication and policy development so that judges would only adjudicate and policy developers never make decisions that could be considered adjudicative ones, but an example will illustrate the overlap between the two processes.

In 1985 the Supreme Court had to decide whether refugee claimants from India, who were about to be deported without having had an oral hearing, were entitled to a hearing either under the *Charter* or the *Bill of Rights*. The question was basically a legal one: Did the guarantees of fundamental justice in section 7 of the *Charter* and section 2(e) of the *Bill* require an oral hearing? From a legal perspective, the answer was relatively clear. The common-law principle of natural justice, implied both by section 7 of the *Charter* and section 2(e) of the *Bill*, indicated that an oral hearing was required. (See the *Singh* case[79] in chapter 5.)

In the same case, the court had to consider another question: Does the denial of an oral hearing constitute a reasonable limit (under section 1) to the right to fundamental justice? This question is related more to policy development than to adjudication. From a policy development perspective, this question cannot be answered effectively without research to indicate whether the determination of refugee status can be undertaken accurately through a process that does not involve an oral hearing, or whether an oral hearing (and what kind of oral hearing) is the most effective of various alternative approaches. Policy-makers with a university education in public policy and administration are trained to undertake social scientific evaluations of various methods to answer this kind of question and to recommend the approach that is best in terms of both accuracy and cost. Lacking these kinds of resources — which are inappropriate for adjudication, in any case — the court could consider only the arguments presented by counsel for the government (the party on which the onus of proof rested). Counsel for the government, unaccustomed to making policy-related submissions, tried to justify the denial of an oral hearing by invoking "administrative convenience." Whether this argument was based on failure of government counsel to consult with policy-making staff, or whether policy-making staff had failed to undertake proper research in order to recommend the most accurate and cost-effective refugee determination system, or whether they did so and their recommendations were rejected by government, is not known. Regardless, the reasoning of government lawyers did not seem convincing, and the court decided that the denial of an oral hearing did not constitute a reasonable limit to fundamental justice. Although the court may well have stumbled into making the right decision, the way in which the decision was made (the court was not presented with relevant social science evidence from either side or from the intervenors) was unsound. This illustrates how the courts, as institutions, are ill-prepared for making policy-related decisions.[80] It is beyond the courts' control whether they are presented with adequate evidence on which to base a decision. It is up to counsel to decide what evidence to present. However, what Charter critics often ignore is that it is not the case that cabinets are always presented with adequate evidence on which to base their decisions either, or whether — even if they do have adequate evidence — they have the desire or ability to use it wisely.

THE ADVERSARY SYSTEM

The adversary system is an approach to adjudication utilized in common-law systems. In this approach, it is the responsibility of the litigants to present the judges with all the facts and theory they need to make decisions. Judges may not carry out an independent investigation of the facts. Although they may research legal theory and precedents on their own, they are not usually provided with many resources to do this, and they are expected to rely primarily on the information presented by counsel for the litigants. Supreme Court of Canada judges and provincial appeal court judges are assigned law clerks to assist with legal research. Trial court judges rarely have such assistance. Thus, if decisions about the meaning of the *Charter* seem to take into account only a narrow range of possibilities, this is usually because the lawyers presenting the case have, through lack of knowledge or through design, narrowed the possibilities in advance.

Counsel on both sides tend naturally to argue as forcefully as they can on behalf of their clients. With regard to Charter litigation, it is usually the case that a private person or corporation is challenging a federal or provincial law or the actions of a federal or provincial official. Therefore, in almost every Charter case, lawyers for the Crown (the name given to the state as a legal person) will tend to argue for the most restrictive and narrow interpretation of the *Charter* in order to uphold what they perceive to be the interests of their client. This is ironic when one remembers that the *Charter*'s supporters in the federal and some provincial cabinets claimed in 1981 that the *Charter* would protect our rights forever in the broadest possible way.

THE BACKGROUNDS OF JUDGES

The principle of judicial impartiality is critical to successful adjudication. There is no doubt in the author's opinion, based on extensive interviews with dozens of judges across Canada,[81] that judges generally do their best to be as impartial as possible.[82] However, when they are faced with having to give meaning to general phrases that could have a number of plausible meanings (such as many of those in the *Charter*) and there are few if any guiding precedents, the principle of impartiality may be of little assistance. In these cases, judges may apply what they perceive to be the standard of a reasonable person informed of the necessary facts and law, but that perception may be influenced by the judges' personal experiences and backgrounds. The following summarizes how judges' backgrounds differ from those of the average Canadian.

According to the 2001 Canadian census, there are 2,011 judges in Canada.[83] Judges in superior courts (provincial supreme courts and courts of appeal, the Federal Court, the Tax Court, the Federal Court of Appeal, and the Supreme Court of Canada) are appointed by the federal cabinet. Lower courts — provincial courts or territorial courts — are presided over by judges appointed by provincial or territorial cabinets. About half of Canada's judges are in each category.[84] All of the provincially-appointed judges are trial judges. Amongst the federally-appointed judges, 86 per cent are trial judges and the rest are appellate court judges. Judges are well paid for their work, both to make the possibility of successfully bribing a judge highly unlikely and to encourage good lawyers to apply for judgeships. In 2014, federally-appointed judges in the provinces and territories earned about $301,000 annually, while Supreme Court of Canada judges earned $358,000. Provincially-appointed judges tend to earn somewhat less. For example, in 2012, judges in the Ontario Court of Justice (Ontario's provincial court) earned about $265,000. Chief judges and justices earn slightly more than the other judges on their courts.[85]

According to data obtained in the Canadian census of 2001, 24 per cent of Canadian judges are women, with the proportion of female judges steadily increasing.[86] The proportion of female judges in each province varies widely, from 28 per cent in Manitoba to 14 per cent in Yukon. In 2010, four of nine Supreme Court of Canada judges (including the chief justice) were women, compared with only one when the *Charter of Rights* came into effect. With regard to ethnicity, prior to reform of judicial appointment procedures in the 1970s, those of British or French origin were significantly overrepresented amongst the judiciary, while new Canadians, Aboriginal Canadians, and visible minorities were underrepresented. Thanks to improvements in appointment procedures, the face of the Canadian judiciary is beginning to change so that judges are somewhat more broadly representative of Canadian society, especially in jurisdictions that encourage new Canadian, Aboriginal, and visible minority applicants. For example, just under 1 per cent of Canadian judges were Aboriginal in 2001, compared with about 3 per cent of Canadians who identified as Aboriginal.[87] Because judges are generally appointed from among the ranks of lawyers with many years of experience in private practice, judges are older than the average adult Canadian. The average age of superior court judges in Canada varies from about fifty-five to sixty-five, depending on the province. Most provincial court judges appear to be, on average, one to three years younger. The average age of Supreme Court of Canada judges, as of February 1989, was sixty-three. Their average age at appointment was fifty-eight. As long as it is considered important for judges to be recruited from the ranks of experienced lawyers, it is inevitable that they will be older. This may mean that judges, as policy-makers, find it more difficult to consider the policy implications of changing social values than do the relatively younger policy-makers in the executive and legislative branches.[88]

Judges are disproportionately married. In 1984, for example, 93 per cent of Alberta judges were married compared with about 80 per cent of the general population in the same age bracket. Only 3 per cent of Alberta judges were single or divorced — a much smaller proportion than the general population. Of the thirteen judges who served on the Supreme Court of Canada in 1988 and 1989 (there were four retirements), ten were married, one was single, and two were widowed. Those who had been married had an average of three children. As a result, judges may have some difficulty in understanding the problems of Canadians who are single (whether heterosexual or gay) or divorced.[89]

As might be expected, judges come disproportionately from upper social class backgrounds. In Alberta in 1990, for example, 46 per cent of the fathers of federally appointed judges and 52 per cent of the fathers of provincial court judges were businessmen or professionals, a group that comprised only 9 per cent of Alberta males in 1931 (around the time most of these judges were born). Conversely, 42 per cent of Alberta judges had fathers who were labourers or farmers, who made up 87 per cent of the province's male population when the judges were children. Only two of the first fifty Supreme Court of Canada judges were born into working-class families. The income of judges is also significantly higher than that of the average Canadian.[90] The question of whether the judiciary should be more representative of the social class backgrounds of Canadians is a difficult one. There are some who think that the upper-class nature of the judiciary indicates the failure of our governing system to implement the liberal-democratic value of equality.[91] Others think that because being born into a middle- or upper-class family provides advantages to children who aspire to a judicial career, a non-partisan appointment process that is structured to recruit the very best judges will always recruit judges disproportionately from the those classes. Moreover, judges from a working-class background may not necessarily be more sympathetic to the claims of workers when decision-making concerns issues that are more policy-oriented than legal. Peter Russell has observed that "some very tough attitudes may be engendered in the person who has had to struggle and 'make it the hard way.'"[92]

During Canada's first century, almost all judges appointed to every level of court in Canada were supporters of the party that controlled the government that appointed them. Before the First World War, many if not most of these had been candidates for office (successful or unsuccessful); since that time, the proportion of judges who were candidates has fallen to a level of no more than 10 to 20 per cent of judges. This change is particularly evident with regard to the Supreme Court. Only two judges appointed since 1949 have been candidates for elected office. Further, thanks to somewhat more non-partisan procedures for judicial selection, partisan considerations play a smaller role in judicial appointments than they once did.[93]

Perhaps the most important feature of Canadian judges that sets them apart from both average Canadians and elected politicians is that they tend to be extremely high achievers, both academically and in their community work. For example, according to data that colleagues and I collected in the mid-1990s, 90 per cent of Canadian appellate judges had received significant academic honours or awards during their university education. One-third had published journal articles or books, and one-quarter had received honourary degrees. As reforms are made to emphasize merit over partisan factors in judicial appointments, future judges may well be even higher achievers than current ones. Only 66 per cent of Canadian MPs elected in 2009 had a university education, and just 23 per cent of Canadians aged twenty-five to sixty-four have university degrees.[94] High levels of education tend to be associated with support for minority rights and tolerance of difference.[95]

THE CRITICS REVISITED

The intensity of criticism of the *Charter of Rights* from both left- and right-wing academics has been labelled "Charterphobia" by Richard Sigurdson.[96] Indeed, the passion with which critics attack both the idea of the *Charter* and leading decisions of the Supreme Court on it is breathtaking. This passion is generated by deeply-held beliefs: belief in human rights, democracy, equality, and fairness, and concern that the Charter regime does not meet their standards. My own position in this debate is closer to that of Professor Peter Russell, the father of the political science study of law in Canada. Like most political scientists at the time of the national debates leading up to the *Charter* in 1982, Russell was worried about the potential negative impact of a constitutionally-entrenched *Charter of Rights* on Canadian democracy. "The danger here is not so much that non-elected judges will impose their will on a democratic majority, but that questions of social and political justice will be transformed into technical legal issues and the great bulk of the citizenry who are not judges and lawyers will abdicate their responsibility for working out mutually acceptable resolutions on the issues which divide them."[97] In 2009, in an article revisiting this comment, Russell observed that the claims of Charter critics had proved to be exaggerated, although "Charter patriotism has probably contributed to the dumbing-down of the Canadian demos."[98] But overall, "At the margin, the *Charter* has contributed to making Canadian democracy more generous and inclusive."[99] Russell stressed that from his perspective, the greatest danger to Canadian democracy at the present time is not the *Charter* or judicial activism, but rather the increasing centralization of power in the Prime Minister's Office.

The arguments of the Charter critics are revisited in the concluding chapter.

WAS IT WORTH IT?

In summary, opponents of the *Charter* claim that the adjudicative process in the courts is not the most conducive environment for the development of effective policies for human rights promotion. Courts have little in the way of research facilities, litigation is dominated by the wealthy, and civil liberties issues come to court in a haphazard manner. In addition, critics claim that judges are not the most likely candidates to champion civil liberties. Few judges have much training in theories of human rights, and because of their work, they tend to be both business-oriented and cautious. As well, because the *Charter* gives judges more opportunity to intervene in the policy process, which is supposed to be the domain of elected legislatures in democracies, it might have an anti-democratic impact.

As judges make more and more decisions based on the *Charter*, Canadians will ask themselves whether it was worth all the trouble its creation caused or whether the skeptics were right after all. The next five chapters summarize a number of key Charter decisions from 1984 to 2014 — decisions that will be pivotal in the ultimate judgment Canadians form about the *Charter*.

CHAPTER 3

THE FUNDAMENTAL FREEDOMS

Section 2 of the *Charter* declares that everyone has freedom of (a) conscience and religion; (b) thought, belief, opinion, and expression; (c) peaceful assembly; and (d) association. Obviously, these are general words that could be interpreted in a wide variety of ways with regard to specific situations. For example, section 2 provides no guidance as to whether freedom of religion rules out Sunday-closing laws or laws restricting hate speech or pornography, or whether freedom of association means that workers have a constitutionally protected right to strike. It is silent about whether the federal government can require graphic warning labels on cigarette packages, or whether the Quebec government may prohibit languages other than French on commercial signs. These are the kinds of policy issues that judges are called on to decide.

This chapter reviews thirteen important Supreme Court decisions that indicate how the judges are approaching section 2. The *Big M* decision concerns the constitutionality of Sunday-closing laws, and the *Multani* case whether freedom of religion means that a Sikh student can wear a ceremonial kirpan to school. Three others — *Dolphin Delivery*, the *Alberta Labour Reference*, and *Health Services Bargaining Association v. BC*

— consider whether the *Charter* implies the right of workers to picket and strike. The *Ford* and *Devine* decisions deal with the relation between freedom of expression and Quebec's restrictions on the use of English on commercial signs, while the *RJR-MacDonald* case considers the constitutionality of the tobacco advertising legislation. The *Keegstra, Zundel,* and *Ross* cases are concerned with restrictions on hate speech, while the *Butler* and *Sharpe* cases consider the constitutionality of governmental restrictions on pornography.

FREEDOM OF RELIGION
THE *BIG M* CASE[1]

The first section 2 case to reach the Supreme Court was *Regina v. Big M Drug Mart Ltd.,* which was decided in April 1985. About six weeks after the *Charter* came into effect in 1982, Big M Drug Mart of Calgary was charged with contravening the federal *Lord's Day Act* by selling goods on a Sunday. Big M claimed that the *Act* violated the *Charter*'s guarantee of freedom of religion and should therefore be declared inoperative. (Although a corporation cannot have a religion, corporations can challenge statutes as violations of freedom of religion because the references to "everyone" in section 2 and "anyone" in section 24 of the *Charter* include corporations.)

This argument was accepted by the Alberta Court of Appeal, but the Crown appealed to the Supreme Court. Big M won again in our highest court, much to the surprise of those who thought that the court might take the same tack as in the parallel case under the *Canadian Bill of Rights* — the *Robertson and Rosetanni* case, which is reviewed in chapter 1.

Chief Justice Brian Dickson wrote the main opinion in *Big M*. There are four important features of his decision: (1) the *Bill of Rights* precedent; (2) the purpose of the *Charter*; (3) freedom of religion; and (4) whether the *Lord's Day Act* might be a reasonable limit to freedom of religion pursuant to section 1 of the *Charter*.

The Bill of Rights Precedent

Chief Justice Dickson handled the *Robertson and Rosetanni* precedent by pointing to one of the differences between the *Charter* and the *Bill*. He reminded his readers of the troublesome declaration in section 1 of the *Bill* that "in Canada . . . there have existed and shall continue to exist . . . the following human rights and fundamental freedoms. . . ."

> [T]he Canadian Charter of Rights and Freedoms *does not simply "recognize and declare" existing rights as they were circumscribed by legislation current at the time of the* Charter's *entrenchment. The language of the* Charter *is imperative . . . [T]he* Charter *is intended to set a standard upon which present as well as future legislation is to be tested.*[2]

Dickson's comments about the *Robertson and Rosetanni* case constitute an early indication that the Supreme Court intended to take a far more activist approach in interpreting the *Charter* than it had with the *Bill*.

The court concluded that the *Lord's Day Act* violated the *Charter's* guarantee of freedom of religion because the act had a clearly religious purpose: to force all Canadians, under the threat of criminal sanction, to observe the Christian sabbath. To demonstrate the religious purpose of the act, Dickson traced the wording of the legislation to a 1677 English statute, *An Act for the Better Observation of the Lord's Day Commonly Called Sunday.*

Dickson's judgment in *Big M* implies that in *Robertson and Rosetanni* the court had been forced to conclude that the *Lord's Day Act* did not violate freedom of religion because of the straitjacket created by the unfortunate wording of section 1 of the *Bill*. Thus, Dickson did not find the reasoning in *Robertson and Rosetanni* very convincing. In *Robertson and Rosetanni*, the Supreme Court had reasoned that although the purpose of the act was originally to apply the criminal law to religious observance (thus making it valid federal legislation), over the years the effects of the law had evolved to make it purely secular in purpose (so that it did not infringe freedom of religion).

Understandably, Dickson was not impressed with this "shifting purpose" approach to the *Lord's Day Act*, even though the US Supreme Court had adopted the same kind of rationale to avoid striking down state Sunday-observance laws as violations of the American *Bill of Rights*. He noted that it would be improper for the courts to second-guess the original legislature about the act's purpose. Furthermore, the shifting-purpose approach would create uncertainty in the law. At any point, a litigant could claim that a law had become unconstitutional because its purpose had changed.

Dickson asserted that a law could be considered an infringement of the *Charter* either because of its purpose or its effect. Both the purpose and the effect of statutes would have to conform to the *Charter*.

The Purpose of the *Charter*

In its 1984 Charter decisions, the Supreme Court announced that it would adopt a purposive approach to Charter interpretation.[3] In other words, the court would attempt to ascertain from historical, political, or philosophic sources the purpose of each of the rights guarantees in the *Charter* and would apply them accordingly. This purposive approach, which is in the philosophic tradition of liberalism, is reflected in Dickson's opinion:

> *A truly free society is one which can accommodate a wide*
> *variety of beliefs, diversity of tastes and pursuits, customs, and*
> *codes of conduct. A free society is one which aims at equality*
> *with respect to the enjoyment of fundamental freedoms and I*
> *say this without any reliance on s. 15 of the* Charter. *Freedom*
> *must surely be founded in respect for the inherent dignity and*
> *the inviolable rights of the human person.[4]*

He also reiterated what had been said about the purpose of the *Charter* in a 1984 case, *Hunter v. Southam*. He declared that the purpose of a constitutional charter is "the unremitting protection of individual rights and liberties."[5] He added that the central feature of the *Charter*'s fundamental freedoms section (section 2) is "the notion of the centrality of individual conscience and the inappropriateness of governmental intervention to compel or to constrain its manifestation."[6]

Freedom of Religion

It follows from the court's general discussion of the *Charter* that the guarantee of freedom of religion is not an isolated right but part of the overall goal in a liberal society to emphasize the "centrality of individual conscience."

Dickson's judgment in *Big M* also alluded to some of the practical reasons for respecting freedom of religion as learned from the lessons of history. He noted how in post-Reformation Europe, both Roman Catholic and Protestant monarchs had attempted to impose their beliefs on all their subjects, not often with great success but always at the cost of many lives. According to Dickson, during the seventeenth century people in England eventually realized that "belief itself was not amenable to compulsion."[7] Therefore, the position that the minority must conform to the traditions of the religious majority, either for the sake of convenience or to promote "the truth," was no longer acceptable. It follows that one of the purposes of the *Charter*'s guarantee of freedom of religion is to protect "religious minorities from the threat of 'the tyranny of the majority.'"[8]

In his discussion of freedom of religion, Dickson made a comment that stands out because it would seem to have more in common with a theological treatise than with legal reasoning: "Attempts to compel belief or practice denied the reality of individual conscience and dishonoured the God that had planted it in His creatures."[9] While this comment is not necessary to Dickson's analysis, a judge of his talent does not make such a statement without reason. One possible explanation for his observation is that it could be intended to provide future courts with a guideline for interpreting the religious connotation of the *Charter*'s preamble: "Whereas Canada is founded upon principles that recognize the supremacy of God and the rule of law."

As indicated in chapter 1, many of the civil liberties in the *Charter* can be thought of as logical derivatives from the principle of the rule of law. But the connection between the concept of "the supremacy of God" and the *Charter* is not clear. In fact, by recognizing a deity, the phrase would seem to contradict the guarantee of freedom of conscience in section 2. As it happens, the reference to the supremacy of God in the *Charter*'s preamble is copied from the *Canadian Bill of Rights* and was included at the insistence of some members of Parliament under pressure from their constituents. Little thought was given to the apparent contradiction between this phrase and section 2(a). That was left for the courts to work out.

Dickson's brief foray into theology in *Big M* may provide a way out of the dilemma for future courts. If the supremacy of God can be interpreted to mean that freedom of conscience must be respected, there is no necessary contradiction between the *Charter*'s preamble and the affirmation of freedom of conscience in section 2(a).

The Section 1 Analysis

Even though the court decided that the *Lord's Day Act* infringes freedom of religion, it is possible that the legislation could nevertheless be sustained as a reasonable limit to rights, pursuant to section 1 of the *Charter*. In fact, counsel for the federal government argued that the *Lord's Day Act* should be considered a reasonable limit for two reasons. First, most religions advocate a day of rest, and because Christians are the majority in Canada, the Christian day is the most practical. Second, it is important for there to be a common weekly day of rest in society so that families can spend time together. (Keep in mind that this decision occurred prior to the court's development of the Oakes test for section 1.)

Dickson dismissed the first argument because the purpose of the guarantee of freedom of religion is to protect religious *minorities,* not the majority. He accepted that the second argument had some merit but pointed out that legislation creating a weekly holiday from work for secular rather than religious purposes would fall under provincial jurisdiction pursuant to section 92(13) of the *Constitution Act, 1867*: that is, under the provincial powers over property and civil rights rather than the federal criminal law power. Thus, the Supreme Court's decision in *Big M* had the effect of transferring primary responsibility for Sunday-closing legislation from the federal government to the provinces.[10] It remained possible for the provinces to enact weekly-day-of-rest legislation that had a purely secular purpose. Dickson's judgment in *Big M* constituted a fairly broad hint that such legislation might be found constitutional by the court.

In fact, Ontario's secular Sunday-closing legislation, the *Retail Business Holidays Act*, was declared to be constitutional by the Supreme Court at the height of the Christmas shopping rush in 1986.[11] The legislation had been challenged by four retailers convicted of operating on Sundays contrary to the provincial legislation. It is ironic that after successfully battling in the courts for the power to enact Sunday secular closing legislation, the government then relaxed its restrictions on Sunday shopping, as has happened in most other provinces. However, the point from this litigation is that the provincial legislatures have the power to enact weekly holiday legislation should they wish to exercise that power, but they must frame the legislation in a way that minimally impairs the freedom of religion of any who may be disadvantaged by the legislation.

THE *MULTANI* CASE[12]

Orthodox Sikhs carry with them a *kirpan*, or small metal dagger, because of a commandment given by the tenth Guru of Sikhism, Guru Gobind Singh, in 1699. The kirpan is a symbol of a responsibility to cut through untruth and a reminder to defend those who are unfairly treated. It must be kept in a sheath at all times except during religious ceremonies. Many orthodox Sikhs wear a small kirpan (one to nine centimetres in length) sewn into their clothing.[13]

In November of 2001, Gurbaj Singh Multani was a twelve-year-old student at École Sainte-Catherine-Labouré in west Montreal. He was wearing a twenty-centimetre kirpan sewn into his clothes, as he had since he started attending the school, but the sewing gave way in the playground and the kirpan fell out. This caused alarm amongst school officials and parents, particularly in the wake of the September 11 attacks on the World Trade Center in New York. The school district had a policy that prohibited students from "carrying weapons and dangerous objects."[14] A month after the incident, the local school board decided that Gurbaj would be allowed to "wear his kirpan to school provided that he complied with certain conditions to ensure that it was sealed inside his clothing."[15] However, in February, the school's governing board overturned the local board's decision, and Singh was prohibited from attending school wearing the kirpan. In March, the father of Gurbaj Singh Multani requested the Quebec Superior Court to issue a declaration that his son be allowed to wear a kirpan to school further to the guarantees of freedom of religion in the *Charter of Rights* and the Quebec *Charter of Human Rights and Freedoms*. In May, the declaration was granted but appealed by the governing board and the Quebec government to the Quebec Court of Appeal, which overturned the declaration in 2004. Singh's father then appealed to the Supreme Court of Canada, which rendered its decision in favour of Multani in 2006. Because of the legal wrangling, Gurbaj Singh Multani had moved to a private school where he could wear his kirpan, but the Supreme Court nevertheless agreed to hear the appeal because of the significance of the case for determining the meaning of freedom of religion under the *Charter*. All eight judges who participated in writing the judgment ruled in favour of Multani. Justice Louise Charron wrote for herself and four colleagues, and there were two separate concurring decisions, one for Justices Marie Deschamps and Rosalie Abella, and one by Justice Louis LeBel.[16]

The Quebec government argued that freedom of religion is not an absolute right, and so the board's ban on wearing the kirpan need not be justified under s. 1 of the *Charter*. Rather, it argued that freedom of religion itself in s. 2(a) should be defined narrowly and "limited by imperatives of public order, safety, and health, as well as by the rights and freedoms of others."[17] However, the court disagreed with this submission, and affirmed that in most cases, an alleged violation of freedom of religion should be dealt with under s. 1.[18]

FREEDOM OF RELIGION

The court found that the governing board's refusal to allow Gurbaj Singh Multani to wear a kirpan sewn into his clothing to school constituted a clear violation of freedom of religion. Those claiming a violation of freedom of religion "must demonstrate (1) that he or she sincerely believes in a practice or belief that has a nexus with religion, and (2) that the impugned conduct of a third party interferes, in a manner that is non-trivial or not insubstantial, with his or her ability to act in accordance with that practice or belief."[19] Charron emphasized that the court will not delve into whether a particular religious practice is actually a requirement of the religion, because "different people practise the same religion in different ways."[20] What is important is evidence of the sincerity of a particular religious belief, which would include consistency of practice. There was a good deal of evidence both that orthodox Sikhs believe that a metal kirpan must be worn at all times, and that Gurbaj Singh and his father believed in the importance of this rule and consistently practised it. As well, the board's interference with Gurbaj Singh's religious practice was neither "trivial nor insignificant."[21] In fact, Singh felt compelled to attend a private school where he was allowed to wear his kirpan rather than comply with the board's order that he not wear it to school.

Can the board's interference with freedom of religion be saved by s. 1? The objective of the board in banning the kirpan to ensure reasonable safety at school was found to be "pressing and substantial" by Charron.[22] As well, Charron found a rational connection between the objective of ensuring reasonable safety and banning the kirpan. However, she wrote that Singh's freedom of religion was not minimally impaired. She wrote that those contemplating an action that may violate someone's religious practice have a duty to provide reasonable accommodation up to the point where the accommodation would "cause undue hardship to the party who must perform it."[23]

The board's argument was that a metal kirpan could not only be used as a weapon but also is a symbol of violence. Charron wrote that there was plenty of evidence that for Sikhs the kirpan is a symbol of values that are the opposite of violence, such as mercy, kindness, and honour.[24] In fact, for the board to claim that the kirpan is a symbol of violence is not only disrespectful of the Sikh religion, but may indicate a lack of proper recognition of the importance of freedom of religion and multiculturalism in Canadian society within the context of the *Charter*.[25]

With regard to the board's argument that allowing the wearing of a kirpan would present a danger to others in the school, Charron noted that orthodox Sikhs had been wearing the kirpan in schools across Canada for a century, and there was no evidence of there ever being any violence associated with that practice.[26] She also pointed out that schools allow other potentially dangerous objects, such as baseball bats and compasses. She concluded that "the only possible explanation for the acceptance of these other potentially dangerous objects in schools is that the respondents consider the activities in which those objects are used to be important, while accommodating the religious beliefs of the appellant's son is not."[27]

Another of the board's arguments was that allowing Sikh students to wear a kirpan, and Muslim women to wear a chador, is unfair to students who wish to wear caps or scarves but are not allowed to. Charron countered this argument as follows: "To equate a religious obligation such as wearing the chador with the desire of certain students to wear caps is indicative of a simplistic view of freedom of religion that is incompatible with the Canadian *Charter*."[28]

Charron noted that courts have upheld the prohibition of the kirpan in some specific situations in which the ban is for a short time period and where there is no sense of community that would help to ensure that the kirpan is truly being used as a religious symbol — for example, on airplanes or in courtrooms.[29] Charron distinguished the situation in schools from that in airplanes and courts by quoting from the Ontario Board of Inquiry:

> *Courts and schools are not comparable institutions. One is*
> *a tightly circumscribed environment in which contending*
> *elements, adversarially aligned, strive to obtain justice as they*
> *see it, with judge and/or jury determining the final outcome.*
> *Schools on the other hand are living communities which, while*
> *subject to some controls, engage in the enterprise of education*
> *in which both teachers and students are partners. Also, a court*
> *appearance is temporary . . . and is therefore not comparable*
> *to the years a student spends in the school system.*[30]

In conclusion, Charron stated that "An absolute prohibition [on wearing the kirpan in schools] would stifle the promotion of values such as multiculturalism, diversity, and the development of an educational culture respectful of the rights of others."[31] However, it is reasonable for school boards to set particular conditions on the wearing of the kirpan so as to ensure that there is minimal risk of it being dislodged from the clothing in which it is concealed. Because the prohibition on kirpans in schools under any conditions was found not to have met the minimal impairment test under s. 1, Charron wrote that there was really no need to consider the third part of the second prong of the Oakes test — overall proportionality. She considered this third part anyway because of the need to stress the importance of respecting freedom of religion.

> *A total prohibition against wearing a kirpan to school*
> *undermines the value of this religious symbol and sends*
> *students the message that some religious practices do not*

merit the same protection as others. On the other hand, accommodating Gurbaj Singh and allowing him to wear his kirpan under certain conditions demonstrates the importance that our society attaches to protecting freedom of religion and to showing respect for its minorities. The deleterious effects of a total prohibition thus outweigh its salutary effects.[32]

Charron's disposition was to declare the governing board's decision to prohibit the wearing of a kirpan by Gurbaj Singh null and to order the board to pay the costs of Singh from the start of the litigation.

Another freedom of religion issue that the Supreme Court has considered concerns whether freedom of religion means that religious schools can operate without the necessity of obtaining a government permit. The court decided in *Jones* that religious schools should not be exempt from meeting provincial education requirements as long as these do not "unduly encroach" on religious convictions.[33] And in 2009, in the *Hutterian Brethren of Wilson Colony* decision, the Supreme Court declared that the Alberta government's requirement of photo identification on driver's licences, with no exemption for religious reasons permitted, is a justifiable limit on freedom of religion.[34] The *Jones* and *Hutterian Brethren* decisions both illustrate that while the court considers freedom of religion to be important, like other human rights, it cannot be considered absolute.

THE RIGHT TO PICKET AND TO STRIKE

Since December 1986, the Supreme Court has made a number of decisions concerning the right to strike or to picket. In this section, three of these decisions will be reviewed in detail: *Dolphin Delivery* (1986), the *Alberta Labour Reference* (1987), and *BC Health Services* (2007). The labour law cases have been troublesome for the court. To begin with, Supreme Court majorities exercised considerable restraint (except when courts were threatened with picketing), but in the 2000s began to interpret the s. 2(d) right to freedom of association more liberally, even going so far in *BC Health Services* to overrule the *Alberta Labour Reference* as unable to "withstand principled scrutiny."[35]

THE *DOLPHIN DELIVERY* DECISION[36]

Dolphin Delivery, a Vancouver delivery and courier company, had been receiving about a fifth of its business from another courier company, Purolator, for whom it was doing deliveries. In June 1981, Purolator locked out its employees in a labour dispute, and Dolphin Delivery continued to make deliveries indirectly for Purolator, which was handling business through a third company, Supercourier. In November 1982, the union representing Purolator employees (the Retail, Wholesale and Department Store Union, or RWDSU) gave notice to Dolphin Delivery that the union would picket Dolphin Delivery unless it ceased doing business with Supercourier. Dolphin Delivery, opposed to the threatened picketing, applied for a court order that such picketing would be illegal.

Although most labour relations matters fall under the jurisdiction of provincial governments, this particular dispute fell under federal jurisdiction because it dealt with an industry engaged in interprovincial transportation and communications. The *Canada Labour Code*, however, did not specify whether the union should be allowed to picket in a case like this and so the legality of the picketing would have to be determined according to common law. Pending this determination, Dolphin Delivery obtained a BC Supreme Court injunction ordering the union not to picket until the legal issue could be resolved. The union appealed the decision to grant the injunction on the grounds that it violated the freedom of expression protected by section 2(b) of the *Charter*. After losing in the BC Court of Appeal, the union appealed to the Supreme Court of Canada.

In addition to considering whether the injunction represented a violation of the *Charter*, the court had to deal with two more basic issues. First, because the determination of the issue depended on the common law, the court had to decide whether the *Charter* applies to the common law. Second, because the dispute was between private parties, the court had to decide whether the *Charter* applies to private litigation.

APPLICATION OF THE *CHARTER* TO THE COMMON LAW

Justice William McIntyre, who wrote the majority opinion, had no difficulty in finding that the *Charter* can override the common law when the two conflict. Section 52 of the *Constitution Act, 1982*, which defines the formal constitution of Canada, declares that the constitution, which includes the *Charter*, is the "supreme law of Canada, and any law that is inconsistent with . . . the Constitution is . . . of no force or effect."[37] The court considered that the phrase "any law" is clearly broad enough to include the common law. What remained to be considered was whether the *Charter* applied to *all* common law or just to common law in the public rather than the private sphere.

APPLICATION OF THE *CHARTER* TO PRIVATE LAW

The question about the application of the *Charter* to private litigation governed by the common law rather than by statutes was more difficult to answer. Section 32 of the *Charter* states that it applies to Parliament, legislatures, and governments in Canada. At the time of its adoption, many legal scholars thought that section 32 meant that the *Charter* would apply to public law litigation — disputes in which a government was a party — but not usually to private law litigation — disputes between private individuals or corporations. It was generally accepted, however, that some private law cases would have Charter implications, such as cases that relied on statutes dealing with private law that might infringe the *Charter*. The court had confirmed this application of the *Charter* to private law in the *Skapinker* case[38] (discussed in chapter 2).

Moreover, the *Charter* might also apply to private law cases determined solely according to common law if the common law authorized a court to make an order that violated the *Charter*. According to this view, the word "government" in section 32 of the *Charter* should be interpreted as meaning the institutions that govern a country, including the courts. Since the time of Montesquieu, students of politics have considered government to contain three branches — the legislative, the executive, and the judiciary. From this perspective, the law created by the courts — the common law — would have to conform to the *Charter* to the extent that the courts take governmental action — that is, make orders. Mr. Justice William McIntyre rejected this interpretation of section 32. The word "government" is sometimes used narrowly to mean only the executive branch of government, and he concluded that this is how the word should be interpreted in section 32. Thus, he claimed, court orders in the private law field made solely pursuant to the common law are not subject to the *Charter* unless government action is involved.

McIntyre reasoned that to expand the definition of government in section 32 to include the courts would result in the *Charter* applying to practically all private litigation, since all private law cases end with court orders unless they are settled out of court. None of the Supreme Court judges who heard the *Dolphin Delivery* case were willing to countenance so broad an application of the *Charter*. Nevertheless, McIntyre stated that the "judiciary ought to apply and develop the principles of common law in a manner consistent with the fundamental values enshrined in the Constitution." This statement raises the question of why the judges would be so insistent on excluding common-law Charter claims dealing with private law if they intend to interpret the common law consistently with the *Charter* anyway. The answer may be that formal Charter litigation with regard to private matters regulated by the common law would present the courts in Canada with countless issues that would not only take them further into the policy-making realm, but could increase the backlogs of cases.

Although the court's approach to private litigation is understandable given that from the beginning it was generally accepted that the *Charter* would not apply to most private litigation, the decision is problematic. In the *Dolphin Delivery* case the court affirmed that the regulations created by "creatures of Parliament and the legislatures," such as municipal councils, marketing boards, and regulatory agencies such as the CRTC (Canadian Radio-television and Telecommunications Commission), are subject to the *Charter*. The courts, however, are also creations of either Parliament or legislatures, and yet the regulations they create, known as the common law, are *not* subject to the *Charter*. It seems incongruous to exempt the courts from the *Charter* in this way.

THE FREEDOM OF EXPRESSION ISSUE

It was clear to Mr. Justice McIntyre that picketing is a form of expression and is therefore protected by section 2(b) of the *Charter* in all public law cases and in private law cases where the constitutionality of a statute or regulation is an issue. McIntryre wrote, "The union is making a statement to the general public that it is involved in a dispute, that it is seeking to impose its will on the object of the picketing, and that it solicits the assistance of the public in honouring the picket line."[39] The only judge who disagreed with this reasoning was Mr. Justice Jean Beetz, who maintained an approach consistent with the one he had developed in the *Dupond* case[40] (see chapter 1). In that case, Beetz, writing for the majority, could find no element of expression in a political demonstration.

Because of the court's reasoning that private law cases decided under common law were not covered by the *Charter*, the union lost the case. Because the court found no Charter violation, there was no need for the court to consider whether an injunction that violated freedom of expression could be upheld under section 1. However, the court decided to comment on this issue anyway in an attempt to clarify the law. Without applying the two-part, three-pronged test in *Oakes*, McIntyre simply concluded that because Supercourier was a third party not directly involved in the labour dispute, it would be reasonable to limit freedom of expression in order to prevent harm to the third party: "It is reasonable to restrain picketing so that the conflict will not escalate beyond the actual parties. While picketing is, no doubt, a legislative weapon to be employed in a labour dispute by the employees against their employer, it should not be permitted to harm others."[41]

In a later case, the Supreme Court found that picketing is protected by section 2(b) but that to prohibit the picketing of courthouses is a reasonable limit under section 1. In this decision, known as the *BCGEU* case,[42] the issue was whether the British Columbia Government Employees Union could be prohibited from picketing at the entrances to courthouses. The union went on strike on November 1, 1983, as part of a general labour protest against the provincial government's new restrictive labour legislation. When the chief justice of the BC Supreme Court arrived at the Vancouver courthouse at 8:00 a.m. on November 1, he immediately issued an injunction prohibiting picketing at courthouses. He issued the injunction on his own motion and acting *ex parte* (meaning that the union's side was not presented). The order made provision for the union to apply for an order to set aside the injunction. The union applied for such an order, but the application was dismissed. The union appealed all the way to the Supreme Court of Canada, primarily on the grounds that the injunction violated the right to freedom of expression in section 2(b) of the *Charter*.

The main decision of the Supreme Court, written by Chief Justice Dickson, relied on the *Dolphin Delivery* decision to the effect that picketing is a form of expression protected by section 2(b). However, Dickson concluded that the injunction was a reasonable limit under section 1. The objective of the injunction — "assuring unimpeded access to the courts"[43] — was of sufficient importance to pass the first part of the Oakes test. This is because access to the courts is necessary to preserve the rule of law and also to protect the rights in the *Charter* itself. The injunction also met all three requirements in the second part of the Oakes test. In particular, the injunction restricted the right of union members as little as possible by leaving "the Union and its members free to express themselves in other places"[44] and by providing for a method whereby the injunction could be challenged. Moreover, the chief justice refrained from using a more restrictive procedure — charging picketers with contempt of court for blocking access to the courts.

> *Finally, there was a proportionality between the effects of*
> *the injunction on the protected right and the objective of*
> *maintaining access to the court . . . A significant element . . .*
> *of the objective of the injunction order was to protect Charter*
> *rights [by allowing litigants to continue to bring Charter*
> *claims to court]. The Charter surely does not self-destruct in a*
> *dynamic of conflicting rights.*[45]

Thus, although the Supreme Court has recognized that union picketing is protected by section 2(b) of the *Charter*, in both *Dolphin Delivery* and *BCGEU*, the *Charter* was interpreted in a way that, in the end, was of no assistance to the union cause.

THE ALBERTA LABOUR REFERENCE[46]

During the 1970s and early 1980s, there were several strikes in Alberta involving nurses and public servants. In 1983 the legislature amended its labour legislation to prohibit strikes and lockouts involving public servants, hospital employees, firefighters, and nurses. (The police were already prohibited from striking.) The legislation provided for compulsory arbitration

111

to settle disputes involving these employees, limited the matters the arbitration boards could consider, and required the boards to consider the government's fiscal goals.

Labour leaders in the province strongly opposed the amendments.[47] They claimed that these amendments violated section 2(d) of the *Charter* — freedom of association. In order to settle the issue, the government referred the question of the constitutionality of the legislation to the Alberta Court of Appeal. This court could find no protection of a right to strike in section 2(d). The unions appealed this decision to the Supreme Court of Canada. In the meantime, Premier Peter Lougheed announced that if the Supreme Court found a right to strike in the *Charter*, the legislation would be re-enacted with a section 33 override attached to it. It became unnecessary for the government to use section 33 when the Supreme Court upheld the Alberta Court of Appeal decision.

The Majority Decision

The opinion of the majority on why freedom of association does not imply the right to strike was written by Mr. Justice McIntyre. He described six approaches to defining the meaning of freedom of association. Beginning with the most conservative, these definitions are as follows:

- the right to associate with others in common pursuits (However, the government may limit the "objects" or "actions" of groups. Freedom of association means "the freedom [of groups] to engage collectively in those activities which are constitutionally protected for each individual.");
- whatever persons may lawfully do as individuals, they "are entitled to do in concert with others";
- groups have a right to engage in "collective activities which may be said to be fundamental to our culture and traditions";
- groups have a right to engage in those activities "which are essential to the lawful goals" of the group;
- groups have a right to engage in any activity, subject to reasonable limits pursuant to section 1 of the *Charter*.

Having established these six choices, McIntyre described the last three as unacceptable. From his perspective, the *Charter* is a document designed primarily to protect *individual* rights. Denominational school rights, continued by section 29, and Aboriginal rights, protected by section 25 of the *Charter*, are listed as the only two exceptions to this general rule.

The purpose of freedom of association, according to McIntyre, is to protect the individual's right of association, not to establish a third category of group rights. To illustrate the problems that might arise when groups may do what individuals cannot, he cited the example of a gun club claiming the right of its members to bear arms, although individuals not belonging to the club could not claim such a right. For McIntyre, only the first three approaches to freedom of association are acceptable, as they do not create special group rights. Lest some think this approach trivializes the concept of freedom of association, McIntyre quoted from de Tocqueville to the effect that the individual right to associate with others is "inalienable . . . [and one of the] foundations of society."

The Minority Decision

Chief Justice Dickson, in a decision concurred with by Madame Justice Bertha Wilson, attacked the majority's definition of freedom of association as being "legalistic, ungenerous, indeed vapid." If freedom of association merely allows individuals to do in concert with others what they are free to do alone, then the "express conferral of a freedom of association [in section 2(d)] is unnecessary." Dickson described how individual workers are powerless if they bargain individually with management. Unless unions have the power to strike, unions and management cannot bargain as relative equals. He related how the collective-bargaining process, including the right of unions to strike, had led to a general atmosphere of labour peace. In addition, collective bargaining, with the strike as the ultimate weapon, had resulted in workers having a say in the conditions of their employment and thus in promoting their "sense of identity, self-worth and emotional well-being." He noted that there is no individual equivalent of the right to strike and that section 2(d) was intended to prevent legislatures from "precluding associational conduct because of its concerted or associational nature." In other words, the freedom to belong to a labour union is of little value if the union cannot engage in the one activity that makes it viable — the strike.

If we consider these formal, legal arguments, the Dickson-Wilson approach seems more convincing. However, almost as an aside, the majority gave another reason for not finding a right to strike in section 2(d): the inappropriateness of courts as policy-makers in the labour relations field. McIntyre pointed out that the history of labour relations in Canada had proven that "specialized labour tribunals are better suited than courts for resolving labour problems."

> *Judges do not have the expert knowledge always helpful and sometimes necessary in the resolution of labour problems. If the right to strike is constitutionalized, then [labour disputes] become matters of law. This would inevitably throw the courts back into the field of labour relations and much of the value of specialized labour tribunals would be lost.*

Mr. Justice Le Dain, with Justices Beetz and (Gérard) La Forest concurring, made the same point: "It is surprising that in an area in which this Court has affirmed a principle of judicial restraint in the review of administrative action we should be considering the substitution of our judgment for that of the legislature." If the right to strike is constitutionalized, then every piece of back-to-work legislation and every statute limiting the right to strike of essential employees could be the subject of a court challenge.

Although this argument has nothing to do with the attempt to give a legal definition to section 2(d), it is more convincing than the main reasons of the majority. For several decades, progressive labour lawyers have been imploring judges to exercise restraint and stay out of labour disputes as much as possible. Since not many judges have labour backgrounds or experience in industrial relations, they have shown a remarkable ability to make unenlightened decisions in this field. The labour relations boards that exist in all jurisdictions in Canada were established as an alternative to courts, and the consensus of legal scholars is that these boards have shown much more wisdom in dealing with labour disputes than have the courts. From this perspective, the majority decision in the *Alberta Labour Reference* shows good sense.

The weakness of this approach is that it does not recognize that denying a constitutional protection for the right to strike is quite different from judicial restraint in the face of ordinary legislation. The denial of a constitutional right to strike is apt to be interpreted by many as a judicial stamp of approval for an anti-labour government's program of severely restricting the right to strike. Armed with this weapon, such a government might be tempted to go very far in trying to reduce the power of organized labour, resulting in an increasingly hostile labour climate.

Chief Justice Dickson explained how he would have decided the section 1 issue (whether limiting the right to strike is reasonable) if the majority had found a right to strike in section 2(d). He stated that "the protection of services which are truly essential . . . is a legislative objective of sufficient importance" to pass the first part of the Oakes test. Dickson concluded, however, that the legislation would not pass the second part of the test. Although it was clear that police and firefighters provide essential services — that is, services "whose interruption would endanger" the life, personal safety, health, and security of all or part of the population, not to mention the rule of law — Dickson said that the Crown had failed to show why public servants and hospital employees other than nurses or doctors should be considered essential. Thus, part of the legislation failed the rational-connection prong of the second part of the Oakes test. Moreover, the legislation, in Dickson's opinion, did not encroach on the right to freedom of association as little as possible. For example, the legislation left it to the discretion of a government board whether an arbitration board should be established during a labour dispute or whether bargaining or mediation should continue indefinitely. Furthermore, the legislation totally excluded certain matters from being referred to arbitration, and the Crown could not justify these exclusions.

THE *BC HEALTH SERVICES* DECISION[48]

Very occasionally, minority decisions become majority decisions in subsequent cases in which the Supreme Court is persuaded that the earlier precedent is wrong. That is precisely what occurred in the *BC Health Services* decision of 2007, in which the reasoning of McIntyre in the *Alberta Labour Reference* was soundly rejected by a six to one majority in favour of reasoning similar to the Dickson-Wilson approach. But the seeds for overruling the *Alberta Labour Reference* were sown in the Dunmore decision of 2001.[49] In 1994, Ontario's NDP government enacted legislation giving farm workers the right to form labour unions. In 1995, Ontario's Conservative government repealed the NDP legislation and enacted a law prohibiting farm workers from forming unions, claiming that unionization would threaten the family farm. In *Dunmore*, in an eight to one decision the Supreme Court struck down the Conservative legislation on the grounds that an outright prohibition on any group from forming a labour union is a violation of s. 2(d). With regard to the *Alberta Labour Reference*, the majority reasoned that McIntyre's very restrictive interpretation of s. 2(d) was not explicitly accepted by all of the majority nor were parts of Dickson's more liberal approach explicitly rejected.[50] The majority concluded that the Conservative farm-worker legislation did not limit the freedom of association rights of farm workers as little as necessary in order to protect the family farm, and without overruling the *Alberta Labour Reference*, legislation that prevents individuals from forming an association is a violation of s. 2(d) (freedom of association).

The issue in the *BC Heath Services* case was whether the BC government could constitutionally enact legislation that gave health care employers (public and private) the ability to contract out of collective agreements at their discretion and without notice or consultation with labour unions. From 1991 to 2001, the cost of health care grew three times as fast as the provincial economy.[51] In 2001, the BC Liberal party defeated the New Democratic party and was determined to reduce the provincial deficit. The 2002 *Health and Social Services Delivery Improvement Act*[52] was intended to make it easier for health care employers to reorganize their labour forces in order to cut costs. Sections of existing collective agreements inconsistent with the *Act*'s grant of power to health care employers, including contracting-out provisions prohibited by the collective agreements, were declared invalid. The new provisions were enacted quickly, with "no meaningful consultation with unions."[53]

The decision of the majority of six was written by Chief Justice Beverley McLachlin and Justice LeBel. The first part of the decision analyzed the relation between s. 2(d) and collective bargaining issues.

We conclude that s. 2(d) . . . protects the capacity of members
of labour unions to engage, in association, in collective
bargaining on fundamental workplace issues . . . This
protection does not cover all aspects of "collective bargaining."
. . . What is protected is simply the right of employees to
associate in a process of collective action to achieve workplace
goals. If the government substantially interferes with that
right, it violates s. 2(d) of the Charter: Dunmore.[54]

McLachlin and LeBel, building on the Dunmore decision, then explained why the court decided to overrule the majority decision in the *Alberta Labour Reference*, thus siding with the minority in the latter case. They broke their explanation into four categories.

First, "a review of the s. 2(d) jurisprudence of this Court reveals that the reasons evoked in the past for holdings that the guarantee of freedom of association does not extend to collective bargaining can no longer stand."[55] McLachlin and LeBel criticized McIntyre's argument in the *Alberta Labour Reference* that the *Charter* is intended to protect only individual rights, not collective rights. Referring to the decision in *Dunmore*, McLachlin and LeBel concluded that allowing governments to prohibit collective bargaining is clearly a violation of freedom of association, and so the right must obviously extend beyond individual rights.[56] A problem with the majority decision in the *Alberta Labour Reference*, McLachlin and LeBel wrote, was that that majority had adopted a decontextualized approach to interpreting s. 2(d) (i.e., an approach devoid of thinking about the ramifications of government actions like those challenged in *Dunmore* and *BC Heath Services*), rather than the "purposive approach taken to other Charter guarantees."[57]

Second, "Canada's historic recognition of the importance of collective bargaining to freedom of association" augurs in favour of overturning the *Alberta Labour Reference* precedent.[58] To defend this position, McLachlin and LeBel summarized the history of labour relations in Canada beginning in the 1870s to show that the right to collective bargaining, in the Canadian context, is not merely a modern right not intended to be covered by the *Charter*, as McIntyre had claimed. Rather, the recognition of s. 2(d) as encompassing some aspects of collective bargaining is "the culmination of a historical movement towards the recognition of a procedural right to collective bargaining."[59]

Third, "collective bargaining is an integral component of freedom of association in international law."[60] McLachlin and LeBel's summary of Canada's history of collective bargaining was interspersed with references to the history of collective bargaining in the US, the UK, and other industrial nations, which was the forerunner of international agreements, such as the International Labour Organization's *Convention Concerning Freedom of Association and Protection of the Right to Organize*.[61] Canada has ratified this convention, as well as other international agreements that enshrine the right to free collective bargaining. Although international law is not part of domestic Canadian law unless enacted by appropriate legislatures, McLachlin and LeBel wrote that "international conventions to which Canada is a party recognize the right of the members of unions to engage in collective bargaining, as part of the protection for freedom of association. It is reasonable to infer that s. 2(d) of the *Charter* should be interpreted as recognizing at least the same level of protection."[62]

Fourth, "interpreting s. 2(d) as including a right to collective bargaining is consistent with . . . other Charter rights . . ."[63] such as the s. 15 right to equality. McLachlin and LeBel pointed out that Charter rights are underpinned by values that underlie it, such as "[h]uman dignity, equality, liberty, respect for the autonomy of the person, and the enhancement of democracy."[64] Collective bargaining contributes to ameliorating the historic inequality between employers and employees, and promotes workplace democracy, as well as enhancing the dignity of individual workers.[65]

McLachlin and LeBel pointed out that the "right to collective bargaining . . . is a limited right . . . as the right to a process."[66] The judges explained that the Charter right to collective bargaining is not a right to particular objectives, but rather guarantees the right of employees "to unite, to present demands to . . . employers collectively and to engage in discussions in an attempt to achieve workplace-related goals."[67] S. 2(d) prohibits governments from "substantial interference"[68] with collective bargaining.

McLachlin and LeBel found that the provisions of the *BC Act* that invalidated the provisions of past collective agreements and that prohibited certain procedures — contracting out, "bumping," and certain aspects concerning layoffs — from being included in future collective agreements were clearly interferences in the collective bargaining process. They reasoned, as well, that this interference is substantial,[69] and thus subject to s. 2(d). In applying the s. 1 test, they concluded that the *Act*'s purpose, to enhance "the ability of health employers and authorities to respond quickly and effectively to changing circumstances," is pressing and substantial, thus passing part one of the Oakes test.[70] They considered that there was evidence of a rational connection between the objectives of the legislation and the sections of the *Act* being challenged, but that these sections did not minimally impair the s. 2(d) right to collective bargaining. Thus, three sections of the *Act* were struck down.[71]

The Supreme Court's labour relations decisions indicate just how difficult it has been for the court to wrestle with the application of the abstract concept of freedom of association, and apply it to the very complex world of labour relations. These decisions also show how the court can re-evaluate the soundness of its earlier judgments in the context of new factual situations, and in the light of the criticism it has been subjected to in law journals from the time of the *Alberta Labour Reference* to the *BC Health Services* decision.

THE LANGUAGE OF COMMERCIAL SIGNS IN QUEBEC

The Canadian political system can be regarded as a complex experiment around the issue of whether the members of two linguistic groups, anglophones and francophones, can each fulfill their aspirations in a federal liberal democracy in which the most numerous group is dominant in nine out of ten provinces. There are many complicating factors in this experiment. Because the language of the majority is also the dominant language of North America and the language of commerce and science in most of the world, the members of the majority group have never known what it is like to have a mother tongue that is in danger of extinction. Thus, they have difficulty in appreciating the concerns of the francophone minority, which regards the preservation of the endangered French language and culture in North America as a goal of overriding concern.

Since they form a majority in Quebec, francophones have used the provincial government as a vehicle for preserving and promoting their language within Quebec by requiring the use of French in the workplace and limiting the use of English. However, Quebec is also a liberal society that values human rights, such as freedom of expression. Thus, the collective desire of the francophone community to preserve and promote its language has come into direct collision with the liberal ideal of individual freedom of expression.

Another dimension to the issue is the lingering resentment among some in the francophone community against previous generations of anglophone Quebeckers, some of whom regarded themselves as the superior class in Quebec society. Such a "social hangover" is apt to lead to emotional overreactions on both sides. The public tensions emanating from this situation cannot help but be taken into account consciously by the government when drafting language policy, and by judges at the unconscious level when adjudicating Charter issues that affect language policy.

BILL 101 AND CIVIL LIBERTIES LEGISLATION

In 1977 the Parti Québécois government enacted Bill 101, the *Charter of the French Language.* Among many other provisions, the bill prohibited the use of English on most commercial signs, although in some cases (such as for stores with not more than four employees) English or another language could be used alongside French. These provisions were designed primarily to tackle the language issue in Montreal, where the great majority of Quebec anglophones reside. From the perspective of the Parti Québécois, the problem was not the use of English by anglophones, but the image of anglophone dominance that English signs presented to immigrants (whom the Quebec government wanted to assimilate into the francophone community) and to francophones themselves.

It should be pointed out that Bill 101 guaranteed anglophones and other linguistic minorities the untrammelled right to use their language for political, social, cultural, and educational purposes. Newspapers, television stations, radio stations, and educational institutions were exempted from the bill's signs and advertising provisions. The commercial signs provisions of Bill 101 were designed to give the streets of Quebec a French look, with the hope that everyone would absorb the message that the French language is a permanent fixture in Quebec, not a quaint relic of an ethnic minority on the road to assimilation.

There was some question as to whether these provisions violated the Quebec *Charter of Human Rights and Freedoms*, which had been enacted by Quebec's Liberal government in 1975. Section 3 of the Quebec *Charter of Rights* states that "[e]very person is the possessor of . . . freedom of expression," and section 10 declares that "[e]very person has a right to full and equal recognition and exercise of his human rights and freedoms, without distinction . . . based on [among other categories] language." However, section 9.1 of the Quebec *Charter of Rights* is a limitations clause that the PQ claimed would save Bill 101 against a challenge from the Quebec *Charter* itself. Section 9.1 reads as follows:

> *In exercising his fundamental freedoms and rights, a person
> shall maintain a proper regard for democratic values, public
> order, and the general well-being of the citizens of Quebec. In
> this respect, the scope of the freedoms and rights, and limits to
> their exercise, may be fixed by law.*

When the *Canadian Charter of Rights and Freedoms* came into effect in 1982, the PQ provincial government enacted a blanket override of the *Charter* as a protest against its enactment without the assent of the Quebec National Assembly. The override legislation amended all Quebec statutes enacted prior to 1982, including Bill 101, so that each statute would contain a clause stating that it would operate notwithstanding sections 2 and 7–15 of the *Charter*. As well, the government routinely included a Charter override clause in each piece of legislation passed after the blanket override, including an amendment to Bill 101 enacted in 1983 which came into force in 1984. This practice of overriding the Canadian *Charter* was discontinued by the Quebec Liberal government elected in 1985, but the previous overrides remained in effect for their natural five-year life spans.

THE CHALLENGES TO BILL 101

In 1978 Allan Singer, a stationer in the predominantly anglophone Montreal suburb of Pointe Claire, was charged with continuing to display his store sign (as he had for thirty years) in English only in contravention of Bill 101. He was convicted. Then, in conjunction with several other merchants, he sought a declaration from the Quebec Superior Court that the guarantees of equality and freedom of expression in the Quebec *Charter of Rights* nullified the commercial signs provisions of Bill 101, including those allowing English signs on smaller stores as long as French was also used. The case became known as *Devine v. Quebec*[72] after one of the other merchants also charged. Singer and the other merchants lost in the Quebec Superior Court and the Quebec Court of Appeal, but went on to appeal to the Supreme Court of Canada. In the Supreme Court, the Canadian *Charter* became an issue because one of the override clauses that protected Bill 101 from Charter scrutiny had expired. In addition, lawyers for Devine and Singer argued that the override procedures used by the Quebec legislature were procedurally incorrect and therefore not effective.

Meanwhile, another somewhat different challenge to Bill 101 was developing. In 1984 several merchants, including Brown's Shoe Store, brought a motion before the Quebec Superior Court requesting a declaration that the provisions of Bill 101 that prohibited English contravened both the Quebec *Charter of Rights* and the Canadian *Charter of Rights*. (Unlike Singer and Devine, these merchants did not object to using bilingual signs, but only to the provisions making French the exclusive language of signs.) As in the *Devine* case, lawyers for these merchants argued that the procedures used by the Quebec legislature to override sections of the Canadian *Charter* were ineffective. This case became known as *Ford v. Quebec*.[73] Ford and the other merchants were successful in obtaining the declaratory judgment striking down parts of Bill 101. The Quebec government unsuccessfully appealed to the Quebec Court of Appeal in 1986. Quebec then appealed to the Supreme Court of Canada.

The Supreme Court released its judgment for both the *Ford* and *Devine* cases on December 15, 1988. In both decisions, only one opinion was presented, and it was attributed to the entire panel consisting of Justices Dickson, Beetz, McIntyre, (Antonio) Lamer, and Wilson. (Justices [Willard] Estey and Le Dain had participated in the hearing but resigned from the court after the hearing and took no part in preparing the judgment.) The *Ford* case, in which the major issue was whether the Quebec government could prohibit French-only signs without violating either the Quebec *Charter of Rights* or the Canadian *Charter*, is considered first below. The judgment in *Ford* will then be compared to that in *Devine,* in which the chief issue was whether the Quebec government could require bilingual signs.

THE *FORD* CASE (1988) AND THE ISSUE OF FRENCH-ONLY SIGNS

The *Ford* case dealt with four major issues:

- the effectiveness of Quebec's blanket override of the *Canadian Charter of Rights and Freedoms;*
- whether the prohibition of English on signs violates freedom of expression as protected by section 2(b) of the Canadian *Charter* and section 3 of the Quebec *Charter of Rights;*
- if freedom of expression has been violated, whether it can be justified pursuant to the limitations clauses in the Canadian *Charter* (section 1) or the Quebec *Charter of Rights* (section 9.1); and
- whether the prohibition of English on signs violates the guarantee of equality in section 10 of the Quebec *Charter of Rights.*

THE EFFECTIVENESS OF QUEBEC'S BLANKET OVERRIDE

The merchants succeeded in the Quebec Court of Appeal. They argued that the words "expressly" and "provision" in section 33 of the Canadian *Charter* (see the Appendix) imply that when a legislature wishes to override the *Charter,* it must state precisely which provisions of an act are to take precedence over the *Charter.* As well, the merchants claimed that the legislature must declare which particular rights contained in section 2 or sections 7–15 are to be overridden. To this submission was added the argument that the democratic process requires legislators to deliberate about the specific implications of the overrides being contemplated. It was suggested that these required procedures are defeated both by the blanket override and by the routine override used after 1982.

The Supreme Court was not persuaded by these arguments. The court claimed that the position of the merchants amounted to a claim that section 33 was a directive to legislatures to deliberate about the use of the override in a particular way. The court held that, on the contrary, section 33 is a merely procedural set of instructions. All that is required to meet the requirements of section 33 is for a legislature to state which section numbers in the *Charter* are to be overridden. Thus, both the blanket override applying to pre-1982 statutes and the routine overrides used since that time are effective.[74] (The court also decided that a legislature could not enact a retroactive override of the *Charter*. In other words, the earliest that an override could become effective would be the date of proclamation of the override legislation.)[75]

As a result of the court's view of section 33, section 58 of Bill 101 — which prohibits "public signs and posters and commercial advertising" unless they are in French — was still protected from the Canadian *Charter* at the time of the hearing thanks to a 1984 amendment to Bill 101. Of course, section 58 was still subject to the Quebec *Charter of Rights*. However, section 69 of Bill 101, which allows only "the French version of a firm name" to be used on signs in Quebec, was subject to the Canadian *Charter* because the section 33 override that applied to section 69 had expired, having been enacted in 1982. (Recall that section 33 overrides automatically expire after five years.)

The argument of the merchants about the need for careful deliberation about the use of section 33 constitutes an example of a good point raised in the wrong forum. From a legal standpoint, the Supreme Court's conclusion that section 33 is merely procedural is sound. From the perspective of democratic theory, the merchants' argument that section 33 requires more than routine consideration by legislatures is compelling. It is the kind of issue that should be considered not in a court, but by the politically aware Canadian public with a view to pressing for reforms either in section 33 or in legislative procedure in general that would force legislators to consider more carefully the invocation of section 33. For example, section 33 could be amended to require public hearings before its application in normal circumstances or, if used during emergencies, afterwards, but within a specified period.

FREEDOM OF EXPRESSION

As noted in chapter 2, the Supreme Court has declared that it will interpret similar phrases similarly in the Canadian *Charter* and the various statutory bills of rights, such as the Quebec *Charter of Rights*. Therefore, the court will give freedom of expression in section 2(b) of the Canadian *Charter* the same meaning as freedom of expression in section 3 of the Quebec *Charter of Rights*.

The court broke the question of the meaning of freedom of expression into two sub-issues: (1) whether freedom of expression includes the language in which ideas are expressed or merely the ideas themselves, and (2) whether freedom of expression includes commercial expression.

Counsel for the Quebec government argued that the purpose of freedom of expression in a liberal democracy is to protect the expression of ideas themselves, not the medium (language) in which the ideas are expressed. Counsel suggested that the ability to present ideas is a "freedom" in the traditional liberal sense, whereas the ability to use a particular language to express these ideas is a privilege that can be regulated by government within the confines of the constitution's language rights sections. Because these language rights sections (sections 16–23 of the Canadian *Charter* and section 133 of the *Constitution Act, 1867*) provide specific but limited guarantees of language privileges, such privileges were not intended by the constitution to be broadened by being considered as included in section 2(b).

> *The Court rejected this suggested approach. Of the language rights sections of the constitution, the Court said that they are intended to impose obligations on government . . . [to provide] specific opportunities [for Canadians] to use English or French, or to receive services in English or French, in concrete, readily ascertainable and limited circumstances. In contrast, what the respondents seek in this case is a freedom as that term was explained by Dickson . . . [in the* Big M *decision]: "Freedom can primarily be characterized by the absence of coercion or restraint. If a person is compelled by the state . . . to a course of action or inaction which he would not otherwise have chosen, he is not acting of his own volition and he cannot be said to be truly free."*[76]

Because merchants are compelled not to use English, their freedom of expression is constrained. Moreover, the court quoted from sociological evidence to the effect that "[l]anguage itself is content, a reference for . . . the societal goals and the large-scale value-laden arenas of interaction that typify every speech community."[77] This respect for language, the court claimed, had been adopted by the *Charter of the French Language* itself, which stated in its preamble that "the French language [is] the distinctive language of a people . . . [and] the instrument by which that people has articulated its identity."[78] The court concluded that language is

> *a means by which a people may express its cultural identity. It is also the means by which the individual expresses his or her personal identity and sense of individuality. That suggests that "freedom of expression" is intended to extend to more than the content of expression in its narrow sense.*[79]

Therefore, freedom of expression includes the freedom to express ideas in the language of choice, and not merely the freedom to express ideas in the language specified by the government.

On the question of whether freedom of expression includes commercial expression, the court referred to US case law on this question for possible guidance. The US Supreme Court had decided that the First Amendment guarantee of freedom of speech included commercial speech. It pointed out that freedom of commercial speech protects audiences (listeners) as well as advertisers and that audiences may have a "keener by far" interest in obtaining information about commercial products than "in the day's most urgent political debate."[80] However, the American judges had also decided that commercial speech deserved a lesser degree of protection than political speech.

The court noted that the US judges had been subjected to much criticism for their approach to commercial speech because of the difficulty in drawing the line between commercial speech and political speech. As a result, the Canadian judges rejected the American approach of dividing expression into two types — commercial and non-commercial — and then providing less protection to non-commercial speech. However, they accepted the argument that commercial speech is important because it protects audiences as well as advertisers.

> *Given the earlier pronouncements of this Court to the effect*
> *that the rights and freedoms guaranteed in the* Canadian
> Charter *should be given a large and liberal interpretation,*
> *there is no sound basis on which commercial expression can*
> *be excluded from the protection of s.2(b) . . . Over and above*
> *its intrinsic value as expression, commercial expression which,*
> *as has been pointed out, protects listeners as well as speakers,*
> *plays a significant role in enabling individuals to make*
> *informed economic choices, an important aspect of individual*
> *self-fulfillment and personal autonomy.*[81]

This conclusion demonstrates how judges, because of their social backgrounds and practice experience, may be sympathetic to the claims of commercial interests. (In contrast, they may be uncomfortable with the claims of labour, as the right-to-strike cases discussed earlier demonstrated.) Although the court's reasoning about the value of commercial speech does have some merit, to suggest that the sign on Brown's Shoe Store — "Bravo Bravo. Brown's quality, Bravo's price" — is as important to human freedom as the ability to debate publicly the ideals of Christ, Locke, and Marx, for example, seems to be stretching the point. One of the implications of this decision is that all statutes that regulate advertising are now subject to Charter challenges.

WHETHER THE COMMERCIAL SIGNS PROVISIONS ARE A REASONABLE LIMIT

The Attorney General of Quebec submitted as evidence a number of studies in sociolinguistics concerning the dangers faced by the French language in Quebec. These studies indicated that French in Canada is threatened with extinction because of declines in the francophone population, the tendency of francophones outside Quebec to assimilate, the usual practice of immigrants to Quebec of assimilating with the anglophone population, and anglophone domination of the upper echelons of the business community. The studies showed that prior to Bill 101, the heavy use of English on commercial signs in Montreal suggested to new immigrants that learning English was as acceptable, or perhaps more acceptable, than learning French; to francophones that English was the language of the future; and to anglophones that there was no need to learn French. The purpose of the commercial signs provisions of Bill 101 was to change this *visage linguistique*, or linguistic impression, of Quebec (and particularly Montreal) and to promote the use of French among all language groups.

The court concluded that the studies demonstrated the importance of the government's objective in enacting the commercial signs provisions. Thus, the first part of the Oakes test for the acceptance of reasonable limits to rights — that the government's objective must be of substantial importance — was met. Moving to the second part of the test, the court concluded that there was a rational connection between the signs provisions and the goal of preserving and promoting the French language. However, the judges reasoned that the provisions failed to limit freedom of expression as little as necessary to achieve the goal of preserving and promoting the French language. In other words, the sociolinguistic studies did not

> *demonstrate that the requirement of the use of French only is*
> *either necessary for the achievement of the legislative objective*
> *or proportionate to it. That specific question is simply not*
> *addressed by the materials. Indeed, in his factum and oral*
> *argument the Attorney General of Quebec did not attempt*
> *to justify the requirement of the exclusive use of French . . .*
> *Thus, whereas requiring the predominant display of the*
> *French language, even its marked predominance, would*
> *be proportional to the goal of promoting and maintaining*
> *a French "visage linguistique" in Quebec and therefore*
> *justified under s. 9.1 of the* Quebec Charter *and s. 1 of the*
> Canadian Charter, *requiring the exclusive use of French has*
> *not been so justified.*[82]

Through this reasoning, the court provided the Bourassa government with a broad hint that if Bill 101 were amended so as to provide for the predominant but not exclusive use of French on commercial signs, such a provision would be found by the court to be in conformity both with the Canadian *Charter* and the Quebec *Charter of Rights*. As we shall see, the Bourassa government did not take the bait.

EQUALITY AND THE QUEBEC *CHARTER OF RIGHTS*

The court had no difficulty in finding that section 58 of Bill 101, the section prohibiting the use of any language other than French on commercial signs, is discriminating. In other words, this provision has a harsher effect on non-francophones than on francophones. It has "the effect of nullifying the right to full and equal recognition and exercise of this freedom [to express oneself in the language of one's choice]."[83] Thus, the challenged commercial signs provisions violate the guarantee of equality in the Quebec *Charter of Rights*, as well as the guarantee of freedom of expression.

THE *FORD* DECISION AND THE *CHARTER*

The *Ford* decision tackled a number of complex Charter issues. According to *Ford*, legislatures may invoke the section 33 override simply by following the correct technical procedure of declaring which numerical sections of the *Charter* shall not apply to a piece of legislation. Even if this procedure is put into place by a blanket override of previous legislation, it is nevertheless effective.

The *Ford* decision also determined that freedom of expression includes the freedom to express oneself in the language of choice and that commercial advertising is protected by the *Charter*. As well, it decided that the freedom to express oneself in commercial advertising in the language of choice can be limited by a requirement that the official language, if its existence is endangered, must be included on all signs and given prominence.

These pronouncements carry with them profound implications for the future development of policies in Canada concerning freedom of expression, language, and human rights in general. For example, should legislators be forced to consider more carefully the imposition of the section 33 override? Does commercial advertising really merit full Charter protection? Is the forced use of French in addition to the language of choice truly a reasonable limit to freedom of expression? These are important questions that are the proper subject of public debate as well as judicial consideration. The judicial reasoning about these issues, however, might help to inform such public debates.

THE *DEVINE* CASE (1988) AND BILINGUAL SIGNS[84]

The major issue in *Devine* was whether the Quebec government could require the use of French in commercial advertising, such as signs and commercial forms (like invoices and applications for employment), in addition to the merchant's language of choice. That question was really answered in *obiter dicta* in the *Ford* decision: the requirement that French be used in addition to the language of choice does violate the guarantee of freedom of expression in both the Canadian *Charter* and the Quebec *Charter of Rights*, but this requirement constitutes a reasonable limit pursuant to the limitations clauses in both documents. *(Obiter dicta,* or "words in passing," are the parts of a judicial decision that are not essential to the outcome.) Thus, much of the *Devine* decision simply reiterates the reasoning contained in the more comprehensive *Ford* decision.

There were two unique aspects of the *Devine* decision. The first was whether certain types of language legislation might be *ultra vires* a provincial legislature because only the federal Parliament, acting under its criminal jurisdiction, is empowered to enact such legislation. The second was whether a government regulation requiring the mandatory use of French alone (as opposed to the mandatory use of French in addition to another language) violates the equality clauses in the Canadian *Charter* and the Quebec *Charter of Rights*.

The Jurisdictional Issue

Allan Singer argued that legislation prohibiting signs unless they are in French (with or without another language) is really criminal legislation because it creates a prohibition backed by a threat of punishment in the form of a stiff fine. (Corporations violating the commercial signs provisions of Bill 101 were liable to a fine of up to $5,750 for a second offence, plus a fine of up to $2,300 per day for carrying on a business without a certificate from the Office de la langue française.) Because only the federal Parliament may enact criminal legislation, pursuant to section 91(27) of the *Constitution Act, 1867*, such legislation, it was submitted, is outside of the competence of the provincial legislature. The Supreme Court did not accept this interpretation of the criminal law. A criminal law, the court declared, is one that deals with "some traditional criminal law concern such as morality or public order." The court described the commercial signs provisions as dealing with the regulation of business within Quebec, a subject matter falling within provincial jurisdiction.[85]

The Equality Issue

The question of the possible impact of the equality clauses in the Canadian *Charter* (section 15) and the Quebec *Charter of Rights* (section 10) was also raised in the *Ford* case. However, this issue was ultimately of little importance, because the French-only provisions in Bill 101 were struck down primarily as violations of freedom of expression. In *Devine*, however, since the bilingual signs provisions of Bill 101 were upheld as reasonable limits to freedom of expression, the equality issue became critical to the outcome of that case.

The court skillfully sidestepped the opportunity to provide a substantive interpretation of section 15 of the Canadian *Charter*. It noted that because section 1 applied to section 15 as well as to section 2(b) — freedom of expression — it would first tackle the question of whether section 1 might apply differently to section 15 than to section 2(b). (Recall that the court had already decided that the requirement of bilingual signs and business forms was a reasonable limit to freedom of expression.) The court decided that the section 1 limitation would apply to section 15 in the same way. Therefore, there was no need for the court to decide whether the bilingual signs provisions violated section 15, and it did not offer an opinion on this question.[86]

The court could not quite so easily sidestep the equality clause in the Quebec *Charter of Rights*. This is because the limitations clause in the Quebec *Charter of Rights*, section 9.1, does not apply to the equality clause (section 10). Nevertheless, the court interpreted the guarantee of equality in section 10 of the Quebec *Charter of Rights* narrowly so as to allow the bilingual signs provisions to stand. Their reasoning was that section 10 guarantees the "equal recognition and exercise of [a person's] human rights and freedoms" and that it had already been decided that the bilingual signs provisions did not violate freedom of expression, as limited by section 9.1. Therefore, because freedom of expression as acceptably limited was not violated, the equal recognition of freedom of expression could not be considered as infringed.[87]

The court's handling of the equality issue demonstrates that very often judges will try to decide a complex issue by applying a narrow legal point, rather than having to consider the broader policy implications of a case. This is not meant as a criticism of the judges; it is simply one of the characteristics of adjudication that makes it a rough tool for policy-making.

The result of the *Devine* decision is that the court upheld the power of the Quebec National Assembly to require the use of French, alongside the merchant's preferred language, in commercial signs and commercial documents. Such a requirement could be enforced without violating either freedom of expression in the Canadian *Charter of Rights* or the Quebec *Charter of Rights*, or equality in the Quebec *Charter of Rights*.

POLITICAL JURISPRUDENCE AND THE *FORD* AND *DEVINE* DECISIONS

The question of the constitutionality of the commercial signs provisions of Bill 101 presented the court with its most difficult political predicament since the constitutional reference in 1981. The judges were obviously aware that their twin Bill 101 decisions would become a political football and that they would have to bear some responsibility for the inevitable political fallout — *whatever* conclusions were reached.

The commercial signs provisions of Bill 101 were extremely popular among francophone Quebeckers. These provisions markedly changed the *visage linguistique* in Quebec. With the exception of the signs belonging to businesses like those of Singer and Devine, unilingual English signs virtually disappeared from the streets of Quebec after Bill 101's passage. Even bilingual signs became rare. The commercial signs provisions seemed visibly and dramatically to have reversed the decline of French in Quebec — hence their popularity among the francophone population. The success of Bill 101 also indicated to some Quebec nationalists that Quebec could possibly maintain its culture and language while remaining part of Canada.

Aware of this situation, the Supreme court found a way to allow the Quebec government to preserve the central core of the commercial signs provisions — requiring the predominance of French on every sign — without violating the essential spirit of freedom of expression in the Canadian *Charter* or the Quebec *Charter of Rights*. The evidence presented by the Quebec government, however, did not justify the *exclusive* use of French on signs as a reasonable limit on freedom of expression designed to preserve the French language.

What the court could not elegantly consider in the legal context was that Bill 101 represented a mixture of a rational and an emotional response to the language issue in Quebec. The rational response, according to the evidence before the court, was to require the predominance of French on all commercial signs. The continued existence of English on commercial signs, however, tended to rekindle the image of the *maudit anglais* among francophones who remembered the days of the condescending anglophones. The Supreme Court's suggested compromise was greeted by huge protests among Quebec nationalists, and so the Bourassa government concluded that the Supreme Court's "French predominant" solution was politically unacceptable. Four days after the Supreme Court decision, Premier Bourassa announced that his government would invoke the override provisions of both the Canadian *Charter* and the Quebec *Charter of Rights* to prohibit the use of any language but French on outdoor signs. English and other languages would be allowed only indoors, and only if the indoor signs could not be easily read from the outside. With regard to chain stores and franchise outlets, only French would be allowed either inside or outside. Violators would face stiff fines and even jail sentences.

The Bourassa response was denounced by civil libertarians outside Quebec and by anglophones inside Quebec. Amnesty International announced that it would defend anyone who was jailed as a result of contravening the new language legislation, Bill 178 (which amended Bill 101 and contained a s. 33 override). Some castigated the framers of the *Charter of Rights* for including section 33, the override provision, and they redoubled their efforts to have it removed. Bourassa claimed that if the Meech Lake Accord had been in effect, he would not have needed to resort to section 33, because the Supreme Court would have upheld all of Bill 101. However, according to

Peter Hogg's analysis of the accord, Bourassa's claim seems unconvincing. The distinct society clause, being merely interpretive in nature, would not have provided the court with any means of applying the sociolinguistic evidence differently.

If the reaction of the extreme Quebec nationalists, as well as the prohibition of any non-French language at all on outdoor signs, can be considered as unnecessarily overzealous attempts to protect the French language, the reaction of the anti-section 33 forces can be considered naive. Section 33 gives judges a certain amount of freedom to call it like it is. This is because judges are aware that section 33 offers governments a quick antidote to Supreme Court decisions on the *Charter* that cause political crises. Section 33 takes the pressure off the judges to solve political crises with their decisions. Instead, they can concentrate on developing more lasting interpretations of the *Charter*, leaving the short-term crises to the politicians. Without section 33, it is conceivable that the Supreme Court might have interpreted freedom of expression more narrowly in an attempt to smooth over the linguistic tensions that then existed in Quebec. Judges are aware that it is difficult to impose human rights on an unwilling population. Rights can only flourish when reason triumphs over petty hatreds and jealousies.

Discussion continued in Quebec over Bill 178's ban on outdoor signs in languages other than French. In 1993, the United Nations Human Rights Committee ruled that the law violated the *International Covenant on Civil and Political Rights*.[88] This ruling was extremely embarrassing to the Quebec government. By 1993, emotions had begun to subside, and a more rational debate was able to take place about how best to protect the French language and culture while respecting basic human rights. In 1993, the Quebec National Assembly enacted new legislation that allowed languages other than French on outdoor commercial signs, so long as the French lettering showed "marked predominance" over the lettering in other languages.[89] There was no s. 33 override included in the legislation, as the government considered it to comply with the Supreme Court rulings in *Ford* and *Devine*.[90] In 1994, the Parti Québécois won the provincial election, and the new government left the language legislation enacted in 1993 in place. It could be argued that the use of the override six years earlier had created a cooling-off period during which time Quebeckers could contemplate the

Supreme Court's rulings in *Ford* and *Devine*. In the end, they decided that they could live with the court's reasoning.

LEGISLATIVE RESTRICTIONS ON ADVERTISING
THE *RJR-MACDONALD* DECISION (1995)[91]

In 1988, the government of Brian Mulroney secured the passage of the *Tobacco Products Control Act*, which banned all tobacco advertising in Canada, and also banned the sale of tobacco products unless they were sold in packages printed with warnings about the dangers of smoking. As well, severe restrictions were placed on the promotion of tobacco products, and the distribution of tobacco products for free was prohibited. This was in reaction to mounting evidence that tobacco was contributing to a good many diseases, especially lung cancer. The tobacco companies challenged the law as a violation of freedom of expression under the *Charter*, and the case reached the Supreme Court in 1994. In a five to four decision released in 1995, the court struck down the key provisions of the legislation for being overbroad, leaving in place only the prohibition of the distribution of tobacco products for free. In reaction, in 1997 Parliament enacted the *Tobacco Act*, which permitted "information and brand-preference advertising, while forbidding lifestyle advertising and promotion, advertising appealing to young persons, and false or misleading advertising or promotion."[92] The revised legislation was upheld by the Supreme Court in 2007.[93]

The majority that struck down the main provisions of the 1988 legislation consisted of Chief Justice Lamer and Justices McLachlin, (John) Sopinka, (John C.) Major, and (Frank) Iacobucci. McLachlin wrote a decision that was concurred with by Sopinka and Major regarding Charter issues. Iacobucci, with the concurrence of Lamer, agreed with McLachlin's striking down of the key features of the *Act*, but took a somewhat different approach to the application of s. 1.

Section 1 Analysis by McLachlin
All nine judges agreed that the key sections of the *Act* infringed the Charter right to freedom of expression, and so the analysis centred on the s. 1 analysis. McLachlin wrote that the objective of the impugned sections of

the *Act* was twofold: "to prevent people in Canada from being persuaded by advertising and promotion to use tobacco products," and "to discourage people who see the package from tobacco use."[94] From her perspective, it is important to focus on the objective just of the impugned sections of the *Act* rather than the general purpose of the *Act*, which is "to protect Canadians from the health risks of tobacco use."[95] A more focused definition of the objective sets a higher standard for the government to justify the infringement of rights under s. 1.

McLachlin agreed that the objectives of the impugned sections of the legislation are of sufficient importance to justify the infringement of freedom of expression. With regard to whether there is a rational connection between the objectives and the means used in the *Act* to achieve them, she could not find a rational connection in relation to the complete ban on tobacco advertising; the complete prohibition of making information available about particular tobacco products; or the ban on printing a tobacco company's logo or name on promotional products like cigarette lighters. She wrote that there was no social science evidence that such drastic measures are necessary in order to meet the objectives. On the other hand, she stated that a ban on "lifestyle advertising" and advertising directed at children could likely be justified in order to discourage Canadians from smoking.[96]

As well, McLachlin concluded that the legislation did not limit freedom of expression as little as necessary in order for the government to achieve its objectives. McLachlin emphasized that the government's choice of an appropriate way to achieve an objective while minimally limiting rights "seldom admits of perfection and the courts must accord some leeway to the legislator. If the law falls within a range of reasonable alternatives, the courts will not find it overbroad merely because they can conceive of an alternative which might better tailor objective to infringement. . . ."[97] Nevertheless, it was clear to McLachlin that by prohibiting tobacco companies from advertising the contents of their products and pointing out how particular products differ, the *Act* prevented Canadian consumers from "learning about product availability to suit their preferences and to compare brand content with an aim to reducing the risk to their health."[98] She continued, "[t]he government had before it a variety of less intrusive measures when it enacted the total ban on advertising, including: a partial ban which would allow information and brand preference advertising; a ban on lifestyle advertising only; measures . . . to prohibit advertising aimed at children and adolescents; and labelling requirements only . . . In my view, any of these alternatives would be a reasonable impairment of the right to free expression, given the important objective and the legislative context."

McLachlin was critical of the part of the minority judgment, written by La Forest, that argued the court should defer more to Parliament's choice of measures when commercial advertising is at issue because advertising is a less important type of expression than other kinds of expression. McLachlin countered that "[c]ommercial speech, while arguably less important than some forms of speech, nevertheless should not be lightly dismissed."[99] Advertising, she wrote, often provides important information about products, which consumers need in order to make rational choices.

The key provisions of the *Act* (other than the ban on giving away tobacco products for free), having failed the rational-connection and minimal-impairment tests, were struck down by McLachlin (writing for Sopinka and Major), with the concurrence of Iacobucci and Lamer.

Section 1 Analysis by Iacobucci

Iacobucci agreed with the dissenting opinion of La Forest that the *Act* passes the rational-connection test. However, he agreed with McLachlin that it failed the minimal-impairment test. His remarks about what kind of legislation would pass the minimal-impairment test were valuable to the Chrétien government in redrafting the legislation.

> [I]t is clear that health warnings can and should be placed on the packages, but the strictures of the Charter *necessitate that they be attributed to their author, in all likelihood Health and Welfare Canada. Regarding the advertising ban, it is clear to me that an effort could have been made to regulate tobacco advertising along the lines of alcohol advertising . . .*
> *[P]artial bans in the order of prohibitions on lifestyle advertising only and limitations on advertising aimed at*

adolescents could have been given more constructive attention
[by the government].[100]

Section 1 Analysis by La Forest

La Forest, with three other judges concurring, preceded his s. 1 analysis with
a discussion of how strictly s. 1 should be applied to cases that concern a
corporation's right to freedom of expression for the purpose of increasing
their market share of a harmful product in order to earn greater profits. He
noted that the causal link between tobacco consumption and diseases such
as cancer is complex because there are other factors also involved, and so for
the court to demand "definitive social scientific evidence respecting the root
causes of a pressing area of social concern" may "paralyze the operation of
government in the socio-economic sphere."[101] He referred to former Chief
Justice Dickson's assertion that the "'core' values [of the *Charter* include] the
search for political, artistic, and scientific truth; the protection of individual
autonomy and self-development; and the promotion of public participation in the democratic process."[102] When an issue concerning freedom of
expression is "farther from the 'core' of freedom of expression values, this
Court has applied a lower standard of justification."[103] He concluded that
"the harm engendered by tobacco, and the profit motive underlying its
promotion, place this form of expression as far from the 'core' of freedom
of expression values."[104]

La Forest defined the objective of the *Tobacco Products Control Act* as "protecting public health by reducing tobacco consumption."[105] Given this
broad definition of purpose, and his emphasis on deference to Parliament
in cases like this, it was not difficult for La Forest to find a rational connection between the objective of the *Act* and the means used — the ban on all
tobacco advertising and promotion and the prescription of specific warnings on tobacco products.[106] As well, he found that the legislation limited
the freedom of expression of tobacco companies as little as necessary to
achieve the governmental objective. Tobacco companies were still allowed
to market their products, and over two decades, the government had found
that less restrictive approaches to reducing the use of tobacco products
were not working effectively.[107] It follows that La Forest concluded that
the *Act* did more good by discouraging the use of tobacco products than it

did harm by restricting freedom of expression.[108]

In both the *Ford* and *RJR-MacDonald* decisions, the Supreme Court demonstrated that the *Charter* protects commercial freedom of expression as well as freedom of expression that is more closely related to the core values of freedom of expression. The *RJR-MacDonald* decision, in which the *Tobacco Products Control Act* was struck down in a close five to four vote, demonstrates how difficult it is for the judges to form a consensus about the degree to which commercial expression deserves Charter protection.

THE HATE SPEECH CASES

Clearly, restrictions on hate speech are a violation of the *Charter*'s guarantee of freedom of expression. But can these limits be justified as a reasonable limit under section 1? Three leading hate speech cases are reviewed in this section: the Supreme Court's *Keegstra* decision of 1990, the *Zundel* decision of 1992, and the *Ross* decision of 1996.

THE *KEEGSTRA* DECISION (1990)[109]

In the early 1960s, there was a wave of hate literature, most of which was directed at blacks and Jews, distributed in Canada. In response, Parliament created the Cohen Committee in 1965 to study the problem and make recommendations. The result was the enactment of what eventually became s. 319(2) of the *Criminal Code*, which makes it an offence to promote hatred against an identifiable group. The new section was intended to curtail hate speech and hate literature while limiting freedom of expression as little as necessary.[110]

James Keegstra grew up in southern Alberta in the 1930s and earned his bachelor of education degree from the University of Calgary in 1967. He was hired to teach high school in Eckville, Alberta (a town of fewer than one thousand west of Red Deer), in 1968. In the early 1970s, he became an adherent of Holocaust denial and Jewish conspiracy teachings and included these teachings in his social studies classes.[111]

Keegstra's teachings attributed various evil qualities to Jews. He described Jews to his pupils as treacherous, subversive, sadistic, money loving, power hungry, and child killers. He taught his classes that Jewish people seek to destroy Christianity and are responsible for depressions, anarchy, chaos,

139

wars, and revolution. According to Keegstra, Jews "created the Holocaust to gain sympathy" and, in contrast to the open and honest Christians, were deceptive, secretive, and inherently evil. Keegstra expected his students to reproduce his teachings in class and in exams. If they failed to do so, their marks suffered.[112]

Although most students accepted Keegstra's teachings as accurate history, some did not and complained to their parents. But it was not until 1982 that the mother of one of Keegstra's students read her son's class notes and was so appalled by them that she complained to the county school board. (The mother had moved to Eckville from Britain and so had a very different perspective about the Holocaust.) In the fall of 1982, the board ruled that Keegstra had deviated from the provincial curriculum and ordered him to comply. Keegstra maintained that he was following the curriculum and made no changes in the content of his lessons. As a result, in December the board removed him from his teaching position.[113] In 1983, Keegstra was "charged under s. 319(2) . . . of the *Criminal Code* with wilfully promoting hatred against an identifiable group by communicating anti-Semitic statements to his students,"[114] and convicted in a jury trial in 1984. Keegstra received a one-year suspended sentence, one year of probation, and two hundred hours of community service. He appealed to the Alberta Court of Appeal, which ruled that s. 319(2) was a violation of section 2(b) of the *Charter*. The Crown appealed to the Supreme Court, which in a four to three decision ruled that section 319(2) is a reasonable limit to freedom of expression, and so upheld Keegstra's conviction.[115]

The Majority Decision of Chief Justice Dickson

Dickson explained that hate speech is one of those freedom of speech values that is far from the core of freedom of expression values. "At the core of freedom of expression lies the need to ensure that truth and the common good are attained . . . There is very little chance that statements intended to promote hatred against an identifiable group are true, or that their vision of society will lead to a better world."[116] He noted that the key to understanding the Charter guarantee of freedom of expression is "the connection between freedom of expression and the political process . . . Such open participation must involve to a substantial degree the notion that all persons are equally deserving of respect and dignity."[117] Hate propaganda works in the opposite direction. It argues "for a society in which the democratic process is subverted and individuals are denied respect and dignity simply because of racial or religious characteristics. This brand of expressive activity is thus wholly inimical to the democratic aspirations of the free expression guarantee."[118]

Nevertheless, it was clear that s. 319(2) of the *Criminal Code* is a violation of freedom of expression. Moving on to the s. 1 analysis, Dickson described the purpose of s. 319(2) as "protecting target group members and fostering harmonious social relations in a community dedicated to equality and multiculturalism,"[119] and he had no difficulty in finding that the objective is pressing and substantial, thus satisfying the first part of the Oakes test.[120] As well, it was obvious to him that there is a rational connection between the objective of the legislation and the means used — the suppression of hate propaganda.[121] He then outlined the arguments of the Supreme Court minority as to why they thought that there was no rational connection and critiqued each one of them.

The first argument against a rational connection is that law suppressing hate propaganda might actually advance the cause of hate-mongers by giving them a huge amount of media attention, and that this may generate support for their views and sympathy for their persecution. (From the time that Keegstra was charged in 1984 and past the Supreme Court decision in 1990, the Keegstra story often dominated the headlines in the media.) Dickson's view was that by and large, such media attention had just the opposite effect: the fallacy of the hate-mongers' message is exposed and their targets are encouraged by the state's attempts to protect them through prosecution of the offenders.[122]

The second argument that there is no rational connection is that the suppression of hate speech by the government may cause many to be suspicious of the government's motives and begin to suspect that the hate message may, in fact, be true. Again, Dickson argued that hate speech suppression has the opposite effect. "I stress my belief that hate propaganda legislation and trials are a means by which the values beneficial to a free and democratic society can be publicized. In this context, no dignity will be unwittingly foisted upon the convicted hate-monger or his or her philosophy, and that a hate-monger might see him- or herself as a martyr is of no matter to the content of the state's message."[123]

The third argument against the existence of a rational connection is the fact that in the 1920s and 1930s there were laws in pre–Nazi Germany that suppressed hate speech, and in the end they did not prevent the persecution of Jews. To this, Dickson retorted that there were many factors that led to the rise of the Nazi movement, and the Holocaust cannot be blamed solely on the failure of the German anti-hate laws to prevent it. Conditions in Germany at that time were very different from those in Canada at the present time. Moreover, Germany currently has anti-hate speech legislation similar to Canada's, indicating that today's Germany does not consider such laws futile.[124]

In the same vein, with regard to the second part of the three-pronged proportionality test in *Oakes*, Dickson argued that s. 319(2) limits hate speech as little as necessary to achieve the objective. The prohibition of hate speech does not include private conversations. Second, the prohibition is limited to the willful promotion of hatred against an identifiable group. Third, an identifiable group is defined by the *Criminal Code* as "any section of the public distinguished by colour, race, religion, or ethnic origin." The act to be targeted is therefore the intentional fostering of hatred against particular members of our society, as opposed to any individual, and so this definition of an identifiable group limits the scope of the prohibition.[125] Fourth, "the sense in which 'hatred' is used in s. 319(2) does not denote a wide range of diverse emotions, but is circumscribed so as to cover only the most intense form of dislike."[126] Fifth, the *Code* itself provides several defences for those accused of promoting hatred against an identifiable group: establishing that the alleged hate statements are in fact true; showing that "in good faith, he expressed or attempted to establish by argument an opinion on a religious subject";[127] arguing that the alleged hate statements are relevant to the public interest, are for the public benefit, and "on reasonable grounds he believed them to be true";[128] and if someone quotes hate speech in an effort to have it removed.

Dickson concluded that s. 319(2) "create[s] a narrowly confined offence which suffers from neither over-breadth nor vagueness . . ."[129] Dickson added that the anti-hate speech section of the *Criminal Code* does more good, by attempting to curtail hate speech, than harm, by violating freedom of speech. S. 319(2) "represents an impairment of the individual's freedom of expression which is not of a most serious nature."[130]

The Minority Opinion of Justice McLachlin

Justice McLachlin's minority opinion was concurred with by Justice Sopinka; as well, Justice La Forest agreed with her reasoning about freedom of expression. McLachlin agreed with the majority that s. 319(2) infringed the Charter right of freedom of expression, and that the objective, which she defined as "eradicating speech which advocates racial and cultural hatred,"[131] was pressing and substantial, thus passing the first part of the Oakes test. Note, however, that McLachlin's definition of the purpose of s. 319(2), containing as it does the ambitious goal "eradicating," set a higher standard for meeting the rational-connection test than Dickson's definition of purpose, which stressed the goals of "protecting" and "fostering." As a result, in her view, s. 319(2) failed not only the rational-connection test, but all three prongs of the proportionality part of the Oakes test. As noted in the discussion of Dickson's decision, McLachlin was of the opinion that s. 319(2) could have the opposite of the effect intended, and far from eradicating hate speech, could actually encourage it. Thus, there is no rational connection between the objective of s. 319(2) and the means used. Furthermore, she wrote that s. 319(2) was overbroad. Someone could be convicted "not only of actually inciting others to hatred, but also of attempting to do so. The Court of Appeal accepted the argument that this made the crime, at least potentially, a victimless one."[132] In addition, she gave examples of several books, such as Salman Rushdie's *Satanic Verses*, and films being held up at the Canadian border because officials thought they might violate s. 319(2).[133] She claimed that these incidents created a chilling environment for those with legitimate points to make but who feared that they might run afoul of the *Criminal Code*.

Perhaps McLachlin's strongest argument that s. 319(2) was overbroad was that the *Criminal Code* is not the appropriate vehicle to tackle hate speech. "Discrimination on grounds of race and religion is worthy of suppression. Human rights legislation, focusing on reparation rather than punishment, has had considerable success in discouraging such conduct."[134]

With regard to the third prong of the proportionality test, McLachlin had no doubt that s. 319(2) did more harm than good. "[T]he limitation on freedom of expression created by s. 319(2) of the *Criminal Code* invokes all of the values upon which s. 2(b) of the *Charter* rests — the value of fostering a vibrant and creative society through the marketplace of ideas; the value of the vigorous and open debate essential to democratic government and preservation of our rights and freedoms; and the value of a society which fosters the self-actualization and freedom of its members."[135]

It is clear that both the majority and minority in the *Keegstra* decision had persuasive arguments. Dickson's argument prevailed by one vote given his stature as one of the Supreme Court's most respected and penetrating minds regarding human rights issues. However, Dickson and Wilson (who concurred with Dickson in *Keegstra*) retired prior to the next hate speech case — *Zundel*.

THE *ZUNDEL* DECISION (1992)[136]

Ernst Zundel was an infamous Holocaust denier. Born in Germany in 1939, he lived in Canada from 1958, off and on, until his deportation to Germany in 2005. Beginning in 1985, he was charged under s. 181 of the *Criminal Code* with "spreading false news," in part for publishing a Holocaust-denial pamphlet entitled "Did Six Million Really Die?" He could have been charged under the same hate-speech section of the *Criminal Code* as Keegstra, but because of the emphasis on Holocaust-denial, the prosecutors decided that s. 181 — spreading false news — was more appropriate. The problem was that s. 181 was a reincarnation of laws passed in medieval times to protect English aristocrats and so was more vulnerable to a Charter challenge based on twentieth-century standards about human rights than the more contemporary hate speech section of the *Criminal Code* (s. 319[2]).

Like the *Keegstra* decision, the *Zundel* decision was decided by a seven-judge panel, and was a four to three decision — but this time in favour of striking down the *Criminal Code*'s "spreading false news" law for violating freedom of expression. The majority decision was written by McLachlin, supported (as she was in *Keegstra*) by La Forest and Sopinka. L'Heureux-Dubé, in a sense, had switched sides — in favour of upholding the *Criminal Code* in *Keegstra* but in favour of striking down in *Zundel*. L'Heureux-Dubé gave no reasons for her changed position, but it seems intuitively clear. She is noted for her support of human rights. In *Keegstra*, it was the Jewish community whose human rights deserved support because they were the victims of hate speech. In *Zundel*, it was a different and outdated section of the *Criminal Code* that threatened human rights, and so it was ordinary Canadians — who might not be aware that their views were inaccurate and who faced criminal charges as a result — who deserved support.

The Majority Decision of McLachlin

What distinguished McLachlin's opinion in *Zundel* from that in *Keegstra* was her focus on the heritage of s. 181 of the *Criminal Code* — the section that makes spreading false news a criminal offence. Section 181 was not an issue in *Keegstra*, although it would invoke many of the same issues as s. 319(2) did in in that case. However, s. 319(2) was a fairly recent addition to the *Criminal Code*, specifically designed to curtail hate speech, while s. 181 had a history dating back to 1275 in England. As McLachlin noted, the original English statute "introduced the offence *De Scandalis Magnatum*, or *Scandalum Magnatum*." It provided "[t]hat from henceforth none be so hardy to tell or publish any false News or Tales, whereby discord, or occasion of discord or slander may grow between the King and his People, or the Great Men of the Realm."[137] McLachlin then explained that in the thirteenth century and throughout the Middle Ages, this law was considered necessary in order to preserve order, because "the offended great one was only too ready to resort to arms to redress a fancied injury."[138] It was repealed in the United Kingdom in 1887 but enacted into Canada's *Criminal Code* in 1892, possibly because the drafters of the *Criminal Code* did not realize that the law had been repealed in the UK. She found that s. 181 was a clear violation of the Charter right to freedom of expression and then proceeded to the s. 1 analysis.

McLachlin had difficulty defining the objective of including s. 181 in the *Criminal Code*, given the uncertainty surrounding its inclusion, after the provision from which it was drafted had been repealed in the UK. She was not persuaded by any of the arguments claiming the government had a modern purpose in mind by inserting s. 181 into the *Criminal Code*, and so she was left with the original thirteenth-century purpose — to protect the reputations of aristocrats. She reminded her readers about the court's decision in *Big M* not to allow that a law can have a shifting purpose over time. McLachlin therefore concluded that s. 181 did not have a pressing and substantial purpose that might justify limiting freedom of expression. (*Zundel* is one of the few cases in which the impugned legislation failed to pass the first part of the Oakes test.)

Nevertheless, McLachlin argued that even if it could be shown that the purpose of s. 181 is to promote "social and racial tolerance in society,"[139] and even if that objective were to be considered pressing and substantial, s. 181 would still come to grief by failing to limit rights as little as necessary to achieve the objective. Under s. 181, someone could be convicted "for virtually any statement which does not accord with currently accepted 'truths,' and lends force to the argument that the section could be used (or abused) in a circular fashion essentially to permit the prosecution of unpopular ideas."[140] Further, "perhaps the greatest danger of s. 181 lies in the undefined and virtually unlimited reach of the phrase 'injury or mischief to a public interest.'"[141] Such broad language is bound to have a chilling effect on freedom of expression for some.[142]

The Minority Opinion of Cory and Iacobucci

Justices (Peter) Cory and Iacobucci, in a decision concurred with by Gonthier, presented arguments in defence of s. 181 very similar to the arguments presented by Dickson in *Keegstra*. (McLachlin acknowledged that Cory and Iacobucci made a "laudable effort" to justify s. 181 under s. 1 of the *Charter* because of their abhorrence of hate mongering.)[143] Cory and Iacobucci state that the purpose of s. 181 is "to prevent the harm caused by the willful publication of injurious lies."[144] They argue that this purpose is simply a change in emphasis from the original thirteenth-century purpose, rather than a major shift. They find that this purpose is pressing and substantial, and that it passes all three parts of the proportionality test under s. 1.

The *Zundel* decision illustrates how important the definition of the purpose of impugned legislation is to the subsequent reasoning. With regard to old legislation, such as s. 181 (the false-news section of the *Criminal Code*), it is often difficult to find accurate information about the original intent of legislation. With regard to more recent legislation, such as the hate-speech section of the *Criminal Code* (s. 319(2)), defining the purpose is frequently somewhat more straightforward. Since the advent of the *Charter*, Parliament, provincial, and territorial legislatures have tended to spell out the purpose of legislation in its preamble. Pre-Charter legislation was not usually scrutinized for its impact on human rights, and so older legislation that clearly poses a threat to human rights is vulnerable.

Zundel did not walk free after his victory in the Supreme Court in 1992. His application for Canadian citizenship was rejected because he was found to be a security risk. In 1997 he was charged by the Canadian Human Rights Commission with distributing hate literature, but left for the US to avoid proceedings. He was deported back to Canada in 2003, and in 2005 was deported by Canada to Germany. Upon arrival he was charged under German law with inciting hatred and was convicted in 2007. He was jailed until 2010.[145]

THE *ROSS* DECISION (1996)[146]

Malcolm Ross was a school teacher in New Brunswick from the 1970s to the 1990s. He described himself as a fundamentalist Christian. "In his published writings, which consist of four books or pamphlets published from 1978 to 1989, and three letters to New Brunswick newspapers, Ross . . . argued that Christian civilization was being undermined and destroyed by an international Jewish conspiracy."[147]

In 1988, a Jewish parent complained to the New Brunswick Human Rights Commission. He alleged "that the [school board] violated . . . the [*New Brunswick*] *Human Rights Act* by discriminating against him and his children . . . on the basis of religion and ancestry. [He] alleged that the School Board, by failing to take appropriate action against . . . Ross . . . who publicly made racist, discriminatory, and bigoted statements, condoned his anti-Jewish views, and breached . . . the *Act* by discriminating against Jewish and other minority students within the educational system served by the School Board."[148]

Unlike Keegstra, Ross did not disseminate his anti-Semitic views in the classroom but rather through his publications and media contributions.

The Human Rights Commission created a board of inquiry, which found that the school board "discriminated by failing to discipline the respondent meaningfully in that, by its almost indifferent response to the complaints and by continuing his employment, it endorsed his out-of-school activities and writings. This, it held, resulted in an atmosphere where anti-Jewish sentiments flourished and where Jewish students were subject to a 'poisoned environment' within the School District 'which has greatly interfered with the educational services provided' to [the Jewish complainant] and his children."[149]

The board of inquiry ordered the school board to place Ross "on a leave of absence without pay for . . . eighteen months," appoint him to a non-teaching position during that period, and offer him a non-teaching position if one became available. If no position became available, his employment with the school board would be terminated. In addition, the board of inquiry ordered that should Ross publicly disseminate his anti-Semitic views during employment with the school board at any point in the future, his employment should be immediately terminated.[150] Ross challenged this decision all the way to the Supreme Court of Canada, which handed down its decision in 1996.

The court was unanimous in upholding most of the board of inquiry's decision. The decision of the court was written by the Supreme Court's New Brunswick judge, La Forest.

Did Ross Discriminate?

The first step in this case was for La Forest to determine whether Ross's actions constituted discrimination contrary to the *New Brunswick Human Rights Act*. La Forest cited numerous examples, produced by the courts, of discrimination. For example, he summarized the evidence of two students in the school district in which Ross worked.

> *They gave evidence of repeated and continual harassment in the form of derogatory name calling of Jewish students, carving of swastikas by other students into their own arms and into the desks of Jewish children, drawing of swastikas on blackboards, and general intimidation of Jewish students. The appellant's daughter . . . gave evidence of one occasion on which she had planned to attend the respondent's school to watch a gymnastic*

> *competition, when she was advised that she could not go to the*
> *school because that was ". . . where the teacher who hates Jews*
> *works." The teacher referred to was identified as [Ross]. Yona*
> *Attis stated that she attended the competition, but that she*
> *felt scared while there, and anxious "that someone was going*
> *to come up behind [her] and grab [her] and beat [her] up or*
> *something." Further evidence of taunting and intimidation of*
> *the Jewish students was disclosed in her testimony, including*
> *incidents of shouting and signalling of the "Heil, Hitler"*
> *salute. What this evidence discloses is a poisoned educational*
> *environment in which Jewish children perceive the potential*
> *for misconduct and are likely to feel isolated and suffer a loss*
> *of self-esteem on the basis of their Judaism.*[151]

La Forest wrote that "[t]eachers are inextricably linked to the integrity of the school system. Teachers occupy positions of trust and confidence, and exert considerable influence over their students as a result of their positions. The conduct of a teacher bears directly upon the community's perception of the ability of the teacher to fulfil such a position of trust and influence, and upon the community's confidence in the public school system as a whole."[152] Given that position of trust, if teachers flagrantly discriminate in their out-of-school activities, then the school board, in allowing them to persist in such behavior, is in violation of the *New Brunswick Human Rights Code.*

Did the Order of the Board of Inquiry Violate Freedom of Expression?
La Forest had little difficulty in finding that the order of the Board of Inquiry violated freedom of expression, based primarily on the Keegstra and Zundel precedents.[153]

Is the Violation of Freedom of Expression Justified under s. 1 of the Charter?
The first part of the s. 1 analysis was to identify the purpose of the Board of Inquiry's order. La Forest stated its purpose as follows: "to address the specific steps to be taken to remedy the discrimination in the School Board created through the respondent's writings and publications. More generally,

the order aims at remedying the discrimination found to have 'poisoned' the educational environment in the School Board."[154] La Forest found that this objective was substantially important, thus passing the first part of the of the Oakes test.[155]

The first prong of the second part of the s. 1 analysis was to determine whether there was a rational connection between the objective and the means used. La Forest found that the means used — the Board's order regarding Ross — was rationally connected to the objective of remedying discrimination. He had concerns, however, relating to the second prong — limiting rights as little as necessary. " [T]he evidence does not support the conclusion that the residual poisoned effect would last indefinitely once Ross has been placed in a non-teaching role. For that reason, [the] clause which imposes a permanent ban on disseminating his anti-Semitic views does not minimally impair the respondent's constitutional freedoms."[156] Given his finding regarding the second prong of the Oakes test, La Forest stated that it was not necessary for him to delve into the third prong — the overall-balance test.

La Forest's decision affirmed most of the Human Rights Tribunal's decision to put Ross into a non-teaching position for a year and a half in order to find a non-teaching position, but struck down the tribunal's condition that Ross must cease to disseminate his anti-Jewish ideas while in a non-teaching position.

Unhappy with this decision, Ross went to the United Nations Human Rights Committee with a claim that his transfer to a non-teaching position violated his right under the *International Covenant on Civil and Political Rights* to express freely his religions opinions. The committee of fifteen unanimously rejected his claim in 2000.[157]

The importance of the *Ross* decision is that it affirms teachers have a duty not to discriminate and this duty is owed not only inside the classroom but also outside the classroom when they are not on duty.

THE PORNOGRAPHY CASES

Two of the most prominent cases in which the Supreme Court ruled on the tension between permitting pornography as an element of freedom of expression and restricting it to preserve human dignity, were the *Butler* case of 1992, and the *Sharpe* case of 2001. The *Butler* case dealt with the sale of hard-core sexual videotapes and magazines, while the *Sharpe* case concerned child pornography.

THE *BUTLER* DECISION (1992)[158]

Section 163 of the *Criminal Code* prohibits the sale of obscene materials. An obscene material, according to the legislation, is one in which "a dominant characteristic . . . is the undue exploitation of sex, or of sex and any one or more of the following subjects, namely crime, horror, cruelty, and violence . . ."[159]

In August of 1987, Donald Butler opened a sex shop in Winnipeg which sold hard-core videotapes and magazines, and sex toys. Shortly after the store opened, it was raided by the police, and Butler was charged with 173 counts of violating what became s. 163 of the *Criminal Code*. In October, the store was reopened for a week; police once again raided it and laid another seventy-seven charges. At trial, Butler was convicted on eight charges only. The trial judge ruled that in order to comply with the *Charter's* right to freedom of expression, the definition of obscenity needed to be restricted to materials that depict sex and cruelty, lack of consent, or dehumanization, and fined Butler $1,000 for each count that he was convicted on. The Crown appealed, and three out of five judges on the Manitoba Court of Appeal panel convicted Butler on all charges. They held that freedom of expression does not extend to obscene materials.

The main decision of the Supreme Court was written by Mr. Justice Sopinka, and concurred with by six other judges. Two judges, L'Heureux-Dubé and Gonthier, agreed with most of what Sopinka had written but added some of their own analysis. In this decision, the Supreme Court clarified how courts are to determine whether material is obscene. The judges found that when this approach to obscenity is applied, there is a violation of freedom of expression, but it is a justified infringement on rights under s. 1 of the *Charter*. Given this clarification, the Supreme Court ordered a new trial for Butler.

An important issue that Sopinka had to grapple with was how to determine the "undue" exploitation of sex in s. 163. He wrote that there are three important tests that courts must apply. The first is the "community

standard of tolerance" test. Sopinka adopted the definition of this test provided by Dickson in an earlier case: "What matters is not what Canadians
think is right for themselves to see. What matters is what Canadians would
not abide other Canadians seeing because it would be beyond the contemporary Canadian standard of tolerance to allow them to see it."[160] He
noted that this test is not frozen in time but changes as Canadian society's
standards change. After reviewing the case law and evidence pertaining to
pornography and obscenity, Sopinka concluded that the Canadian community will not tolerate pornographic materials that cause harm; pornographic
materials that cause harm fit the definition of undue exploitation of sex in
the *Criminal Code*. "[T]here is a substantial body of opinion that holds that
the portrayal of persons being subjected to degrading or dehumanizing
sexual treatment results in harm, particularly to women and therefore to
society as a whole."[161]

Sopinka pointed out that there are some publications that contain
depictions of harm, but that these depictions are necessary in order for the
author to complete a true work of art. This "internal necessities" test was
developed by courts to "assess whether the exploitation of sex has a justifiable role in advancing the plot or the theme, and in considering the work as
a whole, does not merely represent 'dirt for dirt's sake' but has a legitimate
role when measured by the internal necessities of the work itself."[162]

To understand Sopinka's analysis, it is important to consider the relation between pornography and obscenity. One legal definition of pornography is "[t]he portrayal of sexual acts solely for the purpose of sexual
arousal."[163] The same legal dictionary defines obscenity as "[a] publication
which is illegal because it is morally corruptive."[164] A major task of the
Supreme Court was to decide how to divide pornographic publications
into those that are obscene and those that are not. Sopinka divided pornography into three categories: "(1) explicit sex with violence, (2) explicit
sex without violence but which subjects people to treatment that is degrading or dehumanizing, and (3) explicit sex without violence that is neither
degrading nor dehumanizing."[165] In deciding what kinds of pornography
should be treated as obscene under the *Criminal Code*, Sopinka wrote that
"the portrayal of sex coupled with violence will almost always constitute
the undue exploitation of sex [contrary to s. 163]. Explicit sex which is

degrading or dehumanizing may be undue [contrary to s. 163] if the risk of harm is substantial. Finally, explicit sex that is not violent and neither degrading nor dehumanizing is generally tolerated in our society and will not qualify as the undue exploitation of sex unless it employs children in its production."[166]

The result of this analysis was a threefold test for materials that are obscene: the community standards test, the internal necessities test, and the degrading or dehumanizing test.

Next, Sopinka reviewed s. 163 of the *Criminal Code* and determined that it violated freedom of expression as protected in s. 2(b) of the *Charter*. He then turned to the question of whether s. 163 could be saved through application of s. 1. Sopinka defined the objective of s. 163 as "the avoidance of harm to society," which he held was substantially important, therefore meeting the standard of part one of the Oakes test. He referred to the "burgeoning pornography industry [which] renders the concern even more pressing and substantial than when the impugned provisions were first enacted."[167] It had been argued by Butler's lawyers that s. 163 was vulnerable to the shifting-purpose doctrine, which was rejected in the *Big M* decision. In reply, Sopinka wrote that "[o]ur understanding of the harms caused by these materials has developed considerably since [1959, the year the legislation was enacted]; however this does not detract from the fact that the purpose of this legislation remains, as it was in 1959, the protection of society from harms caused by the exposure to obscene materials . . . A permissible shift in emphasis was built into the legislation when, as interpreted by the courts, it adopted the community standards test. Community standards as to what is harmful have changed since 1959."[168] This is an ingenious defence of the community standards test. However, does it persuasively justify the exclusion of the ever-changing community standards test from the shifting-purpose doctrine? Not infrequently, judges are caught between a rock and a hard place, and they must do their best to write a judgment that is likely to be seen as both legally sound and accepted as legitimate by Canadian society.

In determining whether there is a rational connection between s. 163 and the objective of reducing harm to society, Sopinka concluded that although the social science evidence in this regard was mixed, there was enough evidence to support a rational connection.

Concerning whether s. 163 infringed rights as little as necessary to achieve the objective, Sopinka emphasized that in this case, the three tests for obscenity had considerably narrowed the definition of obscenity from earlier case law. Obscene materials must be degrading and dehumanizing. There is an artistic defence for materials deemed of importance to an artistic work. He notes that the task of the court is not to determine whether legislation that restricts rights does so in a "perfect" manner, but that it does so in a reasonable manner.[169]

Finally, Sopinka found that s. 163 did more good than harm in restricting freedom of expression because the avoidance of harm is one of the hallmarks of a democratic society.[170]

The *Butler* decision set the stage for one of the most publicized Charter of Rights decisions — the *Sharpe* decision about child pornography.

THE *SHARPE* DECISION (2001)[171]

Not long after the *Butler* decision, in which Sopinka referred to child pornography as an example of obscenity, the Canadian Parliament enacted a new provision, s. 163.1 of the *Criminal Code*, to ensure that child pornography would be outlawed.[172] The relevant parts of s. 163.1 are as follows:

> *163.1 (4) Every person who possesses any child pornography is guilty of*
>
> *(a) an indictable offence and liable to imprisonment for a term not exceeding five years; or*
>
> *(b) an offence punishable on summary conviction.*

John Robin Sharpe was a British Columbia resident who admitted that he enjoyed child pornography and felt that he was entitled to possess and produce it (drawings and manuscripts) for his own purposes. He was charged with possession of child pornography under the new s. 163.1 of the *Criminal Code*, and in 1999 was acquitted because the trial judge found that s. 163.1 was overbroad, thus violating s. 2(b) of the *Charter* in that

Sharpe's personal activities did not constitute harm to society. Later in 1999, the British Columbia Court of Appeal agreed. The Crown appealed to the Supreme Court, and its decision was handed down in 2001. There was a tremendous amount of media attention paid to this case from the time of the trial decision up to the Supreme Court decision.[173] The Opposition demanded that the s. 15 override clause be used to protect s. 163.1, but the Chrétien government's position was to wait for the Supreme Court decision.[174] The decision seemed to satisfy most critics, so that the pressure to invoke s. 15 subsided.

All nine judges heard the appeal, and they were unanimous in upholding s. 163.1 as a reasonable limit to freedom of expression. Chief Justice McLachlin wrote the opinion for herself and five other judges in which part of s. 161.1 was "read down" so as not to include materials produced by older teenagers for their own purposes (technically still children if under eighteen) in which they filmed themselves; three judges (Claire L'Heureux-Dubé, Charles Gonthier, and Michele Bastarache) wrote a separate concurring opinion that objected to the reading down in the majority opinion.

The Majority Opinion of Chief Justice McLachlin

The first issue that McLachlin dealt with was whether s. 163.1 violates freedom of expression. She wrote that s. 163.1 is a clear violation of freedom of expression: "Without the right to possess expressive material, freedom of thought, belief, opinion, and expression would be compromised . . . The private nature of the proscribed material may heighten the seriousness of a limit on free expression."[175]

McLachlin then outlined the tension in this case between freedom of expression, and "society's interest in protecting children from the evils associated with the possession of child pornography. Just as no one denies the importance of free expression, so no one denies that child pornography involves the exploitation of children."[176] What made this case difficult was that Sharpe conceded that the government had a right to ban the distribution of child pornography, and that there must be limits to the kinds of child pornography that could be legally possessed by individuals. For him, what was at issue were the manuscripts and drawings that he had produced for personal use. He claimed that these did not harm children, and to have the state confiscate them and charge him with a criminal offence was an invasion of his privacy and personal freedom of expression.

In her s. 1 analysis, McLachlin stated that the "main purpose in passing the child pornography law was to prevent harm to children by banning the production, distribution, and possession of child pornography, and by sending a message to Canadians 'that children need to be protected from the harmful effects of child sexual abuse and exploitation and are not appropriate sexual partners.'"[177] She concluded that this objective is "pressing and substantial."[178] With regard to the rational-connection test from *Oakes*, she concluded that ". . . the social science evidence adduced in this case, buttressed by experience and common sense, amply meets the *Oakes* requirement of a rational connection between the purpose of the law and the means adopted to effect this purpose. Possession of child pornography increases the risk of child abuse. . . . Only by extending the law to private possession can these harms be squarely attacked."[179]

Concerning the minimal-impairment test, McLachlin wrote that "the law may also capture the possession of material that one would not normally think of as 'child pornography' and that raises little or no risk of harm to children: (1) written materials or visual representations created and held by the accused alone, exclusively for personal use; and (2) visual recordings, created by or depicting the accused, that do not depict unlawful sexual activity and are held by the accused exclusively for private use."[180] (An example of the latter is a video recording made by a seventeen-year-old married couple of their sexual activities for their own use.) McLachlin concluded that with regard to these two aspects, s. 163.1 is overbroad. The remedy she devised was that "s. 163.1 should be read as though it contained an exception for: (1) any written material or visual representation created by the accused alone, and held by the accused alone, exclusively for his or her own personal use; and (2) any visual recording, created by or depicting the accused, provided it does not depict unlawful sexual activity and is held by the accused exclusively for private use."[181] Given this reading down of s. 163.1, McLachlin concluded that the third prong of the second part of the Oakes test was met by the legislation: it did more good than harm.[182]

The Separate Concurring Opinion of L'Heureux-Dubé, Gonthier, and Bastarache

L'Heureux-Dubé, Gonthier, and Bastarache did not agree that s. 163.1 should be read down, as held by McLachlin and her supporters. Rather, they considered that the risk of excluding the materials contained in McLachlin's reading down from the scope of s. 163.1 was too great. These materials could too easily be obtained by others and exploited. With regard to the materials produced by Sharpe for his own use, they considered these materials to be harmful to Sharpe and others with similar practices. With regard to photos and videos made by consenting teenagers between fourteen and seventeen, they considered that they are too young to properly understand their actions. As a result, these judges would have upheld s. 163.1 without any reading down.[183] As well, they considered that child pornography is very distant from the core of the values that the Charter guarantee of freedom of expression was meant to protect. However, they were outvoted by the majority.

The *Sharpe* and *Butler* cases illustrate that from time to time judges are required to make decisions regarding subject matter that no doubt they would prefer to avoid. McLachlin referred to the trial court judge's decision in *Sharpe* as "courageous,"[184] likely because he knew full well that he would be severely chastised by the media for striking down s. 163.1. Nevertheless, judges are required to do their best to apply the *Charter* fairly to everyone, regardless of the degree to which society approves or disapproves of their actions. In dealing with the tension between freedom of expression on the one hand, and obscenity and child pornography on the other, it is clear that all of the judges, from trial to the Supreme Court, did their best to grapple with distasteful issues as impartially as humanly possible.[185]

THE SUPREME COURT AND THE FUNDAMENTAL FREEDOMS

The Supreme Court has given the fundamental freedoms much greater protection under the *Charter* than it did under the *Bill of Rights*. At the same time, the court is obviously struggling to create an appropriate balance between giving broad protection to individual rights, on the one hand, and respecting the policy decisions of the legislative and executive branches of government, on the other. Although the court has defined the freedoms of religion and expression broadly (as in the freedom of religion cases, and belatedly in the labour relations cases), it has upheld provincial Sunday closing legislation, some of the commercial signs provisions in Quebec's Bill 101, obscenity and anti-child pornography legislation, and legislation severely curtailing tobacco advertising.

The Supreme Court is interpreting the fundamental freedoms in the *Charter* from the perspective of the ideology of liberalism. Although this approach is useful in giving meaning to freedom of religion, it was less helpful in unravelling the concept of freedom of association in the early labour relations cases. This was because freedom of association is closely connected with the growth of the labour movement that occurred after the development of classical liberal theory. But aside from the theoretical issue, the majority on the court in the early cases may have chosen not to find a right to strike in section 2(d) for a very practical reason — the fear of entangling the courts more deeply in labour litigation. In 2007, the court overruled its earlier decisions, adopting an approach to political liberalism that included the historical development of the labour movement in Canada, and daring to take a more active role in labour litigation.

The ideology of liberalism guided the court's interpretation of freedom of expression in relation to the commercial signs provisions of Quebec's Bill 101. But here we witnessed a direct collision between the liberal, and therefore individualistic, bent of the *Charter* and the collective desire of the majority of francophones in Quebec to take the steps they considered necessary to preserve their language. The issue was how to balance the right of individuals to advertise in their own language against the right of francophones to preserve their culture and language. To put this in more basic terms, all Quebeckers, both francophones and anglophones, as members of a rights-conscious society deserve to be respected and owe respect to each other. What language policies will best promote this mutual respect? There are no easy answers to such a question because it is a question about promoting human values. An answer cannot be deduced from "correct" legal reasoning any more than a computer stuffed full of all the relevant facts could settle the issue. It is instructive that although the court's response to Bill 101 — permitting a law that would require French to be predominant on outdoor signs, but allowing less prominent wording in other languages — was initially so vehemently rejected by Quebec's Liberal government (and likely by most francophones) that the s. 15 override was invoked, after several years of calmer debate the Supreme Court's compromise solution was accepted by a Parti Québécois government, and the override was not renewed.

Likewise, there are sensible arguments on both sides of the debate about how to accommodate reasonably the requirements of minority religions, and acceptable governmental limits on pornography. The most workable answers are likely to emerge after a thoughtful public airing of these questions during which the basic goal of optimizing mutual respect is kept front and centre. It is important for Canadians to consider these issues further, and the Supreme Court's reasoning about them at least provides a useful point of departure for such a debate.

CHAPTER 4

DEMOCRATIC RIGHTS

Democratic rights are protected by sections 3–5 of the *Charter*. Section 3 states that every citizen has the right to vote in provincial and federal elections and to run for office in these assemblies; section 4 provides that there must be federal and provincial elections at least every five years (with exceptions possible during war or civil strife); and section 5 mandates Parliament and provincial legislatures to sit at least once a year. To date, all of the reported Charter challenges raised pertaining to democratic rights have occurred under section 3.

The democratic rights section of the *Charter* has not been the subject of litigation as frequently as most other Charter sections. There were only about one hundred reported cases between 1982 and 1988 in all Canadian courts that touched on democratic rights, none of which went to the Supreme Court. However, between 1991 and 2014, the Supreme Court made a number of important decisions that dealt directly with or were related to the democratic rights sections of the *Charter*, nine of which are examined in this chapter.

Litigation touching on democratic rights is reviewed in this chapter according to the following categories:

- the question of voter parity, including whether large discrepancies between the number of voters in urban and rural constituencies infringe the right to vote;
- how a province could secede from Canada following the principles of democracy;
- whether certain classes of people, such as prisoners or the developmentally challenged, can be barred from voting;
- whether restrictions on election spending by non-party groups are constitutional;
- whether Elections Canada rules ensuring only qualified voters can vote should be interpreted strictly or generously when judges are conducting a vote recount;
- whether particular restrictions on voting or registering to vote are constitutional;
- whether specific qualifications for candidacy are acceptable; and
- whether regulations restricting the political activity of public servants are permissible.

THE QUESTION OF VOTER PARITY

Section 3 declares that "every citizen of Canada has the right to vote." This declaration seems to carry with it the implication that every citizen has the *equal* right to vote. Voting rights would not mean much if, for example, a legislature decreed that university professors or property owners or men were entitled to ten votes each. If section 3 alone does not guarantee equality in the right to vote, section 15, the equality section, likely has that effect.

In most provinces and at the federal level, there are more voters in urban constituencies than in rural ones. There is an extreme example of this situation in British Columbia. In the early 1980s, the most populous riding in the province had about 36,000 voters, while the least populous had only 2,500. This meant that a vote in the rural constituency was worth more than fourteen times as much as a vote in the urban constituency. In 1986 the BC Civil Liberties Association initiated a case in the BC Supreme Court in which it was alleged that the gross under-representation of voters in the large urban ridings violated the implied equal right to vote in section 3.[1]

In April 1989 British Columbia's Chief Justice, Beverley McLachlin, decided in favour of the BC Civil Liberties Association. In her decision, which was her last before taking up her duties in the Supreme Court of Canada, she wrote that although allowances could be made for geographic and regional factors, the electoral boundaries must be drawn so as to promote equality of population in the electoral districts.[2] This decision set the stage for the *Saskatchewan Electoral Boundaries Reference* of 1991, which was the first case regarding voter parity to reach the Supreme Court of Canada.

REFERENCE RE PROVINCIAL ELECTORAL BOUNDARIES (SASKATCHEWAN) (1991)[3]

In Canada's electoral tradition, which reflects the approach in the United Kingdom, the population of voters in electoral districts does not need to be as close as possible to the same in all districts. Electoral boundaries can take into account factors such as sparsely populated areas, geography, and cultural and language affinities. The tradition in Canada is for the federal order of government and the provinces to create independent electoral commissions to periodically redraw electoral boundaries in reaction to population changes and directions from the appropriate legislature. As a result, the population of voters in northern and rural constituencies tends to be less than that in urban ridings. This situation contrasts with that in the US, where the guarantee of the right to vote in the Constitution was interpreted by the US Supreme Court in the 1960s to mean that the voter populations in electoral districts must be as close as possible to equal across the board,[4] and US courts have generally not tolerated a discrepancy of more than 20 per cent.

When s. 3 of the *Charter* was debated in 1981 and 1982, there was no discussion about whether s. 3 should be interpreted to reflect the equal apportionment approach that had been in place in the US since the 1960s. However, litigation regarding how much deviation from equality of electoral-district populations would be acceptable was inevitable. Changes to Saskatchewan's electoral boundaries legislation in the late 1980s provided the circumstances for judicial analysis of this issue.

Grant Devine's Progressive Conservative government was elected in 1981 in Saskatchewan, replacing the previous New Democratic Party (NDP) government, and was re-elected in 1986. The second-term Devine government was scandal-ridden, and so when it pushed through amendments to legislation governing the Saskatchewan Electoral Boundaries Commission in 1989, there was suspicion in some quarters that the amendments were intended to create a favourable situation for that government to be re-elected in the next election, which had to take place by late 1991.

Prior to the 1989 amendments, the Electoral Boundaries Commission was mandated to recommend electoral boundaries that would take into account a number of factors including equality of voter population in Saskatchewan ridings, geography, concentration or sparseness of population, and local conditions. The result was that with the exception of the two northern Saskatchewan ridings, which had very sparse populations, the variation of the populations from the average (known as the quotient) was not more than 15 per cent. The amendments specified a set number of urban and rural constituencies, removed equality of voter population per constituency as a factor to be striven for, required constituency boundaries to respect municipal boundaries, and allowed for a deviation from the quotient of up to 25 per cent.

The 1989 legislation required the Electoral Boundaries Commission to take into account the following factors when recommending changes in electoral boundaries to the legislature:

> *The Commission . . .*
>
> *(a) shall determine a constituency population quotient . . . from which:*
>
> *(i) no proposed southern constituency population shall vary . . . by more than 25%;*
>
> *(ii) no proposed northern constituency population shall vary . . . by more than 50%;*
>
> *(b) may use the allowable variation from the population quotient . . . to accommodate:*
>
> *(i) the sparsity, density, or relative rate of growth of population of any proposed constituency;*
>
> *(ii) any special geographic features including size and means of communication between the various parts of the proposed constituency;*

> *(iii) the community or diversity of interests of the*
> *population, including variations in the requirements of the*
> *population of any proposed constituency; and*
> *(iv) other similar or relevant factors.*[5]

Clearly, this legislation enhanced the voting power of rural voters, among whom the Devine Conservatives had much of their support, and diminished the voting power of urban voters, among whom the NDP tended to have more support. As a result, litigation began with regard to the constitutionality of these changes. In order to clear the air prior to the 1991 election, the Saskatchewan government sent a reference question to its Court of Appeal asking whether the amendments to the Electoral Boundaries Commission terms of reference were constitutional. The Court of Appeal, in early 1991, found that the amendments were unconstitutional, and that decision was appealed to the Supreme Court. The Supreme Court expedited its hearing of the appeal because of the election that had to take place later in 1991. The hearing was held in April, and the decision was released in June. The election was held in October.

By the time of the Supreme Court hearing, the recommendations of the Saskatchewan Electoral Boundaries Commission, based on the 1989 amendments, had already been approved by the Saskatchewan legislature. As a result, both the majority and minority opinions of the Supreme Court focused on the results of the redrawing of the electoral boundaries for the 1991 election, rather than on what could have been the commission's recommendations, given the new, broader terms of reference.

The case was heard by the full court of nine. The majority of five, led by Justice McLachlin, decided in favour of the constitutionality of the electoral boundaries (Justice Sopinka wrote a short concurring decision). The remaining three judges dissented, led by Justice Peter Cory.

Justice McLachlin began by outlining the general principles that she applied in determining how far the populations of individual electoral districts could vary from the average, or quotient, for the Saskatchewan ridings. (The fact that the two northern ridings were allowed to vary from the quotient by up to 50 per cent was not contested; all parties were of the opinion that because of the sparse northern population, up to a 50 per cent variance was acceptable.) First, she emphasized that pursuant to the *Persons* decision of 1930, the constitution should be interpreted as a "living tree."[6] As well, the courts had to recognize that legislatures, when developing policy, must take into account "practical living facts" that change over time. "This is nowhere more true than in considering the right to vote, where practical considerations such as social and physical geography may impact on the value of the citizen's right to vote."[7] Finally, McLachlin underlined the importance of considering the nature of a free and democratic society by quoting from Justice Brian Dickson's decision in the *Oakes* case.

> *The Court must be guided by the values and principles*
> *essential to a free and democratic society which I believe*
> *embody, to name but a few, respect for the inherent dignity of*
> *the human person, commitment to social justice and equality,*
> *accommodation of a wide variety of beliefs, respect for*
> *cultural and group identity, and faith in social and political*
> *institutions which enhance the participation of individuals and*
> *groups in society.*[8]

McLachlin then addressed the meaning of the right to vote in s. 3 of the *Charter*. She concluded that this right entailed "effective representation." Effective representation includes relative parity of voting power but also recognizes that "factors like geography, community history, community interests, and minority representation may need to be taken into account to ensure that our legislative assemblies effectively represent the diversity of our social mosaic."[9] McLachlin concluded that the Canadian electoral tradition since Confederation was effective representation, not absolute voter parity.

Justice McLachlin then closely examined the results of the 1989 changes. She pointed out that the differences between the pre-1989 Saskatchewan electoral boundaries and the changes enacted in 1991 were minimal. "The rural areas have 53.0 percent of the seats and 50.4 percent of the population. Urban areas have 43.9 percent of the seats and 47.6 percent of the population. The rural areas are, therefore, somewhat over-represented, and the urban areas somewhat under-represented, but these deviations are relatively small."[10]

Although the post-1989 changes allowed for a discrepancy as much as 25 per cent between the voting populations of constituencies, that limit was seldom approached, and each time for a good reason based on geography or projected future population growth or decline. Justice Sopinka's concurring decision emphasized that although the post-1989 changes were not significant enough to warrant the conclusion that s. 3 was violated, the discretion left to the Electoral Boundaries Commission might result in future recommendations that could lead to unconstitutional electoral boundaries.

The minority also closely examined the pre- and post-1989 electoral boundaries, and although the minority judges also found the changes to be minor, they concluded that the differences were important enough to invoke s. 3 of the *Charter* because the right to vote is so fundamental to democracy. They concluded that the pre-1989 legislation, which allowed a 15 per cent difference from the quotient in southern Saskatchewan was reasonable, but the new 25 per cent quotient deviated too much from the principle of voter equality to be upheld. Key to the minority's finding was that the Saskatchewan government did not present any evidence about the purpose of the changes, or about the relation between the purpose and a rational connection with the results, or with regard to how the new legislation minimally impaired the right to vote with relative equality.

The constitutional importance of the *Saskatchewan Electoral Boundaries* decision, however, is the fact that all nine judges agreed about how the s. 3 guarantee of a citizen's right to vote should be interpreted with regard to the drawing of electoral boundaries. Their disagreement was over how to apply these principles rather than the principles themselves. As a result, the electoral boundary principles laid down in this decision will govern how electoral boundaries are redrawn federally, provincially, and territorially for the foreseeable future.

It should be noted that in 2003 in the *Figueroa* decision, the Supreme Court's definition of effective representation was applied by the Supreme Court in 2003 to the definition of official party status in the *Canada Elections Act* so as to strike down advantages given to larger political parties.[11]

ASSESSMENT

Given the questionable ethical record of the Grant Devine government during its second term in office, it is not unreasonable to speculate that the 1989 changes to the Saskatchewan Electoral Boundaries Commission mandate were politically motivated. The commission was given leeway to change electoral boundaries in a way that clearly skewed electoral districts in favour of the governing party. However, the evidence analyzed by the Supreme Court majority showed that the commission did its best to draw fair electoral boundaries within the confines of the new legislation. Had the commission recommended electoral boundaries that were clearly designed to favour the incumbent government, the Supreme Court minority would have become the majority.

The Supreme Court majority, in the absence of strong evidence that the new electoral boundaries were significantly different from the previous ones, erred on the side of deference to the legislative branch, thus quelling inevitable charges of judicial activism. Had the court found the electoral-boundaries legislation unconstitutional, that decision itself may have become an election issue.

Even with the new electoral boundaries, the Devine government was soundly defeated in the October 1991 election. Subsequently, nearly all of the former Devine cabinet and backbench members were implicated in a fraud for misuse of their communications allowances for personal purposes. Several served jail terms, one committed suicide, and the provincial Progressive Conservative Party ceased to exist.[12] However, none of these ethical breaches involved electoral fraud.

CANADIAN DEMOCRACY AND THE SECESSION OF A PROVINCE
REFERENCE RE SECESSION OF QUEBEC (1998)[13]

After the *Saskatchewan Electoral Boundaries* litigation, the next major opportunity that the Supreme Court had to analyze democratic rights in Canada came with the *Quebec Secession Reference* in 1998. The primary issue here was not the meaning of s. 3 but rather the interpretation of the amendment procedures in the constitution and international law issues related to secession. Nevertheless, the case is presented here because it is central to the

Supreme Court's jurisprudence on the nature of Canadian democracy and impacted the court's approach to subsequent s. 3 decisions.

Following the near victory of the pro-secession side in the 1995 Quebec secession referendum, the federal government sent a reference question to the Supreme Court asking whether Quebec could secede unilaterally after a pro-secession vote, either according to the Canadian constitution or to international law.[14]

The three questions that the cabinet sent to the Supreme Court to answer were as follows:

> *Under the Constitution of Canada, can the National Assembly, legislature, or government of Quebec effect the secession of Quebec from Canada unilaterally?*

> *Does international law give the National Assembly, legislature, or government of Quebec the right to effect the secession of Quebec from Canada unilaterally? In this regard, is there a right to self-determination under international law that would give the National Assembly, legislature, or government of Quebec the right to effect the secession of Quebec from Canada unilaterally?*

> *In the event of a conflict between domestic and international law on the right of the National Assembly, legislature, or government of Quebec to effect the secession of Quebec from Canada unilaterally, which would take precedence in Canada?*[15]

The government of Quebec refused to participate in the court's hearing because it considered that the Supreme Court of Canada had no legitimacy to consider the issue of a future sovereign Quebec. The Supreme Court considered it so important that Quebec be represented in this case that it appointed an *amicus curiae*, or friend of the court, to argue on behalf of Quebec's interests. A team of six lawyers acted as *amicus curiae*, headed by prominent Quebec lawyer André Joli-Cœur.

The answer to question one was absolutely clear according to the wording of the amending procedures in the *Constitution Act, 1982*: no. The answer question two was also obvious to any international law expert: no. Thus, the answer to question three was also clear: there was no conflict. However, the unanimous nine-judge panel issued a lengthy ninety-page decision attributed to "The Court." The reason for the in-depth decision was likely that the judges wished to present a blueprint for how a province could secede from Canada through democratic means.

After addressing some preliminary objections regarding the court's jurisdiction to answer the questions raised by the *amicus curiae*,[16] the court reviewed "the context in which the Canadian union has evolved. To this end, we will briefly describe the legal evolution of the Constitution and the foundational principles governing constitutional amendments."[17] The court presented a concise history of the negotiations leading up to the *Constitution Act, 1867*, emphasizing the approval of the Quebec *Resolutions of 1865* by the legislatures of the four colonies that formed Canada in 1867. The court also reviewed the unsuccessful attempt by Nova Scotia to secede from Canada because, as noted by the British Colonial Secretary in 1868, of the reliance that the other three provinces, especially New Brunswick, had put on the Nova Scotia legislature's approval of the new federal country, and the unfairness that Nova Scotia's secession would create.[18] The judges emphasized the importance of the principle of federalism in addressing the serious political and economic issues faced by the colonies that formed Canada in 1867, as well as the military threat posed by the United States.

The court declared that "four foundational constitutional principles . . . are most germane for resolution of this Reference: federalism, democracy, constitutionalism and the rule of law, and respect for minority rights,"[19] all linked to each other in a symbiotic relationship. "The principles are not merely descriptive, but are also invested with a powerful normative force, and are binding upon both courts and governments."[20] The justices analyzed each of these principles in turn.

With regard to federalism, the court noted how the centralist vision of some of the Fathers of Confederation eventually gave way to a more balanced approach. "The principle of federalism recognizes the diversity of the component parts of Confederation, and the autonomy of provincial governments to develop their societies within their respective spheres of jurisdiction. The federal structure of our country also facilitates democratic participation by distributing power to the government thought to be most suited to achieving the particular societal objective having regard to this diversity."[21]

The court noted that an ideal of democracy had always informed the evolution of the Canadian state, an ideal that itself has continually evolved in that the Canadian constitution is a "living tree," growing to accommodate changing societal needs, challenges, and ideals. Quoting from the *Saskatchewan Electoral Boundaries Reference*, the court pointed out that the Canadian tradition is "one of evolutionary democracy moving in uneven steps toward the goal of universal suffrage and more effective representation."[22] Democracy is a system of government by majority rule, but it is much more than that. Again referring to the Saskatchewan reference, the court emphasized that democracy is concerned more with substantive goals rather than mere process, foremost amongst them the promotion of self-government that "accommodates cultural and group identities."[23] Justice Dickson's invocation of the breadth of democratic principles in a free and democratic society, as enunciated in *Oakes*, was once again recalled, as it was in the Saskatchewan reference.

The Court stressed that a successful democracy can thrive only within the context of the rule of law and respectful discussion.

> *[T]he need to build majorities necessitates compromise, negotiation, and deliberation. No one has a monopoly on truth, and our system is predicated on the faith that in the marketplace of ideas, the best solutions to public problems will rise to the top. Inevitably, there will be dissenting voices. A democratic system of government is committed to considering those dissenting voices, and seeking to acknowledge and address those voices in the laws by which all in the community must live.*[24]

Thus, the duty of democratic discussion must "acknowledge and address democratic expressions of a desire for change in other provinces."[25]

With regard to the rule of law, the principle was summarized as follows: "At its most basic level, the rule of law vouchsafes to the citizens and residents of the country a stable, predictable, and ordered society in which to conduct their affairs. It provides a shield for individuals from arbitrary state action."[26] The judges reminded readers of the three basic parts of the rule of law that they outlined in the *Manitoba Language Rights Reference*: "the law is supreme over the acts of both government and private persons," the existence of "an actual order of positive laws," and "the relationship between the state and the individual must be regulated by law."[27] Constitutionalism is related to the rule of law in that all orders of government in Canada are bound both by the rule of law and the constitution. The constitution can be amended, "but only through a process of negotiation which ensures that there is an opportunity for the constitutionally defined rights of all the parties to be respected and reconciled."[28]

Finally, respect for minority rights, the court noted, is a long Canadian tradition, beginning with the guarantees of minority language, education, and religious rights built into the *Constitution Act, 1867*, and continuing with the carefully thought-out minority rights protections in the *Canadian Charter of Rights and Freedoms*. The protection of minority rights is fundamental to the existence of Canada.[29]

The court then applied these principles to the question of Quebec secession. First, it affirmed that secession could be accomplished only through a constitutional amendment. A majority vote in favour of secession would not be enough, but such a vote would indicate a democratic preference and would be a prelude to discussion about constitutional change. However, the court emphasized that "[t]he referendum result, if it is to be taken as an expression of the democratic will, must be free of ambiguity both in terms of the question asked and in terms of the support it achieves."[30]

A referendum result — based on a clear question — showing a clear majority of Quebeckers in favour of secession would place an obligation on the federal government and the other provinces to negotiate a change in the constitutional order of Canada that might lead to Quebec seceding. However, the outcome would not be predetermined; the rights and interests of both Quebeckers and non-Quebeckers would have to be taken into account, and the negotiations might or might not lead to actual secession. The nature of a clear referendum question and a clear majority would be determined by the political process, not by the courts.

On the question of whether Quebec has a right to unilateral secession pursuant to the principles of international law, the court noted that this right applies only to a colonial people that "is subject to alien subjugation, domination, or exploitation; and possibly where 'a people' is denied any meaningful exercise of its right to self-determination within the state of which it forms a part."[31] Quebec does not fit into this category and therefore has no right to secede under international law. Quebec could attempt a unilateral secession in any case, but would need to rely on other states for recognition. Given the state of international law, international recognition would be unlikely.

ASSESSMENT

There is no doubt that the Supreme Court's decision in the *Quebec Secession Reference* gave both the federal government and Quebec more than they had bargained for. The Supreme Court's careful analysis of the principles behind Canadian democracy built on its analysis of the nature of democracy in previous decisions such as *Oakes* and the *Saskatchewan Electoral Boundaries Reference*, and established the principle of a duty to negotiate after a pro-independence referendum result that involved a clear question and a clear majority. This is clearly a sensible and bloodless approach to resolving a contentious issue, but it relies on a modicum of sensible politicians capable of true discussion and compromise.

In response to the Supreme Court's decision in the *Quebec Secession Reference*, in 2000 the Chrétien government introduced into Parliament the *Clarity Act*. It stated that in the event a province called for a referendum on secession, the House of Commons must declare within thirty days whether it considers the referendum question sufficiently clear. In the event of a majority vote in favour of the question, the House of Commons must then declare whether the majority is a clear majority. It must take into account the size of the majority, the proportion who voted, the views of the political parties, and the assessment of Canada's Senate. Two days after the *Clarity Act* became law, the Parti Québécois introduced a motion into the Quebec National Assembly that if a referendum were to be held, a 50 per cent vote plus one person that favoured independence would be sufficient to trigger Quebec independence — a bill that has led to further litigation.[32]

THE SUPREME COURT, DEMOCRACY, AND THE INSTITUTIONS OF GOVERNANCE

The Supreme Court's analysis of the implications of democracy, reflected as it is in its Charter decisions and the *Quebec Secession Reference*, has also impacted other decisions in which the Court is asked to pronounce on the relation between democracy and Canadian political institutions.

For example, in 2013 the Harper government attempted to appoint Marc Nadon, a semi-retired Federal Court of Appeal judge, to fill a Quebec vacancy on the Supreme Court. This appointment was challenged in court as unconstitutional by Toronto lawyer Rocco Galati. To clear the air, the government sent a reference question to the Supreme Court. In 2014, in a six to one decision that included the two remaining Quebec judges, the Court ruled that the appointment was indeed unconstitutional.[33] This is because the *Supreme Court Act*, according to the Court, requires that the three judges from Quebec have a recent background in Quebec civil law so that, in turn, the five-judge panels that hear Quebec civil law appeals always have a majority of Quebec judges who are likely to be experts in this area. Although Nadon had at one time practiced civil law in Quebec, he had not done so during his two decades on the Federal Court, which deals primarily with federal administrative law issues. The majority quoted from Peter Russell to emphasize the importance of ensuring that the Quebec judicial appointments are current in the Quebec civil law:

> [T]he antipathy to having the Civil Code of Lower Canada
> interpreted by judges from an alien legal tradition was not
> based merely on a concern for legal purity or accuracy. It
> stemmed more often from the more fundamental premise
> that Quebec's civil-law system was an essential ingredient of
> its distinctive culture and therefore it required, as a matter
> of right, judicial custodians imbued with the methods of
> jurisprudence and social values integral to that culture.[34]

The decision referred to several Charter of Rights decisions of the Court, including as well as the Quebec Secession Reference decision, indicating the effort that the Court has been going to in order to maintain a consistent approach toward its analysis of democracy and federalism.

Also in 2014, the Supreme Court released its decision on another reference question, this time about the constitutionality of the Harper government's attempts to reform the Senate. The reform initiatives included enabling the provinces to host elections for "senators in waiting" from their provinces — who would then be appointed when vacancies arise from their province, introducing term limits to Senate appointments, and abolition of the requirement that Senators hold at least $4,000 worth of real property in the province for which they are appointed. The government was hoping for the green light to make all these changes through the amending formula that allows Parliament to amend its own internal constitution (s. 44 of the *Constitution Act, 1982*). However, the Supreme Court ruled that because of the federalism principle, the Senate elections reform, as well as the term limits reform, would need the approval of at least seven of the ten provincial legislatures representing 50% of Canada's population, plus Parliament. However, the property qualification could be abolished through s. 44, except for the unique provisions referring to Quebec, which would also require Quebec's consent. A final question sent to the Court asked which amending formula would apply to the abolition of the Senate, and the answer was that the unanimity formula would apply — the legislatures of all ten provinces plus Parliament — because the Senate is an essential ingredient of the confederation bargain that has implications for all the provinces.[35]

Like the Nadon decision, the 2014 Senate reference decision cited several Charter of Rights decisions, as well as the *Quebec Secession Reference*, in order to show that the Court's analysis of Canadian democracy and the federalism principle is consistent.

Neither the Nadon decision nor the 2014 Senate reference decision were Charter of Rights decisions. However, the Court's heavy reliance on its analysis of Canadian democracy and Canadian federalism in the Charter is an indication of how important Charter jurisprudence is to the Court's overall approach to democratic rights.

CLASSES OF PERSONS DENIED THE VOTE

Many groups, including prisoners and those with mental disabilities, have been denied the vote at various times in our history. For example, women were excluded from voting until 1916, when Manitoba gave them the right to vote in provincial elections. All the provinces eventually followed Manitoba's lead; Quebec was the last in 1940. Women won the right to vote in federal elections in 1918. Some provinces prevented Canadians of Asian origin from voting until the early part of the twentieth century (see chapter 1). Native Canadians living on reserves could not vote until 1960. There are five groups, however, that until the advent of the *Charter* were disenfranchised by the federal and provincial elections acts: prisoners, those in institutions for the mentally disabled or those with mental illnesses, judges, minors, and non-citizens. A broad interpretation of section 3 has extended the right to vote to some in the first three of these groups. Although non-citizens do not have rights under section 3, they could still press for broader voting rights under the equality rights of the *Charter*. Some Canadian municipalities consider from time to time allowing non-citizens who are permanent residents to vote in municipal elections in order to encourage more participation in civil politics.[36]

One reason for denying prisoners the vote is because voting is one of a number of liberties denied to them as part of their punishment. (The US Constitution allows the state legislatures to deny the vote indefinitely to those convicted of criminal offences.) Some legislators have considered that the mentally disabled, those with mental illnesses, and minors are incapable of voting intelligently.

The purpose of the denial of the vote to judges prior to the *Charter* was to promote judicial independence and impartiality. If judges cannot vote, there is no incentive for politicians to try to influence them and possibly infringe their independence in so doing. As well, there is no need for judges who cannot vote to make up their minds about election issues, a process that might affect their impartiality. Within a few years after the *Charter* became law, provincial and federal governments amended their elections acts to allow judges to vote. They must have concluded that they could not have provided empirical evidence in court that would demonstrate that denying the vote to judges really did promote judicial impartiality.

Prisoners and the mentally disabled have been active in claiming the right to vote through Charter challenges in the courts.

PRISONERS

The first province to allow prisoners to vote in provincial elections was Quebec.[37] Prisoners can now vote in all municipal, provincial, territorial, and federal elections, but only as a result of litigation pursuant to s. 3 of the *Charter*.

Shortly after the *Charter* came into effect in 1982, inmates in remand centres in Saskatchewan successfully applied for a court order to allow them to vote.[38] Remand inmates are prisoners waiting for trial; they have not been convicted. The Crown was unable to demonstrate that the failure to provide remand inmates with facilities for voting constituted a reasonable limit to the right to vote.

Also in 1982, through Charter litigation, those on probation in British Columbia won the right to vote.[39] Prior to the case, BC was the only province that denied probationers the vote. The Crown claimed that denial was to prevent "unfit persons" from voting. However, the Crown was unable to explain to the satisfaction of the BC Court of Appeal why probationers were unfit to vote in BC but fit to vote in the rest of Canada. This decision indicates how the *Charter* can promote national standards with regard to matters within provincial jurisdiction.

Attempts to persuade judges that convicted prisoners serving sentences should be allowed to vote met with limited success until the two *Sauvé* cases reached the Supreme Court in 1993 and 2002 respectively. For example, in 1983 the BC Supreme Court ruled that the franchise for prisoners could be denied for practical reasons: the need to keep the identity of some prisoners confidential and the difficulty in setting up electioneering activities in prisons.[40] In several cases, judges ruled that prisoners had gone to court to demand the right to vote too close to the election day, thus not giving judges adequate time to consider their arguments carefully, or giving prison officials time to make appropriate arrangements should the right to vote be granted.[41] However, these early cases provided hints that attempts by governments to justify denying prisoners voting rights might not meet the standards of the Oakes test. In an Ontario Supreme Court decision in July 1988, Mr. Justice John Bowlby struck down the section of the *Ontario Election Act* that denied the vote to prisoners. Judge Bowlby was of the opinion that "the rehabilitation of convicts would be assisted by enabling them to participate in the electoral process." The judge wrote that "even with the most flagrant crime there must exist hope of reform. This is the philosophy of our penal system."[42]

THE *SAUVÉ* CASES (1993 AND 2002), AND PRISONERS WINNING THE RIGHT TO VOTE

Richard Sauvé was convicted of first degree murder in 1978, along with several other co-accused. He was sentenced to 25 years.[43] He maintains that he was innocent — in the wrong place at the wrong time — and is working to have his conviction overturned. After reconciling himself to the fact that he would spend years in jail, he decided to take advantage of educational opportunities available to prisoners, and began taking university courses. Through these courses, he learned about the *Charter of Rights and Freedoms* and the guarantee in section 3 of the right to vote of all citizens. He wanted to vote and to participate in the political system in other ways in order to help tackle what he considered to be the injustices of the Canadian criminal justice system.[44] He found a lawyer who agreed to go to court on his behalf to apply for a declaration that prisoners in Ontario had the right to vote.

Sauvé lost his case at trial in 1988.[45] He appealed, and won at the Ontario Court of Appeal in 1992.[46] and the decision was appealed by the Crown to the Supreme Court of Canada in 1993. In a brief decision, the Supreme Court declared that the blanket denial of the vote to prisoners was a violation of s. 3 because it was overbroad.[47] The *Canada Elections Act* denied the vote to all prisoners, whether they were serving sentences of one day or life. As well, denying the vote based on administrative convenience did not meet the standard of the Oakes test. The federal government was given one year to implement changes to the *Elections Act* that would stand up to Charter scrutiny.

The amended legislation, implemented in 1993, gave prisoners serving less than two years the right to vote, but denied it to those sentenced to two years or more. It appears that the amendment was enacted quickly without much thought about why the cut-off should be two years. The preamble to the *Penitentiary Act* was clear that an important purpose of the Canadian penitentiary system was to rehabilitate offenders, given that nearly all inmates will eventually be released from prison and expected to act as good citizens from that time. Why did prisoners serving less than two years deserve to vote as part of the rehabilitative process, but those serving between two and three years, for example, not deserve to vote? It appears that setting the threshold at two years, which meant that federal penitentiaries could avoid having to establish voting facilities for most inmates, was administratively convenient for the federal penitentiary system, which incarcerates prisoners sentenced to more than two years (as opposed to provincial jails, which house prisoners serving less than two years).

Sauvé and other prisoners serving more than two years challenged the new *Elections Act* provisions, and they won at trial in the Federal Court in 1996. The federal government successfully appealed to the Federal Court of Appeal in 2000, and then Sauvé appealed to the Supreme Court of Canada, which, in 2002, ruled in his favour in a five to four decision. The majority decision was written by Chief Justice McLachlin.

McLachlin summarized the government's objectives in denying the right to vote to prisoners sentenced to more than two years as follows:

> *Section 51(e) denying penitentiary inmates the right to vote was not directed at a specific problem or concern. Prisoners have long voted, here and abroad, in a variety of situations without apparent adverse effects to the political process, the prison population, or society as a whole. In the absence of a specific problem, the government asserts two broad objectives as the reason for this denial of the right to vote: (1) to enhance civic responsibility and respect for the rule of law; and (2) to provide additional punishment, or enhance the general purposes of the criminal sanction.* [48]

Courts presume that every piece of government legislation is designed to tackle a specific problem, and an analysis of the problem being addressed sheds light on the objective of the legislation that limits a right. In this case, however, the government could not identify a specific problem that it was addressing, but did refer to the objectives of enhancing civic responsibility, and providing additional punishment pursuant to the criminal sanction.

Clearly the limit on the right to vote violates s. 3 of the *Charter*, so the judges went straight to the s. 1 analysis. The first step was to consider whether the government's objective in limiting a right was "pressing and substantial." Given how vague the government's stated objectives were, McLachlin only reluctantly decided that the government had passed the test for proceeding past the first part of the Oakes test. Moreover, in the 1993 Sauvé decision, the Supreme Court had also, with reservations, given the government a pass on the "substantial importance" first part of the Oakes test. But McLachlin warned that vague and general objectives are unlikely to get the government past the first part of the Oakes test in the future. "At the end of the day, people should not be left guessing about why their Charter rights have been infringed."[49]

With regard to the three prongs of the second part of the Oakes test, the government's arguments completely failed to meet the standard. One fascinating aspect of this case is that the government appears to have spared no expense to win, through hiring prestigious expert witnesses to prepare expert reports to support the government's position. For example, Seymour Martin Lipset, at that time arguably one of the Western world's best-known sociologists, presented evidence in support of the government's position. His Report, which summarized some of his career's findings comparing Canadian and American political cultures, noted that because Canada and the United States are both democracies with similar democratic qualities. In the U.S. at that time, most states denied the franchise to prisoners, and fifteen states denied the right to vote to many convicts for life because of the view that their criminal record demonstrated that they were not fit to participate in the democratic process. Lipset argued that Canada, with its more communitarian values, was even more justified in denying the franchise to those imprisoned for the most serious offences.[50] A leading Canadian political scientist, Christopher Manfredi, argued in his Report that democratic legislatures can limit Charter rights in order to promote good citizenship.[51] A similar argument was presented by Thomas Pangle, one of the world's leading political philosophers at the time, who analyzed concepts of citizenship from the time of Aristotle. He concluded that in the Western philosophical tradition those who commit serious breaches of the law are unfit to exercise the democratic exercise of the franchise, which is limited to law-abiding citizens.[52]

None of these arguments impressed McLachlin because she did not consider them relevant to the legal issues before the court. Where was the government's evidence that there was a rational connection between the government's objective of promoting rehabilitation and preventing prisoners from learning to become better citizens through voting? Where was the government's defence of the requirement that the two-year threshold limited the voting rights of prisoners as little as necessary in order to achieve the objective of rehabilitation? The evidence showed that federal penitentiaries only housed about fifteen thousand inmates at any one time, and seventy-five per cent of these would be released after serving less than five years. Where was the evidence that the threshold needed to be two years, as opposed to three, five, or ten years? No such evidence was presented by the government. And finally, McLachlin found no government evidence to show that prohibiting prisoners from voting did more good than harm.

Sauvé's expert witnesses were not as well known as those hired by the government, but they did present evidence relevant to the legal issues according to McLachlin. Criminologists from both Canada and Scandinavia presented empirical evidence that allowing prisoners to vote promoted rehabilitation by educating them about the principles of Canadian democracy and the electoral system, which many had never before been encouraged to take seriously. They presented evidence to show that some prisoners sentenced to more than two years are granted day parole prior to two years. Even according to the existing legislation, these parolees were entitled to vote, but no provision had been made to allow them to vote in penitentiaries. As a result, even in penitentiaries mechanisms would need to be developed to allow these parolees to vote. Further, more than 95 per cent of prisoners in penitentiaries are eventually released, and being shown respect through allowing them to exercise the franchise would encourage them to accept the responsibilities of citizenship after their release. Moreover, if the votes of prisoners were to be distributed amongst their home communities, there would be very little chance that prisoners' votes would be determinative of the outcome of elections in any particular constituency.[53] Another of Sauvé's expert witnesses, Grant Amyot, a political theorist at Queen's University, wrote a concise Report challenging the logic of of the philosophical evidence provided by the government experts.[54]

Nevertheless, the four dissenting judges would have preferred that the court defer to the government's position. Justice Gonthier, who wrote the opinion of the dissenters, considered penal policy best left to the legislature. He considered that the evidence provided by the government's expert witnesses indicated that there was a philosophical and social policy basis for the government's position, and so the court should not second-guess the legislature on such a sensitive issue.[55]

The sense of the media around the time of the Sauvé decision was that many Canadians were opposed to granting prisoners the right to vote.[56] No doubt, the court's majority of five sensed the pulse of the public on this issue, but they did not let this deter them from striking down limits on prisoner voting rights. They were determined to focus on the legal issues involved, and it was a reality that the government provided no evidence relevant (as measured by the Oakes test) to the objective of promoting rehabilitation by preventing prisoners from voting. It may be that many people who oppose the right of prisoners to vote would not be able to provide a carefully reasoned defence of their position. If honest, they might admit that it just seems obvious that if someone has committed a crime requiring a severe prison term, they have forfeited the right to vote. However, the purpose of the *Charter of Rights* is to force governments to think carefully about whether any good could come out of limiting a right, and if so, to provide hard evidence. One could argue that the *Charter* is a vehicle for encouraging us to think more carefully and systematically than ever before about whether limits on rights are clearly justifiable. If a democracy surrenders one of its key rationales for existence — protection of minority rights — it "commits suicide."[57]

It would be possible for Parliament to enact new legislation limiting prisoners' voting rights, but such legislation would need to be based both on research showing a rational connection between the government's objective and the likely impact of such a restriction, and on evidence that the government had chosen the method that would limit prisoners' voting rights as little as necessary to achieve the objective. For example, Parliament could investigate taking the franchise from those classified as dangerous offenders, because they are unlikely to ever be released from prison and rehabilitation is unlikely. But where rehabilitation is a real possibility, it is unlikely that the Supreme Court will approve a limit to prisoners' voting rights.

As for Richard Sauvé, he achieved day-release from prison in 1995.[58] He first apprenticed as a carpenter, then became a child and youth worker, and from 1998 to 2013 was employed by Lifeline Inreach, an organization that arranged for ex-prisoners to visit long-term prisoners still serving sentences. From 2013, he has been employed by an organization that helps those released from prison to transition to productive lives. He was granted full release by the Parole Board of Canada in 2002.[59] During the 18 years he was in prison, Sauve started a "Lifers' Group" and a "Ten Plus Group" at Collins Bay Penitentiary, both of which aimed to represent the interests of long-term prisoners. He obtained his BA and did much of the work toward an MA in Criminology while in prison. He was involved in advocating for prisoners' rights and interests before prison administration and to politicians and was the Deputy Coordinator of an annual sporting event that brought together mentally challenged children from across Ontario for a weekend of Olympic-style games in the Collins Bay prison yard."[60] He has been an active voter ever since winning the right to vote, thanks to his hard-fought battle for prisoners' voting rights.

In 2004, "Of the 36,378 incarcerated persons in Canada who were eligible to vote [in the federal election], 9,635 registered and 9,250 cast ballots. In federal institutions, 13,198 inmates were eligible to vote and 5,189 registered. In provincial institutions, 23,180 inmates were eligible to vote and 4,446 registered."[61]

OTHER GROUPS

Non-resident Canadian citizens won a court case in 1985 that declared they had the right to vote.[62] In 1988, federally appointed judges won the right to vote through litigation in the Federal Court.[63] Also in 1988, the Federal Court ruled that legislation prohibiting the mentally disabled from voting was unconstitutional.[64] As a result, federal enumerators called on institutions for the mentally disabled and institutions housing those with mental illnesses before the 1988 election. Patients who could state their name, age, citizenship, and residence were placed on the voters' list. (Only about fifty of eight hundred residents at the Huronia Regional Centre in Orillia, Ontario, were able to meet these requirements.[65]) Since the late 1980s, all the provinces and territories have enfranchised the mentally disabled and those suffering from mental illnesses for provincial elections.

Up to 2014, there has been no reported litigation with regard to whether those under the age of eighteen — or selected persons under eighteen – should be allowed to vote.

RESTRICTIONS ON ELECTION SPENDING BY NON-PARTY GROUPS

In 1974, Parliament enacted legislation that limited campaign expenditures by parties and candidates, but it contained a loophole that made it fairly easy for individuals and interest groups to advertise for or against parties or candidates without reference to the spending limits. According to Canada's chief electoral officer, "a number of persons who were not acting . . . with the knowledge and consent of candidates or registered agents of political parties have . . . spent unlimited sums of money to promote or oppose a particular candidate or registered party, sums which they do not have to account for in terms of sources or amount."[66] The result was that the election spending limits were becoming meaningless, and some low-income candidates were worried about being squeezed out of the political process. To remedy that deficiency, and to provide for greater equality of access to the democratic process, in 1983 Parliament enacted provisions that would plug the loop-hole by prohibiting individuals and interest groups from advertising for or against political parties during election campaigns unless they did so under the auspices of a political party and within the campaign expense limits. This 1983 legislation had the support of all three major federal political parties at the time. Individuals and groups were still free to advertise their views with regard to specific issues as long as parties were not mentioned.

In the Alberta Court of Queen's Bench, the National Citizens Coalition, a right-wing lobby organization, challenged these provisions as violations both of section 2(b) (freedom of expression) and section 3 of the *Charter*. The trial judge, however, based his decision on section 2.[67] He found that the limits on third-party spending constituted a violation of freedom of expression that could not be justified under s. 1 of the *Charter*. Because the Oakes test for the application of section 1 would not see the light of day until the next year, the judge decided that unless the Crown could produce specific examples of how excessive advertising by non-party groups had actually resulted in harm, the restrictions on advertising by non-party groups had to be struck down.

The government decided not to appeal this decision. Because an election was approaching, a decision to appeal might have been politically damaging.[68] As well, because the *NCC* decision came just three months before the 1984 federal election, the chief electoral officer decided not to enforce the provisions affecting interest-group advertising so that the same rules would apply both inside and outside Alberta.

This result meant that, subsequently, interest groups and businesses were free to spend unlimited funds during election campaigns advertising for or against political parties. This had little impact on the 1984 election campaign, but the 1988 election was a different story because a major issue was the Conservative government's proposed free trade agreement with the United States, which was opposed by the Liberal Party. Businesses and other interest groups were free to spend as much as they wished to advertise for or against political parties. As it turned out, the Conservative party was clearly the primary beneficiary. Most Canadian and US businesses supported free trade, and they spent large sums to promote a Conservative victory.

The Royal Commission on Electoral Reform and Party Financing, which reported in 1991, recommended that third parties be allowed to engage in advertising directed at parties or candidates during election campaigns, but that strict limits should be placed on how much they could spend. Initially, the limit was $1,000 per constituency, but in 2000 this was amended to $3,000 per constituency, or $150,000 in total during the campaign period. The National Citizens Coalition continued to litigate against these limits, and succeeded in either Alberta or Ontario five times between 1993 and 2002.[69] Finally, in 2004, an appeal of one of these decisions reached the Supreme Court of Canada in the *Harper v. Canada* case (Stephen Harper had served as president of the National Citizens Coalition from 1997 to 2001, prior to his re-entry into politics).

HARPER V. CANADA (2004)[70]

Prior to its adjudication of third-party spending limits in *Harper v. Canada*, the Supreme Court had already wrestled with the third-party spending regulations in the 1992 Charlottetown Accord referendum rules. The rules forced all third parties to include themselves under either the "yes" or "no" umbrella. This provision meant the Quebec Equality Party was prohibited from publicizing its position in favour of abstention from voting because that position did not fall under either umbrella. Robert Libman, president of the Equality Party, had gone to court to seek a declaration that the referendum rules were unconstitutional. Although the case did not reach the Supreme Court of Canada until 1997, the court heard it anyway because the issue of third-party spending limits was still a live issue. The court ruled that the prohibition against third-party advertising was unconstitutional in that it did not meet the minimal-impairment requirement of the Oakes test, but the court also signalled that it would find reasonable third-party spending limits constitutional.[71]

In *Harper*, the Supreme Court upheld the third-party limits of $3,000 per constituency and $150,000 total for the country as a reasonable limit to the violation of freedom of expression in a six to three decision. The majority decision was written by Justice Michele Bastarache.

Justice Bastarache considered the argument of Stephen Harper and the NCC that the third-party election spending limits violated both s. 3 and s. 2(b) of the *Charter* (freedom of expression). With regard to s. 3, Bastarache focused on the "effective representation" aspect of s. 3 outlined in the *Saskatchewan Electoral Boundaries* decision. He concluded that the third-party spending limits actually enhance the right to vote by promoting equality in the electoral contest and preventing wealthy third parties from dominating election advertising.[72] He rejected the argument of the NCC that the third-party limits prevent citizens from being reasonably informed of the election issues, arguing that the limits allow for third parties to get their points across in a system that promotes equality of debate, but does not prevent third parties from spending unlimited funds prior to the election period. Therefore, the third-party limits do not violate s. 3.

Bastarache conceded that the limits did violate s. 2(b), but the violation was saved by s. 1. He stated that the "objectives of the third-party election advertising scheme are threefold: first, to promote equality in the political discourse; second, to protect the integrity of the financing regime applicable to candidates and parties; and third, to ensure that voters have confidence

185

in the electoral process."[73] He found that these objectives were pressing and substantial enough to justify limiting freedom of expression.

The NCC had argued that in order to show a rational connection between the objectives of the third-party spending limits and the results achieved, it would be necessary to show conclusively that the spending limits prevented harm and prevented election results from being unfair. Bastarache stated that this was too high a standard; a "reasoned apprehension" of harm is sufficient.[74] The Royal Commission on Electoral Reform had provided a great deal of evidence from expert research that in the absence of third-party limits, the electoral contest could be rendered unfair if third-party groups spent large amounts of money on advertising.

Next, Bastarache found that the third-party limits in question minimally impaired freedom of expression. He cited the *RJR-MacDonald* decision that the measures chosen "need not be the least impairing option."[75] He also cited the opinions of several well-known Canadian experts on the electoral process that the limits chosen by the legislation reflect a fair balance between a level playing field during the campaign period and third parties' freedom of expression.[76] Finally, Bastarache concluded that the third-party limits resulted in more benefits to Canadian democracy than harm.

Justice McLachlin, writing for the dissenting judges, concluded that although it is reasonable to limit the amount spent by third parties during election campaigns, the limits in the impugned legislation were too restrictive. She cited the high cost of radio and television advertising and mailings, and concluded that only higher limits would meet s. 1 requirements.[77]

Harper and the NCC had also challenged s. 323 of the *Elections Act*, which prevented any political parties, candidates, or third parties from "knowingly transmitting election advertising"[78] on election day up until the polls close. The blackout period was approximately twenty hours, depending on when the polls close. The media are exempt from the blackout.

There were two objectives of s. 323 identified: ensuring that voters across Canada have access to the same information when going to the polls, and to "provide commentators and others with an opportunity to respond to any potentially misleading election advertising."[79] The second purpose is related to the exemption of the media from the blackout and gives them the opportunity to comment on any misleading election advertising that may have occurred just prior to the blackout period. A unanimous court held that although s. 323 violated freedom of expression, the provision was justified as a reasonable limit under s. 1. The objective was rationally connected to the results, and because of the media exemption, freedom of expression was limited as little as necessary to achieve the results. Finally, s. 323 had positive results in promoting the effective right to vote.[80]

ASSESSMENT

The majority decision in the Harper case not only helps to further clarify the meaning of the effective-representation aspect of s. 3, but it sensibly balances the right to freedom of expression with the right to a fair electoral system that promotes opportunities for a variety of opinions to be expressed and respectful discussions to take place that are not unduly influenced by voices backed by wealthy supporters. It takes into account the research conducted by two of Canada's leading scholars on election procedures, Frederick Fletcher and Peter Aucoin, as well as the wealth of evidence presented in the research studies of the 1991 Royal Commission on Electoral Reform and Party Financing.[81] Even the minority agreed with the principle of regulating third-party advertising but would have taken a less deferential approach to the solution adopted by Parliament.

Given that Stephen Harper, through the National Citizens Coalition, worked so hard to have the restrictions on third-party advertising struck down by the court, it is not surprising that, in February 2014, his Conservative government introduced amendments to the *Canada Elections Act* designed in part to loosen some of the regulations restricting election spending by political parties, and reducing some of the powers and responsibilities of Elections Canada. No doubt there will be litigation about whether these changes comply with ss. 3 and 2(d) of the *Charter*. However, it is noteworthy that the 2014 amendments do not change the restrictions on third-party advertising. They do, however, include third parties in a set of new regulations designed to prevent the abuse of "robocalls."[82]

THE INTERPRETATION OF THE RULES DURING A JUDICIAL VOTER RECOUNT: STRICT OR GENEROUS?

OPITZ V. WRZESNEWSKYJ (2012)[83]

In the 2011 federal general election, Conservative Ted Opitz defeated Liberal incumbent Boris Wrzesnewskyj (pronounced *zhez-NEF-skee*) by twenty-six votes in the Ontario riding of Etobicoke Centre after a judicial recount. Wrzesnewskyj applied for a declaration in the Superior Court of Ontario for the election to be annulled because of voting irregularities. A Superior Court judge found seventy-nine voting irregularities, and as a result declared the election in Etobicoke Centre null and void. Had there not been a successful appeal by Opitz, the result would have been a by-election. However, Opitz appealed directly to the Supreme Court "as of right." (Although the great majority of cases heard by the Supreme Court are cases granted "leave to appeal" [permission to appeal] by the court itself, there are a few instances in which appellants have a right to appeal, and an appeal of a judicial recount is one of these.) The Supreme Court, in its appellate capacity, in a four to three decision concluded that there should be a degree of tolerance for errors at polling stations, and on a balance of probabilities, Opitz had won the election. In sum, voters should not be disqualified by technicalities when they are truly eligible to vote. The minority, taking a stricter rule of law approach, called for a firmer application of electoral regulations and would have annulled the election results.

The majority decision was written by Justices Marshall Rothstein and Michael Moldaver.[84] They noted that "[t]he right of every citizen to vote, guaranteed by s. 3 of the *Charter*, lies at the heart of Canadian democracy."[85] Rothstein and Moldaver focused on an aspect of s. 3 that had previously been emphasized in the *Figueroa* decision: the right of the "citizen to play a meaningful role in the political life of the country."[86] They noted that s. 6 of the *Elections Act* states that "every person who is qualified as an elector is entitled to have his or her name included in the list of electors."[87]

Of the seventy-nine ballots set aside by the Superior Court judge, Rothstein and Moldaver concluded that there was not enough evidence presented by Wrzesnewskyj to set aside fifty-nine of them. That was because they had been set aside due to administrative errors at polling stations, such as unsigned registration certificates, incorrect recording of vouching,[88] or missing registration certificates. The *Canada Elections Act* allows a judge to annul an election if "there were irregularities, fraud, or corrupt or illegal practices that affected the result of the election."[89] The majority stated that "[a]n applicant [applying to have an election annulled] must prove that a procedural safeguard designed to establish an elector's entitlement to vote was not respected" in order to establish an irregularity; then the applicant must demonstrate that there were a sufficient number of these irregularities to put the result of the election in question. The majority concluded that Wrzesnewskyj had not met the standard of proof required and summed up its decision as follows:

> We are asked to disqualify the votes of several Canadian citizens based on administrative mistakes, notwithstanding evidence that those citizens were in fact entitled to vote. We decline the invitation to do so. The Canadian Charter of Rights and Freedoms *and the* Canada Elections Act . . . *have the clear and historic purposes of enfranchising Canadian citizens, such that they may express their democratic preference, and of protecting the integrity of our electoral process . . . We are dealing here with a challenge based on administrative errors. There is no allegation of any fraud, corruption, or illegal practices . . . Given the complexity of administering a federal election, the tens of thousands of election workers involved, many of whom have no on-the-job experience, and the short time frame for hiring and training them, it is inevitable that administrative mistakes will be made. If elections can be easily annulled on the basis of administrative errors, public confidence in the finality and legitimacy of election results will be eroded. Only irregularities that affect the result of the election and thereby undermine the integrity of the electoral process are grounds for overturning an election.*[90]

The minority decision was penned by Chief Justice McLachlin. After consulting the definition of "irregularity" in the *Oxford Dictionary*, McLachlin concluded that "an election may be set aside as a result of non-compliance with the provisions of the [*Elections*] *Act*, even in the absence of fraud or corrupt or illegal practices. The objective of efficiency and certainty in the electoral process suggests that there ought to be strict compliance with the requirements of the *Act*."[91]

Emphasizing the importance of deferring to the clear wording of an act of Parliament, McLachlin said, "The *Act* expressly states that a person who is not entitled to vote shall not receive a ballot or be allowed to vote, even if he is qualified to vote, in the sense of meeting the citizenship and age requirements . . . My colleagues, with respect, merge the concepts of qualification and entitlement."[92] She noted that if Canadians cannot rely on the plain wording of the *Canada Elections Act*, they are less likely to have confidence in the integrity of the electoral process.

The minority found that Wrzesnewskyj was able to prove that sixty-five of the ballots cast were irregular, so that the election should have been annulled and a by-election called.

ANALYSIS

Opitz v. Wrzesnewskyj is an important decision in that the majority opinion emphasizes the right to vote under s. 3 of the *Charter*. Technicalities in the application of the *Canada Elections Act* that are shown to interfere with this right are likely to be the object of litigation in the future. As well, the *Fair Elections Act* of 2014, which makes voting more difficult for some citizens, will clearly attract Charter challenges, as it runs contrary to the majority Supreme Court opinion that all Canadian citizens over eighteen are entitled to vote.

RESTRICTIONS ON VOTING

Sometimes, otherwise eligible voters find themselves disenfranchised because they have been missed by enumerators, are unable to be in their home riding at election time, or have not fulfilled local residency requirements in time for the election. In the early days of the *Charter*, a number of people challenged these kinds of restrictions as violations of the section 3 right to vote. During the six weeks prior to the 1988 federal election, at least a dozen citizens raised issues like this in court. Most were unsuccessful, either because the challengers had failed to give adequate notice to the Crown — various statutes require that if a constitutional issue is to be raised, adequate notice must be given — or because the judges decided that such important matters could not be decided within the short time period before the election.

In most Canadian provinces and territories, there are residency requirements ranging from six months to a year for voting in provincial or territorial elections. In 1982 a Saskatchewan resident who had not resided in the province for the required six-month period applied to the Court of Queen's Bench for an order that would allow his name to be entered on the provincial voters' list. The court decided against the claim on the grounds that residency requirements are common in "free and democratic" societies and that it is a legislative task, not a judicial one, to decide what specific period should apply.[93]

In a similar case in the Yukon Territory, the territorial Supreme Court decided in 1985 that a twelve-month residency requirement was unconstitutional. The Crown had argued that a residency requirement was necessary to prevent election results from being distorted by a last-minute influx of non-residents or by people merely passing through, and that residency requirements allow voters to develop a commitment to the community. The judge was not persuaded by any of these arguments and concluded that a residency requirement was simply another relic of past anti-democratic restrictions on voting, such as property or educational qualifications, or being male. However, this decision was overturned on appeal. The territorial Court of Appeal decided that the residency requirement passed all of the elements of the Oakes test. In particular, the requirement was rationally connected with the objective of ensuring that voters "show some connection with the province or territory before deciding upon local matters."[94]

By and large, judges tend to accept the current rules and regulations governing how Canadians may cast their ballots unless these rules are clearly out of line with the rules in other Canadian jurisdictions. In this way, the *Charter* is promoting greater uniformity in provincial voting procedures.

CANDIDACY

Some of the various elections acts in Canada prevent certain individuals from running as candidates in elections. For example, anyone convicted of a criminal offence could not run in provincial elections in Nova Scotia for the five years following their conviction until this provision was struck down in the *MacLean* case, discussed below. Other statutes or regulations preclude some classes of employees from seeking or accepting elected office unless they resign their position. These provisions have been challenged in several cases.

One of the most publicized of the challenges involved Billy Joe MacLean, the former Nova Scotia cabinet minister who was convicted of fraud for submitting false expense claims in 1986. Not only was MacLean forced to resign from the cabinet, but the Nova Scotia legislature declared his seat vacant. The Nova Scotia *Elections Act* prohibited him from running for office for five years. MacLean challenged this provision as a violation of section 3 of the *Charter*. He won his case in the Nova Scotia Supreme Court.[95] The judge concluded that the *Elections Act* failed to meet the rational-connection test prescribed by the Oakes case because it was a sweeping prohibition that applied to all offenders, no matter how minor the offence. MacLean was therefore able to contest the by-election for his vacated seat. In the campaign, he claimed that he had been guilty only of poor bookkeeping, and he was re-elected to the legislature. However, he went down to defeat in the provincial general election of 1988.

Fred Harvey was elected to the New Brunswick legislature in the provincial election of 1991. He was subsequently convicted of violating the New Brunswick *Elections Act* by inducing a sixteen-year-old to vote when he knew this was illegal. According to the *Elections Act*, Harvey was forced out of the legislature and prohibited from running again for five years. He went to the Superior Court in New Brunswick for an application declaring that the *Act* violated his s. 3 Charter rights, and the case reached the Supreme Court of Canada in 1993. The court upheld the New Brunswick Court of Appeal decision that found that although the *Act* violated the right in s. 3 to be a candidate, this violation was upheld under s. 1.[96]

In the 1982 Alberta provincial election, H. Jonson, a high school principal in the town of Ponoka, won a seat in the legislature. The County of Ponoka School Board gave the principal a leave of absence without pay so he could complete his term as an MLA (member of the Legislative Assembly). A provincial election was called in 1986, and during the election campaign, the board passed a new policy that would continue Jonson's leave of absence for only one year, should he win the election. Jonson won the election and challenged the board's new policy in court. He claimed the new policy violated sections 3 and 15 of the *Charter*, as well as similar provisions in the *Alberta Bill of Rights*. The board defended its position by claiming the *Charter* did not apply to its policies. The Queen's Bench judge held that the *Charter* did, in fact, apply to the decisions of school boards, because such boards exercise powers they have been delegated by the provincial legislature. While the judge could find no violation of a Charter right in the board's new policy, he concluded that the new policy was unreasonable from the standpoint of administrative law because it was implemented in the midst of an election campaign. The judge ordered that the MLA was entitled to retain his designation as principal and to be granted a leave of absence without pay for the duration of his current term as MLA.[97]

POLITICAL ACTIVITIES OF PUBLIC SERVANTS

All jurisdictions in Canada have to some extent limited the freedom of public servants to participate in political activities. The four western provinces and Quebec have usually had the fewest restrictions. Most public servants in these provinces may participate in political activities as long as these activities do not interfere with their work and are not carried out during their hours of employment.

In 1986 provincial public servants in Nova Scotia and federal public servants challenged the restrictions on their political activities as violations of section 2 (freedom of expression, assembly, and association) and section 3 of the *Charter*. Regarding section 3, they argued that the constraints on the political activities of public servants confined the campaign resources available to some candidates, thereby limiting their right under section 3 to be a candidate.

The outcomes of the two cases were quite different. In Nova Scotia, the *Civil Service Act* prohibited public servants from engaging in any partisan political activity and from contributing funds to a political party. A Nova Scotia Supreme Court judge accepted that the purpose of this restriction — to promote an impartial public service — met the requirements of the first part of the Oakes test (an objective of substantial importance). However, the legislation failed the second part of the test, the proportionality requirements. The restrictions amounted to a blanket prohibition of political activities; they did not limit rights as little as was necessary to achieve the purpose of the legislation.[98]

Federally, the *Public Service Employment Act* prohibits public servants from working for or against candidates for Parliament or a provincial legislature, or for or against a political party. Public servants, however, are allowed to attend political meetings and to contribute funds to political parties. The public servants who challenged these provisions wished to engage in low-level political activities such as attending a party convention as a delegate and canvassing on behalf of a candidate. The Federal Court interpreted the provisions of the *Act* broadly so as to permit many of the activities the public servants wished to participate in. The judge concluded that there had been no violation of section 3. He also concluded that while in some respects the *Act* did violate section 2, these breaches were reasonable limits under section 1. In his opinion, the *Act* limited Charter rights as little as necessary in order to promote impartiality in the public service.[99] However, when this case reached the Supreme Court of Canada in 1991, the court ruled that an absolute prohibition on the political activities of public servants at lower levels was not a reasonable limit under s. 1. "[A]n absolute rule prohibiting all public participation and discussion by all public servants would prohibit activities which no sensible person in a democratic society would want to prohibit."[100]

Another Supreme Court decision about the political rights of public servants deserves mention: *OPSEU v. Attorney-General for Ontario*.[101] Although it was not a Charter case, it has implications for the *Charter*. Before the *Charter* came into effect in 1982, the Ontario Public Service Employees Union (OPSEU) initiated a court challenge to the provisions of the *Ontario Public Service Act* that prevented provincial public servants from participating in federal political activities. OPSEU claimed that under the Duff Doctrine a provincial law could not interfere with federal political activity nor with freedom of expression. When the case reached the Supreme Court of Canada in 1986, the union hoped that the court would also consider the implications of sections 2, 3, and 15 of the *Charter*. The court, however, decided not to consider the Charter issues because the facts of the case dated from pre-Charter times.

OPSEU lost the case essentially because the provincial law was considered to have only an incidental effect on federal elections, its basic purpose being to promote the impartiality of the provincial public service. However, the case is noteworthy because for the first time a majority on the Supreme Court adopted the Duff Doctrine. The majority decision was written by Mr. Justice Beetz. Given his abrupt dismissal of the Duff Doctrine in the *Dupond* decision (see chapter 1), the following words of Beetz are remarkable:

> *There is no doubt in my mind that the basic structure of our*
> *Constitution as established by the* Constitution Act, 1867
> *contemplates the existence of certain political institutions,*
> *including freely elected legislative bodies at the federal*
> *and provincial levels. In the words of Duff C. J. C. in* Re
> Alberta Statutes *at p. 133, "such institutions derive their*
> *efficacy from the free public discussions of affairs . . ." and,*
> *in those of Abbott J. in* Switzman v. Elbling *at p. 328,*
> *neither a provincial legislature nor Parliament itself can*
> *"abrogate this right of discussion and debate." Speaking more*
> *generally, I hold that neither Parliament nor the provincial*
> *legislatures may enact legislation the effect of which would*
> *be to substantially interfere with the operation of this basic*
> *constitutional structure. On the whole, though, I am inclined*
> *to the view that the . . . legislation [in question] . . . affects*
> *federal and provincial elections only in an incidental way.*

It is significant that Beetz made it part of his holding that the preamble to the *Constitution Act, 1867* prohibits both Parliament and provincial legislatures from interfering with free elections, including free public discussion. Beetz not only revived the Duff Doctrine, he adopted the most far-reaching version of it proclaimed thus far, holding that neither the federal Parliament nor the provincial legislatures can limit free expression in relation to the democratic process. The significance of this revival of the Duff Doctrine lies in the fact that the preamble to the *Constitution Act, 1867* cannot be overridden by section 33 of the *Charter*.

It also appears, however, that in future when the court is faced with a Charter case relating to the political activities of public servants, it may be somewhat sympathetic to what will no doubt be the position of the Crown — that the restrictions are a reasonable limit designed to promote public service impartiality.

THE *CHARTER* AND DEMOCRATIC RIGHTS

Patrick Monahan, a former Dean of Osgoode Hall Law School, has argued that if Canadian courts attempt to interpret the *Charter* so as to maximize democratic values, the dissonance between the democratic process and the fact that unelected officials (judges) are called on to make fundamental policy decisions about the *Charter* can be reduced.[102] To date, have Canadian courts, through their interpretation of democratic rights, advanced the ideals of democratic participation in government?

This question can certainly not be answered unequivocally. The *Saskatchewan Electoral Boundaries Reference* and *Opitz v. Wrzesnewskyj* may have erred on the side of deference to government. On the other hand, the *Harper* decision seems to present a fair and balanced approach toward electoral regulation which defers to the government, but also corrects several judgments of lower courts that could be considered too absolutist in favour of freedom of expression. The fact that courts extended the franchise to prisoners, some mentally challenged persons, and citizens living abroad indicates a careful analysis of what is entailed by the right to vote.

One contribution the judiciary can make to policy development with regard to democracy is to point out what kinds of restrictions on voting or candidacy seem to be arbitrary or not carefully considered by the policy-makers, and thus maybe unfair.

The *Charter* has raised numerous questions about the appropriateness of the rules governing voting and candidacy in Canada. Without the *Charter*, some of these issues might not have received much attention from legislators and policy-makers in the public service. Consequently, although the courts lack the policy-making tools of the legislative and executive branches, they can contribute positively in some ways to the policy-making role.

Most importantly, the Supreme Court has developed, and is continuing to refine, a principled approach to Canadian democracy based on

Chief Justice Brian Dickson's analysis in the Oakes case of 1986. He stated that a free and democratic society is based on "respect for the inherent dignity of the human person, commitment to social justice and equality, accommodation of a wide variety of beliefs, respect for cultural and group identity, and faith in social and political institutions which enhance the participation of individuals and groups in society."[103] This approach has underpinned the Supreme Court's decisions related to Canadian democracy from the Oakes decision, through the *Quebec Secession Reference*, through to the Senate reference of 2014. Although only some of the Supreme Court's decisions on Canadian democracy are directly based on s. 3 of the *Charter*, all of the Court's decisions about Canadian democracy reflect Dickson's approach in *Oakes*.

CHAPTER 5

LEGAL RIGHTS

About 90 per cent of all Charter arguments raised in reported cases across all Canadian courts deal with one of the legal rights sections — sections 7–14.[1] In the Supreme Court of Canada, about two-thirds of the Charter cases heard concern legal rights.[2] The heavy use of these sections by litigants is partly a result of the familiarity lawyers have with legal rights in that most of these rights are simply codifications of common-law principles. As well, these sections give lawyers the opportunity to raise additional arguments in cases that would have gone to court anyway because of the criminal process. In contrast, many of the cases litigated under sections of the *Charter* dealing with the fundamental freedoms, democratic, mobility, equality, and language rights are cases mounted specifically to raise a Charter challenge.

When the *Charter* was in its infancy, observers like Peter Russell predicted that cases based on the legal rights sections were likely to produce the least controversial decisions because judges would simply continue to apply the same principles with which they were familiar under the common law.[3] However, some legal rights decisions have had a surprising impact either on the criminal justice system or on government policies. This is mainly because of two factors: (a) the inclusion of some "new" legal rights in the *Charter* as well as a broader description of some older ones (see chapter 1), and (b) the fact that the *Charter*, as part of the constitution, invites judges to expand the traditional common-law protections. This chapter will consider about twenty of the Supreme Court's most prominent legal rights decisions.

UNREASONABLE SEARCH AND SEIZURE: *HUNTER V. SOUTHAM* (1984)[4]

On April 19, 1982, two days after the *Charter* became law, officers from the Combines Investigation Branch appeared at the *Edmonton Journal*. They demanded to search the newspaper's offices and had with them a search certificate granted by the Restrictive Trade Practices Commission, the body responsible for enforcing the federal *Combines Investigation Act*. The certificate read as follows:

> *You are hereby authorized to enter upon the premises*
> *hereinafter mentioned, on which I believe there may be*
> *evidence relevant to this inquiry, and examine thereon and*
> *copy . . . any other book, paper, record, or other document*
> *that in your opinion may afford such evidence. The premises*
> *referred to herein are those occupied by or on behalf of*
> *Southam Inc., 10006-101 Street, Edmonton, Alberta, and*
> *elsewhere in Canada.*

The search went ahead. Southam Inc., owner of the *Journal*, decided to test the *Charter* by requesting a court order to strike down the section of the *Combines Investigation Act* that authorizes such searches. Southam claimed that the act violated section 8 of the *Charter*, which declares that everyone has a right to be secure against unreasonable search or seizure. The Supreme Court of Canada decision was handed down in September 1984.

In order to appreciate the significance of the decision, it is useful to keep in mind that in the decade immediately prior to this case there was an enormous expansion of newspaper chains like Southam and Thomson.[5] This change began to generate public concern, which came to a head in August 1980. Both Thomson and Southam owned a newspaper each in

Ottawa and Winnipeg. One newspaper from each chain closed in each city, leaving Southam with a virtual monopoly in Ottawa, and Thomson in a similar position in Winnipeg. The public outcry which resulted led to the creation of the Kent Royal Commission on Newspapers, which reported in 1981. The commission hinted that both newspaper chains may have breached the *Combines Investigation Act* in closing the two newspapers. The subsequent investigation by the Combines Branch led to the search of the *Edmonton Journal* offices.

Chief Justice Dickson wrote the unanimous opinion for the full Court. He pointed out that in order for the court to give legal definitions of terms like "unreasonable search or seizure," it could not rely either on a dictionary or on the rules of construction that had been developed for non-Charter cases. Neither approach would lead to conclusive results. Dickson declared that the court would take a "purposive" approach toward resolving such issues, meaning that the court would define the various provisions of the *Charter* according to their historical and political purposes. Dickson quoted Viscount Sankey's decision in the 1930 "persons" cases (see chapter 1), in which Sankey described the Canadian constitution as "a living tree capable of growth and expansion within its natural limits." Dickson claimed that the court needed to give the *Charter* a broad interpretation rather than to "read provisions of the Constitution like a last will and testament lest it become one."

Dickson said that the purpose of section 8 was to protect a right to privacy. He pointed out how common-law judges had for centuries protected individual privacy from illegal encroachment by the state, and he mentioned specifically the judgment of Lord Camden in *Entick v. Carrington*[6] (see chapter 1). He said that a reasonable search would be one in which "the interests of the state in [intruding] come to prevail over the interests of the individual in resisting [state intrusions]." Building on the common law relating to trespass, Dickson defined a reasonable search as one which is (a) authorized by a statute (this principle protects the rule of law) and (b) conducted after a search warrant is issued, unless the need for a search is so pressing that it would be unrealistic to obtain a warrant. The search warrant can be issued only by an impartial party (someone capable of "acting judicially," though not necessarily a judge), and that party must be satisfied that there are probable grounds to believe that an offence has been committed and that the evidence is located in the specific place to be searched.

The search procedures utilized by the Restrictive Trade Practices Commission did not pass this test. First, the search warrant was not issued by an independent party. The members of the commission, who could issue search warrants, also had investigative powers. Therefore, they could not be considered impartial, since they had an interest in the investigation. Second, the *Combines Investigation Act* did not require the presentation of evidence showing probable cause in order to obtain the warrant; rather, the *Act* required only the possibility of finding evidence.

Dickson claimed that to accept such a low standard would be to "authorize fishing expeditions of considerable latitude." Third, the warrant did not specify a location but would allow all Southam offices in Canada to be searched. Dickson described such a warrant as "tantamount to a licence to roam at large on the premises of Southam Inc." — an unreasonable invasion of privacy.

One naturally wonders whether the Supreme Court's standard for protecting individual privacy might prevent public officials like those in the Combines Investigation Branch from effectively carrying out their duties. Peter Russell discovered that by the time of the Supreme Court decision in *Hunter* v. *Southam*, the Combines Investigation Branch had already modified its procedures for obtaining warrants to comply with the higher standards.[7] It appears that the lower standards were more convenient for the branch, but the new standards do not present any serious difficulties. The ability of the *Charter* to promote higher standards of procedural fairness in public administration is one of its positive effects.

Since the *Hunter* v. *Southam* decision, the Supreme Court has indicated some of the characteristics of what it will consider a reasonable invasion of privacy. In the *Hufsky* decision in 1988,[8] the court decided that a police officer's demand to see a person's driver's licence and insurance card during a spot check is not "an intrusion on a reasonable expectation of privacy . . . There is no such intrusion where a person is required to [comply] with some legal requirement that is a lawful condition of the exercise of a right or privilege."[9] The court has also held that "writs of assistance" (blanket search warrants sometimes issued to the police for as long as they hold office) are unconstitutional,[10] that taking a blood sample without legal authorization contravenes section 8[11] and that, at Canada's ports of entry, persons whom the authorities wish to strip search must be given the opportunity to contact counsel before the search can take place.[12]

FUNDAMENTAL JUSTICE AND THE REFUGEE-DETERMINATION PROCESS: THE *SINGH* DECISION (1985)

Canada's *Immigration Act* defines three kinds of immigrants who may apply to become permanent residents of Canada: people who qualify according to a points system that takes into account employability and likelihood of adapting successfully to Canadian life; people sponsored by relatives in Canada who are citizens or permanent residents; and people who are refugees according to the Geneva Convention, that is, those in need of protection because they have a well-founded fear of persecution in the country they are fleeing, owing to such factors as their beliefs or race.

Some refugees who wish to apply to Canada for protection do so at Canadian government offices abroad. Others come directly to Canada and make a refugee claim upon entry. According to the refugee-determination process in place up to the *Singh*[13] decision in 1985, those in the latter group were eventually examined under oath by an immigration officer, and the transcript of the examination was sent to the Refugee Status Advisory Committee. The committee would then advise the minister or his or her delegate whether the applicant met the convention's definition of a refugee, and the minister or delegate would make a final determination. If the decision was against the applicant, the applicant could appeal to the Immigration Appeal Board within fifteen days. The appeal board would review the applicant's transcript and evidence submitted by the minister, but the applicant was allowed neither to examine the minister's evidence nor to have an oral hearing.

The events leading to the *Singh* decision involved Satnam Singh and several other Sikhs from India who had fled their home country because, they claimed, of the persecution they had suffered at the hands of Indian government authorities. The Refugee Status Advisory Committee kept a list of refugee-producing countries, and India was apparently not on the list. The troubles between the Sikhs and the central government had only recently begun, and at the time it had not been established by Canadian immigration officials whether Indian government officials sometimes persecuted innocent Sikhs who were not participating in terrorist activities. (Later, the Refugee Status Advisory Committee recognized that there were some cases of unjustified persecution of Sikhs in India.) Thus, Singh's application for refugee status was rejected, his appeal was dismissed by the Immigration Appeal Board, and he was ordered to be deported to India. Singh then appealed to the courts for a declaration that the refugee claimant procedures violated section 7 of the *Charter*, which guarantees "everyone" the right to "life, liberty, and security of the person" unless "deprived thereof . . . in accordance with the principles of fundamental justice." It should be noted that section 7 refers to everyone, which means every human being, whether a citizen of Canada, a permanent resident, or a visitor (whether visiting legally or illegally).

When the case was first heard by the Supreme Court, some judges were disappointed that no arguments were presented about the possible relevance of section 2(e) of the *Canadian Bill of Rights*, which provides a right to a "fair hearing in accordance with the principles of fundamental justice for the determination of [a person's] rights and obligations." The court reserved its decision and requested written submissions from both sides about this section of the *Bill*. These submissions were considered before the court handed down its decision.

The panel assigned to the case consisted originally of seven judges, but Mr. Justice Julien Chouinard became ill and was unable to participate in the decision. Thus, the *Singh* decision is one of the few in which an even number of judges rendered a judgment. The six judges decided unanimously in favour of Singh. Three based their decision on the *Bill of Rights*, while the other three grounded their reasoning on the *Charter*.

THE *CHARTER* DECISION

Madame Justice Bertha Wilson wrote the decision based on the *Charter*, with Dickson and Lamer concurring. Wilson was faced with two major questions. First, was Singh deprived of the right to life, liberty, and security of the person? And if so, were the procedures followed in accordance with the principles of fundamental justice?

The phrase "life, liberty, and security of the person" can reasonably be interpreted in a number of different ways. For example, life, liberty, and security of the person could be considered as separate concepts, the deprivation of any of which could be enough to trigger a potential violation of section 7. On the other hand, the phrase could be considered as a single concept. Wilson left open the question of whether one or the other of these views should prevail, but she specified that even if the "single right" approach were eventually to be adopted, each of the three elements of the right would have to be defined by the court. Because the "security of the person" element was the one that most directly applied to Singh's situation, Wilson discussed possible meanings of the term.

A broad interpretation of security of the person might contain one of the rights included in the *Universal Declaration of Human Rights*: "a standard of living adequate for . . . health and well-being . . . including food, clothing, housing, and medical care and necessary social services, and the right to security in the event of . . . circumstances beyond [a person's] control." Wilson said that it was not necessary for the court to decide whether such a broad definition should be adopted, because "even if one adopts the narrow approach advocated by the counsel for the Minister, 'security of the person' must encompass freedom from the threat of physical punishment or suffering as well as freedom from such punishment itself." Thus, she concluded that the refugee-determination procedures infringe the right to security of the person if they permit the authorities to deport someone to a country where his or her life would be endangered.

In approaching the question of whether the procedures followed in the refugee-determination process were in accordance with the principles of fundamental justice, Wilson concluded that fundamental justice must at least include the factors that the Supreme Court had already determined were implied by the phrase "fundamental justice" in section 2(e) of the *Canadian Bill of Rights*.[14] For example, a "tribunal which adjudicates upon . . . rights must act fairly, in good faith, without bias and in a judicial temper, and must give to [litigants] the opportunity adequately to state [their] case." Wilson allowed that procedural fairness "may demand different things in different contexts," but she nevertheless was "of the view that where a serious issue of credibility is involved, fundamental justice requires that credibility be determined on the basis of an oral hearing." This is because without an oral hearing a refugee applicant would not have the opportunity of learning about the minister's evidence and therefore would not be able to respond thoroughly to the case against him or her. As a result, Wilson decided that the breach of security of the person (allowing deportation of a refugee applicant to a country where the applicant may be killed) was not in accord with the principles of fundamental justice.

Counsel for the government had "devoted relatively little time in the course of argument" to the question of whether a violation of section 7 could be upheld as a reasonable limit pursuant to section 1. In the absence of such evidence, Wilson determined that the violation of section 7 could not be justified under section 1.

THE *BILL OF RIGHTS* DECISION

Mr. Justice Beetz wrote the decision for the three judges who based their reasoning on the *Bill of Rights*; Estey and McIntyre concurred. Although Wilson, in her decision, agreed that the *Bill* "continues in full force and effect," those judges who based their decision on the *Bill* expressed no opinion about the applicability of the *Charter*. Thus, it is reasonable to conclude that the *Bill of Rights* was more central to the *Singh* decision than was the *Charter*. The *Singh* decision could therefore be considered as the first case since *Drybones*[15] in which the Supreme Court struck down a part of a statute based on the authority of the *Canadian Bill of Rights*. (In his decision, Beetz declared part of section 71[1] of the *Immigration Act* inoperative.)

This resurrection of the *Bill* is a puzzling phenomenon. According to the *Therens* decision, discussed later in this chapter, fear about abandoning legislative supremacy was the major reason why the court gave a narrow interpretation to the *Bill* prior to 1982. Perhaps the judges assumed the advent of the *Charter* in 1982 signalled a softening of the importance of legislative supremacy in Canada, and that they were now free to give effect to the *Bill*. Beetz even referred to the statutory bills of rights as "constitutional or quasi-constitutional documents." He interpreted the words "fundamental justice" in section 2(e) of the *Bill* similarly to Wilson's interpretation of the same phrase in section 7 of the *Charter*. But Beetz pointed out that section 2(e) of the *Bill* has a broader application than section 7 of the *Charter*. Section 2(e) of the *Bill* provides persons — human or corporate — with the right to fundamental justice in any case that affects their rights or obligations (which includes a wide range of situations). On the other hand, section 7 of the *Charter* provides only human persons with the right to fundamental justice, and then only if they are faced with the loss of their life, liberty, or security of the person.

THE IMPACT OF THE *SINGH* DECISION

The *Singh* decision sent shock waves through Canada's Department of Employment and Immigration. The department had been totally unprepared for the Supreme Court ruling that refugee claimants should receive oral hearings. For two years after the *Singh* decision, the department was unable to develop a new refugee-determination process that would incorporate the elements of fundamental justice specified by the Supreme Court. Instead, the old system continued but now granted oral hearings on appeal to refugee claimants whose applications were dismissed by the Refugee Status Advisory Committee. As a result, the backlog in the determination of refugee cases increased from one year to more than three. Some who appealed were bona fide refugees who would have been deported to their home country to face persecution or death had it not been for the *Singh* decision. Others, however, were not true refugees, but people who wanted to immigrate to Canada for economic or family reasons and were unable to meet the regular criteria for immigration or family sponsorship.

Some self-styled immigration consultants and a few unscrupulous lawyers began to advise their overseas clients that if they could not qualify to enter Canada under the immigration points system or the relative sponsorship program, they should come to Canada and claim refugee status even though they were not true refugees. The strategy was that because the refugee-determination process was so backlogged, by the time they had exhausted their final appeal, they would have demonstrated that they could live as good Canadian citizens and perhaps the government would allow them to stay for humanitarian reasons. The result of the government's failure to act quickly to resolve the backlog of refugee cases was that thousands of refugee claimants arrived in Canada from countries like Portugal, Turkey, and Brazil, which produce few, if any, refugees. Finally, in May 1987 the Mulroney government introduced its new refugee determination bill, Bill C-55. The legislation created the Convention Refugee Determination Division of the Immigration and Refugee Board, which was designed to provide refugee applicants with oral hearings.[16]

In addition, the strategy behind Bill C-55 was to force the processing of most refugee cases to Canadian government offices abroad so that the procedures would not be constrained by the *Charter*. The *Singh* case and the fallout from it illustrate how the *Charter* can have a positive influence on the protection of human rights in the courts, but at the same time give rise to the development of compensatory constraints by policy-makers in the executive branch. Rather than devising a system that would provide refugee claimants with procedural safeguards which the court said were guaranteed by the *Charter* and the *Bill of Rights*, the government decided to create a system that would make it difficult for refugee claimants to invoke Charter rights in the first place.

Clearly, Canada and the other liberal democracies will continue to be faced with the problem of balancing a fair refugee-determination system against the need to prevent abuse, and against the pressures of local prejudices and misinformation, for years to come. Judicial policy-making under the *Charter of Rights* and the *Bill of Rights* will continue to play an important part in shaping how Canadians respond to this issue.

THE RIGHT TO LIFE AND SECURITY VERSUS THE CRUISE MISSILE: THE *OPERATION DISMANTLE* CASE (1985)[17]

In 1983 a number of organizations that were opposed to the testing of the US cruise missile in Canada joined forces to mount a constitutional challenge to stop the tests. They referred to themselves as "Operation Dismantle." The organizations included some peace groups, labour unions, women's groups, church organizations, and medical doctors. The cruise missile is a small, low-flying, computer-guided weapon that can evade radar detection until eight minutes before it reaches its target.

The anti-cruise groups feared that once the cruise became operational, the danger of nuclear war would be greatly increased. This was because officials in the former Soviet Union would have only seconds to decide whether to launch a retaliatory attack after their radar screens had picked up what *might* be a US cruise missile attack. Moreover, because satellite detection of cruise missiles is impossible, agreements to limit nuclear weapons would become unlikely, thus leading to an escalation of nuclear weapons capabilities. Cruise tests were planned in northern Canada because the geography is similar to that in Russia. The anti-cruise groups reasoned that since the testing was an integral part of the development of the cruise, the testing contributed to the likelihood of a nuclear war. The increased risk of war deprived all Canadians of their security of the person, and a war itself would deprive many Canadians of their lives, contrary to the guarantees of life and security of the person in section 7 of the *Charter*.

When Operation Dismantle brought its case to the Federal Court of Appeal, lawyers for the government argued that the claim should not proceed to trial because there was no reasonable cause of action. The Federal Court upheld the government's position, and the anti-cruise groups appealed to the Supreme Court of Canada. Meanwhile, the cruise tests took place in March 1984. The Supreme Court released its decision in May 1985. The court unanimously upheld the decision of the Federal Court.

The court had three important questions to answer. First, are cabinet decisions subject to the *Charter*, even though no statutes are involved? Second, are issues like the government's defence policy "justiciable," that is, do they raise true legal questions? And third, if the first two questions are answered in the affirmative, should this particular case proceed to trial?

In Canada, federal and provincial cabinets derive their authority from two sources: legislation and the prerogative power. The prerogative power is inherited from pre-democratic English times when the monarch was the supreme power. Prerogative powers may be limited or abolished through legislation, but Parliament has not chosen to abolish the cabinet's prerogative powers over foreign affairs and national defence. Counsel for the government had argued that the *Charter* should not apply to these cabinet powers. However, the judges all agreed that the wording of section 32(1)(a) of the *Charter*, which declares that the *Charter* applies, among other things, to the government of Canada, is broad enough to include all cabinet decisions. In chapter 2 it is noted that because of the adversary system, government lawyers tend to argue for the narrowest possible interpretation of the *Charter*, even though the government that spearheaded the *Charter* boasted that it would protect the rights of Canadians in the broadest possible way. This particular issue is a good illustration of that tendency.

Government lawyers also claimed that matters such as defence policy are not justiciable because they are outside the legal jurisdiction of a court of law. The justiciability issue was suggested to them by a reading of US Supreme Court cases dealing with the US *Bill of Rights*, which have drawn a line between cases that raise legal issues and those that raise political issues. The former are justiciable, while the latter are not. The justiciability doctrine is based on the US theory of the separation of powers. One branch of government is not supposed to encroach on the duties of another branch. Legal issues belong to the judiciary, while political ones belong to the legislature or executive.

The Canadian Supreme Court decided that to apply the US justiciability test to Charter issues was inappropriate. Instead of asking whether a particular issue is legal or political, the Canadian court decided to ask whether a particular government action violated the *Charter*. Madame Justice Wilson described this approach as follows:

> The question before us is not whether the government's defence policy is sound but whether or not it violates the [anti-cruise groups'] rights under s.7 [I]f we are to look at the Constitution for the answer to the question whether it is appropriate for the courts to "second guess" the executive on matters of defence, we would conclude that it is not appropriate. However, if what we are being asked to do is to decide whether any particular act of the executive violated the rights of the citizens, then it is not only appropriate that we answer the question; it is our obligation under the Charter to do so.[18]

Thus, the Supreme Court of Canada has provided a wider scope for issues capable of being litigated under the *Charter* than the US Supreme Court has for issues that may be litigated under the American *Bill of Rights*.

The main decision, written by Chief Justice Dickson, concluded that there was no basis for Operation Dismantle's statement of claim because the arguments of the anti-cruise groups were mere speculation. There was no evidence that foreign powers would act in the way hypothesized by the groups. According to Dickson, it could just as easily be supposed that

> *lack of verification would have the effect of enhancing enforceability [rather] than of undermining it, since an inability on the part of nuclear powers to verify systems like the cruise could precipitate a system of enforcement based on cooperation rather than surveillance. In brief, it is simply not possible for a court, even with best available evidence, to do more than speculate upon the likelihood of the Federal Cabinet's decision to test the cruise missile resulting in an increased threat of nuclear war.*

Justice Wilson gave different reasons for agreeing that the anti-cruise groups did not have a case. She said that section 7 of the *Charter* protects individual rights. In order for a claim to go to trial under section 7, the claimants would have to argue that a cabinet decision threatened the lives, liberties, or personal security of specific individuals.

Did the anti-cruise groups actually expect to stop the testing of the cruise through Charter litigation, or did they use the case to generate publicity for their cause? It is likely that those in the coalition with some legal training saw the court challenge mainly as a publicity measure, while many of the rank-and-file members believed that they might actually win their case. There is a lesson here about how Canadians perceive civil liberties. Canadians unfamiliar with the intricacies of the legal system may tend to believe that whatever is morally right is probably also legally right when set against the *Charter*. Although some of those with legal training may also believe that the *Charter* enshrines moral values, others might be more apt to see the *Charter* as just another opportunity for winning cases regardless of moral right or for generating publicity regardless of legal foundation.

THE RIGHT TO COUNSEL AND THE THERENS DECISION, 1985[19]

The *Charter* not only protects the right to counsel as the *Canadian Bill of Rights* does, but it goes beyond the *Bill* to establish a right to be informed of the right to counsel. Exactly one week after the *Charter* came into effect in 1982, Paul Mathew Therens lost control of his motor vehicle and collided with a tree in Moose Jaw, Saskatchewan. The police, suspecting that Therens had been drinking, took him to the police station for a Breathalyzer test. Therens co-operated in taking the test. He was not informed of his right to counsel, and he did not request to contact a lawyer. The Breathalyzer test provided evidence for the Crown to charge Therens with driving while having a blood alcohol content in excess of eighty milligrams of alcohol in one hundred millilitres of blood.

The reason why Therens was not informed of his right to counsel was that this right takes effect, according to section 10(b) of the *Charter*, only "on arrest or detention." Therens was not arrested before the Breathalyzer test, and the police did not consider that he was being detained. This is because Therens could have refused to take the test. Had he done so, however, he would have been charged with refusing to take a Breathalyzer test, the penalty for which is the same as the penalty for driving with a blood alcohol content of over eighty. Nevertheless, the definition of detention formulated by the Canadian Supreme Court under the *Canadian Bill of Rights* did not include being requested to give a breath sample.[20] Thus, the police were acting on what they considered to be good legal authority by not informing Therens of a right to counsel at the stage of the Breathalyzer test.

At trial, Therens's lawyer claimed that to admit the evidence against Therens would constitute a violation of the *Charter*. Section 24(2) states that where "evidence was obtained in a manner that infringed or denied any rights or freedoms guaranteed by this *Charter*, the evidence shall be excluded if it is established that, having regard to all the circumstances, the admission of it in the proceedings would bring the administration of justice into disrepute." The trial judge agreed that the evidence should not be admitted and dismissed the charge against Therens for lack of evidence. The Crown lost its appeal in the Saskatchewan Court of Appeal in April 1983 and appealed to the Supreme Court. In May 1985 the Supreme Court handed down its decision.

The Supreme Court dealt with four key issues: the status of Bill of Rights precedents as applied to the *Charter*; the meaning of detention under the *Charter*; whether the failure to inform of and allow the right to counsel before the Breathalyzer test is a reasonable limit; and whether refusing to admit the evidence in this case would bring the administration of justice into disrepute.

THE STATUS OF CANADIAN BILL OF RIGHTS PRECEDENTS

The Crown argued that the framers of the *Charter* must have been aware of the meaning that the Supreme Court had given to detention under the *Bill of Rights* and that therefore it is that meaning which should apply to the *Charter*. Mr. Justice Le Dain, who wrote the decision for the majority about this issue, disagreed. He said that constitutional documents must necessarily use "general language which is capable of development and adaptation by the courts." He referred to the analysis of legal theorist Ronald Dworkin,[21] who claimed that constitutional language contains broad concepts that should not be reduced to narrow interpretations based on particular conceptions of the broader concept. Le Dain then explained that the Supreme Court had given a narrow interpretation to the *Bill* because of the desire to defer to the principle of legislative supremacy. Because the *Charter* represented a "new constitutional mandate for judicial review," the definitions established under the *Bill* should not be taken as reliable guides to the meaning of the *Charter*.

THE MEANING OF DETENTION

Having rejected the definition of detention developed under the *Bill*, the court needed to develop a new approach. The Crown claimed that a person was detained only when compelled to do something and that a person could not be compelled to take a breath test. Le Dain disagreed. Because the consequences for refusing to take a breath test are the same as for being convicted of drinking and driving, "it is not realistic to speak of a person who is liable to arrest and prosecution for refusal to [take a breath test] as being free to refuse to comply. Any criminal liability for failure to comply with a demand or direction of a police officer must be sufficient to make compliance involuntary."

Le Dain then supplied a broad definition of detention that includes what we could call psychological detention.

> *Most citizens are not aware of the precise legal limits of police*
> *authority. Rather than risk the application of physical force*
> *or prosecution for willful obstruction, the reasonable person is*
> *likely to err on the side of caution, assume lawful authority,*
> *and comply with the demand. The element of psychological*
> *compulsion, in the form of a reasonable perception of*
> *suspension of freedom of choice, is enough to make the*
> *restraint of liberty involuntary.*[22]

Because detention was defined to include Therens's situation, the court concluded that a breach of the *Charter* had occurred when Therens was given a breath test without first being told of his right to counsel.

REASONABLE LIMITS TO THE RIGHT TO COUNSEL

On this issue, Mr. Justice Le Dain examined the relevant Breathalyzer provisions of the *Criminal Code* and could find no express or implied limitation to the right to counsel. He noted that breath samples must be taken within two hours from the time that the offence was allegedly committed and that this time period does not "preclude any contact at all with counsel prior to the Breathalyzer test." Because there were no limits prescribed by law, section 1 arguments could not be entertained.

WHETHER TO ADMIT EVIDENCE THAT WOULD BRING THE ADMINISTRATION OF JUSTICE INTO DISREPUTE

The final question the court had to decide was whether this violation of a Charter right had brought "the administration of justice into disrepute," in order to exclude the evidence pursuant to section 24(2) of the *Charter*. The majority of the court concluded that the evidence should be excluded. According to Mr. Justice Estey:

> *Here the police authority has flagrantly violated a* Charter
> *right without any statutory authority for so doing. Such an*

> *overt violation as occurred here must, in my view, result in the rejection of the evidence thereby obtained. To do otherwise than reject this evidence on the facts and circumstances in this appeal would be to invite police officers to disregard the Charter rights of the citizen and to do so with an assurance of impunity.*

Mr. Justice Le Dain suggested an alternative approach. For this particular case, the evidence should be admitted, but in all future cases where a person being requested to take a Breathalyzer test was not told of his or her right to counsel, the evidence would be excluded. The majority rejected this approach, however, because it would not send a clear signal to the police that they must take the *Charter* seriously. Mr. Justice McIntyre took a polar opposite view. From his perspective, to *exclude* the evidence so that Therens would go free on a technicality "would itself go far to bring the administration of justice into disrepute."

The disagreement among the judges about what it means to bring the administration of justice into disrepute underlines one of the problems of legal interpretation that may always be contentious. In interpreting vague phrases that seem to imply a community standard, judges often try to apply what they consider to be the standard of the average reasonable person who is informed of the relevant circumstances surrounding the issue. Professor Dale Gibson of the University of Manitoba has suggested that litigants could conduct public opinion polls about whether excluding a particular piece of evidence would bring the administration of justice into disrepute. The majority on the court rejected this suggestion, both because it would increase the costs to litigants and because of the difficulty in explaining all the relevant circumstances to those being polled. In the absence of hard evidence, then, the standard of the average reasonable person becomes a subjective standard set by the judges themselves. Because judges are specialized professionals drawn from the upper echelons of society, it is unlikely that they will be able accurately to guess the views of average, reasonable people. A less subjective standard is obviously needed, but our legal imaginations have not yet been capable of finding one.

In view of the *Therens* decision, readers may wonder whether people who are asked to take a roadside Breathalyzer test have a right to retain counsel before taking it. (Roadside tests are used by police as an initial screening procedure; those who fail are asked to accompany a police officer to a police station, where Breathalyzer evidence is collected that may be used as evidence in court.) In a 1988 case,[23] the Supreme Court of Canada decided that the denial of the right to counsel before a roadside test is a reasonable limit under section 1. The court pointed out an important difference between the *Criminal Code* provision governing roadside breath tests (*Thomsen*) and police station Breathalyzer tests (*Therens*). The former Criminal Code provision states that a person shall provide a breath sample "forthwith" if requested to do so, whereas in the latter section, the breath test shall be provided "forthwith *or as soon as practicable*" (emphasis added). Thus, the roadside test does imply a limit prescribed by law to the right to counsel, since a breath sample could not be provided forthwith if counsel were contacted and consulted.

The court decided that the limit implied by the roadside testing procedure was reasonable under section 1. The objective of the roadside testing procedure — "not only to increase the detection of impaired driving, but to increase the perceived risk of its detection"[24] — is a pressing and substantial concern, and the means chosen to achieve the objective are proportional to it, particularly in view of the fact that the *Therens* decision guarantees that a person who fails the roadside test has a right to retain counsel before the police station test.

In another 1988 case, the Supreme Court decided that police spot checks on highways, while they do violate the *Charter*'s section 9 right not to be arbitrarily detained, constitute a reasonable limit.[25] This is because of the importance of detecting and reducing impaired driving.

Since *Therens*, the Supreme Court has developed a test for the exclusion of evidence that would bring the administration of justice into disrepute — section 24(2). In the *Collins* decision,[26] Mr. Justice Lamer, writing for the majority, declared that the admissibility of evidence obtained in violation of a Charter right depends on three factors. First, if the admission of such evidence would prejudice the fairness of a trial, it should be excluded. Second, the more serious the Charter violation, the more compelling the need for the judges to exclude the evidence. Third, the evidence should *not* be excluded if doing so would bring disrepute to the justice system. The court has tended to exclude evidence when, as in the *Therens* case, there was a violation of the right to counsel,[27] but has sometimes admitted evidence in such cases if the *Collins* test has been met.[28] On the other hand, the court has tended to admit evidence when there was an unreasonable search or seizure,[29] although such evidence may be excluded for compelling reasons.[30]

THE *BC MOTOR VEHICLE ACT* CASE AND FUNDAMENTAL JUSTICE (1985)[31]

Because a large number of serious motor vehicle accidents in Canada are alcohol related, provincial governments have legislated serious penalties for drinking and driving. The suspension of driving privileges is one such common penalty. In addition, to encourage safer driving overall, some provincial governments suspend drivers' licences for a specific period upon the accumulation of a certain number of demerit points. Unless the suspension of licences can be enforced, however, these sanctions do not serve as an effective deterrent.

In 1982 the British Columbia legislature amended its *Motor Vehicle Act* to create an "absolute liability" offence for driving without a valid driver's licence. A first conviction would result in a mandatory minimum fine of $300 and a mandatory minimum jail sentence of seven days. For subsequent convictions, the minimum jail sentence would be fourteen days.

Normally, judges assume that Parliament does not wish accused persons to be convicted unless they intentionally committed an illegal act or acted recklessly. This principle, known as *mens rea*, has been developed through the common law (see chapter 1). An absolute liability offence is one for which the accused person cannot claim as a defence that he or she was not aware of committing the prohibited act. The *BC Motor Vehicle Act* created an absolute liability offence because it declared that a person charged with driving without a valid licence could not claim as a defence that he or she was not aware the licence was suspended. Perhaps the government feared that if a finding of *mens rea* was required, some of those guilty of driving without a valid licence might escape conviction — for example, by ignoring registered mail notices informing them of their licence suspensions.

Before 1982, legislatures in Canada could create absolute liability offences simply by stipulating that *mens rea* was not an element of particular offences. After 1982, it was not clear whether the *Charter* prohibited legislatures from creating absolute liability offences. Section 7 of the *Charter* guarantees everyone the right to life, liberty, and security of the person unless deprived thereof pursuant to the principles of fundamental justice. It was possible that "fundamental justice" included *mens rea*. To settle this issue, the BC government sent a reference to the provincial Court of Appeal in 1982. The case was appealed to the Supreme Court, which rendered its decision in 1985.

The question of whether *mens rea* is included in section 7 of the *Charter* raises the question of whether section 7 is *substantive* or *procedural* in nature. A procedural interpretation would mean that a legislature could enact a law that would deprive people of their life, liberty, or security as long as the correct procedures of fundamental justice were followed — for example, a fair hearing before an independent and impartial judge, adequate notice of the hearing, the right to counsel, and so on. A substantive interpretation would mean that even if the correct procedures were followed, in certain instances a legislature could not deprive a person of his or her life, liberty, or security.

The substantive-versus-procedural issue is a product of the US Supreme Court's interpretation of the due process clause in the American *Bill of Rights*. The fifth and fourteenth amendments to the US *Constitution* protect life, liberty, and property unless persons are deprived of them through due process of law. Between 1905 and 1937 (a period known as the *Lochner* era, after a decision that set the tone for the period), the American Supreme Court interpreted "due process" in a substantive way to strike down social policy laws that restricted anti-union activity and provided for maximum hours of work, minimum wages, and maximum prices. The laws were considered by the judges to interfere with employers' liberty to contract with employees, and with property rights.

When President Franklin Delano Roosevelt's New Deal legislation was threatened by, among other things, this substantive interpretation of due process, Roosevelt considered expanding the court and packing it with judges who would interpret due process in a merely procedural way. The court-packing scheme was never carried out, because in 1937 the court changed its tactics. It overruled earlier decisions and abandoned the substantive interpretation of due process that had precluded some social welfare legislation. The US Supreme Court has continued to interpret due process in a substantive way with regard to other matters, however. For example, in 1965 the court struck down a law prohibiting the use of contraceptives, and in 1973 it struck down an anti-abortion law.[32]

The framers of the *Charter* hoped to foreclose any possibility that the Canadian courts might indulge in a Canadian version of the *Lochner* era and thereby limit the potential of Canadian social programs. For that reason, they carefully avoided any mention of due process in the *Charter*. Instead, they adopted the phrase "fundamental justice." This phrase is potentially synonymous with "due process." However, the Canadian Supreme Court had already defined fundamental justice in a purely procedural way in a case decided under the *Canadian Bill of Rights*.[33] In testimony before the Special Joint Committee on the Constitution in 1981, Jean Chrétien, minister of justice; B. L. Strayer, assistant deputy minister; and F. J. E. Jordan, senior counsel, said that the phrase "fundamental justice" had been carefully chosen for section 7 as a signal for the courts to interpret the section in a procedural rather than in a substantive way.

In spite of this background, in the *BC Motor Vehicle Act* decision the Supreme Court gave fundamental justice a substantive interpretation. Concerning the Bill of Rights precedent, Mr. Justice Lamer, who wrote the majority opinion, reminded his readers that in the *Therens* decision the court had declared that before 1982 concern about legislative supremacy had prevented the court from applying the *Bill* broadly. Therefore, Bill of Rights precedents could not be taken as reliable guides to Charter interpretation.

There were two issues related to the impact of the parliamentary testimony of Jean Chrétien and his officials. The first was whether evidence from parliamentary committee hearings should be entertained by judges. Traditionally, common-law courts did not consider such evidence when determining the intent of the legislature because such evidence was considered to be an unreliable guide to the thinking of members of Parliament (MPs) as a whole. The only reliable guide was considered to be the legislation itself. In 1976, however, the Supreme Court decided that a blanket exclusion of certain types of evidence is unwise; whether to admit evidence should be determined by its potential relevance.[34] Thus, the court decided that to accept evidence from a legislative committee would be in keeping with the new approach to admitting evidence.

The second issue was how much weight should be given to the evidence. The court assigned the evidence minimal weight for two reasons. First, there was no evidence that Jean Chrétien and his officials represented the views of most MPs and provincial legislators. Second, according to Justice Lamer:

> *Another danger with casting the interpretation of s.7 in terms of the comments made by those heard at the Joint Committee Proceedings is that, in so doing, the rights, freedoms, and values embodied in the* Charter *in effect become frozen in time to the moment of adoption with little or no possibility of growth, development, and adjustment to changing societal needs.*[35]

Having given minimal weight to Jean Chrétien's recommendation for interpreting section 7, Lamer had no difficulty in deciding that section 7 should be given more than a procedural interpretation. He described the procedural-versus-substantive issue as an American one, not relevant to the *Charter* because of its different wording. From the purposive perspective, Lamer claimed that section 7 was intended to protect "the basic tenets of our legal system,"[36] such as "the dignity and worth of the human person"[37] and "the Rule of Law."[38] He claimed that sections 8–14 of the *Charter* are specific examples of how fundamental justice is to be applied, and he noted that some of these provisions go beyond the provision of mere procedural safeguards.

Lamer concluded that a combination of a mandatory prison term (which deprives a person of liberty) and an absolute liability offence violates fundamental justice. He noted that such a violation of section 7 might be shown to be a reasonable limit under section 1 but that lawyers for the Crown had failed to produce any evidence as to why this violation of fundamental justice should be accepted as a reasonable limit. In the absence of such evidence, the court could only hold that the existence of a reasonable limit had certainly not been "demonstrably justified."[39]

Mr. Justice Lamer's opinion in this case seems to be full of paradoxes. He first claimed that the procedural-substantive debate is not relevant to section 7 of the *Charter* and then interpreted section 7 in a substantive way. He accepted uncontested evidence from a parliamentary committee hearing and then assigned it minimal weight and decided contrary to that evidence. He claimed that the courts do not make policies but merely apply the law, and then proceeded to make a very important policy decision: that fundamental justice includes, and extends beyond, the legal safeguards in sections 8–14. But these apparent paradoxes may oversimplify a complex issue. The interpretation of fundamental justice in the context of the *Charter* continues to be one of the court's most difficult policy-making tasks to date.

JUDICIAL INDEPENDENCE AND THE *VALENTE* CASE (1985)[40]

In 1981 Walter Valente was charged with dangerous driving after an accident in which three children were killed. Dangerous driving is a serious Criminal Code offence that can result in a jail sentence. The case came before an Ontario Provincial Court judge in December of 1982. In an effort to keep his client out of jail, Valente's lawyer argued that the trial violated Valente's right to an independent and impartial judge, which is guaranteed by section 11(d) of the *Charter*. The provincial court judge decided that the argument had enough merit for it to be heard by a judge of a higher court. The Ontario Court of Appeal heard the case involving judicial independence early in 1983. In the meantime, two other Ontario Provincial Court judges and a justice of the peace announced that they would decline jurisdiction whenever a lawyer questioned their independence. This series of events became known as the "judges' revolt."[41]

The Ontario Court of Appeal found that provincial court judges qualify as independent and impartial for the purposes of the *Charter*, and this decision was confirmed by the Supreme Court of Canada in December 1985. In order to understand the significance of the Supreme Court decision, some familiarity with the relevant background issues is necessary.

The provincial court[42] is the basic workhorse court in each province. Over 90 per cent of all cases generated in Canada are heard at this level. The bulk of the workload of these courts is composed of minor traffic and criminal cases, although provincial court judges can hear cases involving a number of serious offences, including several for which the maximum penalty is life imprisonment. Provincial court judges also hear family cases (such as custody disputes), young offenders cases, and small claims cases. Canadians who become involved with the justice system are much more likely to form their impressions of Canadian justice in the provincial court than in any other court.

In spite of the importance of the provincial court, the working conditions and salaries of provincial court judges are generally not as good as for judges of superior courts in the provinces. There are historical reasons for this discrepancy. Before the 1960s, provincial court judges were known as "magistrates" or "police magistrates," and until reforms in the 1960s and 1970s, many had no legal training. The "real" judges were considered to be those in the superior courts. Beginning in the late 1960s, however, all provincial governments raised the standards for appointments to their provincial courts; now all provincial court judges have legal training and have practised law for several years before becoming judges. Concurrently, the kinds of cases provincial court judges can hear have steadily increased in seriousness in terms of penal consequences in criminal cases or monetary ones in civil cases.

The fact that provincial court judges are sometimes paid significantly lower salaries and have fewer benefits than judges in the higher courts has led to resentment among some provincial court judges. Valente's lawyer, no doubt aware of this situation, built his argument on those aspects of the relatively poorer working conditions of provincial court judges that might impinge judicial independence.

In part, the independence of superior court judges is protected by sections 96 to 100 of the *Constitution Act, 1867*. For example, section 99 protects the security of tenure of superior court judges by stipulating that they shall hold office until retirement "during good behaviour," which means they cannot be removed for making decisions the government disapproves of. Moreover, they may only be removed with the approval of both the Senate and the House of Commons, a public process intended to protect judges from arbitrary firings. Section 100 states that the salaries of the superior and district court judges must be set by an act of Parliament rather than by cabinet order, and it implies that the salaries of judges may not be lowered except during a general economic crisis. Valente's position was that, in order to be independent, provincial court judges required the same constitutional guarantees of their independence. In addition, counsel for Valente argued that superior court judges have their own benefit plans — presumably to protect their independence — while provincial court judges are enrolled in ordinary public service benefit plans.

Mr. Justice Le Dain wrote the opinion of the unanimous Supreme Court panel. The decision is an important one for two reasons. First, Le Dain distinguished between judicial independence and judicial impartiality. Impartiality, he wrote, is a state of mind, while independence concerns the relations between judges and others — relations that should be regulated so as to promote impartiality. Second, Le Dain declared that there are three essential conditions for the existence of judicial independence: security of tenure, financial security, and institutional independence. All should be secured through reasonable measures such as legislation; however, Le Dain considered that constitutional guarantees, like sections 99 and 100 of the *Constitution Act, 1867* were useful but not absolutely necessary. The security of tenure of judges could be guaranteed by ordinary statutes as long as the statutes stipulated that judges held their appointments during good behaviour and as long as the removal process required an independent inquiry. The requirement of financial security could be met as long as a statute guaranteed judges a salary. And institutional independence could be achieved if judges could control those aspects of court administration directly related to decision-making.[43]

Valente lost his case, but what emerged from the Supreme Court's decision was a working definition of judicial independence for the purposes of section 11(d) of the *Charter*. The three essential conditions of judicial independence outlined in *Valente* remain the touchstone for the Supreme Court's analysis of judicial independence: security of tenure, financial security, and institutional independence. However, these terms are sufficiently vague as to have attracted additional litigation.

POST *VALENTE: PROVINCIAL COURT JUDGES REFERENCE* (1997)[44]

There have been a number of cases since *Valente* when the Supreme Court has responded to claims of violation of judicial independence.[45] The most significant is the *Provincial Court Judges Reference* decision.

As a response to the recession of the early 1990s, several provinces responded to the serious recession then underway by introducing salary cuts across the public sector, including salary cuts that impacted provincially-appointed judges. In Prince Edward Island, Alberta, and Manitoba, these cuts reduced the salaries of provincially-appointed judges by between 3.8 per cent and 7.5 per cent. This salary reduction met opposition either from provincial judges associations or from criminal accused persons, who initiated court actions in which they argued that the cuts violated the principle of financial security of judges, as set out in the *Valente* decision. This litigation reached the Supreme Court of Canada in 1996, and the court handed down its decision in 1997.

Lamer wrote the decision for six of the seven judges on the panel. He noted that the *Valente* decision addressed the independence of individual judges. But what was at issue in the *Provincial Court Judges Reference* was the collective independence of the judiciary and the institutional arrangements surrounding this collective independence. Lamer emphasized that in addition to the three essential conditions of judicial independence, there were two "dimensions" — individual and institutional, or collective.[46] In order to analyze the implications of collective independence, Lamer argued that the court must take into account the "unwritten norms" of the Canadian constitution because the bare-bones wording of section 11(d) of the *Charter*, and sections 96 to 100 of the *Constitution Act, 1867* do not cover all aspects of what we in Canada currently understand as judicial independence. As an aid to interpretation, Lamer turned to the preamble to the *Constitution Act, 1867*.

> *The preamble, by its reference to "a Constitution similar in Principle to that of the United Kingdom", points to the nature of the legal order that envelops and sustains Canadian society. That order, as this Court held in* Reference re Manitoba Language Rights, *[1985] 1 SCR 721, at p. 749, is "an actual order of positive laws," an idea that is embraced by the notion of the rule of law.*[47]

Lamer concluded that the essential condition of financial security had both an individual and collective dimension. The individual dimension was decided in *Valente*: judges must have salaries set by law in such a manner to prevent executive interference with judicial decision-making.[48] He went on to state that

> [g]*iven the importance of the institutional or collective*
> *dimension of judicial independence generally, what is the*
> *institutional or collective dimension of financial security? To*
> *my mind, financial security for the courts as an institution*
> *has three components, which all flow from the constitutional*
> *imperative that, to the extent possible, the relationship*
> *between the judiciary and the other branches of government be*
> <u>*depoliticized*</u>.[49]

After a very lengthy set of reasons, the chief justice eventually concluded that in order to depoliticize sufficiently the relationship between the judiciary and the government, Judicial Compensation Commissions are essential to protecting the institutional independence of the judiciary.[50] A Judicial Compensation Commission (JCC) is an independent body that makes recommendations regarding appropriate adjustments of judicial salaries at least every three years. Judicial Compensation Commissions had been established some years earlier by the federal government and by some provincial governments to help insulate executive decision-making from chief judges and justices in determining the appropriate level of judicial salaries. They are typically tribunals composed of a representative of the government, a representative of the relevant grouping of judges, and a third member selected by the other two. Lamer wrote that the recommendations of Judicial Compensation Commissions are not mandatory for governments to follow but must be given serious consideration.

This logic of this decision, perhaps the most far-reaching of the Supreme Court's decisions in its exercise of discretion, is hard to follow.

> *No matter how you read S. 11(d), however, it is hard to*
> *conclude that the plain wording of this section mandates*

*the existence of JCCs. As well, prior to this decision, no one
ever suggested that the convention of judicial independence
included JCCs. JCCs are an invention of the late 20th century,
not a time-honoured constitutional tradition. The creation of
these arms-length bodies as a buffer between governments and
judiciaries is, without a doubt, a good idea, and represents
another important Canadian contribution to the theory and
practice of judicial independence. But for the judiciary to state
that JCCs are required by the constitution not only underlines
the potential scope of judicial discretion, and also illustrates its
potential for abuse.*[51]

Following this decision, the Supreme Court has addressed issues of judicial compensation in several cases. To begin with, the court was strict in requiring governments to prove that they had given JCC recommendations serious consideration when rejecting some of their recommendations. However, more recently, the court has become more lenient, perhaps as a result of the perception of some that it took too much licence in the *Provincial Court Judges Reference.*[52]

THE *OAKES* CASE (1986)[53]

As noted in chapter 1, one of the presumptions developed through the common law to protect civil liberties is that an accused person should be presumed innocent until proven guilty. Like all common law, this presumption may be reversed in specific instances with appropriate legislation. Such reversals are known as "reverse onus clauses."

Up to 1986, the Canadian *Narcotic Control Act* contained a reverse onus clause. A person who was proven to be in possession of a narcotic was also presumed to be guilty of trafficking unless he or she could prove otherwise. Thus, the traditional presumption of innocence applied only to a person charged with possession of an illegal narcotic. However, once possession was proven, the onus was reversed and there was a presumption of guilt with regard to trafficking. The purpose of this reverse onus clause was, of course, to curtail the use of illegal drugs, which was and is a very serious social problem.

David Edwin Oakes was charged with trafficking in narcotics in Ontario in 1981. At his trial, it was proven that he had been in possession of eight one-gram vials of hashish oil. It was then up to Oakes to prove that he was not also guilty of trafficking. Oakes claimed that he had bought the hashish oil for his own use and claimed that the reverse onus clause in the *Narcotic Control Act* violated section 11(d) of the *Charter*. Section 11(d) states that any person charged with an offence has the right to be presumed innocent until proven guilty according to law in a fair and public hearing by an independent and impartial tribunal. Oakes won at trial, but the Crown appealed.

Oakes argued in the Ontario Court of Appeal in 1983 that the reverse onus clause violated section 11(d) of the *Charter*, and he won again. The Crown appealed to the Supreme Court of Canada. It was clear that the reverse onus clause in the *Narcotic Control Act* violated section 11(d), but the Crown claimed that this provision was a reasonable limit pursuant to section 1. This was because of the serious problem of drug trafficking in Canada and the need of law enforcement agencies to have effective means to suppress it.

As noted in chapter 2, the Supreme Court developed a two-part test for reasonable limits in its decision in this case. The first part of the test was that the government objective in violating a Charter right must be of sufficient importance. Chief Justice Dickson, writing for a unanimous seven-judge panel, declared that the government's objective — "curbing drug trafficking by facilitating the conviction of drug traffickers" — was of sufficient importance to pass part one of the test.[54]

The second part of the analysis, known as the proportionality test, has three prongs: (a) the rational-connection test, (b) the least-impairment test, and (c) the general-proportionality test (that is, the cure must not be worse than the disease). The chief justice failed the reverse onus clause on the first prong of part two of the test.

> In my view, [the reverse onus clause] does not survive the
> rational connection test. . . .[P]ossession of a small or
> negligible quantity of narcotics does not support the inference
> of trafficking. In other words, it would be irrational to infer

that a person had an intent to traffic on the basis of his or her
possession of a very small quantity of narcotics. . . .

In light of the seriousness of the offence in question,
which carries with it the possibility of imprisonment for
life, I am further convinced that the first component of the
proportionality test has not been satisfied by the Crown.
Having concluded that [the reverse onus clause] does not
satisfy this first component of proportionality, it is unnecessary
to consider the other two components.[55]

It should be noted that the issue Dickson was considering in the above passage was whether the reverse onus clause would result in irrational conclusions in *any* case, not just in this particular one. Obviously, Oakes had been in possession of more than a negligible quantity of hashish oil. According to the rule of law, laws must be applied equally to everyone. Therefore, if a law violates the Charter rights of some but not others, it cannot be declared inoperative for some but upheld for the others. Laws must be framed so as to be fair to all. Therefore, laws that violate the Charter rights of some, and cannot be saved under section 1, must be struck down.

The court has made other important decisions about section 11(d). In the *Vaillancourt* decision,[56] the court declared that the Criminal Code offence of culpable homicide, a type of murder, violates the presumption of innocence. (Persons are guilty of culpable homicide if they act recklessly in a manner that may cause death and a death results, even if unintended.) The court has also upheld the reverse onus clause in the *Criminal Code* that states a person proven to have occupied the driver's seat in a vehicle is presumed to have "care and control" of the vehicle unless he or she can prove otherwise.[57] As a result, persons who are intoxicated and found in a driver's seat can be convicted of impaired driving whether or not their vehicle was in motion.

THE *MORGENTALER* CASE (1988)[58]

In 1985 Dr. Henry Morgentaler and two other doctors were convicted of procuring abortions contrary to section 251 of the *Criminal Code*. They appealed to the Supreme Court of Canada on the grounds that section 251 violated the rights of pregnant women to liberty and security of the person contrary to the principles of fundamental justice in section 7 of the *Charter*. The Supreme Court rendered its decision in January 1988.

Section 251 prohibits abortions unless they are carried out by a qualified medical practitioner in an approved hospital, and unless such abortions have been sanctioned by a majority of the hospital's abortion committee on the grounds that the procedure is necessary to safeguard a woman's life or health. Approved hospitals are those which are designated by the provincial minister of health (who is under no obligation to approve any hospitals) and which provide specified services. There must be at least three doctors on the abortion committee, none of whom do abortions. Because of these restrictions, only about 40 per cent of Canadian hospitals are eligible to provide abortions. Moreover, only about half of the eligible hospitals have actually established abortion committees. The result is that at the time women could obtain abortions in about only 20 per cent of Canadian hospitals.

The seven-judge panel that heard the *Morgentaler* case was seriously divided. Five judges decided in favour of Morgentaler's appeal, but for three very different sets of reasons, as outlined below.

SECTION 251 VIOLATES THE PROCEDURAL RIGHTS OF WOMEN (DICKSON, LAMER CONCURRING)

Chief Justice Dickson began by pointing out that it would be necessary only to consider the procedural implications of fundamental justice in relation to section 251; a substantive review would not be necessary because the case could be decided on procedural grounds alone. (See the *BC Motor Vehicle Act* case, earlier in this chapter, regarding the procedural and substantive approaches.)

True to the purposive approach to Charter adjudication developed by the court, the chief justice reasoned that the purpose of the guarantee of security of the person was, at the very least, to prevent "state interference with bodily integrity and serious state-imposed psychological stress." He concluded that section 251 violates security of the person because

every pregnant woman is told by the section that she cannot

submit to a generally safe medical procedure that might
be of clear benefit to her unless she meets criteria entirely
unrelated to her own priorities and aspirations. Not only
does the removal of decision making power threaten women
in a physical sense; the indecision of knowing whether an
abortion will be granted inflicts emotional stress . . . Forcing
a woman, by threat of criminal sanction, to carry a foetus to
term unless she meets certain criteria unrelated to her own
priorities and aspirations, is a profound interference with a
woman's body and thus a violation of security of the person.[59]

In addition, Dickson noted that the delays caused by the elaborate decision-making procedure required to obtain abortions, and the psychological stress caused by the decision-making procedures, also contributed to the violation of security of the person. For all these reasons, section 251 was held to violate the right to security of the person. (He left unanswered the question of whether section 251 violated the right to liberty.) Section 7, however, stipulates that certain violations of life, liberty, and security of the person are acceptable: those that conform with fundamental justice. Dickson therefore proceeded to a consideration of whether the violation of security of the person in section 251 conformed with fundamental justice.

Dickson reasoned that section 251 failed to meet the procedural standards for fundamental justice for several reasons. First, the administrative system established by section 251 is so cumbersome that the great majority of hospitals in Canada do not provide abortions. In other words, section 251 prohibits some abortions but permits others under certain conditions. These conditions, however, are difficult to meet in most locations. Therefore, the legal protection that section 251 supposedly provides to women whose life or health would be endangered by continuing a pregnancy does not, in fact, exist in many parts of the country.

Another difficulty, according to Dickson, is that section 251 provides no definition of health. The evidence before the court was that

therapeutic abortion committees apply widely differing

> *definitions of health. For some committees, psychological*
> *health is a justification for therapeutic abortion; for others it*
> *is not. Some committees routinely refuse abortions to married*
> *women, while [others do not] . . . It is not typically possible*
> *for women to know in advance what standard of health will be*
> *applied by any given committee . . . It is no answer to say that*
> *"health" is a medical term and that doctors . . . must simply*
> *exercise their professional judgment . . . [T]he absence of any*
> *clear legal standard to be applied by the committee in reaching*
> *its decision is a serious procedural flaw.*[60]

In other words, if a woman must meet a certain standard in order to obtain an abortion, she must know what that standard is. And the same standard, under the rule of law, must be applied to everyone.

Having concluded that section 251 failed to provide fundamental justice, Dickson considered whether the provision could be saved under section 1. In defining Parliament's objective in enacting section 251, Dickson accepted the statement of purpose in the abortion law itself: to protect the life and health of pregnant women. He accepted this statement of purpose as being sufficiently important to pass the first part of the *Oakes* test. (Dickson noted that section 251 says nothing about protecting the fetus.) However, he concluded that section 251 failed all three prongs of the second part of the *Oakes* test. The complex administrative machinery was arbitrary and not rationally connected with the objective of the section. It infringed women's rights far more than necessary. And its negative effects were generally out of proportion to its benefits.

SECTION 251 VIOLATES THE PROCEDURAL RIGHTS OF WOMEN, BUT PARLIAMENT IS JUSTIFIED IN PROTECTING THE FETUS (BEETZ, ESTEY CONCURRING)

Mr. Justice Beetz agreed with Chief Justice Dickson that "if an effective and timely therapeutic abortion may only be obtained by committing a crime, then s. 251 violates the pregnant woman's right to security of the person." Therefore, section 251 would pass muster only if it met the requirements of fundamental justice, or failing that, if it were considered a reasonable limit under section 1.

Beetz also agreed that section 251 violated fundamental justice but for different reasons than those advanced by Dickson. Beetz noted that section 251 provided women with a limited right to therapeutic abortions, and in addition he claimed that the right to liberty in section 7 of the *Charter* entrenched some minimum right to an abortion. However, he concluded that the Crown had failed to demonstrate that it was necessary for all abortions to be performed in a hospital. As well, he could find no justification for the requirement that committees established to approve abortions must consist of medical doctors practising at the hospital where the abortion would be performed. Nevertheless, he did think that the requirement for a second opinion about the necessity for an abortion was a reasonable one, given the possible conflict between the state's interest in protecting the fetus and a woman's interest in her liberty, security, and health.

> *The risk resulting from the delay caused by [the in-hospital provision and the resident committee provision] is unnecessary. Consequently, the requirement violates the principles of fundamental justice . . . [These are] by no means a complete catalogue of all the current system's strengths and failings. It demonstrates, however, that the administrative structure put in place by Parliament has enough shortcomings so that [the abortion law] violates the principles of fundamental justice.*[61]

Beetz disagreed with Dickson, however, about whether the abortion law required a clearer definition of health. He felt that a certain amount of flexibility was required in framing such a law and that medical doctors were entitled to exercise medical judgment. He regarded as having exceeded their authority those committees that routinely refused abortions unless approved by the woman's spouse, refused abortion requests from married women, or refused to consider second abortions. Such decisions could therefore be reviewed by a court as exceeding the legal jurisdiction of the committees.

The most important aspect of the disagreement between the reasons of Beetz and Dickson, however, concerns the section 1 analysis. Whereas Dickson had taken the wording of the abortion law at face value and had considered its objective as protecting the life and health of women, Beetz concluded that this was only a secondary purpose. The primary purpose, he claimed, was to protect the fetus. From this perspective, Beetz found that the objective of section 251 was of sufficient importance to pass the first part of the *Oakes* test. However, he failed section 251 on the first prong of the second part of the *Oakes* test. Because section 251 contained unnecessary restrictions (like the in-hospital and resident committee provisions), the limit to a woman's section 7 rights was *not* rationally connected either with the primary objective of protecting the fetus or the secondary objective of protecting a woman's life or health.

Although Beetz and Dickson reached the same conclusion about the fate of section 251, their emphasis is quite different. Both condemned section 251 for its procedural shortcomings, but Dickson's criticisms were harsher. Beetz stressed the legitimacy of Parliament's desire to protect the fetus, while Dickson emphasized the rights of women. Moreover, Beetz hinted that if Parliament corrected the procedural deficiencies that he had pointed out, the abortion law might be found constitutional: "It is possible that a future enactment by Parliament along the lines of the laws adopted in [other] jurisdictions could achieve a proportionality which is acceptable under s.1."

SECTION 251 IS A FLAGRANT VIOLATION OF WOMEN'S RIGHTS (WILSON)

Madame Justice Wilson was far more critical of the civil liberties abuses contained in section 251 of the *Criminal Code* than any of the other judges on the panel, although even she concluded that the state had the constitutional authority to regulate abortions some time in the second trimester.

Wilson agreed with Dickson and Beetz that section 251 violated a woman's right to security of the person, but for her the deficiencies of section 251 were more than procedural.

> [T]he flaw in the present legislative scheme goes much deeper
> than that. In essence, what [section 251] does is assert that
> the woman's capacity to reproduce is not to be subject to her

own control . . . She is truly being treated as a means — a
means to an end which she does not desire but over which she
has no control. She is the passive recipient of a decision made
by others as to whether her body is to be used to nurture a new
life. Can there be anything that comports less with human
dignity and self-respect?[62]

Wilson considered that section 251, in addition to violating security of the person, infringed the right to liberty in section 7. In coming to this conclusion, she analyzed the right to liberty from a purposive perspective and looked to the political theory of liberalism for support. She referred to John Stuart Mill and the jurisprudence of the US Supreme Court concerning abortion[63] and wrote that the guarantee of liberty is

tied to the concept of human dignity . . . [which] finds
expression in almost every right and freedom guaranteed in
the Charter. *Individuals are afforded the right to choose*
their own religion and their own philosophy of life, the
right to choose with whom they will associate and how they
will express themselves, the right to choose where they will
live and what occupation they will pursue. These are all
examples of the basic theory underlying the Charter, *namely*
that the state will respect choices made by individuals and,
to the greatest extent possible, will avoid subordinating
these choices to any one conception of the good life . . . The
fact that the decision whether a woman will be allowed to
terminate her pregnancy is in the hands of a committee is
just as great a violation of the woman's right to personal
autonomy in decisions of an intimate and private nature
as it would be if a committee were established to decide
whether a woman should be allowed to continue her
pregnancy. Both these arrangements violate the woman's
right to liberty.[64]

Having decided that section 251 breached both liberty and security of the person, Wilson considered whether it did so in conformity with fundamental justice. She proposed that an infringement of a section 7 right that also infringed another Charter right could not possibly be considered to be in accord with fundamental justice. From her perspective, section 251 violated the guarantee of freedom of conscience contained in section 2(a) of the *Charter*. The decision about whether to have an abortion is a matter of conscience for the mother, and therefore no set of procedures will justify its abrogation. From Wilson's perspective, the right of women to decide about the continuance of a pregnancy is a substantive right that could only be limited if the state could make a case under section 1.

Wilson agreed with Beetz that the primary government objective in section 251 was to protect the fetus. She considered this objective to be of sufficient importance to pass the first part of the Oakes test. But to meet the requirements of proportionality, the second part of the Oakes test, valid abortion legislation could not interfere with a woman's conscience during the first trimester of pregnancy. The appropriate point at which the state could begin to regulate or prohibit abortions would most probably occur some time during the second trimester: "The precise point in the development of the foetus at which the state's interest in its protection becomes 'compelling' I leave to the informed judgment of the legislature which is in a position to receive guidance on the subject from all the relevant disciplines."

Wilson did not deny "that the foetus is potential life from the moment of conception." However, she noted that "[i]t is a fact of human experience that a miscarriage or spontaneous abortion of the foetus at six months is attended by far greater sorrow and sense of loss than a miscarriage or spontaneous abortion at six days or even six weeks."[65]

Canadian women have widely divergent views about the issue of abortion. It is not surprising that Wilson's opinion had a far more passionate tone than the other decisions and that it outlined in more detail the ways in which section 251 affected the liberty, dignity, and security of women. Her emphasis on the primacy of a woman's conscience during the first trimester should not be taken as an endorsement of the pro-choice movement but rather as an acknowledgment that in matters of conscience no point of view can be proven correct. Therefore, when courts are called upon to give meaning to the vague and general phrases of the *Charter* — which, after all, is an entrenchment of liberal-democratic values — those values must guide the courts' deliberations.

LET PARLIAMENT DECIDE THE DIFFICULT ISSUE OF ABORTION (MCINTYRE, LA FOREST CONCURRING)

Mr. Justice McIntyre, supported by Mr. Justice La Forest, would have upheld section 251. McIntyre based his reasoning on a narrow interpretation of the rights to liberty and security of the person in section 7 of the *Charter* and on a procedural interpretation of fundamental justice.

McIntyre was distressed at the possibility that the court might give the *Charter* meanings its framers never intended it to have.

> *[T]he courts must confine themselves to such democratic values as are clearly found and expressed in the* Charter *and refrain from imposing or creating other values not so based . . . The Court must not resolve an issue such as that of abortion on the basis of how many judges may favour "pro-choice" or "pro-life." But there is a problem, for the Court must clothe the general expression of rights and freedoms contained in the* Charter *with real substance and vitality. How can the courts go about this task without imposing at least some of their views and predilections upon the law? . . . [According to Mr. Justice Harlan of the US Supreme Court, it is a]* "mistaken view of the Constitution . . . that every major social ill in this country can find its cure in some constitutional 'principle,' and that this Court should 'take the lead' in promoting reform when other branches of government fail to act."[66]

McIntyre suggested that the Canadian Supreme Court had found a way to minimize writing the judges' own views into the constitution, and that was to pay strict attention to the "purposive approach" to Charter interpretation. The purpose of section 7, he claimed, was to protect specific rights clearly included in the concepts of life, liberty, and security of the person.

He could find no right to abortion specifically included in these concepts. Moreover, he reviewed the history of abortion legislation in the United Kingdom and Canada to show that there never had been a right to abortion recognized in our political tradition.

As further evidence that Canadian legislatures had not intended there to be a right to abortion included in section 7, McIntyre quoted the testimony of Jean Chrétien, then minister of justice, when he appeared before the Special Joint Committee on the Constitution in 1981:

> *Parliament has decided a certain law on abortion and a*
> *certain law on capital punishment, and it should prevail*
> *and we do not want the courts to say that the judgment of*
> *Parliament was wrong . . . [W]e do not want the words "due*
> *process of law." [This is because] it is a danger, according to*
> *legal advice I am receiving that [the phrase "due process"]*
> *will very much limit the scope of the power of legislation by*
> *Parliament and we do not want that.*

Clearly, it was the former justice minister's hope that the insertion of "fundamental justice" into section 7 instead of "due process" would signal the courts to give section 7 a merely procedural interpretation, thus leaving Parliament's abortion law intact.

Because McIntyre found that section 251 did not infringe either the right to liberty or security of the person, it was unnecessary for him to consider whether section 251 abridged fundamental justice. Nevertheless, he considered this issue in *obiter* to refute some of the conclusions of the majority. He agreed with Beetz that the word "health" was not too vague a standard to meet the requirements of fundamental justice. However, he disagreed with Beetz and Dickson that the administrative procedures established by section 251 unnecessarily restricted access to abortions. This is because he gave little weight to the evidence contained in the research studies cited by Dickson and Beetz; rather, he felt that the court should "place principal reliance upon the evidence given under oath in court." None of the testimonies of medical doctors who had performed abortions produced examples of abortion applications ultimately refused, and no woman testified that her application for an abortion had been refused. Therefore, to McIntyre it was not clear that section 251 unnecessarily restricted access to abortions, and "the court's role is not to second-guess Parliament's policy choice as to how broad or how narrow" the access to abortions should be.[67]

Clearly, McIntyre's position was that unless the *Charter* is *very* clear, the court should defer to the judgment of Parliament concerning policy issues such as access to abortion, as in this case, or concerning the right to strike. The three majority opinions, however, presented strong reasons for finding an infringement of security of the person in Parliament's abortion law. In the end, none of these approaches can be classified as the *right* one; the *best* one is probably the one that Canadians, over time, find the most convincing.

Each of the four opinions in the *Morgentaler* case raises cogent points. The decision of the court should not be regarded as settling the issue, but rather as contributing toward a solution that is appropriate to our times. The judges' opinions are worthy of careful reflection by citizens and government policy-makers as a stimulus to further consideration of the issue.

LEGAL RIGHTS AND RESTRICTIONS ON EVIDENCE
SEXUAL ASSAULT EVIDENCE: *SEABOYER* (1991), AND *MILLS* (1999)

Canadian courts have had and will continue to have to navigate the stormy waters between admitting evidence in sexual assault cases in order to ensure a fair trial and preserving the privacy of sexual assault victims. Victims of sexual assault are unlikely to support charges against those who have offended them unless the privacy of their sexual history, as contained in confidential interviews with their therapists and social workers, is protected. On the other hand, such evidence may help to exonerate an innocent individual who is unfairly accused by someone intent on victimizing an alleged perpetrator.

Seaboyer[68]

In the early 1980s, pressure was building on the Canadian government to reform the *Criminal Code* to allow the more successful prosecution of perpetrators of rape and, at the same time, to encourage rape victims (overwhelmingly women) to register complaints with police.[69] Similar reforms were occurring around this time in a number of US states, the United Kingdom, and Australia. Prior to the Canadian reforms in 1983, the common law — dating from before the recognition of women's equality — permitted the accused's lawyer in sexual assault cases to question the complainant about her previous sexual activity in order to convince a jury that she had consented to the sexual activity in question. Under such circumstances, it was understandable that many victims of sexual assault would be unwilling to notify police and request that charges be laid.

The 1983 amendments to the *Criminal Code* added what became known as the "rape shield" provisions.[70] The new section 276 of the *Criminal Code* prohibited any attempts to produce evidence about the sexual history of sexual assault victims other than with the person accused of the assault, except under very restrictive circumstances, and only after a judge approved the admission of the evidence in a hearing closed to the jury and members of the public.

After these new provisions came into effect, Steven Seaboyer was charged with the sexual assault of a woman he had met at a bar. He wanted to cross-examine the complainant about her prior sexual activity in order to try to prove that her bruises may have been caused by a previous sexual encounter, but during the preliminary hearing was not permitted to do so. Seaboyer appealed, claiming that the rape shield sections of the *Criminal Code* violated sections 7 and 11(d) of the *Charter*. When the case reached the Supreme Court in 1991, the court dealt with another relatively similar case, that of Nigel Gayme, in which the accused was challenging the constitutionality of the rape shield legislation. Nigel Gayme, eighteen at the time of the alleged sexual assault, contended that the fifteen-year-old complainant was actually the one who initiated the sexual activity at their school. In order to pursue this argument, Gayme wanted to cross-examine the complainant about her prior sexual activity, but at the preliminary hearing was not permitted to do so. Gayme also appealed, claiming that the rape shield provisions are unconstitutional. Neither the trial judge in Seaboyer's case nor the trial judge in Gayme's case held a closed hearing to determine whether there should be an exception to the rape shield rule; both considered that the blanket exclusion of evidence relating to sexual activity other than with the accused would not permit them to allow an exception.

The Supreme Court had the difficult task of balancing the right to a fair trial of accused persons with the right of sexual assault victims to their privacy. The decision of the majority of seven was written by Madame Justice McLachlin. She began by summarizing her conclusion.

> *My conclusion is that one of the sections in issue, s. 276,*
> *offends the* Charter. *While its purpose — the abolition of*
> *outmoded, sexist-based use of sexual conduct evidence — is*
> *laudable, its effect goes beyond what is required or justified by*
> *that purpose. At the same time, striking down s. 276 does not*
> *imply reversion to the old common law rules, which permitted*
> *evidence of the complainant's sexual conduct even though it*
> *might have no probative value to the issues on the case and,*
> *on the contrary, might mislead the jury. Instead, relying on*
> *the basic principles that actuate our law of evidence, the courts*
> *must seek a middle way that offers the maximum protection*
> *to the complainant compatible with the maintenance of the*
> *accused's fundamental right to a fair trial.*[71]

There are two essential thrusts to McLachlin's reasoning. The first is the importance of ensuring that the accused have the ability to make a "full answer and defence."

> *The right of the innocent not to be convicted is dependent*
> *on the right to present full answer and defence. This, in*
> *turn, depends on being able to call the evidence necessary to*
> *establish a defence and to challenge the evidence called by the*
> *prosecution.*[72]

McLachlin compared the new rape shield provisions in the *Criminal Code* with similar provisions that had been enacted in several US states, the United Kingdom, and Australia, and concluded that the Canadian approach was amongst the most restrictive in terms of allowing judges discretion to admit relevant evidence.

> *[Section] 276 is among the most draconian approaches to*
> *the problem of eradicating improper inferences as to consent*
> *and credibility from the evidence of the sexual activities of the*
> *complainant. Section 276 follows the so-called "Michigan"*
> *model, which consists in a general prohibition followed*
> *by a series of exceptions. The Michigan model is generally*
> *regarded as the most invasive of the rape-shield laws in so*
> *far as it admits of no judicial discretion to receive relevant*
> *evidence which may not fall into the enumerated exceptions.*
> *Provisions in England, Australia, and many of the United*
> *States generally allow for some measure of judicial discretion*
> *to deal with the impossibility of foreseeing all eventualities and*
> *avoiding the unfairness of excluding evidence which may be*
> *highly relevant to the defence.*[73]

Having concluded that s. 276 "overshoots the mark,"[74] McLachlin turned
to whether it could be saved by s. 1. Having already stated that the objectives of the legislation are laudable, she had no difficulty in deciding that the
objectives of the legislation were pressing and substantial. As for the three-
pronged proportionality test, however, she concluded that the s. 276 does
not minimally impair the rights of accused persons to a fair trial.

She then considered the impact of striking down s. 276. She noted that
common-law principles must conform to the *Charter*, and so Canadian
judges must now modify the sexist way in which the common law had been
applied prior to the *Charter*.

> *The rules in question are common law rules. Like other*
> *common law rules of evidence, they must be adapted to*
> *conform to current reality. As all counsel on these appeals*
> *accepted, the reality in 1991 is that evidence of sexual*
> *conduct and reputation in itself cannot be regarded as logically*
> *probative of either the complainant's credibility or consent.*
> *Although they still may inform the thinking of many, the twin*

myths which s. 276 sought to eradicate are just that — myths
— and have no place in a rational and just system of law. It
follows that the old rules which permitted evidence of sexual
conduct and condoned invalid inferences from it solely for
these purposes have no place in our law.[75]

To assist judges in modernizing their application of the common law to evidence in sexual assault cases, McLachlin suggested some guidelines.

1. On a trial for a sexual offence, evidence that the
complainant has engaged in consensual sexual conduct on
other occasions (including past sexual conduct with the
accused) is not admissible solely to support the inference that
the complainant is by reason of such conduct:

(a) more likely to have consented to the sexual conduct at
issue in the trial;

(b) less worthy of belief as a witness.

2. Evidence of consensual sexual conduct on the part of
the complainant may be admissible for purposes other than
an inference relating to the consent or credibility of the
complainant where it possesses probative value on an issue in
the trial and where that probative value is not substantially
outweighed by the danger of unfair prejudice flowing from the
evidence.

3. Before evidence of consensual sexual conduct on the part
of a victim is received, it must be established on a voir dire
(which may be held in camera) by affidavit or the testimony
of the accused or third parties, that the proposed use of the
evidence of other sexual conduct is legitimate.

4. Where evidence that the complainant has engaged in sexual

> *conduct on other occasions is admitted on a jury trial, the*
> *judge should warn the jury against inferring from the evidence*
> *of the conduct itself, either that the complainant might have*
> *consented to the act alleged, or that the complainant is less*
> *worthy of credit.*[76]

McLachlin upheld the decisions of the judges at the preliminary enquiries of Seaboyer and Gayme to commit them to trial, and so it would be expected that the trial judges in their cases would take into account these principles in deciding whether to allow the cross-examinations that they had requested.[77]

The court's majority decision was subjected to harsh criticism from women's groups that did not trust judges to implement McLachlin's suggested principles for reinterpreting the common law in a way that would encourage sexual assault victims to report violations to the police. Justice Minister Kim Campbell decided on a new approach — to clarify in legislation the meaning of "consent" in sexual encounters and to ensure that the decision about whether consent had been granted could not be based on a woman's prior sexual activity or conduct. Someone making sexual advances would now be required to take reasonable measures to ensure that consent was given, and "intoxication, recklessness, or willful blindness" could not be used as excuses.[78] This new legislation, which in some ways restricted evidence in sexual assault cases more than the Supreme Court stated was permissible in *Seaboyer*, underwent extensive parliamentary review, and received all-party approval in 1992. The legislation was upheld by the Supreme Court in 2000,[79] and is sometimes pointed to as an example of a dialogue between courts and legislatures.

After the 1992 legislation came into effect, some defence lawyers began to use a new technique to defend their clients and to dissuade sexual assault complainants from agreeing to pursue charges: attempting to obtain the confidential records of complainants that might embarrass them in court. Up to this time, the Supreme Court had been relatively lenient regarding requests to obtain the confidential records of sexual assault victims, and in 1995 ruled in a five to four decision in *O'Connor* that the records of a complainant's therapeutic records should not be difficult for the defence to obtain.[80] There was a generally negative public response to the *O'Connor* decision, leading to intensive study of the issue in Parliament. The consensus in Parliament was that the minority decision in *O'Connor*, which argued for a higher threshold for obtaining the therapeutic records of complainants, was preferable, and legislation was enacted to that effect. This legislation was challenged in 1999 in the *Mills*[81] case, and Parliament's tougher rules for the admissibility of therapeutic records as evidence was upheld by the Supreme Court in an eight to one decision. Essentially, the Supreme Court in *Mills* supported its minority decision four years earlier in *O'Connor*. Bateman et al. identify two reasons for this surprising result.[82] First, in *O'Connor* the court was adjudicating a common-law issue rather than parliamentary legislation, and so it was deciding in a "legislative vacuum." Second, the court acknowledged the impact of "constitutional dialogue," and emphasized that legislatures, in addition to courts, have an important role in interpreting the constitution. As the Court's majority in *Mills* noted:

> *This Court has also discussed the relationship between the courts and the legislature in terms of a dialogue, and emphasized its importance to the democratic process . . . [See also P. W. Hogg and A. A. Bushell, "The Charter Dialogue Between Courts and Legislatures," (1997): 35 Osgoode Hall L.J. 75.] If the common law were to be taken as establishing the only possible constitutional regime, then we could not speak of a dialogue with the legislature. Such a situation could only undermine rather than enhance democracy. Legislative change and the development of the common law are different. As this Court [has] noted . . . the common law changes incrementally, "while complex changes to the law with uncertain ramifications should be left to the legislature." While this dialogue obviously is of a somewhat different nature when the common law rule involves interpretation of the* Charter, *as in* O'Connor, *it remains a dialogue nonetheless.*[83]

CAPITAL PUNISHMENT AND THE *BURNS*

CASE (2001)[84]

Capital punishment for murder and other serious offences had been a feature of the Canadian *Criminal Code* from the earliest times until the mid-twentieth century, when a number of legal reformers, including Progressive Conservative prime minister John Diefenbaker, led a campaign against the practice. Diefenbaker, a former defence lawyer in Saskatchewan, was disgusted by the executions of people whom he considered innocent.

The last executions in Canada occurred in 1962. From then until 1976, Prime Ministers Diefenbaker, Pearson, and Trudeau commuted all death penalties to life imprisonment, and in 1976 Parliament abolished the death penalty for nearly all offences after a free vote in the House of Commons.[85] In 1987, a motion to reinstate the death penalty at the pre-1976 state was defeated in a free vote in the House, and in 1998 the last remnant of the death penalty — which had been retained for some military offences — was abolished.[86]

After the *Charter of Rights and Freedoms* came into effect, there was a question of whether Canada should not extradite accused persons to countries applying the death penalty to offences for which it had been abolished in Canada, unless assurances were provided by the foreign country that the death penalty would not be applied.

Joseph Kindler had been convicted of murder in the United States and sentenced to death, but escaped from death row to Canada. Once captured and secured in Canada,[87] he fought extradition back to the US on the grounds that this would violate s. 7 of the *Charter*. The Supreme Court ruled in 1991, in a four to three decision, that such an extradition would not violate s. 7 unless it "shocked the conscience" of Canadians, and in this case the court decided that because the US had a legal system similar to Canada's, the conscience of Canadians would not be shocked.[88] Shortly after the Supreme Court ruling, Kindler was extradited back to Pennsylvania, where he had been convicted of murder and sentenced to death in 1983. Kindler then began a serious of court actions appealing the death penalty that reached the US Supreme Court in 2009, and his death sentence was set aside in 2011.[89] Part of Kindler's argument in the US was that in the *Burns* case of 2001, the Supreme Court ruled that prior to extraditing someone to a jurisdiction that retained the death penalty, in all but the most exceptional cases the Canadian government must receive assurances that the death penalty will not be applied.

The *Burns* case arose from the following situation. In 1994, Canadians Glen Burns and Atif Rafay, both eighteen, travelled to Rafay's parents' home in Bellevue, Washington, and murdered Rafay's parents and sister so that Rafay would inherit their property. They then returned to Vancouver and eventually confessed to the murders to an undercover police officer. The state of Washington applied to have them extradited to the US for trial, and after a hearing by an extradition judge, the minister of justice ordered them extradited. Burns and Rafay made a submission to the minister that extradition without an assurance from Washington State that the death penalty would not be imposed was a violation of sections 6, 7, and 12 of the *Charter of Rights*. The minister nevertheless ordered the extradition without the assurance, and Burns and Rafay then applied for a court order that the minister's action violated the *Charter*. The case eventually reached the Supreme Court of Canada.

The Supreme Court ruled in a unanimous decision that the *Charter* requires the minister to seek and obtain an assurance that the death penalty will not be applied prior to extradition when extradition is to a jurisdiction that has retained the death penalty, in all but exceptional cases.[90] The court gave a number of reasons for its change of heart after the *Kindler* case. Amongst these reasons were that in the intervening ten years, there had been several well-publicized cases of wrongful convictions in murder cases.[91] Applying the death penalty is final; there is no chance to correct an error in conviction. "[W]here capital punishment is sought, the state's execution of even one innocent person is one too many."[92] Second, since 1991 a number of countries had renounced the death penalty, and from an international perspective, the death penalty was increasing being recognized as cruel and unusual punishment.[93] Canada had been at the forefront of encouraging the international community to abolish the death penalty. Third, part of the cruelty of the death penalty was "death row syndrome" — the psychological stress on the prisoner resulting from waiting for the death penalty to be imposed.[94] "[I]t is difficult to avoid the conclusion that in the Canadian view of fundamental justice, capital punishment is unjust and it should be stopped."[95]

Like Diefenbaker, during the ten years since *Kindler* the Supreme Court had become convinced that capital punishment not only risked sending innocent people to their deaths, but was abhorrent in nearly all cases. The court left open the possibility of deportation without assurance that the death penalty would not be imposed in exceptional cases, but in good judicial tradition, declined to define such cases — thus avoiding theoretical discussion in the absence of facts and allowing future courts, with a more solid factual basis, to decide. It is ironic that the Supreme Court's change of heart was introduced in evidence in Kindler's many appeals in the US, and the end result was that Kindler was saved from execution in a country that is currently going through the same excruciating debate about abolition of the death penalty that Canada went through earlier.

OBTAINING HEALTH CARE WITHIN A REASONABLE TIME: *CHAOULLI* (2005)[96]

Does the right to security of the person in section 7 imply that Canadians have a right to receive important and especially life-saving medical services in a timely manner, and that governments must by law prevent unreasonable delays? This question was addressed by the Supreme Court in 2005 in its decision in the Chaoulli case.

Jacques Chaoulli was a Montreal doctor who wanted to operate his own private hospital to perform some operations sooner than they could be performed in the public health system under the *Canada Health Act*. It was difficult for him to do so because Quebec's health legislation prohibited Quebeckers from obtaining private medical insurance, meaning that only the very wealthy would be able to afford the services of a private hospital. Dr. Chaoulli was joined in the litigation by George Zeliotis, who was frustrated by having to contend with a long waiting list for a hip operation and also a heart operation.[97] They sought a declaration that the prohibition of private medical insurance in Quebec's *Hospital Insurance Act* and *Health Act* violated both the Canadian and Quebec Charters of Rights.

The reason for the prohibition, according to the submissions of the Quebec government, was that Quebec's legislation had to comply with the *Canada Health Act* in order for Quebec to claim part of the cost of administering its health services from the federal government. The *Canada Health Act* requires provincial health plans "to be administered publicly, . . . be comprehensive and universal, . . . provide for portability from one province to another . . . be accessible to everyone."[98] This approach implies equality of the provision of services: those with higher incomes should not be able to use their income to "jump the queue" to obtain services. In order to prevent queue-jumping, six provinces with 90 per cent of Canada's population prohibited their residents from obtaining private health care insurance.[99] The reasoning is that private health insurance would make hospitals like the one that Dr. Chaoulli wanted to operate financially viable, and these private facilities would draw physicians away from the public system, thus resulting in fewer physicians and potentially even longer wait times in the public system.[100]

There were three major considerations in the Supreme Court's analysis:

1. *Do the current wait times in Quebec for some types of surgery result in a violation of the s. 7 Canadian* Charter *right to security of the person and the s. 1 Quebec* Charter *right to the protection of the inviolability of the person? If so, is there credible evidence that lifting the prohibition against private health insurance would lead to a two-tier health delivery system, in which those who cannot afford private health insurance would be subjected to even longer waiting times?*

2. *If there is a violation of s. 7 of the Canadian* Charter *or s. 1 of the Quebec* Charter, *can they be justified as reasonable limits?*

3. *Does the Quebec* Charter *provide greater protection for individual security than the Canadian* Charter?

Seven judges heard the *Chaoulli* case. Six of the judges focused on the Canadian *Charter*, and they were split 3-3 over whether there was a violation of security of the person under s. 7. The seventh judge, Justice Deschamps, addressed only the application of the Quebec *Charter*. Because she decided that the prohibition of private health insurance did indeed violate the Quebec *Charter*, she wrote that there was no need to address the

Canadian *Charter* because the protection of the "inviolability of the person" provides a broader degree of the protection of individual security than s. 7 of the Canadian *Charter*.[101]

Three of the six judges who focused on the Canadian *Charter*, McLachlin, Major, and Bastarache, agreed with Justice Deschamps' conclusions about the application of the Quebec *Charter*, and so the decision of Deschamp became the holding for this case. However, these three judges also argued that the prohibition of private health insurance also violated s. 7 of the Canadian *Charter*. Although a great deal of evidence was provided to the court, the McLaughlin-Major-Bastarache trio could not find any definitive proof that allowing private health care insurance would harm the public health care system by creating longer waiting times.[102] However, they were convinced by the evidence that there were "Delays in the public system [that] are widespread and have serious, sometimes grave, consequences."[103] These delays clearly violated security of the person in s. 7 of the *Charter*, and could not be justified as conforming with the s. 7 guarantee of fundamental justice. These judges asserted that the restrictions on private health insurance were arbitrary because there was no compelling proof that they were needed, and any arbitrary stipulation is a violation of fundamental justice.[104] For similar reasons, the prohibition could not be justified under s. 1; because they were arbitrary, they failed all parts of the Oakes test.[105]

The three judges who argued that the prohibition of private health insurance does not violate s. 7 of the *Charter* — Binnie, LeBel, and Fish — were convinced by the evidence presented by the Quebec government, such as the Romanow Commission of Inquiry into the state of Canadian health care, that government policy to ensure that all Quebeckers receive health services in a timely fashion, regardless of their income, was so strong that the Court ought to defer to it. As well, they pointed out that the evidence about whether waiting times were excessive was mixed.[106] As a result of this analysis, these three judges concluded that the prohibition of private health insurance was not arbitrary, and thus not a violation of fundamental justice in s. 7. As well, these judges argued that "security of the person" should not be expanded to include non-legal concepts:

> *Thus, the formal requirements for a principle of fundamental*
> *justice are threefold. First, it must be a* legal *principle.*
> *Second, the reasonable person must regard it as vital to our*
> societal notion *of justice, which implies a significant societal*
> *consensus. Third, it must be capable of being identified with*
> *precision and applied in a manner that yields predictable*
> *results . . . The aim of "health care of a reasonable standard*
> *within a reasonable time" is not a legal principle.*[107]

The Court suspended its judgment to give the Quebec government time to make changes to its health care plan. The Quebec government made minimal changes — allowing private health insurance only for "cataract surgery and knee and hip replacements."[108]

The fact that four judges out of seven — the Binnie-LeBel-Fish trio, plus Madame Justice Deschamps — did not conclude that the prohibition of private health care insurance violates the Canadian *Charter* means that the decision has no impact on parts of Canada outside of Quebec. It also indicates that the Court is split on how broadly s. 7 should be interpreted outside of the traditional legal meanings of the words in s. 7. This issue is sure to arise again in future litigation. However, following *Chaoulli*, a number of s. 7 cases were decided by the Supreme Court that involved issues closer to the traditional legal issues associated with life, liberty, security of the person and fundamental justice. These decisions might be thought of as a revolution in thinking about these concepts.

FIGHTING TERRORISM WHILE RESPECTING HUMAN RIGHTS: *CHARKAOUI* AND *KHADR*

CHARKAOUI (2007 AND 2008)[109]

In 1978, Parliament enacted legislation creating security certificates. Security certificates, issued by the appropriate cabinet minister, would allow for the detention of someone suspected of being a security risk. The government's evidence of the security risk would be reviewed by a Federal Court judge; at the government's request, the evidence would be withheld from the person accused of being a security risk. However, until legislative changes in 2001, an independent special counsel would review the government's evidence and act as an advocate for the person who was allegedly the security risk. In 2001, in the aftermath of 9/11, Parliament abolished the special counsel procedure through the enactment of the *Immigration and Refugee Protection Act* (*IRPA*). Under both the pre- and post-2001 systems, if the Federal Court judge was satisfied that the security risk was proven, the subject of the security risk was subject to deportation, even if the deportation meant the likelihood of torture or death. At least twenty-nine security certificates had been issued between 1991 and 2009.[110]

In 2003, Adil Charkaoui, a Moroccan immigrant and Canadian permanent resident pursuing graduate studies, was arrested in Montreal under a security certificate, suspected of being an al Qaeda sleeper agent.[111] He subsequently spent nearly two years in jail, then four years wearing a GPS bracelet, until the security certificate was quashed by a Federal Court judge in 2009. In 2010, Charkaoui launched a lawsuit against the federal government for $24 million.[112] The critical milestone leading to Charkaoui's exoneration was a Supreme Court decision in 2007.

In the Federal Court, Charkaoui argued that the security certificate scheme was unconstitutional in that it violated section 7 of the *Charter*, amongst other sections.[113] A unanimous nine-judge panel of the Supreme Court held that the post-2001 security certificate system violated section 7 of the *Charter* and could not be justified under section 1.

The court's opinion, written by Chief Justice McLachlin, emphasized that a fair hearing requires that the affected person be informed of the case against him or her, and be permitted to respond to that case.[114]

The court acknowledged that

> [o]ne of the most fundamental responsibilities of a government is to ensure the security of its citizens. This may require it to act on information that it cannot disclose and to detain people who threaten national security. Yet in a constitutional democracy, governments must act accountably and in conformity with the Constitution and the rights and liberties it guarantees.[115]

The Report of Mr. Justice O'Connor on the Maher Arar case had been released in 2006,[116] and it was clear from McLachlin's judgment that the judges were acutely aware of the lessons that had been learned from the Arar episode. First, McLachlin referred to the harsh potential consequences of deporting someone to a country where they might face torture, which is what happened to Maher Arar after he was deported from the US to Syria, and tortured, after US security officials received erroneous information from the RCMP about Arar's alleged ties to a terrorist organization.[117] Second, McLachlin points out that the Arar inquiry utilized a "special counsel" procedure similar to that in place regarding security certificates prior to 2001.

> The Arar Inquiry provides another example of the use of special counsel in Canada. The Commission had to examine confidential information related to the investigation of terrorism plots while preserving Mr. Arar's and the public's interest in disclosure. The Commission was governed by the CEA [Canada Evidence Act]. To help assess claims for confidentiality, the Commissioner was assisted by independent security-cleared legal counsel with a background in security and intelligence, whose role was to act as amicus curiae on confidentiality applications. The scheme's aim was to ensure that only information that was rightly subject to national security confidentiality was kept from public view. There is no indication that these procedures increased the risk of disclosure of protected information.[118]

McLachlin reviewed the pre-2001 procedure whereby a special counsel was appointed to represent the interests of the subject of a security certificate, and after reviewing all of the government's evidence, to present a case to the Federal Court judge defending the person accused of being a security risk. McLachlin's favourable comments about the pre-2001 system might indicate that if that system were to be reintroduced, it might pass Charter muster. Clearly, the Supreme Court wanted to know why the pre-2001 system had been abandoned.

> *Why the drafters of the legislation did not provide for special
> counsel to objectively review the material with a view to
> protecting the named person's interest, as was formerly done
> for the review of security certificates . . . and is presently
> done in the United Kingdom, has not been explained. The
> special counsel system may not be perfect from the named
> person's perspective, given that special counsel cannot reveal
> confidential material. But, without compromising security, it
> better protects the named person's s. 7 interests.*[119]

It may be that the drafters of the 2001 legislation, as well as the majority in the Canadian Parliament, overreacted to the horrific events of 9/11, curtailing human rights more than was necessary to ensure the security of Canadians.

Following the *Charkaoui* decision of 2007, Parliament amended *IRPA* early in 2008 to provide for a special advocate to represent targets of security certificates before a Federal Court judge, similar to the pre-2001 procedure. By the time the issue of the validity of Charkaoui's security certificate again reached the Federal Court, the Canadian Security Intelligence Service (CSIS) had destroyed some of the relevant evidence it claimed to have against Charkaoui. Charkaoui then applied for a stay of proceedings, and this litigation soon reached the Supreme Court. In a unanimous decision, the court decided that a stay of proceedings was not an appropriate remedy but that all the evidence CSIS had against Charkaoui must be disclosed to the designated Federal Court judge.[120] In 2009, CSIS refused to comply, and the designated Federal Court judge stayed proceedings. Charkaoui, then a full-time French teacher and PhD student, became a free man.[121]

KHADR (2008 AND 2010)[122]

In 2002, Canadian Omar Khadr was a fifteen-year-old soldier fighting for al Qaeda in Afghanistan because his father had ordered him to do so. He was captured by US forces and accused of killing a US soldier. While in detention in Guantanamo Bay, he was tortured by US authorities on a number of occasions in attempts to obtain intelligence information. In 2003 and

2004, Khadr was interviewed twice by Canadian officials who knew that the results of the interviews would be used as evidence against him in a military tribunal hearing in Guantanamo Bay. Khadr was not given access to legal counsel at the first interview. The second interview occurred after Khadr had been deprived of sleep for three weeks, a fact known by the Canadian officials.[123]

In 2005, Khadr applied to the Federal Court for an order for Canadian officials to disclose to him all the evidence they had collected during their interviews with him. The case ended up in the Supreme Court of Canada, and the Supreme Court released its decision in May of 2008. Given that the United States Supreme Court on two occasions had declared that the regime to which Omar Khadr was subjected in Guantanamo Bay was illegal under US domestic and international law, the Canadian Supreme Court declared that Khadr's Charter s. 7 right to life, liberty, and security of the person had been violated in a manner that was not in accord with the principles of fundamental justice. The Canadian government was ordered to release to Khadr the transcripts of the interviews conducted by Canadian government officials in 2003 and 2004,[124] and the government complied with the order.

Around the same time, the House of Commons Subcommittee on International Human Rights[125] was considering the Khadr situation and issued its report in June. The majority recommended that the government comply with Canada's obligations under the UN's *Convention on the Rights of the Child*, and request repatriation of Khadr so that he could be dealt with under Canadian law. At the time, Khadr was the only foreign national still being held at Guantanamo Bay. However, the Conservative minority on the committee rejected this recommendation, emphasized the possible risk associated with repatriating Khadr, and concluded that the usual standards of criminal law were impractical in a war situation and in particular when combating terrorism.[126] The Conservative minority seemed to be arguing that in order to fight terrorism, the rule of law must be set aside. As expected, the government did not request Khadr's repatriation from Guantanamo Bay.

After Barack Obama won the US presidential election in November of 2008, Khadr's lawyers advised Khadr to apply for a court order in

Canada's Federal Court to compel the Canadian government to have him repatriated to Canada. The Obama administration — which was opposed to the anti–rule of law Guantanamo Bay regime — wanted Khadr repatriated to be dealt with under Canadian law. As well, given the Supreme Court's unanimous ruling in the 2008 *Khadr* decision that the *Canadian Charter of Rights and Freedoms* applied extraterritorially when there is a clear violation of Canada's international human rights obligations, it seemed a good possibility that Canadian courts would order Khadr to be repatriated.

The Federal Court of Appeal agreed with Khadr's argument. However, a unanimous Supreme Court of Canada agreed only in part. Given the 2008 *Khadr* decision, the Supreme Court confirmed that Khadr's Charter rights had been violated and that they applied extraterritorially.

> *Interrogation of a youth, to elicit statements about the most serious criminal charges while detained in these conditions and without access to counsel, and while knowing that the fruits of the interrogations would be shared with the US prosecutors, offends the most basic Canadian standards about the treatment of detained youth suspects.*[127]

The remedy ordered by the court, however, turned out to be ineffective.[128] The court simply declared that Khadr's Charter rights had been violated, and left it to the Canadian government to find an appropriate remedy.[129]

Shortly after the Supreme Court decision was released, Prime Minister Harper announced that the Canadian government would not request Khadr's repatriation but would ask the US government to treat Khadr fairly. As well, the Canadian government requested that the Guantanamo Bay military tribunal not use the evidence collected by Canadian officials against Khadr. This request was refused by the military tribunal. According to Audrey Macklin, it was "predictable" that the US government would reject this request. "After all, attempting to tamper with the trial process of another state . . . constitutes a significantly greater intrusion into the sovereignty of another state than a request from one executive branch to another to repatriate the accused before a trial commences."[130]

Realizing that he could not get a fair trial before the US military tribunal in Guantanamo, in October of 2010 Khadr pleaded guilty to the charges against him in exchange for a commitment from US officials to return him to Canada to serve the remainder of his eight-year sentence after an additional one-year detention at Guantanamo. Khadr was transferred to Ontario's maximum security Millhaven Institution in September 2012, and in 2013 to another maximum security institution in Alberta.[131] In June, 2014 the Alberta Court of Appeal ruled that Khadr had the right to be treated as if sentenced as a youth, which increased his chances of early release. The court cited the two Supreme Court decisions on Khadr.[132] In 2013 and 2014, Khadr requested permission to speak to the media, a request opposed by Canadian government officials.[133]

On May 21 and 22, 2012, the United Nations Committee against Torture in Geneva reviewed allegations that Canada had failed to comply with its obligations under the *Convention against Torture* and issued a report harshly critical of recent Canadian practices, even concluding that Canada was complicit in allowing torture.[134]

INSITE (2011)[135]

In 2003, North America's first safe injection site, called Insite, opened in Vancouver's downtown east side, one of Canada's poorest and most squalid neighbourhoods. Insite was an intergovernmental response to the deteriorating situation in the downtown east side in the 1990s, which is home to about 4,600 intravenous drug users.[136] The purpose of Insite was not only to provide intravenous drug users with clean needles, but to encourage them to use the treatment facility that was located in the same building. In order for the facility to operate legally, the federal minister of health would have to exempt Insite from the *Controlled Drugs and Substances Act* (*CDSA*). Section 56 of the *Act* provides the health minister with the discretion to issue exemptions from the *CDSA* for medical and scientific purposes. Prior to Insite opening in 2003, the minister of health issued the facility a five-year exemption. Evaluations of Insite have shown that it has been successful in reducing both the proportion of deaths from overdoses and infections from dirty needles. As well, there has been an increase in the proportion of intravenous drug users entering treatment programs.

In spite of Insite's demonstrated success, the Conservative Party was ideologically opposed to the idea of a safe injection site, and in 2008 Health Minister Tony Clement refused to continue Insite's exemption from the *CDSA*. As a result, two Insite clients and two non-profit organizations initiated a court action aimed at keeping the facility open. The case reached the Supreme Court of Canada in 2011.

In September of 2011, the Supreme Court released a unanimous judgment that condemned the minister's refusal to continue the exemption and ordered him to reissue it. A cabinet minister's discretionary decisions, the Supreme Court ruled, must comply with the *Charter of Rights and Freedoms*. "Insite has been proven to save lives with no discernable negative impact on the public safety and health objectives of Canada. The effect of denying the services of Insite to the population it serves and the correlative increase in the risk of death and disease to injection drug users is grossly disproportionate to any benefit that Canada might derive from presenting a uniform stance on the possession of narcotics."[137] Such ministerial denial is a violation of s. 7 of the *Charter*, which protects the right to life, liberty, and security of the person.

It is noteworthy that one of the arguments presented in court on the minister's behalf was that "granting a s. 56 exemption to Insite would undermine the rule of law and that denying an exemption is therefore justified."[138] An exemption from the *CDSA* "would effectively turn the rule of law on its head by dictating that where a particular individual breaks the law with such frequency and persistence that he or she becomes unable to comply with it, it is unconstitutional to apply the law to that person."[139] This rule of law argument was flatly rejected by the court. On the contrary, the court cited evidence that Insite had contributed to reducing crime in the downtown east side. The court did not mince words in condemning the health minister's refusal to grant the exemption: "the Minister's refusal to grant Insite a s. 56 exemption was arbitrary and grossly disproportionate in its effects, and hence not in accordance with the principles of fundamental justice."[140]

Perhaps because the government took no meaningful action in response to the Supreme Court's recommendation that Omar Khadr be repatriated to Canada, the court did not trust the government to reconsider the decision not to grant the exemption to Insite in the light of the court's findings about the applicability of s. 7 of the *Charter* to ministerial discretionary decisions. The court's remedy was to order the minister of health to grant the s. 56 exemption to Insite.[141]

BEDFORD (2013)[142]

In December 2013, the Supreme Court released a bombshell with its decision about the rights of prostitutes. However, the Bedford decision was not unexpected for those paying attention to the development of the Supreme Court's jurisprudence regarding s. 7 on "life, liberty and security of the person" in *Insite* and *Kahdr*.

In the Canadian Criminal Law, selling sex for money has never been illegal. However, over time, various laws have attempted to discourage this practice. The Supreme Court was convinced by an overwhelming amount of evidence that the anti-prostitution legislation enacted in the 1980s did not meet the requirements of s. 7 for government to respect life and security of the person enunciated by the Court in *Insite* and *Kahdr*.

Prostitution is often cited as the world's oldest profession, but through-out Canadian history, prostitution has always been an unresolved, and perhaps unresolvable, conundrum. There is general agreement that there ought to be public policies that address the issue, but there has never been a consensus about what these policies should be. Prostitution has never been a criminal offence in Canada, but activities surrounding prostitution have been subjected to legal constraints, either because soliciting for prostitution has created neighborhood distress, or because of pressure from citizens who object to the moral dimensions of prostitution.

Prior to Confederation, prostitution was sometimes tolerated in port cities or frontier areas as long as it was not perceived as a public nuisance, in which case prostitutes, and sometimes their sponsors and customers, were charged with offences not related to prostitution, or with vagrancy.[143] Soon after Confederation, Parliament enacted a law to prevent the "defile-ment" of women under 21, and then expanded the vagrancy laws to include pimps.[144] In 1892, when the *Criminal Code* came into effect, the

Code contained provisions designed to deter prostitution through vagrancy prohibitions (directed both to prostitutes and pimps), and "bawdy-house" (brothel) prohibitions. From that time, prostitution was not a major political issue until the 1970s and 1980s, when prostitution activities became increasingly visible because the increasingly affluent society presented more opportunities for prostitutes, many of whom came from backgrounds that had not benefitted from the new prosperity such as some aboriginal communities.[145]

For a decade prior to 1982, Canadian politics had been preoccupied with resolving the constitutional crises that was eventually resolved through enactment of the *Constitution Act, 1982*. There was no political will to address the prostitution issue until after 1982. In 1983, the federal cabinet appointed a special committee on pornography and prostitution. The committee recommended that restrictions be put on soliciting for prostitution in neighbourhoods where such activities would constitute a nuisance, and that brothels employing up to four prostitutes be legalized and regulated. The Mulroney government rejected the second recommendation, but implemented the first one by making it a criminal offence either for prostitutes or their clients to communicate in a public place for the purposes of prostitution. These provisions were soon challenged in court as violating freedom of expression under the *Charter*, and this litigation was settled in favour of the government by the Supreme Court in 1990.[146] The majority of the Supreme Court found that the new criminal code provisions prohibiting communicating for the purposes of prostitution did violate freedom of expression, but could be justified as a reasonable limit under s. 1.

The Supreme Court in 1990 was not presented with much empirical evidence about the impact of the new criminal code provisions limiting prostitution-related activities. After that time, social scientists collected a good deal of empirical evidence, much of which has indicated that the 1983 criminal code changes drove prostitution activities to places where police were unlikely to witness communication about prostitution, thus putting prostitutes in more dangerous situations than they had been before the criminal code amendments. Then the notorious conviction of Robert Pickton in 2007 for the murder of six prostitutes — he may have killed about 60 in all — provided nation-wide publicity about the dangers faced by prostitutes under the then current legislative regime.[147] In the early 2000s, three activist current or former prostitutes, Terri Jean Bedford, Amy Lebovitch, and Valerie Scott, supported by law professor and social activist Alan Young and colleagues, concluded that there was enough new evidence to challenge successfully the constitutionality of the 1983 prostitution legislation.

Bedford, Lebovitch, and Scott applied to the Ontario Superior Court in 2008 for a declaration that three provisions of the *Criminal Code* relating to prostitution — the prohibition of brothels, communicating for the purposes of prostitution, and "living off the avails" of prostitution[148] — violated security of the person as guaranteed by s. 7 of the *Charter*, and that the communication section also violated freedom of expression in s. 2. The "living off the avails" section was challenged not in order to try to justify pimping, but because the applicants considered this provision overbroad, preventing prostitutes from hiring body guards or receptionists, for example. Justice Susan Himel considered 88 volumes, or 25,000 pages, of evidence.[149] Justice Himel decided in 2010 in favour of the applicants on all three issues. Part of the Superior Court decision was upheld by the Ontario Court of Appeal in 2012, which upheld the stiking down the criminal code provisions relating to the prohibition of brothels, and "living off the avails." The appellate court of five concluded unanimously that these provisions put prostitutes at unnecessary risk. However, a majority of three concluded that the section prohibiting communication for the purposes of prostitution could only be struck down by the Supreme Court of Canada; a lower court could not overrule the 1990 Supreme Court precedent.

The Ontario Court of Appeal's decision was of course appealed to the Supreme Court of Canada, which rendered its decision in December of 2013. The Supreme Court concluded that Justice Himel's analysis of the evidence, which showed overwhelmingly that the criminal code provisions on prostitution unnecessarily endangered prostitutes when engaging in a legal activity, was correct. With regard to the communication section, the Court overruled its 1990 decision on the basis that new evidence showed that the 1983 criminal code provisions on prostitution violated ss. 2 and 7 of the *Charter*. The Court held that lower courts are entitled to set aside the application of a precedent of the Supreme Court when there is compelling new evidence that applying the precedent would result in a violation of the constitution.[150] This is an important clarification of the doctrine of *stare decisis,* because the decision of the majority on the Ontario Court of Appeal — that only the Supreme Court can set aside its own precedents — was the conventional wisdom at the time. The Supreme Court affirmed that only the Supreme Court can over-rule its own precedents, but a lower court, when confronted with a clear conflict between a Supreme Court precedent and the constitution, based on new and compelling evidence, must follow the constitution rather than the precedent.

In commenting on the criminal code provisions restricting activities around prostitution, the Court observed:

> The prohibitions at issue do not merely impose conditions on how prostitutes operate. They go a critical step further, by imposing dangerous conditions on prostitution; they prevent people engaged in a risky — but legal — activity from taking steps to protect themselves from the risks . . . [T]he bawdy-house prohibition prevents resort to safe houses, to which prostitutes working on the street can take clients. In Vancouver, for example, "Grandma's House" was established to support street workers in the Downtown Eastside at about the same time as fears were growing that a serial killer was prowling the streets — fears which materialized in the notorious Robert Pickton. Street prostitutes — who the application judge found are largely the most vulnerable class of prostitutes, and who face an alarming amount of violence . . . were able to bring clients to Grandma's House. However, charges were laid . . . [and] Grandma's House was shut down.[151]

The court concluded that based on the evidence, the three impugned provisions of the *Criminal Code* were "arbitrary, overbroad or grossly disproportionate"[152] to the legislation's objective of preventing public nuisance, and thus a violation of the guarantee in s. 7 to life and security of the person. The Attorneys General of Canada and Ontario had argued that in such a complex policy area, the Court ought to defer to their arguments that the legislation ought not to be tampered with by courts. The Court, composed of a majority of appointments made by Stephen Harper, forcefully disagreed:

> *Calls for deference cannot insulate legislation that creates*
> *serious harmful effects from the charge that they negatively*
> *impact security of the person under s. 7 of the* Charter.[153]

However, the Supreme Court suspended for one year its declaration that the three impugned sections of the criminal code were invalid in order to give Parliament an opportunity to consider the issue and enact new legislation if it chose to do so. The Court emphasized that Parliament had the right to regulate prostitution, so long as it did so without violating the Charter.[154]

Early in 2014, the Harper government requested the public's feedback about how the Criminal Code provisions about prostitution should be amended. The submissions were roughly divided into two streams — those that advocated the "New Zealand" model to allow prostitution but regulate it, and the "Nordic" model of allowing the selling of sex, but making the buying of sex a criminal offence. The government opted for the "Nordic" model, and in June introduced legislation that would make the purchasing of sex illegal, while continuing to allow the legal selling of sex by adults, and allowing communicating for prostitution as long as it did not happen in a place where children might be present. Limited advertising for the sale of sex would be legal, and brothels employing a maximum of two prostitutes would be legal. The inherent contradictions in this approach are obvious, and it is clear that the legislation, if enacted, will be challenged in court.

THE SUPREME COURT AND LEGAL RIGHTS

At the beginning of this chapter, it is noted that a number of observers thought that the Supreme court's decisions about sections 7–14 would be among the least controversial from the perspective of judicial policy-making. Of all the decisions considered in this chapter, that conclusion fits only the *Southam* and *Valente* cases. Moreover, even the *Southam* and *Valente* cases were landmark decisions in that they defined important Charter phrases: "unreasonable search and seizure" and "judicial independence." However, a subsequent decision on judicial independence — the *Provincial Court Judges Reference* — was likely the most controversial decision of the Supreme Court issued up to 2014.

CHAPTER 6

EQUALITY

The current concern for equality in our society can be traced in part to the effects of liberal ideology. But there have been other influences about attitudes toward equality in the liberal democracies. The equality principle in Western political thought has had a wide range of interpretations.

The various theories of equality can be divided into three rough categories: formal equality, numerical equality, and normative equality.[1] Put very simply, formal equality urges treating equals equally and unequals unequally. It has its origins in the writings of Aristotle. The Supreme Court's decision in *A.G. Canada v. Lavell*[2] (see chapter 1), in which it was decided that there had been no breach of equality under the *Canadian Bill of Rights* as long as all Indian women were treated equally, is an example of the formal equality approach. If judges employ this perspective, they can apply the law unevenly so long as they do so consistently within groups of "equals" — for example, Indian women, seniors, pregnant women, and so on.

Theories of numerical equality begin with the proposition that because all human beings have traits in common, they deserve to be treated by and large as equals. There are many variations of this theory. The most conservative approach is that the rules of the economic system should apply equally to everyone. A more radical view is that an equality of *conditions*, such as those offered by affirmative action programs, must come about before the rules of the marketplace can apply equally. There are even some who advocate close to absolute equality in the distribution of goods and services.

Those who support normative equality, like the advocates of numerical equality, accept that under ideal conditions human beings should be treated equally. Instead of asking, as the theories of numerical equality do, how *far* equality of treatment should extend, they attack the problem from the opposite direction. Normative theorists, such as Ronald Dworkin, have attempted to establish acceptable conditions for justifiable deviations from equality. Because theories of numerical and normative equality have so much in common, I refer to them together as "social equality." At the basis of social equality is the idea that all human beings deserve to be treated as equals and that departures from that principle require convincing justification. Since 1985, the Supreme Court has rejected a narrow, formal equality approach and has moved toward what could be considered a form of social equality, which the court refers to as "substantive equality."

Canadians are more likely to favour social equality than formal equality, according to the results of a late 1980s survey of the attitudes of Canadians toward civil liberties conducted by Paul Sniderman and his colleagues. The survey found that 72 per cent of Canadians disagreed with the statement "Some people are better than others" and 73 per cent disagreed with the proposition "All races are certainly not equal."[3]

It appears that since the Second World War, the attitudes of Canadians about equality, like those of citizens of other liberal democracies, have shifted from a formal equality perspective to one of social equality. From the 1960s to the late 1970s, more radical notions of social equality became popular, such as those advocating affirmative action programs for women, visible minorities, and other disadvantaged groups. However, the neo-conservative trend beginning in the 1980s may have moved Canadians toward an approach to social equality that merely advocates economic rules that apply uniformly.[4] The attitudes of Canadians toward equality will continue to shift as new equality claims are presented by groups that claim discrimination, and as catastrophic events such as terrorist attacks challenge our values.[5]

The wording of the equality clause in the *Charter of Rights and Freedoms* (section 15) is in tune with the more radical concepts of social equality dating from the late 1970s and continuing to expand. It was an attempt to broaden the scope of legally enforceable equality provisions in Canada in reaction to the more limited equality provisions in the *Canadian Bill of Rights*, which were interpreted according to the formal equality approach by the Supreme Court. In particular, it should be noted that section 15(1) guarantees the "equal benefit of the law," which makes it one of the most far-reaching equality clauses of any modern bill of rights.[6] If this clause were taken in a rigid and literal sense, it would seem to imply a very radical theory of numerical equality that would mandate government to enforce absolute equality in the provision of services and benefits. However, as chapter 1 argues, no right in the *Charter* can be considered absolute, and judges are usually reluctant to apply legal principles the results of which are markedly out of step with popular expectations.

It is in this context that the Supreme Court of Canada is making decisions about the scope of section 15. Chief Justice Beverly McLachlin has stated that s. 15 is the most difficult section of the *Charter* to interpret.[7] Because section 15 did not become operative until April 17, 1985, up to 1989 the Supreme Court rendered only two substantive decisions about the meaning of s. 15 — the *Andrews* and *Turpin* cases — which are still important today. There were three other decisions that also involved s. 15 but are more important for broader issues of constitutional interpretation. One is the *Ontario Roman Catholic High School Funding* case, in which the court decided that section 15 could not take precedence over the denominational school rights in the constitution. Then there was the case of Joseph Borowski, who sought a declaration from the Supreme Court that a fetus is entitled to the full protection of the *Charter*, including equality rights under section 15. The Supreme Court declined to settle the issue because Borowski's case had become moot thanks to the court's earlier decision in *Morgentaler*, but soon afterward the court was forced into an answer by the case of Chantal Daigle, a woman who wished to terminate her pregnancy but was facing legal challenges from her former boyfriend.

The Supreme Court began the 1990s with an expansion of the notion of equality in the *Schachter* case, which broadened parental leave to include birth fathers. Because this decision had financial implications for the federal budget, the court was criticized for being too activist and, perhaps as a result of this, the male members of the court decided against interfering with the *Income Tax Act* to expand the notion of gender equality in *Symes* and *Thibaudeau*. However, the two female judges on the court in those days dissented. In the late 1990s, the court ruled in favour of expanding the equality rights of the deaf in the *Eldridge* case, but declined to find a violation of equality in the Canada Pension Plan's limitations on survival benefits to spouses under thirty-five years of age in the case of Nancy Law. Nevertheless, in the 1990s, the Supreme Court began to recognize homosexual equality rights in the *Egan*, *Vriend*, and *M. v. H.* decisions, and continued this trend in the 2000s by recognizing the right of gays to marry, and also the responsibility of governments to permit gay marriage without interfering in the refusal of some religions to solemnize gay marriage. Also in the 2000s, the court upheld legislation that restricted social welfare support to those under thirty, refused to order governments to pay additional funds to support autistic children in the *Auton* case, and upheld the right of Newfoundland and Labrador to delay — because of financial woes — the reimbursement of female employees who were the victims of wage discrimination (*Newfoundland v. NAPE*). However, the court also upheld a federal government affirmative action program aimed at Aboriginals on the west coast (*R. v. Kapp*).

Clearly, s. 15 of the *Charter* is one of the most challenging for the judiciary to interpret, in part because s. 15 decisions often have financial implications for governments, and in part because notions of social equality continue to evolve in our society. For these reasons, the Supreme Court's equality decisions are fascinating to consider, and they provoke our individual consciences about the optimal level of social equality.

EARLY EQUALITY DECISIONS: THE 1980s
THE *ANDREWS* CASE (1989)[8]

Lawyers constitute a self-governing profession. The provinces have the power to regulate the professions under the *Constitution Act, 1867*, and every provincial government has delegated to its provincial law society the power to make regulations regarding the practice of law. This means that the provincial law societies act as agents of the government when they establish these regulations. Therefore, the *Charter* applies to the provincial law societies to the extent that they exercise authority delegated to them by the provincial governments.

In three provinces, including British Columbia and Ontario, the provincial law society requires lawyers to be Canadian citizens. As noted in chapter 2, the first Charter challenge that came to the Supreme Court of Canada was brought by a South African citizen who had fulfilled all the requirements for the practice of law in Ontario except that he had not lived in Canada long enough to become a citizen. He challenged the constitutional validity of the Law Society of Upper Canada regulations under section 6 of the *Charter* (mobility rights) and lost.[9]

Mark David Andrews, a UK citizen, brought a similar suit against the Law Society of British Columbia in 1985, except that he based his challenge on section 15. While taking his law degree in the United Kingdom, Andrews had met a Canadian woman; they decided to marry and to move to Canada. Andrews then completed all the requirements for the practice of law in BC, but he did not meet the citizenship requirement, and he could not apply to become a Canadian citizen until after having lived three years in Canada. He claimed in the BC Supreme Court that the Law Society of British Columbia's regulation requiring lawyers to be citizens discriminates against non-citizens and thus violates section 15. Section 15 states that "[e]very individual is equal before and under the law and has the right to the equal protection and equal benefit of the law without discrimination."

The trial court judge in the BC Supreme Court decided against Andrews's claim. He concluded that there was a rational connection between the citizenship requirement and the duties of a lawyer in that lawyers have responsibilities that require a special commitment to the community. Thus, he could find no discrimination. Andrews appealed to the BC Court of Appeal and won. The unanimous decision of the three-judge panel was written by Madame Justice McLachlin (who was later appointed to the Supreme Court of Canada and eventually became the chief justice). She argued that the proper approach to equality in section 15 was formal equality, and that Andrews, as an applicant for admission to the bar, was not being treated the same as other applicants. The discrimination could not be justified under section 1 of the *Charter*. The law society then appealed to the Supreme Court of Canada, which rendered its judgment in February 1989.

Andrews won again in the Supreme Court, but the court interpreted equality differently than the BC Court of Appeal had. The six-judge panel, consisting of Dickson, McIntyre, Lamer, Wilson, La Forest, and L'Heureux-Dubé, agreed about the general principles that should govern judicial interpretation of section 15, although they disagreed about how the principles should be applied to the case at hand. Mr. Justice McIntyre wrote the opinion that described how the court would adjudicate equality claims.

McIntyre was critical of the BC Court of Appeal's conclusion that the courts should apply the formal equality approach to section 15. He noted how this approach had led to unacceptable results in several Bill of Rights cases, such as *Lavell*[10] and *Bliss*.[11] (As chapter 1 recounts, the *Lavell* decision found no violation of equality in section 12 of the *Indian Act*, which entitled Indian men to more benefits than Indian women, because the equality provision in the *Bill* merely implied treating all Indian women equally in this case. In *Bliss,* the court found that the unemployment insurance regulations of the time did not violate equality as long as all pregnant women were treated equally.) He emphasized that the formal equality interpretation had been explicitly rejected in the *Drybones* decision. He said that the formal equality test

> is seriously deficient in that it excludes any consideration of the nature of the law. If it were to be applied literally, it could be used to justify the Nuremberg laws of Adolf Hitler. Similar treatment was contemplated for all Jews. The similarly situated test would have justified the formalistic separate but equal doctrine of Plessy v. Ferguson,[12] a doctrine that [entrenched racial discrimination in the US until the case of Brown v. Board of Education,[13] which overruled Plessy in 1954].[14]

Having rejected formal equality, McIntyre adopted a definition of equality similar to what was referred to earlier in this chapter as social equality. He reached this result by conducting a purposive analysis, concluding that descriptions of equality in section 15, especially the references to equality under the law, the equal protection of the law, and the equal benefit of the law — all of which went beyond the definition of equality in the *Bill of Rights* — were intended to signal to the courts that a broader definition of equality than formal equality was intended.

> *It is clear that the purpose of s.15 is to ensure equality in*
> *the formulation and application of the law. The promotion*
> *of equality entails the promotion of a society in which all*
> *are secure in the knowledge that they are recognized at law*
> *as human beings equally deserving of concern, respect, and*
> *consideration.*[15]

McIntyre then explained that the equality referred to in section 15 could not have been intended to require the elimination of all distinctions (like a radical version of numerical equality).

> *If the* Charter *was intended to eliminate all distinctions, then*
> *there would be no place for sections such as 27 (multicultural*
> *heritage); 2(a) (freedom of conscience and religion); 25*
> *(aboriginal rights and freedoms); and other such provisions*
> *designed to safeguard certain distinctions. Moreover, the*
> *fact that identical treatment may frequently produce serious*
> *inequality is recognized in s.15(2), which [allows affirmative*
> *action programs].*[16]

Like the theorists of numerical equality, McIntyre then tackled the question of how far equality should extend. He approached this issue by focusing on the words "without discrimination" in section 15. In other words, equality should extend far enough so as to preclude discrimination: "Discrimination is unacceptable in a democratic society because it epitomizes the worst effects of the denial of equality, and discrimination reinforced by law is particularly repugnant . It is against this evil that s.15 provides a guarantee."

McIntyre was then faced with having to define discrimination. After reviewing several approaches, he concluded that discrimination may be described as a distinction — intentional or not but based on grounds relating to personal characteristics of an individual or group — which has the effect of imposing burdens, obligations, or disadvantages on such individual or group not imposed upon others, or which withholds or limits access to opportunities, benefits, and advantages available to other members of society. Distinctions based on personal characteristics attributed to an individual based solely on association with a group will rarely escape the charge of discrimination, while those based on an individual's merits and capacities will rarely be so classed.

The personal characteristics upon which unacceptable discrimination is based would include all of the enumerated categories in section 15 — race, national or ethnic origin, colour, religion, sex, age, and mental or physical disability — and categories analogous to these. This is what McIntyre referred to as the "enumerated and analogous grounds" method of defining discrimination. He stressed that not all unequal treatment based on these classifications violated equality, but only that which *discriminated* — that is, imposed disadvantages not imposed on others or withheld benefits available to others — did. Discrimination could result directly from the wording of a law, or it could be indirect and unintentional, that is, the unintended result of legislation that happened to place unfair disadvantages on members of one of the enumerated or analogous categories in section 15. (Such unintentional discrimination is also known as systemic discrimination.)

McIntyre's approach is close to the one recommended by the Women's Legal Education and Action Fund (LEAF), which advocated a definition of equality that stressed the protection of the disadvantaged rather than one allowing the advantaged to gain further ground. (LEAF had been allowed by the court to "intervene" in this case. An intervenor is a party that is not one of the original litigants but that has a stake in the outcome of the case and can present the court with useful evidence.)

Once discrimination is established, the onus is on the party seeking to maintain the inequality to demonstrate that it is a reasonable limit under section 1. Unless the inequality can be justified under section 1, the discriminatory law must be struck down.

With regard to the case at hand, all the judges agreed that by creating a distinction based on citizenship (a category analogous to that of national origin), the Law Society of British Columbia had imposed a burden on permanent residents, thus discriminating against them. Justices Dickson, Wilson, L'Heureux-Dubé, and La Forest concluded that the citizenship requirement did not pass the Oakes test because there was no rational connection between the citizenship requirement and the objective of ensuring that lawyers have a knowledge of and commitment to the principles of government in Canada. McIntyre and Lamer dissented on this point. They agreed that citizenship was neither a necessary nor a sufficient condition to ensure the requisite knowledge of and commitment to the country's political system. However, McIntyre pointed out that the law against theft is neither a necessary nor sufficient condition to prevent stealing, and yet it does help to promote the goal of protecting private property. McIntyre concluded that a reasonable limit must be one which "it was reasonable for the legislature to impose. The courts are not called upon to substitute judicial opinions for legislative ones as to the place at which to draw a precise line."

The *Andrews* decision remains one of the most important equality decisions that the Supreme Court has made. As McIntyre pointed out, "The section 15(1) guarantee is the broadest of all guarantees [in the *Charter*]. It applies to and supports all other rights guaranteed by the *Charter.*" From this perspective, it is somewhat disconcerting to realize that the Canadian judiciary below the Supreme Court level had generally defined equality according to the very narrow approach of formal equality in spite of the clear signals in the wording of section 15 itself that the drafters of the *Charter* intended the courts to move beyond formal equality. This situation helps to illustrate that the task of analyzing theories of equality, and then applying them to policy-making, is not something most judges are appropriately trained for. It is a little ironic that the first Supreme Court case involving section 15 — the section heralded as having the greatest potential to protect the disadvantaged in society — would be brought by a member of one of the least disadvantaged groups in Canada (lawyers) and that he should win his case. Nevertheless, the way in which the court has decided to approach section 15 has at least provided disadvantaged groups with much more hope of overcoming discrimination through judicial review than had been the case with judicial interpretations of the equality clause in the *Canadian Bill of Rights.*

THE *TURPIN* CASE (1989)[17]

On May 4, 1989, the Supreme Court rendered its second decision based on section 15. The case concerned the sections of the *Criminal Code* which require that an accused person charged with murder must be tried by a judge and jury in all provinces except Alberta, where the trial may be by judge alone. Sharon Turpin and her co-accuseds, who had been charged with first-degree murder in Ontario, made a pretrial motion in 1985 to be tried by a judge alone. They argued that they had a right to choose either a jury trial or a trial by judge alone under either section 11(f) of the *Charter* (which provides a right to trial by jury for serious offences) or under section 15. The guarantee of equality before the law in section 15, they claimed, means that advantages granted to accused persons in Alberta under a federal law must also be available in the rest of the country.

The judge accepted the argument that section 11(f) allowed an accused to elect whether to be tried by judge and jury or by judge alone. Turpin was subsequently tried by judge alone and acquitted. The Crown appealed on the grounds that the judge had erred in interpreting the *Charter*. In a 1987 decision, the Ontario Court of Appeal agreed with the Crown and ordered a new trial before judge and jury. Turpin appealed this decision to the Supreme Court and lost.

The judgment of the unanimous court was written by Madame Justice Wilson. After holding that section 11(f) simply provides a right to a jury trial, and not a right to elect either a jury trial or a trial by judge alone, Wilson turned to the section 15 argument. She applied the two-step test developed in *Andrews* about whether a law has violated section 15(1). The first step is to determine whether there has been a violation of any of the four equality rights that section 15(1) enumerates. In this case, Turpin claimed that her right to equality before the law had been infringed. Wilson emphasized that this right must be given a broader interpretation than it was given under the *Canadian Bill of Rights*.

> *The guarantee of equality before the law is designed to advance the value that all persons be subject to the equal demands and burdens of the law and not suffer any greater disability in the substance and application of the law than*

*others. This value has historically been associated with the
requirements of the rule of law that all persons be subject to
the law impartially applied and administered.*[18]

Because the *Criminal Code* treats accused persons outside of Alberta differently — and, some would argue, more harshly — than those charged in
Alberta, Wilson concluded that the *Code* violates equality before the law.

The second step was to determine whether there had been discrimination.
Wilson stressed that "it is only when one of the four equality rights has
been denied with discrimination that the values protected by section 15
are threatened and the courts' legitimate role as a protector of such values
comes into play."

Wilson affirmed the definition of discrimination provided by Mr. Justice
McIntyre in *Andrews*, and advanced the definition a little further. She wrote
that one question that should be considered is whether the group that is
a victim of the inequality has suffered a historical disadvantage because
of the inequality. In this case, accused persons outside of Alberta are not
members of a "discreet and insular minority" who have been socially disadvantaged because of the inequality in the *Criminal Code*. To conclude
that the impugned section of the *Criminal Code* discriminated, she claimed,

> *would not, in my view, advance the purposes of section
> 15 in remedying or preventing discrimination against
> groups suffering social, political, and legal disadvantage
> in our society. A search of indicia of discrimination such
> as stereotyping, historical disadvantage, or vulnerability
> to political and social prejudices would be fruitless in this
> case. [It would] "overshoot the actual purpose of the right of
> freedom in question."* See Regina v. Big M Drug Mart Ltd.,
> at p. 344.[19]

Wilson admitted there might be some examples of inequalities in the
criminal law and procedure, based on provincial variations contained in the
Criminal Code, that might result in discrimination. She said that the court
would have to examine the discrimination issue on a case-by-case basis.

In denying that Turpin and her co-accuseds had been discriminated against, the Supreme Court reiterated that it intends to interpret section 15 to help clearly disadvantaged groups in society. The judges provided an example of a group that, although subjected to unequal treatment, is not disadvantaged: accused persons outside of Alberta.

THE ONTARIO ROMAN CATHOLIC HIGH SCHOOL FUNDING CASE (1986)[20]

The funding of Roman Catholic high schools has been an issue in Ontario since the early part of this century. Part of the Confederation bargain of 1867 was an agreement that Protestants in Quebec and Roman Catholics in Ontario would be guaranteed the right to operate denominational schools with public funding at the same level as that which existed in 1867. Members of denominations who felt that their rights had been eroded could appeal to the federal government for redress under section 93 the *Constitution Act, 1867*. If such an appeal failed to produce results, Parliament could enact remedial legislation to address the grievances. Similar denominational school provisions were written into the terms of entry of new provinces after 1867. As noted in chapter 1, Parliament has never acted to protect the erosion of denominational school rights because of the political calculations involved.

In 1915 the Ontario government decided to fund Roman Catholic high schools only to the end of what we now call grade ten. In addition, the government decided to reduce funding for the Roman Catholic schools up to and including grade ten so that the funding would be up to 10 per cent less than that for public schools. Sentiment in some quarters against the Roman Catholic Church was partly responsible for this decision.

The Roman Catholic school board in Ontario's Tiny Township launched a court challenge to the provincial government's funding cutbacks. The case eventually reached the Judicial Committee of the Privy Council (JCPC), Canada's highest court at the time, in 1928.[21] The JCPC upheld the provincial cutbacks with some questionable reasoning. The Judicial Committee declared that the province, in deciding to fund Roman Catholic Schools only up to the grade ten level, had not reduced the schools' funding below the 1867 level, because in 1867 schools taught only up to what, in the

1920s, would be referred to as grade ten. Moreover, the cutbacks in the level of funding up to grade ten were acceptable because the government was merely regulating education in the province, and besides, the differential funding did not result in undue hardship. As unpersuasive as this reasoning was, it may have reflected the Judicial Committee's reading of the political reality of the time. A decision in favour of the Roman Catholic schools might actually have inflamed anti–Roman Catholic feeling in the province even more. Judges are sometimes reluctant — possibly unconsciously so — to stray too far from what they perceive to be majority public sentiments, even in the face of an obvious constitutional violation, because of worries that a decision may have serious unintended consequences.

In 1984 the provincial Conservative government did an about-face — it decided that henceforth it would fund Roman Catholic high schools right up to the completion of high school and at the same level of support as public schools. The Liberals and NDP decided to support this initiative. However, a number of public school boards opposed the new policy because it would lead to the closing of some public high schools and the transfer of buildings and personnel to the Roman Catholic system. There was fear that this would lead to lowering the standards of education in the public school system. The legislation putting the new policy into effect was not passed until shortly after section 15 of the *Charter* became operative in 1985. Those opposed to the policy change, including the Metropolitan Toronto School Board, claimed that the new legislation was unconstitutional because it violated section 15 of the *Charter*. The board alleged that the extension of funding provided Roman Catholics with more benefits under the law than members of other religions or those without a religion, and that this constituted a violation of equality contrary to section 15.

In order to settle the doubts created by the claims of the Metro Toronto School Board, the Ontario government sent a reference question to its Court of Appeal concerning the constitutional validity of Bill 30, the legislation that extended the funding of Roman Catholic high schools. A five-judge panel heard the case in 1986, and a majority of three concluded that Bill 30 was constitutional. This decision was upheld by the Supreme Court of Canada in 1987. In both courts the key to upholding the legislation was section 29 of the *Charter*, which states that "[n]othing in this

Charter abrogates or derogates from any rights or privileges guaranteed by or under the Constitution of Canada in respect of denominational, separate, or dissentient schools." Obviously, this section means that the rights or privileges enjoyed by Roman Catholic schools in Ontario in 1867 were to be continued. But in the *Tiny* case, the Privy Council had declared that Roman Catholic schools were not entitled to funding beyond grade ten. The argument of those opposed to Bill 30 was that the *extension* of funding beyond grade ten was not rendered immune from section 15 by section 29 of the *Charter*.

The majority on the Ontario Court of Appeal gave a broad interpretation to the phrase "under the Constitution" in section 29. Their view was that this phrase referred to additional privileges granted to denominational schools after 1867 under the constitutional powers that the provinces have over education. The minority on the court disagreed; the two dissenting judges thought that even if "under the Constitution" could be interpreted in this way, at the most it could refer only to privileges granted between 1867 and the coming into force of the *Charter*. Because Bill 30 was not enacted prior to April 17, 1985, it would have to conform to section 15. To the minority, it was obvious that Bill 30 violated section 15 because it discriminated on the basis of religion, one of the prohibited categories. The Crown's argument to justify the discrimination under section 1 — that the government was merely redressing historical grievances — was not persuasive to the minority. The situation in 1985 was entirely different from that in the 1920s; a 1920s wrong could not be corrected in 1988, according to the minority.

The minority view did not impress the Supreme Court of Canada. The Supreme Court gave even stronger reasons for upholding Bill 30 than the Court of Appeal had. In fact, the Supreme Court took the very rare step of overruling a precedent: the *Tiny* decision. With the *Tiny* precedent gone, Bill 30 simply restored to Roman Catholics what they should rightly have received all along. Moreover, the majority opinion, written by Madame Justice Wilson, stated that even without section 29, Bill 30 would have been found constitutional. Wilson's reasoning was as follows:

> *It was never intended, in my opinion, that the Charter could be used to invalidate other provisions of the constitution,*

276

particularly a provision such as s. 93 which represented a
fundamental part of the Confederation compromise . . .
As the majority of the Court of Appeal concluded, "The
incorporation of the Charter into the Constitution Act, 1982
does not change the original Confederation bargain. A specific
constitutional amendment would be required to accomplish
that."[22]

Section 93 of the *Constitution Act, 1867* clearly implies that the provinces have the power to grant special privileges with regard to denominational schools. The privileges granted at the time a province entered into Confederation cannot be reduced, but new privileges can be created. These new privileges, however, can be reduced back to their time-of-Confederation level at the discretion of the provincial legislature. This interpretation of section 93 relied heavily on historical evidence about the "Confederation bargain."

Although the Supreme Court did not, for these reasons, deal with the section 15 issue, the case illustrates that section 15 cannot be used by litigants to challenge inequalities built into the constitution itself. These can be addressed only through a constitutional amendment.

THE *BOROWSKI* CASE (1989)[23]

Joseph Borowski had been one of the leading spokesmen for the pro-life movement in Canada until his death in 1996. He had been an NDP cabinet minister in Manitoba from 1969 to 1971, but he broke with his party over the abortion issue. In 1978 he began his legal battle in favour of fetal rights in Saskatchewan's Court of Queen's Bench by challenging the constitutionality of section 251 of the federal *Criminal Code* — the section that at the time regulated abortion. Because Borowski was not directly affected by section 251, his case went to the Supreme Court of Canada in 1981 for determination of whether he had standing to proceed with his case. *Standing* refers to the legal right of a litigant to have a case heard in a court. In 1981 the Supreme Court determined that Borowski had standing to challenge the abortion provisions in part because a fetus could not initiate a court case.[24]

In 1984 Borowski failed in his bid to obtain a declaration from the Saskatchewan Court of Queen's Bench that the Criminal Code provisions that allow for abortions in certain circumstances are contrary to the *Charter* and therefore of no force and effect. His position was that the right to life of the fetus is protected under section 7 of the *Charter*.

Borowski appealed to the Saskatchewan Court of Appeal. Because section 15 of the *Charter* was in effect by the time the appeal case was argued, Borowski contended that the abortion law also violated section 15 of the *Charter* because it denied the fetus the equal protection of the law. The court rendered its decision on April 30, 1987, and Borowski lost again.

Borowski appealed to the Supreme Court of Canada. However, before his case could be heard, the Supreme Court struck down section 251 of the *Criminal Code* — the abortion law Borowski was challenging — in the *Morgentaler* decision in January 1988 (see chapter 5). It would then have been logical for the federal Attorney General to have petitioned the Supreme Court to quash the appeal on the grounds that because section 251 of the *Criminal Code* had been struck down, Borowski no longer had standing. However, such a move might have been interpreted by some voters as a government stand against fetal rights. Instead, the government of Canada petitioned the Supreme Court to delay the Borowski hearing until after new abortion legislation had been considered by Parliament. This was obviously a strategy to keep the abortion issue out of the public spotlight until after the imminent federal election. However, the petition to delay was dismissed by the Supreme Court in September. On October 1, 1988, Prime Minister Mulroney called an election for November 21. Thus, when Borowski's case came before the court on October 3, Canada was in the midst of an election campaign.

The Women's Legal Education and Action Fund, an intervenor opposed to Borowski's position, argued in court that the case had become moot, a legal term meaning that the causes of the original controversy had disappeared, and therefore the original issue should not be decided because this would be of no practical value. LEAF took this position because the abortion law had already been struck down. Lawyers for the Canadian government refused to take a stand on this point, probably out of concern that any stand would have unpredictable political implications. Borowski, however, continued to seek a declaration that the references to "everyone" in section 7 and to "every individual" in section 15 include the fetus, and he requested permission to proceed. The court took the unusual step of agreeing to hear arguments from both sides, while reserving its decision (until after the election) about whether the case was moot.

One can sympathize with the court's position. If the judges had made a decision on the mootness of the case during an election campaign, it would have been interpreted as a victory for one side or the other, whether or not this actually was the case. The nation's top court, which absolutely needs to maintain an image of neutrality to maintain its legitimacy, could only lose respect by becoming the centre of focus during an election.

During the Supreme Court hearing, the arguments put by those for and against Borowski's position clearly show that the court was being asked to decide a question of policy rather than a legal issue. Morris Shumiatcher, Borowski's lawyer, showed the judges a series of anti-abortion films, including *The Hiccup Film* and *Jumping for Joy*. Borowski came to the courthouse with two jars containing pickled fetuses. "It was my hope that by passing it from judge to judge . . . they would see very clearly it is a perfect baby," said Borowski. The Interfaith Coalition on the Rights and Wellbeing of Women and Children, one of the intervenors, reminded the court that the preamble to the *Charter* states that Canada is founded on principles that recognize the supremacy of God: "The court should not be afraid — and lawyers should not be afraid — to turn to religious principles that underlie our society and say human life in all its stages must be protected."[25]

On the other side, the Women's Legal Education and Action Fund emphasized that the fetuses the judges had seen on film were inside a woman's body. In its factum (a written submission to the court), it criticized the films for "portraying the foetus as an autonomous 'space-hero' and the pregnant woman as the 'empty space' in which he floats." LEAF argued that the abortion issue is a sexual equality issue.

> *The social context of sex inequality has denied women control over the reproductive uses of their bodies . . . Women's reproductive capacity is thus an integral part of women's "equality problem," along a spectrum of situations. For women*

of reproductive age, the guarantee of sex equality should
be interpreted so as to reduce or minimize state-sanctioned
interference with women's full development as human beings,
socially, economically, and politically. Forced maternity in
this broader sense must be clearly understood as a problem of
sex inequality. Access to abortion is necessary as a means for
women to survive in their unequal circumstances. [26]

In March 1989 the Supreme Court of Canada rendered its decision. The court declared that Borowski's case was moot and therefore the question of whether the fetus had a right to equality and to life could not be decided. The unanimous decision was written by Mr. Justice John Sopinka, and concurred with by Justices Dickson, McIntyre, Lamer, Wilson, La Forest, and L'Heureux-Dubé. Sopinka outlined the two-step approach the court would adopt in deciding how to approach the question of mootness. "The first stage in the analysis requires a consideration of whether there remains a live controversy," he wrote. In this case, the controversy had disappeared because the sections of the *Criminal Code* Borowski was challenging had been struck down by the court in the *Morgentaler* decision. But the absence of a live controversy would not settle the issue. The second stage, which becomes relevant only if there was no live controversy, was to decide whether the court should exercise its discretion to hear the case anyway. In making this decision, the court should consider three factors, Sopinka wrote. The three factors would, on balance, have to mitigate in favour of the court exercising discretion to hear the case.

The first factor was whether the adversaries in the case still had a stake in the outcome. Sopinka noted that they did. "The appeal was fully argued with as much zeal and dedication on both sides as if the matter were not moot," indicating that both sides were very concerned about how the Supreme Court would decide the issue.

The second factor was "judicial economy, which requires that a court examine the circumstances of a case to determine if it is worthwhile to allot the required judicial resources to resolve the moot issue." From this perspective, Sopinka implied that even if the court were to decide that a fetus could claim Charter protection, such a decision would not make future litigation on the same issue unnecessary. It would still be necessary for the court to consider the new abortion legislation, and to balance a woman's right to security of the person against a fetal right to life. Thus, such a decision could result in uncertainty that would not be in the public interest, and so this factor augured against the court exercising discretion to hear the case.

The third factor was that the judiciary "should be sensitive to the extent that it may be departing from its traditional role." In this case, Sopinka observed that if the court were to answer the abstract question about fetal rights, this "would in effect sanction a private reference." (Recall that only cabinets may send reference questions to the appropriate court. Sopinka was wary of private citizens gaining the ability to do the same through requiring the courts to answer moot questions.) This third factor, therefore, also suggested that the court should not hear the case. Taking into account all three factors, Sopinka reasoned that on balance it would be unwise for the court to hear it.

In addition, Sopinka declared that Borowski no longer had standing to pursue the appeal. He noted that there had been two significant changes in the nature of the case since Borowski was originally granted standing by the Supreme Court in 1981: section 251 of the *Criminal Code* had been struck down in the *Morgentaler* decision, and Borowski's claim had shifted since 1981 to one primarily based on the *Charter*. Moreover, standing could be based neither on section 24(1) of the *Charter* (which provides standing only to those whose rights have been personally infringed or denied) nor on section 52(1) of the *Constitution Act, 1982* (which provides standing to those challenging an actual law).

In concluding the judgment, Sopinka had some harsh words for the federal Crown for refusing to take a stand on whether the litigation should proceed before and during the election campaign.

> In my opinion, in lieu of applying to adjourn the appeal,
> the [Crown] should have moved to quash. Certainly, such a
> motion should have been brought after the adjournment was
> denied. Failure to do so has resulted in the needless expense
> to [Borowski] of preparing and arguing the appeal before this

> *Court. In the circumstance, it is appropriate that the [Crown]*
> *pay to [Borowski] the costs of the appeal.*[27]

In spite of the minor victory of being awarded costs, Borowski was upset by and angry over his loss. He made the following comments to the press:

> *I'm glad I did not come to Ottawa for the decision . . . I*
> *probably would have gone into the court and punched the*
> *judges in the nose. It looks to me like it [hearing the case] was*
> *a gimmick, a charade, a trick they played on us . . . I think*
> *it would be a waste of my time to ever go back before those*
> *gutless . . . judges who wasted ten years of our time.*[28]

With regard to being awarded costs, Borowski revealed that the Alliance Against Abortion, of which he was president, had spent $850,000 in ten years on the litigation. The costs awarded by the Supreme Court, in the neighbourhood of $1,000, were no consolation to him.

If Borowski had won, no doubt the pro-choice supporters would have been equally as disappointed. This situation underlines how much the Supreme Court stands to lose in terms of legitimacy and prestige when deciding controversial moral issues framed as Charter claims — no matter how it decides them.

TREMBLAY V. DAIGLE (1989)[29]

The reprieve that the outcome of *Borowski* gave the Supreme Court in having to deal squarely with the issue of fetal rights was short-lived. The Supreme Court was forced to decide whether a fetus is a "person" protected by the *Charter* in an extraordinary case in the summer of 1989.

Chantal Daigle and Jean-Guy Tremblay had been living together for five months. When they separated, Daigle was eighteen weeks pregnant and decided to get an abortion. Tremblay went to the Quebec Superior Court to obtain an injunction to stop the abortion. He argued that a fetus is a human being under the Quebec *Charter of Human Rights and Freedoms* and the *Canadian Charter of Rights*, and therefore has a right to life. The fetus is recognized as a juridical person in some parts of the Quebec *Civil*

Code, which allows for the appointment of a "curator" for an unborn child in some cases. The judge noted a conflict between the fetal right to life and the right of the mother to liberty and security of the person under s. 7 of the *Charter* but ruled that the fetal right took precedence. Daigle appealed to the Quebec Court of Appeal and lost. When she was twenty-one weeks pregnant, she appealed to the Supreme Court of Canada for leave to appeal, but by then it was getting so late in the pregnancy that it was likely that no doctor in Canada might be found to perform an abortion. No Quebec hospital would permit an abortion after twenty weeks, so an abortion would be possible only in the United States. Because of the urgency, the Supreme Court agreed on August 1, 1989, to hear the application on August 8 with all judges present. There were several intervenors in the case — including both pro-life and pro-choice groups — which prepared their submissions on very short notice.[30] The Attorney General of Quebec intervened to support of the government of Quebec's power to legislate with respect to abortion but did not take an explicit position on fetal rights.

Just after the lunch break on the day of the hearing, the judges were shocked to learn from Daigle's lawyer that Daigle had already had an abortion in the US. The case was therefore moot, but further to the guidelines set by the *Borowski* decision about whether the court should hear moot cases, Daigle's lawyer requested the court to decide the case because there was still a live controversy about fetal rights. The court accepted this reasoning and continued the hearing.

After taking another break, the court delivered its decision orally from the bench. Tremblay lost because the court declared that a fetus is not a person for the purposes of either the Quebec or Canadian *Charters*. A fetus must be born alive to attain legal personhood.

It should be kept in mind that Parliament and provincial legislatures have the power to enact legislation to protect a fetus that is not yet born. Such legislation could provide rights to the fetus, but *legislated* rights, not Charter rights. However, any such legislation would need to comply with s. 7 of the *Charter*, which guarantees women's rights to life, liberty, and security of the person.

MCKINNEY (1990) AND AGE DISCRIMINATION

In 1986 an application was made in the High Court of Ontario by several professors and a librarian that compulsory retirement provisions at York University, the University of Guelph, the University of Toronto, and Laurentian University violated section 15 of the *Charter*. The professors and the librarian lost their case and appealed. The Ontario Court of Appeal handed down its decision in December of 1987.[31]

There were three major issues: whether the *Charter* applies to the personnel policies of universities; if so, whether compulsory retirement is a violation of the *Charter* that cannot be upheld under section 1; and whether the provisions of the Ontario *Human Rights Code* that permit compulsory retirement constitute a violation of the *Charter* that cannot be justified under section 1.

With regard to the first issue, the Court of Appeal decided that the *Charter* does not apply to the personnel policies of universities because no government action is involved there. The judges claimed that there was an insufficient link between government control and the private nature of university personnel policies to invoke the *Charter*. "With respect to employment of professors, they are masters in their own houses." Because the *Charter* did not apply, the second issue became irrelevant.

The third issue, which concerned the Ontario *Human Rights Code*, became the most important. The *Human Rights Code* prohibits discrimination on the basis of age in the private sector between the ages of eighteen and sixty-five. The five-judge panel agreed that the exclusion of those over sixty-five from the protection of the *Code* violates section 15 of the *Charter*. However, four of them concluded that the violation is a reasonable limit under section 1.

In applying the Oakes test for reasonable limits, the majority wrote that the objectives of the exclusion of the over-sixty-five age group from the protection of the *Code* were twofold: to strike a compromise between, on the one hand, the right to work regardless of age and the right to retire with a guaranteed pension and, on the other, the need to promote renewal of the workforce through providing employment opportunities to younger people. After reviewing evidence from social scientists, the majority concluded that these objectives were "pressing and substantial" and that therefore the requirements of part one of the Oakes test had been met.

With respect to the rational-connection test, the majority found that the exclusion of those over sixty-five from the protection of the *Code* was a sensible way to achieve the two objectives. With regard to the second factor — minimal impairment of the right to equality — the judges noted that many free and democratic countries have legislated provisions for compulsory retirement, including the United Kingdom, Ireland, West Germany, Japan, and Norway. In the United States, the Supreme Court had found that federal and state laws that provide for compulsory retirement meet the equal-protection requirements of the US *Bill of Rights*. In Canada, about half of the workforce is subject to contractual provisions that provide for mandatory retirement, usually at age sixty-five. As a result, tax reductions apply at sixty-five, as well as a number of other benefits for seniors. The judges concluded:

> *In the university context, bearing in mind the extent to*
> *which 65 years of age has been adopted as the normal age of*
> *retirement both by the universities and generally, the extent to*
> *which the financing of pension plans has been based upon it,*
> *and the impact which the elimination of mandatory retirement*
> *would have on faculty renewal, the impairment of the right*
> *to freedom from discrimination on the basis of age by [the*
> Human Rights Code] *was as little as possible.*[32]

The majority also concluded that the exclusion of over-sixty-fives passed the third test — overall proportionality. They pointed out that no one is exempt from the aging process, so that compulsory retirement provisions are liable to affect everyone. Moreover, they noted that the universities are free to make special arrangements to retain certain faculty who are over sixty-five.

The Ontario Court of Appeal decision was appealed to the Supreme Court of Canada, which issued its judgment in 1990.[33] A seven-judge panel of the Supreme Court upheld the Ontario Court of Appeal decision by a five to two majority.[34] The majority decision exempted universities from Charter scrutiny and upheld the Ontario *Human Rights Code*'s exclusion of age discrimination protection for those over sixty-five for essentially the same reasons as those expressed by the majority in the Ontario Court of

Appeal. However, Justice Wilson dissented, arguing that universities are covered by the *Charter of Rights* because there was sufficient connection with government, and that the exclusion of those over sixty-five in the Ontario *Human Rights Code* does not pass the Oakes test. L'Heureux-Dubé also dissented, agreeing with Wilson that the Ontario *Human Rights Code* exemption does not pass the Oakes test, but agreeing with the majority that universities are not sufficiently connected with government to be covered by the *Charter*.

The issue of the fairness or unfairness of compulsory retirement will remain with us for as long as there are labour market issues impacted by government retirement policy. It is a complex issue that is viewed differently according to changing economic circumstances affecting pension plans. At the time of this book's publication, many Canadian universities have abolished compulsory retirement for budgetary and labour market reasons. However, should circumstances change, the Supreme Court has given universities — and other employers — permission to reintroduce compulsory retirement without violating the *Charter*.

OTHER CHARTER EQUALITY DECISIONS UP TO 1990

Two Supreme Court decisions concerning the equality provisions in the human rights codes are significant because they constitute a prelude to the court's treatment of the concept of systemic discrimination — that is, indirect and unintentional discrimination — in Charter cases. In the *Bhinder* decision of 1985,[35] the Supreme Court held that a Sikh who was fired from his job for refusing to replace his turban with a hard hat was the victim of systemic discrimination contrary to the Canadian *Human Rights Act*. Although the regulations of K. S. Bhinder's employer, Canadian National, concerning the wearing of hard hats had not been established to discriminate against Sikhs, they had that effect. Bhinder had hoped to be reinstated in his job through the litigation. The court did not order Bhinder reinstated, however, because the *Act* allowed discrimination in the case of a "bona fide occupational requirement," and the regulation requiring the wearing of a hard hat was such a requirement.

In another case also decided in 1985, *Ontario Human Rights Commission and O'Malley v. Simpsons-Sears Ltd.*,[36] the court considered whether an employee of Simpsons-Sears who had been demoted for refusing to work on Saturdays when she became a Seventh Day Adventist had been subjected to systemic discrimination contrary to the Ontario *Human Rights Code*. Theresa O'Malley claimed that the policy of Simpsons-Sears to require employees at certain levels to work on Saturdays had the effect of discriminating against Seventh Day Adventists, even though the company had not deliberately set out to discriminate. Because the Ontario *Human Rights Code* has no "bona fide occupational requirement" clause, O'Malley won her case. The court concluded that in instances where a company's policies resulted in systemic discrimination, the company had a duty to accommodate disadvantaged employees up to the point of "undue hardship" for the company.

The *Charter* was not in effect when litigation began in these two cases, so the issue of whether the two codes conformed with the *Charter* did not arise. However, the *Charter* was in effect when the Supreme Court issued its decisions in *Bhinder* and *O'Malley*, and the court has been careful since 1982 to apply the same basic principles when determining human rights issues, whether or not the *Charter* is invoked. The *Bhinder* and *O'Malley* cases are therefore important for two reasons. First, they outline the court's approach toward systemic discrimination. Second, they indicate that businesses have a duty to accommodate the religious practices of their employees up to the point of undue hardship. In the case of Bhinder, allowing Sikh employees to wear turbans instead of hard hats would have exposed the employer to liability risks, which would constitute undue hardship. In the case of O'Malley, Simpsons-Sears was a large company with many employees, and arranging for O'Malley to have Saturdays off would not have resulted in undue hardship, so the company had to accommodate.

Another case involving human rights codes deserves mention because it overruled the *Bliss* decision — the infamous Bill of Rights case about pregnancy decided in 1979.[37] Recall from chapter 1 that in *Bliss*, the Supreme Court gave the stamp of approval to discrimination based on pregnancy because such discrimination could not be considered discrimination based on sex. In the *Brooks* case,[38] decided in May 1989, the Supreme Court considered a claim under the Manitoba *Human Rights Act*. Female employees claimed that a company's group insurance plan, which provided weekly benefits for loss of pay because of accident or illness but which excluded pregnancy, constituted discrimination based on sex. The Supreme Court agreed. Chief Justice Dickson's judgment, which all judges on the panel supported, declared that "those who bear children and benefit society as a whole should not be economically or socially disadvantaged." Holding that pregnancy cannot be separated from gender, the court overruled *Bliss*.

Because the court has attempted to interpret words that appear in both the *Charter* and the human rights codes similarly — like "discrimination" — the *Brooks* decision signaled that discrimination in section 15 of the *Charter* includes discrimination based on pregnancy.

SIGNIFICANT SUPREME COURT DECISIONS ON EQUALITY IN THE 1990s
SCHACHTER V. CANADA (1992)[39]

Prior to 1992, Canada's *Unemployment Insurance Act* provided up to fifteen weeks paternity leave for adoptive fathers that could be shared with adoptive mothers, but there was no provision for paternity leave for birth fathers. Shalom Schachter, a lawyer and a birth father, was aware of this discrepancy and applied for paternity leave, but of course his application was denied. He eventually filed suit in the Federal Court, Trial Division, claiming that the *Unemployment Insurance Act* violated s. 15 of the *Charter*. He won. This decision was appealed by the Crown to the Federal Court's Appeal Division, and Schachter again won.

The remedy ordered by the Federal Court of Appeal under s. 24(1) of the *Charter* was to "read in" birth fathers to the relevant section of the *Unemployment Insurance Act* so that birth fathers could share fifteen weeks of parental leave, just as adoptive fathers could. This decision was subjected to severe criticism in the media and the academic world because in a sense, the Federal Court of Appeal was ordering the federal government to spend more money, and in the Westminster system of government, which Canada in inherited from the United Kingdom, all expenditures must be approved by Parliament. The reason for the additional expenditure is that even today, men typically make more money than women, so the cost of parental leave for fathers — being tied to their incomes, would be higher on average than the cost of parental leave for mothers.

As a reaction to the Federal Court of Appeal decision, the federal government amended the *Unemployment Insurance Act* to give birth fathers and adoptive fathers the same rights to apply for shared parental leave, but over a ten-week period rather than a fifteen-week period so that the new provisions would cost the government about the same as it had spent under the old fifteen week-program.

In spite of the legislative change, the Federal Court of Appeal decision was appealed by the federal Crown to the Supreme Court of Canada because of the nature of the remedy ordered by the Federal Court of Appeal. The Supreme Court, in a five to two decision, overturned the reading-in remedy imposed by the lower court and replaced it with the following formula for a remedy in situations like this. First, the basic principle should be the least interference with government legislation. Second, if either of the first two parts of the Oakes test are not met (a substantially important objective that can override a right, and the test of a rational connection between the government objective and the means used), then the offending part of the legislation should be struck down. Third, if either of the final two parts of the Oakes test are not met (a justified violation of a right should interfere with the right as little as necessary, and violation of the right must do more good than harm), the appropriate remedy could be reading in, selective severance of the offending provision, or striking down the offending provision, plus suspending the declaration of invalidity to give the legislature time to find a solution that both complies with the *Charter* and meets its own budgetary goals.

In this case, the Supreme Court agreed that the old parental leave provision violated the *Charter* and should be struck down. However, the court would have suspended the declaration of invalidity to give Parliament time to act. But in this case, suspension was not necessary because Parliament had acted the year before the Supreme Court decision to enact the new ten-week parental leave provisions that allowed both fathers and mothers to share the leave.

Schachter is important for two reasons. First, it sets out the test for the judicial imposition of remedies under s. 24(1) of the *Charter*. Second, it illustrates a limitation of judicial review under the *Charter* impacting policy issues.

There were good reasons why the old fifteen-week parental leave provisions were available to adoptive fathers but not birth fathers. When a child is adopted, the adoptive parents generally do not have nine months to prepare for his arrival; they often have only a few days or weeks. Therefore, if the adoption is by two parents, both are needed to prepare for the arrival, and to help the adoptive child, who may be several years old, settle in. However, neither the Federal Court, the Federal Court of Appeal, nor the Supreme Court of Canada had access to this policy information, because no section 1 evidence was provided by the Crown. When adoptive parents first heard about the *Schachter* litigation, some attempted to raise funds to intervene in the judicial proceedings, but by the time some funds were raised, it was too late. The federal government had already changed the *Unemployment Insurance Act* in a way that advantaged birth fathers, but disadvantaged adoptive parents because of the reduction of parental leave from fifteen weeks to ten.

The quality of judicial review under the *Charter* is only as good as the evidence the courts have to consider, and sometimes that evidence is incomplete.

SYMES V. CANADA (1993)[40]

Elizabeth Symes was a partner in a law firm in the mid-1980s who had hired a nanny to help care for her two children so that she could continue with her career. Symes attempted to deduct the full cost of the nanny's wages (between $10,000 and $14,000, depending on the year) from her own income as a business expense. Revenue Canada did not allow the deductions, instead allowing her to claim child care expenses of between $1,000 and $4,000 annually, depending on the year. Symes filed suit in the Federal Court, Trial Division, claiming that the situation amounted to discrimination based on sex. Her reasoning was that women bear the burden of child care more than men, and that unless women are allowed to deduct the full cost of child care from their income, they will be discouraged from pursuing their careers, and feel forced, for economic reasons, to abandon or delay their careers in order to care for their children. Symes won in the Trial Division, but the decision was appealed to the Federal Court of Appeal, where she lost. She appealed to the Supreme Court of Canada, and lost in a seven to two decision in which the two female judges, L'Heureux-Dubé and McLachlin, dissented.

The seven male judges in the majority found that there was no convincing evidence that the limit to the child care deduction resulted in an adverse effect on women, or that women were impacted more than men. Therefore, there was no definitive evidence that the child care expenses section of the *Income Tax Act* constituted discrimination based on sex.

The two female judges pointed out that during the previous few decades, the Canadian labour market had gone through fundamental changes, and that the majority of women were then in the labour force. They took judicial notice of the fact that not allowing the full cost of child care as a business expense had a differential impact on women. As convincing as this perspective may be, it is possible that the male majority on the court was reluctant to intervene in such a major way to tamper with the *Income Tax Act*, especially after the controversy surrounding the Federal Court, Trial Division's interventionist approach in *Schachter*, and the Supreme Court's subsequent damping down of the lower court's activism.

THIBAUDEAU V. CANADA (1995)[41]

Thibaudeau was another case involving alleged discrimination based on sex in the *Income Tax Act* that split the Supreme Court down gender lines.

In 1987, Suzanne Thibaudeau and her husband divorced. Ms. Thibaudeau was awarded custody of their two children, and her former husband was ordered to pay alimony of an indexed amount of $1,150 a month to Thibaudeau for the exclusive benefit of the children.[42]

At that time, the *Income Tax Act* provisions relating to the child-maintenance payments of divorced or separated couples specified that the spouse receiving the payments had to pay income tax on the alimony, and the spouse making the payments could deduct the alimony amount from his or her income for tax purposes. In the majority of divorces, the mother receives custody, and she generally earns less than the father. The result was that the amount of money saved by the father by not paying taxes on income devoted to alimony was greater than the tax paid by the mother receiving the alimony. This left the two of them with a higher after-tax pooled income than would have been the case if the father's income devoted to alimony was taxed, and the alimony received by the mother was not. In this case, however, Thibaudeau earned more money than her former husband, and she saw the *Income Tax Act*'s provisions as discriminatory against women by enforcing a policy based on stereotypes. To correct this perceived discrimination, in 1989 Thibaudeau reported the alimony she received in her children's income tax returns rather than in her own. This procedure was "corrected" by Revenue Canada, and the alimony was added on to Thibaudeau's income. Thibaudeau then appealed to the Tax Court of Canada, claiming that the *Income Tax Act* provisions relating to taxation of alimony constituted discrimination against women, and further appeals eventually reached the Supreme Court of Canada.

The five judges in the majority, all men, did not find a violation of s. 15 of the *Charter* in the impugned provisions of the *Income Tax Act*. "The purpose of s. 15(1) is to protect human dignity by ensuring that all individuals are recognized at law as being equally deserving of concern, respect, and consideration."[43] What is important is the actual *effect* of the impugned provisions, which does not necessarily result in a burden on custodial women who earn more than their former husbands, because judicial orders in relation to alimony are supposed to take into account this situation.

The two dissenting judges, L'Heureux-Dubé and McLachlin, saw a deeper issue here: that the impugned provisions of the *Income Tax Act* were based on a stereotype — that women generally earn less than men — and they saw these provisions as maintaining the stereotype rather than promoting a society with genuine gender equality. They found that the impugned provisions violated s. 15 and could not be saved under s. 1.

Ironically, either the federal government expected to lose the case, or had already concluded that Thibaudeau and the women's groups supporting her were right. Shortly after the Supreme Court decision, the government announced changes to the custodial provisions of the *Income Tax Act* that reduced the tax burden on spouses receiving child support payments, 98 per cent of whom were women.[44] Even though these changes reduced the tax burden on many custodial mothers, they increased the tax burden on those paying alimony, resulting in less after-tax money being available for child support, and resulting in an increase in tax revenue for the federal government, in a sense at the expense of the children of divorced couples.

This case illustrates the complexity of some gender discrimination issues, especially those related to economic matters. It also shows that male and female judges may tend to view these issues from different perspectives based not only on life experience, but possibly because of the conscious or unconscious influences of gender stereotyping.

ELDRIDGE (1997)[45]

In the mid-1990s, Robin Susan Eldridge and two other deaf people sought a declaration from the British Columbia Court of Appeal "that the failure to provide sign language interpreters as an insured benefit under the Medical Services Plan violates s. 15(1) of the *Canadian Charter of Rights and Freedoms*."[46] Their argument was that although the BC Medical Services Plan covered many health care costs for them and all other British Columbians, in order to access these particular services they needed to pay for sign language interpreters out of their own pockets, while most British Columbians could access health care services without having to hire an interpreter. Given the challenges that deaf people face to find employment, and given the limited financial support available to them, Eldridge and her co-litigants argued that the BC government's refusal to pay for interpreters when they tried to access health care constituted discrimination based on their physical disability.

Eldridge lost in the Superior Court and the Court of Appeal but won in the Supreme Court of Canada in a unanimous decision written by Justice La Forest of New Brunswick. La Forest had a reputation as a conservative-minded judge but also as a champion for those with disabilities..

The Supreme Court focused on the broad issue of whether the deaf had a right to an interpreter in order to access the health care services that were available, according to legislation, to all residents of BC. La Forest acknowledged that the health care legislation did not itself violate the *Charter*. However, the failure of the BC government to be proactive in ensuring that deaf people could access publicly available health care did violate the *Charter* and could not be saved under section 1.

This case is important not only because it was a major victory for the deaf and others with disabilities, but also because the Supreme Court decision forced the BC government to spend additional funds to ensure deaf people access to health care services. Evidence the Supreme Court had access to indicated that the cost to the government would be minimal. However, the costs have been greater than originally anticipated.[47] Accurate cost estimates may not have been introduced into evidence at trial because the eventual outcome of the case at the Supreme Court level was not anticipated. It is an open question as to whether the Supreme Court would have decided as it did if it had accurate information about costs, given that the court is reluctant to make decisions that would clearly mandate significant new government expenditures. In such cases, the court is more likely to declare a violation of the *Charter* and suspend a declaration or order to give the government time to find a remedy it can afford. Regardless, *Eldridge* is an important victory for the disabled community and a reminder to government policy-makers that the situation of the disabled must be considered in the development of all government programs.

LAW V. CANADA (1999)[48]

The Canada Pension Plan (CPP) includes survivor benefits for some — but not all — spouses left behind after the death of a partner who was receiving CPP. Surviving partners who are under thirty-five, have no children, and are not disabled receive no survivor benefits, and for those between thirty-five and forty-five, the benefits are reduced. The purpose of this provision is to encourage younger people who lose a spouse to recover from the loss as soon as possible and to get on their feet again because they are young enough to do so.

Nancy and Jason Law were married in 1980 and ran a family business together. Jason died in 1990 at the age of fifty, leaving behind Nancy, who was only thirty at the time. She carried on with the business, but it did not do as well financially. Jason had paid into CPP for twenty-two years, and Nancy was understandably disappointed when, because of her age, she was denied survivor benefits. As well, various women's groups that supported her saw the CPP survivor benefits provisions as discrimination based both on age and gender, given that the labour market prospects of widowed women are not as promising as those of widowed men.[49] Nancy Law took her case to the Pension Plan Review Tribunal, which agreed that discrimination had occurred but nevertheless upheld the benefits scheme under s. 1 of the *Charter*. Various appeals ensued, and the case ended up in the Supreme Court of Canada. A unanimous decision for a nine-judge panel was penned by Justice Iacobucci.

Iacobucci took the opportunity to establish guidelines for judicial interpretation of s. 15(1) of the *Charter*. He reiterated that the Supreme Court takes a purposive approach to applying the *Charter*, and from that perspective, the primary purpose of s. 15 is to prevent the violation of human dignity and freedom through stereotyping and to promote equal concern and respect. Iacobucci then reviewed the history of s. 15(1) and outlined three questions that must be asked when judges are determining, for the purposes of that section, whether a particular situation results in discrimination.

First, has there been differential treatment? Second, if there has been differential treatment, is it based on an enumerated or analogous ground in s. 15(1)? Third, does the law have a discriminatory purpose or effect such that it perpetuates the view that the person affected is less worthy of respect, and therefore be treated with less dignity, than their peers?

In addressing these questions, Iacobucci set out four factors that need to be considered in answering them.

> *(A) Pre-existing disadvantage, stereotyping, prejudice, or vulnerability experienced by the individual or group at issue*
>
> . . .
>
> *(B) The correspondence, or lack thereof, between the ground or grounds on which the claim is based and the actual need, capacity, or circumstances of the claimant or others . . .*
>
> *(C) The ameliorative purpose or effects of the impugned law upon a more disadvantaged person or group in society . . .*
>
> *(D) The nature and scope of the interest affected by the impugned law.*[50]

In this case, Iacobucci wrote that there was clearly differential treatment as a result of the CPP's survivor rules that provide no benefits to childless, able-bodied survivors under thirty-five. The differential treatment was based on age, one of the enumerated grounds. With regard to the third question, Iacobucci, taking into account the four factors, wrote that the CPP provisions did not have a discriminatory effect that resulted in Nancy Law being treated as less worthy of respect, because able-bodied people under thirty-five with no child-care responsibilities are seen by society as in a better position to recover more quickly from a spouse's death.

The guidelines set out by the court in the *Law* decision are difficult to understand, ambiguous, and appear more subjective than objective. Although the Supreme Court applied the Law test in several subsequent equality cases as a supplement to the Andrews test, in 2008 in the *Kapp* decision (discussed later in this chapter) the Supreme Court officially recognized that the "dignity" analysis set out in *Law* is too subjective, and so the court restated and simplified the Law test for equality.[51]

SAME-SEX CASES IN THE 1990s AND 2000s: *EGAN* (1995), *VRIEND* (1998), *M. V. H.* (1999), AND *REFERENCE RE SAME-SEX MARRIAGE* (2004)

Since the mid-1990s, the Supreme Court has cautiously but increasingly recognized that discrimination against homosexuals is a form of discrimination that is not acceptable under the *Canadian Charter of Rights and Freedoms*. The four most important cases during this period were *Egan* (1995), *Vriend* (1998), *M. v. H.* (1999), and the *Reference re Same-Sex Marriage* (2004). It is likely that the court took this cautious approach so as not to move too far ahead of public opinion and also to keep up with a changing social consensus that increasingly recognized the equal worth and dignity of homosexuals. Miriam Smith, a past president of the Canadian Political Science Association, argues that gays and lesbians may have benefitted from the *Charter of Rights* more than any other disadvantaged group.[52]

EGAN V. CANADA (1995)[53]

At issue in this case was whether the failure of the federal *Old Age Security Act* to include same-sex couples in the definition of "spouse" for the calculation of Old Age Security (OAS) payments was a violation of s. 15(1) of the *Charter,* constituting discrimination based on sexual orientation — analogous to the enumerated ground of "sex." Egan and his same-sex partner had cohabited for many years and were in danger of falling into poverty without the OAS spousal benefit when they reached retirement age.

The decision was close. Four judges, La Forest, Lamer, Gonthier, and Major, found no violation of s. 15(1). However, five judges — L'Heureux-Dubé and Cory, joined by Sopinka, McLachlin, and Iacobucci, found that the Old Age Security provision violated s. 15(1) of the *Charter* in that sexual orientation is analogous to gender discrimination. Thus, for the first time, a majority on the Supreme Court recognized that the *Charter* prohibits discrimination based on sexual orientation. Four of these five found that the OAS definition of spouse could not be saved through s. 1 analysis. Justice Sopinka held the swing vote. Although he found that the OAS definition of spouse constituted a violation of s. 15, in this case he found it could be justified under s. 1 because the purpose of the provision was to ensure that women who had left the labour market in order to care for children would be adequately supported in their retirement years. This purpose satisfied all parts of the Oakes test, according to Sopinka. However, in Sopinka's judgment there were hints that governments should take the opportunity to rethink their policies affecting same-sex couples in the light of the majority judgment that discrimination based on sexual orientation is a violation of s. 15(1) which depending on the impugned legislation, may or may not be justifiable through the application of the Oakes test.

In spite of Egan's loss regarding the narrow issue of whether Old Age Security legislation should treat gay and straight couples equally, the case can be viewed as the court's first recognition of the equality rights of gays and lesbians, and a foundation upon which future gay rights cases could be established.

VRIEND V. ALBERTA (1998)[54]

Delwin Vriend worked as a laboratory assistant at a community college in Edmonton, Alberta, that advertises itself as "Christian." When college administrators learned that he was homosexual, despite several years' worth of positive performance evaluations, he was dismissed because college policy prohibited homosexuality.

Vriend filed a complaint with the Alberta Human Rights Commission. The commission did not pursue the issue because although its governing legislation, Alberta's *Individual Rights Protection Act*, prohibited discrimination in employment, it did not specifically mention discrimination based on sexual orientation. Vriend applied to Alberta's superior court, the Court of Queen's Bench, for a declaration that would broaden the judicial interpretation of the *Individual Rights Protection Act* and won. However, an appeal from that decision eventually reached the Supreme Court of Canada.

All nine judges heard the appeal, and they were unanimous that the Alberta *Individual Rights Protection Act*, by not specifying sexual orientation, violated s. 15(1) of the *Charter*. The court concluded that the Alberta government's objective in not including sexual orientation in the *Act* was to deny homosexuals equal treatment, and that this objective was neither pressing nor substantial. Even so, the court considered all three prongs of the second part of the Oakes test and found that the exclusion of sexual orientation failed in each case.

The majority of the court declared that the appropriate remedy was to "read" sexual orientation into the *Individual Rights Protection Act*. Justice Major dissented in part, because he would have preferred an approach that would have given the Alberta legislature an opportunity to draft a remedy — such as repealing the *Individual Rights Protection Act* altogether. L'Heureux-Dubé also dissented in part, because she would have preferred to have broadened the *Individual Rights Protection Act* to include any group not being treated with equal concern and respect.

Alberta's premier at the time, Ralph Klein, had publicly threatened to re-enact the *Individual Rights Protection Act* as it stood, while invoking s. 33 of the *Charter* — the "notwithstanding" clause — if the Supreme Court decided to protect gay rights. However after the court's decision, the premier hesitated for several days and then announced that s. 33 would not be invoked. This was a time when more and more gay men and lesbian women were coming out, and perhaps many Alberta families had discovered that they had a homosexual relative or friend. Polls at the time indicated that a majority of Albertans supported the Supreme Court decision, and so Klein — ever the astute politician — backed off from his earlier threats.

M. V. H. (1999)

M. v. H. was an Ontario case where the issue was whether homosexual couples should be able to invoke the provincial *Family Law Act* to claim support from a former partner.[55] The case involved a lesbian couple who started living together in 1982 and also ran a business together. They split up about ten years later. After the breakup, M. claimed financial hardship and a share of the business, and invoked the Ontario *Family Law Act* (FLA) to claim support from her former partner. The Ontario *Family Law Act*, amongst other things, sets out rules for division of assets not only between married couples, but also between couples who are not married but who have been living together in a relationship with a degree of permanency. However, s. 29 of the *FLA* defined a spouse as a man or a woman who had been in a conjugal[56] relationship, which had a specific degree of permanence, with someone of the opposite sex. In order to invoke the *FLA*, M. also had to challenge the constitutional validity of the *FLA's* definition of spouse.

The Attorney General of Ontario conceded that s. 29 violated s. 15(1) of the *Charter* in the light of the *Egan* and *Vriend* decisions, but argued, further to Sopinka's decision in *Egan*, that the definition could be upheld under s. 1 because the government needed more time to consider legislative changes. However, the majority of eight in this case were clearly impatient due to the fact that there had been no legislative changes contemplated for the *FLA* since the *Egan* decision four years earlier. The majority of eight found that the *FLA* definition of spouse violated s. 15(1), and for reasons similar to those given in *Vriend*, could not be justified through s. 1 analysis.

> In this case, there is significant pre-existing disadvantage and vulnerability, and these circumstances are exacerbated by the impugned legislation. The legislative provision in question draws a distinction that prevents persons in a same-sex relationship from gaining access to the court-enforced and -protected support system . . . [T]he focus of the inquiry must always remain upon the central question of whether, viewed from the perspective of the claimant, the differential treatment imposed by the legislation has the effect of violating human dignity . . .[57]

The remedy specified by the majority was a declaration that the *Family Law Act* was invalid unless it included same-sex couples, but the declaration was suspended for six months to give the legislature an opportunity to revise the *Act* to bring it into conformity with the *Charter*.[58] The lone dissenter, Justice Gonthier, would have deferred to government objectives, similar to the Supreme Court's decision in *Egan*.[59]

The majority's remedy initiated a flurry of activity by Canada's provincial, territorial, and federal governments to draft amendments to the many pieces of legislation that impacted same-sex couples, and to send them to the relevant legislative bodies in order to comply with the Supreme Court's six-month deadline.

REFERENCE RE SAME-SEX MARRIAGE (2004)[60]

After the *M. v. H.* decision, there was a good deal of pressure put on the federal government to legalize same-sex marriage in civil (but not religious) ceremonies. The *Constitution Act, 1867* divides responsibility for marriage between the federal and provincial governments, with the federal government having responsibility for "marriage and divorce," and the provincial governments for the "solemnization of marriage." For that reason, it was left to the federal government to define marriage, including who could get married. However, the federal government had never defined marriage through legislation, but rather allowed courts to defer to the common-law definition of marriage, which was "the voluntary union for life between one man and one woman, to the exclusion of all others."[61]

In 2002, the government of Jean Chrétien drafted legislation that would replace the common-law definition of marriage with a definition that would allow for homosexual couples to marry. The crux of the proposed legislation was as follows:

> 1. Marriage, for civil purposes, is the lawful union of two persons to the exclusion of all others.

> 2. Nothing in this Act affects the freedom of officials of religious groups to refuse to perform marriages

that are not in accordance with their religious beliefs.[62]

Because of strong resistance to the proposed legislation from Opposition leader Stephen Harper, and also from some within the Liberal government caucus, in 2003 the Chrétien cabinet decided to send three reference questions, as follows, to the Supreme Court about the constitutionality of the proposed legislation.

> 1. *Is the annexed* Proposal for an Act Respecting Certain Aspects of Legal Capacity for Marriage for Civil Purposes *within the exclusive legislative authority of the Parliament of Canada? If not, in what particular or particulars, and to what extent?*

> 2. *If the answer to question 1 is yes, is section 1 of the proposal, which extends capacity to marry to persons of the same sex, consistent with the* Canadian Charter of Rights and Freedoms? *If not, in what particular or particulars, and to what extent?*

> 3. *Does the freedom of religion guaranteed by paragraph 2(a) of the* Canadian Charter of Rights and Freedoms *protect religious officials from being compelled to perform a marriage between two persons of the same sex that is contrary to their religious beliefs?*

Some of those opposed to same-sex marriage had argued that the proposed federal legislation was unconstitutional either on division of powers grounds or Charter grounds, and hence the first question dealt with federal legislative competence, and the second question referred to the *Charter*. Others argued that s. 2 of the proposed legislation did not, in fact, prevent religious groups from being forced to marry homosexual couples, and hence the third question.

However, before the Supreme Court could address these three questions, Paul Martin replaced Jean Chrétien as prime minister, and Martin had concerns about whether the proposed legislation was actually required by the *Charter,* or whether the government had the choice of leaving things as they stood. As a result, the Martin cabinet appended a fourth question to the other three that in a roundabout way asked the court whether the *Charter* requires the legalization of same-sex marriage.

> *4. Is the opposite-sex requirement for marriage for civil purposes, as established by the common law and set out for Quebec in section 5 of the* Federal Law Civil Law Harmonization Act, No. 1, *consistent with the* Canadian Charter of Rights and Freedoms? *If not, in what particular or particulars and to what extent?*

But the option of leaving things as they stood was problematic. Following the *M. v. H.* decision, gay couples who wanted to marry had begun litigation to request superior courts in several provinces and territories and to strike down the opposite-sex requirement for marriage. As a result, beginning in 2002 in Quebec, and 2003 in British Columbia and Ontario, they succeeded. Significantly, the federal Crown decided to accept these decisions and not appeal them further. By the time of the release of the Supreme Court's same-sex marriage reference in 2004, superior courts in Yukon, Nova Scotia, Saskatchewan, and Manitoba had also made decisions validating same-sex weddings that were not appealed by the federal Crown.[63] As a result thousands of gay couples got married in the jurisdictions in which the common-law definition of marriage had been struck down. Thus, prior to the Supreme Court's decision, Canada had already become amongst the first countries in the world to permit same-sex marriage.

The unanimous decision of the Supreme Court panel, which included all nine judges, was attributed to "The Court" — a signal from the court that the court was firm in its opinion. The Supreme Court always has the option of refusing to answer a reference question if the question does not have a legal basis. The court affirmed that all four reference questions had a legal basis. However, the court noted that there was no precedent for the court to reconsider a matter that had already been settled in a lower court, but had not been appealed to a higher court. The Supreme Court noted that because the common-law definition of marriage had already been struck down in lower courts and not appealed by the federal Crown, that matter was settled, and therefore the fourth reference question was redundant and the Supreme Court refused to answer it.[64] Furthermore, the court noted that "[t]he government has stated its intention to address the issue of same-sex marriage by introducing legislation regardless of our opinion on this question."[65] In other words, it was clear to the court that the government, through the fourth question, was attempting to set up the Supreme Court as the body to blame for forcing the government to legalize same-sex marriage, and the court would have none of that.

The court's task in answering the first three reference questions was much simpler. Clearly, s. 91(26) of the *Constitution Act, 1867*, "Marriage and Divorce," gives the federal Parliament the exclusive legislative authority to enact the proposed same-sex marriage legislation, and that takes care of question one.

With regard to question two, s. 92(12) of the *Constitution Act, 1867* gives the provinces exclusive jurisdiction to the "Solemnization of Marriage," which includes legislation about who can perform marriage ceremonies and under what circumstances. Therefore, s. 2 of the proposed same-sex marriage legislation is not within the legislative authority of Parliament. The federal Crown had argued that s. 2 of the proposed legislation was merely attempting to make clear that the legislation would in no way erode provincial powers to determine how marriages are performed, but the Supreme Court pointed out that the clarification of provincial powers had no place in federal legislation.[66]

Reference question three, regarding whether s. 2(a) of the *Charter* protects religious officials from being forced to perform a marriage between homosexuals if doing so would be contrary to their religious beliefs, was answered in the affirmative:

> *If a promulgated statute were to enact compulsion, we*
> *conclude that such compulsion would almost certainly run*
> *afoul of the* Charter *guarantee of freedom of religion, given*
> *the expansive protection afforded to religion by s. 2(a) of the*
> Charter.

> *The right to freedom of religion enshrined in s. 2(a) of*
> *the* Charter *encompasses the right to believe and entertain*
> *the religious beliefs of one's choice, the right to declare one's*
> *religious beliefs openly, and the right to manifest religious*
> *belief by worship, teaching, dissemination, and religious*
> *practice:* Big M Drug Mart . . . *The performance of religious*
> *rites is a fundamental aspect of religious practice. It therefore*
> *seems clear that state compulsion on religious officials to*
> *perform same-sex marriages contrary to their religious beliefs*
> *would violate the guarantee of freedom of religion under s.*
> *2(a) of the* Charter.
> *It also seems apparent that, absent exceptional*
> *circumstances which we cannot at present foresee, such a*
> *violation could not be justified under s. 1 of the* Charter.[67]

Following the Supreme Court's reference decision, Parliament enacted legislation to define marriage as a union between two persons. But that was not the end of the controversy. During the federal election campaign of 2006, in which Stephen Harper's Conservatives were elected with a minority, Harper promised that if elected, his government would hold a free vote (a vote not controlled by party discipline) on the question of repealing this legislation and reinstating the traditional definition of marriage. A free vote was held in December of 2006, and a motion to call on the government to reinstate the traditional definition of marriage was defeated by a vote of 175–123.[68] Subsequently, the Conservative government has considered the matter settled.

OTHER EQUALITY CASES IN THE 2000s

The most important Supreme Court decisions on equality thus far in the 2000s have been *Gossselin v. Quebec* (2002), *Auton v. BC* (2004), *Newfoundland v. NAPE* (2004), and *R. v. Kapp* (2008). The first three of these decisions indicated that the Supreme Court had softened its advocacy of a broad social-equality jurisprudence and, in a sense, was waiting for Canadian society to adjust to this broader approach to social equality in cases such as those involving same-sex relations and the right of the deaf to have interpreters to access health care. The *Kapp* decision, although continuing to reformulate the court's approach to s. 15(1) by restating the *Law* decision of 1999, also enhanced the importance of s. 15(2), which specifically constitutionalizes affirmative action programs.

GOSSSELIN V. QUEBEC (2002)[69]

Between 1984 and 1989, the Quebec National Assembly's social welfare legislation reduced benefits to those recipients between eighteen and thirty to about one-third of the amount that those over thirty were eligible to receive. However, the under-thirties could increase their welfare benefits to that of the over-thirties (or close to it) by participating in one of several educational or work experience programs.

Louise Gosselin was a welfare recipient who was twenty-five when these provisions came into effect. She had psychological problems and as a result was not able to hold on to a job for very long. When the new provisions came into effect, she did participate in several of the programs that would allow her to claim a higher benefit, but she was not able to follow through with any of them because of her personal challenges.

Recall that the Parti Québécois government had introduced a blanket override of ss. 2 and 7 to 15 of the *Charter of Rights* in 1982 as a protest against Quebec not signing on to the new constitutional deal. The override expired in 1987 and was not renewed. Gosselin initiated a class action suit in the Quebec Superior Court on behalf of seventy-five thousand young Quebeckers whom she claimed were being discriminated against under s. 15 of the *Charter* and having their security of the person threatened contrary to s. 7 of the *Charter* because of the 1984 welfare legislation. She sought payment of benefits denied up to the level of the benefits received by the over-thirties between 1987 and 1989, at an estimated cost of $389 million.[70] Gosselin lost at trial, won in the Quebec Court of Appeal, and lost at the Supreme Court level in a five to four decision.

Chief Justice McLachlin wrote the opinion of the majority. In answering the three fundamental questions about alleged s. 15(1) violations set out by Iacobucci in *Law*, she conceded that first there had been discriminatory treatment, and second it was based on the enumerated ground of age. However, further to the third question, she was not persuaded that the 1984–89

Quebec social welfare scheme had a discriminatory purpose or effect that perpetuated the view that Gosselin and other under-thirties were treated with less dignity and respect than the over-thirties.[71] To reach this conclusion, she considered the four contextual factors set out in the *Law* decision:

(A) Whether there is a pre-existing disadvantage, stereotyping, prejudice, or vulnerability experienced by the individual or group at issue: McLachlin could find no persuasive evidence that under-thirties in Quebec had been traditionally discriminated against in the same way that people of advanced age sometime are, or women had been and sometimes still are. On the contrary, she stressed that the programs set up by the government were intended to help under-thirties find employment.[72]

(B) An analysis of the relation between age — the ground on which the claim was based — and the actual need, capacity, or circumstances of the claimant's group (the under-thirties in Quebec): McLachlin's review of this factor stressed that the Quebec government had devised a reasonable policy to try to assist the under-thirties with the desperate situation regarding unemployment they faced in the mid-1980s. Whereas in the 1970s, jobs were relatively easy to obtain for all age groups in Quebec, the situation changed dramatically with the serious economic downturn in the early 1980s. The recession drove the unemployment rate

> among the young from 6 percent (1966) to 23 percent [in 1982]. At the same time, the federal government tightened eligibility requirements for federal unemployment insurance benefits, and the number of young people entering the job market for the first time surged. These three events caused an unprecedented increase in the number of people capable of working who nevertheless ended up on the welfare rolls . . . Moreover, [the under-thirties] accounted for the largest — and steadily growing — proportion of <u>new entrants</u> into the welfare system: by 1983 fully two-thirds of new welfare recipients were under thirty, and half were under the age of twenty-three.[73]

Further, McLachlin noted that the under-thirties who were most at risk of unemployment were school dropouts. Simply giving the under-thirties a larger welfare cheque would not improve their employment prospects; they needed the education and skills required for employment. Government policy was intended to provide these opportunities. Further, McLachlin noted that it was not the judiciary's role to determine whether government policy was optimal — that would take the courts too far out of their adjudicatory role and too far into the policy-making role. From the adjudicative perspective, it is enough that the evidence shows that the government's policy in relation to the actual needs of the claimant's group is reasonable.[74]

(C) An analysis of whether the ameliorative purpose or effects of the welfare policy challenged by Gosselin is designed to improve the situation of a more disadvantaged group: McLachlin compared the unemployment situation of the under-thirties with that of the over-thirties and applied the "reasonable person" test. She concluded that a reasonable person in Ms. Gosselin's situation would realize that under-thirties are in greater need of assistance in finding employment than over-thirties, and that the scheme set up was meant to encourage the under-thirties to take advantage of the help being offered before they became chronically unemployed later on.[75] The implication of this analysis is that from McLachlin's point of view, Gosselin had not adopted a "reasonable" perspective on the situation.

(D) A consideration of the nature and scope of the interests affected by the impugned law: In this case, how severe was the impact of the welfare policy on the under-thirties? McLachlin relied on the analysis of the Superior Court trial judge's decision that there was insufficient evidence to establish that the impact of the welfare policy had been detrimental overall to the under-thirties, or that it devalued young Quebeckers. No new evidence had been introduced to show that the trial judge's decision on the facts was wrong, and in the absence of such evidence, appellate courts such as the Supreme Court cannot tamper with the trial judge's findings.[76]

McLachlin's conclusion, after her analysis of the four contextual factors set out in *Law* was

> *that the impugned law did not violate the essential human*
> *dignity of welfare recipients under thirty. We must base*
> *our decision on the record before us, not on personal beliefs*
> *or hypotheticals. On the facts before us, the law did not*

discriminate against Ms. Gosselin, either individually or as a
member of the group of eighteen- to thirty-year-olds in Quebec.
The differential welfare scheme did not breach s. 15(1) of the
Canadian Charter.[77]

McLachlin also rejected Gosselin's claim that the welfare scheme violated her security of the person, as guaranteed by s. 7 of the *Charter*. She concluded that there was insufficient evidence to indicate that Gosselin had been deprived of her security because of the government policy.[78]

The minority of four dissenting judges took issue with McLachlin's analysis on a number of points. However, the following quote from Justice L'Heureux-Dubé provides an example of how the four minority judges emphasized different facts from the trial than those relied on by McLachlin to conclude that a consideration of the four contextual factors outlined in *Law* did, in fact, show that government welfare policy perpetuated the view that under-thirties were less worthy of respect, and therefore treated with less dignity, than the over-thirties, in violation of s. 15.

Of those eligible to participate in the programs, 88.8 percent
were unable to increase their benefits to the level payable to
those thirty and over. Ms. Gosselin was exposed to the risk of
severe poverty as a sole consequence of being under thirty years
of age. Ms. Gosselin's psychological and physical integrity were
breached.[79]

The *Gosselin* decision remains one of the more controversial s. 15 decisions of the court, and the question of whether the majority or minority were closest to making a reasonable decision will continue to be debated for some time.

AUTON V. BC (2004)[80]

In 1995, the parents of Connor Auton, a preschool-age child suffering from autism, and the parents of three other preschool children who also suffered from autism, along with their autistic children, initiated a suit against the British Columbia government because the BC *Medicare Protection Act* (*MPA*) would not cover the cost of applied behavioural analysis or intensive behavioural intervention (ABA/IBI) therapy for their children.

Those with autism suffer from a neurological disorder which results in them focusing inwardly so that relationships with others become difficult, and sometimes nearly impossible. Little is known about the causes of autism, and treatments are experimental. However, a 1987 study argued that ABA/IBI therapy, which involved intensive and repetitive stimuli administered to children between three and six, might be helpful, and at the trial level in 2000, the judge found that the therapy produced "significant results" in "some" cases.[81] However, the therapy was expensive — $45,000 to $60,000 annually at the time. By 1999, only Alberta and Ontario provided funding for ABA/IBI therapy, although PEI provided partial funding, and pilot projects had begun in Manitoba and Newfoundland.[82]

Auton and the other litigants won at trial in the BC Supreme Court in 2000, and also won at the Court of Appeal level in British Columbia. However, they lost at the Supreme Court of Canada, which heard the case in a seven-judge panel that included the two dissenting judges in the *Gosselin* decision. This time the court was unanimous. The decision was written by Chief Justice McLachlin.

McLachlin was able to reject the claim of Auton and others relatively simply. The first of the three questions about s. 15(1) claims listed in *Law* was whether there had been differential treatment of the claimants. McLachlin pointed out that the BC *MPA* does not include therapists who provide ABA/IBI therapy as medical practitioners. Because these therapists are not included, Auton and other autistic children cannot argue that they are effectively denied medical benefits available to others, as was the case in *Eldridge*. On that point alone, there was no violation of s. 15(1).[83]

Nevertheless, because this case was the first of its kind, McLachlin considered it prudent for the court to consider what the outcome might have been had ABA/IBI therapists been included within the *MPA*. In that case, Auton could have argued that the first two questions in the Law test would have been satisfied by affirming that the *MPA* resulted in differential treatment based on the ground of mental or physical disability. From the perspective of the third question specified in *Law*, she noted that "[i]f a benefit program excludes a particular group in a way that undercuts the overall purpose of the program, then it is likely to be discriminatory: it amounts to an arbitrary exclusion of a particular group. If, on the other hand, the exclusion is consistent with the overarching purpose and scheme of the legislation, it is unlikely to be discriminatory."[84]

The *MPA*, she argued, is intended to provide BC residents with core medical services; the funding of non-core medical services is discretionary. ABA/IBI therapy was not at the stage where it could be proven as medically required for children suffering from autism, and therefore there was no discrimination. And even if services available to autistic children are compared with services available to non-disabled people under the *MPA*, it turns out that therapies that are still in the experimental stage may or may not be covered, depending on the discretion of the policy-makers.

It is worth noting that although McLachlin addressed the third question in the Law test, she did so without specifically noting any of the four factors that the court declared in *Law* should be considered in addressing this kind of question. That kind of analysis might indicate that the court was beginning to move away from reliance on the Law test.

NEWFOUNDLAND V. NAPE (2004)[85]

In early 1988, the government of Newfoundland and Labrador agreed with the Newfoundland and Labrador Association of Public and Private Employees (NAPE) that female-dominated workplaces tended to underpay their employees in violation of the principle of equal pay for work of equal value. The government and the union agreed on a settlement that would result in wage increases to female employees in the designated workplaces (such as hospitals) over a period of four years, starting in 1988, at a cost of about $24 million. Later the same year, the province unexpectedly faced a financial crisis, the most serious in the province's history. The government was forced to introduce austerity measures and cut jobs and some services in order to avoid downgrading its credit rating and to maintain essential services. One of the cost-saving measures was to postpone the agreed-upon wage increases for underpaid female employees until 1991, and to negate liability for the costs that would have been incurred by the government between 1988 and 1991.

NAPE initiated a grievance based on s. 15(1) of the *Charter* — discrimination based on sex — and won in 1997. The government petitioned for judicial review of the grievance decision and succeeded in having it overturned at trial. The Newfoundland and Labrador Court of Appeal upheld the lower court decision in 2002. The Court of Appeal found that although there was discrimination, it could be justified under s. 1 of the *Charter* because of the serious financial crisis.

However, one of the judges on the three-judge appeal panel, Justice William Marshall, proposed a revised test for s. 1 — one in which courts must consider the doctrine of the separation of powers between the judicial and political branches of government, which would lead to deference to government policy and the avoidance of judicial activism. Marshall's admonition to revise the Oakes test, and his accompanying critique of judicial activism, made national headlines in December of 2002, and resulted in a letter of clarification by Newfoundland Chief Justice Clyde Wells that was published in the *Globe and Mail*. Wells pointed out that the revised s. 1 test was advocated by only one of the three judges on the panel, even though the other two judges had signed on to the opinion. Subsequently, Wells's old political nemesis from his days as premier of Newfoundland — John Crosby — complained to the Canadian Judicial Council, accusing Wells of violating judicial independence by explaining a judicial decision in the media. The council dismissed the complaint, noting that in extreme circumstances, a chief justice may contact the media to correct an erroneous media report about a judicial decision.[86]

It was against this backdrop that the Supreme Court issued its decision in October 2004. The unanimous panel of seven included the same judges who participated in the *Auton* decision, but the court's opinion was written by Mr. Justice Ian Binnie. Binnie upheld the Court of Appeal decision on s. 15(1), but completely rejected the revised test for s. 1 advocated by Justice Marshall.

First, with regard to s. 15(1), Binnie noted that "[t]his case thus fits easily within the framework established in [*Law*] . . . which identified the affirmation of human dignity and self-worth as a central purpose of s. 15(1) of the *Charter*."[87] He then reviewed the three questions mandated by *Law* and concluded that the government's delay in implementing pay equity clearly violates s. 15(1). He then moved on to the Oakes test for

s. 1 but without considering any of the four factors for discrimination outlined in *Law*.

He argued that the courts must be very cautious in accepting financial constraint as a justification for government violation of a Charter right. If the government's objective in doing so was substantially important — such as in a severe financial crisis like this one — the first part of the Oakes test might sometimes be satisfied. For the second part of the test, he found a rational connection between the government's objective to manage the financial crisis in the public interest and the delay of pay-equity wage increases. With regard to minimal impairment, he noted that courts must give governments a "margin of appreciation" to implement policies that minimally impair Charter rights and that the three-year delay in implementing the pay increases met that test.[88] He noted that overall, the government policy did more good than harm by taking appropriate action to address the serious financial crisis.

The final part of Binnie's judgment was a critique of Justice Marshall's declaration that a fourth prong should be added to the second part of the Oakes test (exhorting judicial deference to government policy in recognition of the separation of powers between the judicial and political branches of government). Marshall's decision had been a stinging rebuke, from within the judiciary itself, of what he perceived to be judicial activism. Binnie's response was to painstakingly outline how the existing Oakes test provides plenty of room for such judicial deference given the government shows that its policies conform to the *Charter of Rights and Freedoms*. Quoting from *Vriend*, he wrote that "it is not the courts which limit the legislatures. Rather, it is the constitution, which must be interpreted by the courts, that limits the legislatures. This is necessarily true of all constitutional democracies."[89]

This decision is an illustration of the fine line courts must tread when faced with the possibility of tampering with government policy in a way that could have severe financial implications both for governments and for citizens. As well, it is noteworthy that for the second time in a year, the court paid only lip service to the *Law* approach to s. 15(1) analysis, a further indication that the court was backing away from *Law*.

R. V. KAPP (2008)[90]

The *Kapp* decision is important for two reasons. First, it set out — for the first time — a test for the application of s. 15(2) of the *Charter*, the section that allows for government-initiated affirmative action programs to aid groups that have been traditionally discriminated against, even if the affirmative action program clashes with s. 15(1). Second, it openly restates the application of the Law test for s. 15(1).

Prior to contact and then trade with the Europeans in the 1800s, Aboriginal Canadians living near the mouth of the Fraser River in British Columbia relied, to an important degree, on salmon fishing for a livelihood. After European settlement, Aboriginal fishing for commercial purposes was regulated, and eventually severely curtailed, by fishing regulations first by the British colonial government, and then by the governments of Canada and British Columbia. In order to rectify this situation, the federal government introduced the Aboriginal Fisheries Strategy in 1992. In part, this policy was meant to address the *Sparrow* decision of 1990, in which the Supreme Court found that the federal government had a fidiciuary responsibility to Aboriginal peoples, especially with regard to their traditional uses of the land, and traditional fishing activities.[91] Further to the Aboriginal Fisheries Strategy a twenty-four-hour period was set aside on August 19–20, 1998, during which only designates of Aboriginal communities that had been granted special fishing licences could fish for sockeye salmon in the mouth of the Fraser River. Non-aboriginal fishers were prohibited from fishing during that one-day period. This strategy was a pilot sales program to test an approach for providing Aboriginal fishers with enhanced fishing privileges while at the same time preserving most of the fishery for non-Aboriginals.

John Michael Kapp and more than fifty other non-Aboriginal fishers, in protest against the special Aboriginal licences, fished in the mouth of the Fraser during the prohibited period and were charged with fishing at a prohibited time. When they appeared in the provincial court, Kapp and the other fishers claimed that the special Aboriginal licences violated s. 15(1) of the *Charter of Rights*. They won, but the Crown appealed to the BC Supreme Court, where the Aboriginal Fisheries Strategy was upheld and the convictions against Kapp and the other fishers were reinstated on the basis that the "pilot sales program did not have a discriminatory purpose or effect because it did not perpetuate or promote the view that those who were forbidden to fish on the days when the pilot sales program fishery was open are less capable or worthy of recognition or value as human beings or as members of Canadian society."[92] This ruling was upheld on appeal, but the non-Aboriginal fishers appealed to the Supreme Court of Canada.

The Supreme Court of Canada, in a nine to zero decision, ruled that the pilot sales program was an ameliorative program that was justified under s. 15(2) of the *Charter*.[93] The court's main decision, signed onto by eight of the judges, was written by Chief Justice McLachlin and Justice Abella. It emphasized that ss. 15(1) and 15(2) work together to promote the ideal of substantive equality, not the old concept of formal equality.

It is useful here to review the wording of s. 15 in its entirety:

> **15** *(1) Every individual is equal before and under the law and has the right to the equal protection and equal benefit of the law without discrimination and, in particular, without discrimination based on race, national, or ethnic origin, colour, religion, sex, age, or mental or physical disability.*
>
> *(2) Subsection (1) does not preclude any law, program, or activity that has as its object the amelioration of conditions of disadvantaged individuals or groups including those that are disadvantaged because of race, national, or ethnic origin, colour, religion, sex, age, or mental, or physical disability.*

The McLachlin-Abella analysis began with a return to the court's equality jurisprudence twenty years earlier in the *Andrews* decision.

> *Substantive equality, as contrasted with formal equality, is grounded in the idea that: The promotion of equality entails the promotion of a society in which all are secure in the knowledge that they are recognized at law as human beings equally deserving of concern, respect, and consideration . . .[94]*

While formal equality centres on equal treatment, substantive equality focuses on the broader concept of equal concern and respect, which does not mean identical treatment.

> *To approach the ideal of full equality before and under the law — and in human affairs an approach is all that can be expected — the main consideration must be the impact of the law on the individual or the group concerned. Recognizing that there will always be an infinite variety of personal characteristics, capacities, entitlements, and merits among those subject to a law, there must be accorded, as nearly as may be possible, an equality of benefit and protection and no more of the restrictions, penalties, or burdens imposed upon one than another. In other words, the admittedly unattainable ideal should be that a law expressed to bind all should not because of irrelevant personal differences have a more burdensome or less beneficial impact on one than another.*[95]

Governments, under the *Charter*, have a duty to promote substantive equality. One way for them to proceed is to combat discrimination pursuant to s. 15(1). "However, governments may also wish to combat discrimination by developing programs aimed at helping disadvantaged groups improve their situation."[96] They pursue this second method under s. 15(2), "without fear of challenge under s. 15(1)."[97]

McLachlin and Abella then began their simplification of the Law test for equality by aggregating the three essential questions from *Law* into the original two from *Andrews*.

> *The template in* Andrews, *as further developed in a series of cases culminating in* Law v. Canada *(Minister of Employment and Immigration), [1999] 1 SCR 497, established in essence a two-part test for showing discrimination under s. 15(1): (1) Does the law create a distinction based on an enumerated or analogous ground? (2) Does the distinction create a disadvantage by perpetuating prejudice or stereotyping? These*

> *were divided, in Law, into three steps, but in our view the test*
> *is, in substance, the same.*[98]

They noted that *Andrews* noted two types of discrimination, one based on the perpetuation of prejudice or disadvantage, and the second based on stereotyping that does not correspond with an individual's or a group's actual circumstances. In addition, *Andrews* introduced the concept that discrimination could be based on the grounds actually enumerated in s. 15 (analogous grounds). Then, "[a] decade later, in *Law*, this Court suggested that discrimination should be defined in terms of the impact of the law or program on the human dignity of members of the claimant group, having regard to four contextual factors: (1) pre-existing disadvantage, if any, of the claimant group; (2) degree of correspondence between the differential treatment and the claimant group's reality; (3) whether the law or program has an ameliorative purpose or effect; and (4) the nature of the interest affected."[99]

After pointing out the contribution of *Law* to the promotion of substantive equality, McLachlin and Abella acknowledged the shortcomings of the Law test.

> *But as critics have pointed out, human dignity is an abstract*
> *and subjective notion that, even with the guidance of the four*
> *contextual factors, cannot only become confusing and difficult*
> *to apply; it has also proven to be an additional burden on*
> *equality claimants, rather than the philosophical enhancement*
> *it was intended to be.*[100]

They went on to declare that the Law test was not a new test for equality, but an attempt to restate the fundamental approach already developed in *Andrews*.

> *Viewed in this way, Law does not impose a new and*
> *distinctive test for discrimination, but rather affirms the*
> *approach to substantive equality under s. 15 set out in*
> Andrews *and developed in numerous subsequent decisions.*

The factors cited in Law *should not be read literally as if they were legislative dispositions, but as a way of focussing on the central concern of s. 15 identified in* Andrews — *combatting discrimination, defined in terms of perpetuating disadvantage and stereotyping.*[101]

Combatting discrimination is the central purpose both of s. 15(1) and s. 15(2). While s. 15(1) is aspirational and preventative, s. 15(2) allows governments to be proactive. Not all differential treatment amounts to discrimination. Kapp and the other fishers established that they were subjected to differential treatment, but whether they were actually discriminated against depends on the s. 15(2) analysis.

McLachlin and Abella reviewed several ways in which s. 15(2) could be viewed in relation to s. 15(1), as well as earlier references to the concept of affirmative action and s. 15(2), eventually concluding that s. 15(2) should be treated independently from s. 15(1), keeping in mind both sections are meant to further the goal of promoting substantive equality.

We would therefore formulate the test under s. 15(2) as follows. A program does not violate the s. 15 equality guarantee if the government can demonstrate that: (1) the program has an ameliorative or remedial purpose; and (2) the program targets a disadvantaged group identified by the enumerated or analogous grounds. In proposing this test, we are mindful that future cases may demand some adjustment to the framework in order to meet the litigants' particular circumstances.[102]

In determining whether a program authorized by law meets s. 15(2) standards, McLachlin and Abella stressed the need to review the object (purpose) of the program,[103] the type of amelioration contained in the program,[104] and the disadvantages historically faced by the individuals or groups that the program is targeted toward.[105]

In the case of the federal government's aboriginal pilot sales program, there was plenty of evidence to demonstrate that the program's object was to contribute to the amelioration of the impact long-term discrimination had on Aboriginal fishers in the Fraser delta area of BC. Because the court decided that the Aboriginal pilot sales program met the test of s. 15(2), it was unnecessary for the court to consider Kapp and the others' allegation of discrimination against them under s. 15(1).

Clearly, the *Kapp* decision is one of the most important equality rights decisions made by the Supreme Court since *Andrews* both because it simplifies the rather convoluted approach to equality created by the *Law* decision, and because it spells out — for the first time — the criteria that governments must establish in order to ensure that any affirmative action programs they introduce are upheld under s. 15(2).

THE COURTS AND EQUALITY

The question of how much social equality Canadians should enjoy and how to resolve conflicting equality claims is one of the fundamental policy questions every Canadian politician and citizen must grapple with. It is tempting for politicians to avoid this difficult issue by leaving it to the courts. But equality becomes a truly legal issue only after its scope has been defined and after some guidelines are established for resolving conflicting equality claims.

In general, the courts are not as equipped by their legal backgrounds as might be hoped to settle these policy questions. Policy analysis is a specialized field of study that is taught in schools of public administration, not law schools. Despite this, some judges have been able to make useful contributions to the analyses of these issues. For example, the Supreme Court's decision in the *Andrews* case contains some perceptive insights into our country's quest for social equality. If we had post-Charter the same Supreme Court that decided the *Lavell* and *Bliss* cases, however, judicial interpretation could well have done more to retard than to advance the careful consideration of these issues. For this reason, the development of policies about the application of the *Charter* should not be left entirely to the judicial process. The political branches of government (the legislature and the executive) and the public service also have an important role to play, as illustrated by the Supreme Court's endorsement of the "dialogue" proposition, noted in Chapter 5. Moreover, as the *Borowski* decision so vividly illustrates, leaving the resolution of divisive social equality issues to the courts is likely to harm the legitimacy of the Supreme Court as a neutral arbiter of legal disputes.

Nevertheless, Canadian courts have played an important part in tackling the historic discrimination that has been endured by gays and lesbians. In addition to the outcomes of the courts' same-sex decisions in the 1990s and 2000s, Canadian courts have contributed thoughtful reasoning about same-sex relations that may have helped those initially opposed to recognition of same-sex rights realize that substantive social equality must necessarily include same-sex equality.

In cases such as *Schachter*, *Eldridge*, *Symes*, *Thibaudeau*, *Gosselin*, and *Auton*, the Supreme Court appears to have been dragged into finding solutions to social-equality policy issues that are arguably more suited for sensible resolution by government policy-makers — so long as the policy-makers are well-schooled in the theory and history of social equality. Both the Supreme Court and government policy-makers have come up short at times. The court's weakness is its lack of policy expertise and the failure of legal counsel to provide the most helpful background evidence. Government policy-makers are constrained because of a too-narrow focus that prevents human rights issues from receiving the attention they deserve and because of the usual shortcomings in the policy-development process.

Clearly, the right to equality, as Chief Justice McLachlin has indicated, is one of the most difficult rights that the court has to interpret, which is why the court has been inconsistent in its approach. In the *Law* decision, the Supreme Court muddied the water in its approach to social equality, but the *Kapp* decision appears to have contributed toward a somewhat clearer vision.

In our democracy, we all have a right to be treated with equal concern and respect, and we all have an equal right to dignity. On the other hand, we have unequal abilities and dispositions. How can these differences be balanced in a way that protects fairness in the legal sense as well as the right of governments to make pragmatic policy choices in the public interest? That is the essential question faced by judges, public servants in the policy area, and elected politicians when they tackle equality issues.

CHAPTER 7

LANGUAGE RIGHTS

Language rights (sections 16–23), unlike most of the other civil liberties the *Charter* was designed to protect, are not rights in the traditional liberal sense. Rather, they represent a cultural compromise designed to enable two linguistic communities to coexist in one federal country. The language rights in the *Charter* extend the language rights created in 1867 by section 133 of the *Constitution Act, 1867*. Section 133, which was part of the Confederation bargain, permitted the use of either English or French in Parliament and the Quebec National Assembly, and in the courts created by Parliament and those of Quebec.

In the first few years of the *Charter* up to 1989, the Supreme Court made six major decisions dealing with language rights. Only two of these directly concern the language rights in the *Charter*. (This is because not all of the constitutional language rights in Canada are contained in the *Charter*.) The first is the *Quebec Protestant School Boards* case,[1] in which the court resolved the collision between the "Canada clause" in the *Charter* and the "Quebec clause" in the Quebec *Charter of the French Language* by striking down the Quebec clause. The second is the *Société des Acadiens* case,[2] in which the court decided that section 19(2) of the *Charter*, which states that "[e]ither

English or French may be used by any person in . . . any court . . . of New Brunswick," does not entitle litigants to have judges who are fluent in the official language of the litigant. A judge may rely on an interpreter.

Four other early cases are given consideration in this chapter because they help to illustrate the approach the judges developed early on toward language rights. The first of these is the *Manitoba Language Rights Reference*.[3] It concerns section 23 of the *Manitoba Act* (1870), which provides the same kinds of guarantees for the use of English and French in Manitoba as are provided with regard to Quebec in section 133 of the *Constitution Act, 1867*, and with regard to New Brunswick in sections 18 and 19 of the *Charter*. Next, the *MacDonald*[4] and *Bilodeau*[5] cases respectively decided that the clause in section 133 that authorizes the use of either English or French in the courts of Quebec, and the parallel clause in the *Manitoba Act*, do not imply that court summonses must be printed in both official languages. Finally, the *Mercure* case[6] decided that the language rights of francophones protected by the *Saskatchewan Act* (and by implication, the *Alberta Act*) must be respected by the provincial legislature but that they may be changed without a constitutional amendment.

Since 1990, there have been two important Supreme Court decisions that will be highlighted in this chapter, both dealing with French- or English-language school rights. They are *Mahe v. Alberta* (1990), and *Doucet-Boudreau v. Nova Scotia* (2003). Two other minority-language education rights will also be noted: *Gosselin (Tutor of) v. Quebec* (2005), and *Conseil scolaire francophone de la Colombie-Britannique v. British Columbia* (2013).

THE "QUEBEC CLAUSE" AND THE QUEBEC PROTESTANT SCHOOL BOARDS CASE[7]

This case concerns the constitutional validity of the sections of the Quebec *Charter of the French Language* (Bill 101) that restrict English-language schooling to children of long-time anglophone Quebeckers, that is, anglophone parents who had received their primary- or secondary-school education in Quebec.

Enacted in 1977, Bill 101 was the culmination of several attempts by successive provincial governments[8] after the start of the Quiet Revolution to prevent the disappearance of the French culture in Quebec. The Quiet

Revolution, or Révolution tranquille, is the label that refers to the rapid political and economic changes during the 1960s in Quebec when francophones asserted control over Quebec's economy and culture, and modernized its education system. In the 1960s the birth rate of native francophone Quebeckers declined dramatically. At the same time, the great majority of the province's new immigrants were opting to join the anglophone culture because of the perceived economic benefits of this choice. In 1968 a violent conflict occurred involving a school board that tried to force children of Italian immigrants to attend French schools. In reaction, in 1969 the provincial government enacted Bill 63, the *Act to Promote the French Language in Quebec.*

The legislation authorized the ministers of education and immigration to "take the measures necessary" to encourage new immigrants to "acquire the knowledge of the French language upon arrival." As Quebec nationalism grew and there was no apparent increase in the proportion of immigrants assimilating into the francophone culture, the permissive approach of Bill 63 was considered inadequate. In 1974, Bill 63 was replaced by Bill 22, the *Official Language Act.* Bill 22 declared French the official language of Quebec. The section dealing with education prevented the expansion of English-language instruction in schools unless authorized by the minister of education, who had to be satisfied that there was a sufficient number of students whose mother tongue was English to justify such an expansion. In other words, English-language schooling was to be provided only to children of native anglophones, not to children of immigrants whose mother tongue was not English. In addition, Bill 22 prevented francophone children not already fluent in English from attending English-language public schools, and anglophone children not already fluent in French from attending French-language public schools.

In 1976 the Parti Québécois came to power in Quebec. The PQ had been critical of Bill 22 for not going far enough to protect and promote the French language. In 1977, Bill 22 was replaced by Bill 101, the *Charter of the French Language.* The section of Bill 101 dealing with education restricted English-language instruction to children of persons who had received their primary education in English in Quebec, or to children with an older sibling who had received primary education in English in Quebec. These restrictions became known as the "Quebec clause."

When the *Canadian Charter of Rights and Freedoms* came into effect in 1982, it guaranteed that citizens who had received a French primary education anywhere in Canada could have their children educated in French anywhere in the country. Likewise, citizens who had received an English primary education anywhere in Canada could have their children educated in English anywhere in the country. In addition, children with siblings who had received primary or secondary education in either English or French anywhere in Canada could attend, respectively, English- or French-language schools anywhere in the country. These provisions became known as the "Canada clause." It is noteworthy that René Lévesque, premier of Quebec at the time, had at one time agreed to the Canada clause because he was convinced that the premiers of the other nine provinces would not accept it. He withdrew his agreement, however, when the constitution was patriated without the consent of Quebec.

There was an obvious contradiction between the Canada clause in section 23 of the *Charter* and the Quebec clause in Bill 101. Shortly after the *Charter* came into effect in 1982, the Quebec Association of Protestant School Boards applied to the Quebec Superior Court for a declaration that the Quebec clause in Bill 101 was inoperative. The major issue before the Superior Court was whether the Quebec clause could be justified as a reasonable limit pursuant to section 1 of the *Charter*. A great deal of sociolinguistic evidence was presented to the trial judge, Chief Justice Jules Deschênes, suggesting that the replacement of the Quebec clause by the Canada clause would result in higher enrollments in Quebec's English school system and that this would seriously threaten the survival of the French language. After carefully considering the evidence, Deschênes concluded that the increased enrollments resulting from the Canada clause — in the order of less than 5 per cent — would not be enough to threaten the continued existence of the French language in Quebec. It is clear that Deschênes would have accepted the Quebec clause as a reasonable limit had there been evidence that the Canada clause would have substantially increased the number of enrollments in Quebec's English schools.

The Quebec Attorney General appealed to the Quebec Court of Appeal, lost again, and then appealed to the Supreme Court of Canada. The

Supreme Court rendered one decision attributed to "The Court." The panel consisted of Ritchie, Dickson, Beetz, Estey, McIntyre, Lamer, and Wilson. The court's decision was much briefer than that of Deschênes. The judges simply concluded that the Quebec clause was not a mere limit of section 23 of the *Charter*, but a complete denial of it.

> *The provisions of s. 73 of Bill 101 [the Quebec clause]*
> *collide directly with those of s. 23 of the* Charter, *and are not*
> *limitations which can be legitimized by s. 1 of the* Charter.
> *Such limitations cannot be exceptions to the rights and*
> *freedoms guaranteed by the* Charter.

The importance of this decision to the judicial interpretation of section 1 is that any legislation that completely denies a Charter right can never be justified under section 1. However, it may be difficult for the judges always to be able to distinguish clearly between a limitation and a complete denial.

THE ISSUE OF JUDICIAL BILINGUALISM AND THE *SOCIÉTÉ DES ACADIENS* CASE (1986)[9]

In 1982 the Société des Acadiens du Nouveau-Brunswick became embroiled in a dispute with a school board in Grand Falls, New Brunswick. It should be kept in mind that New Brunswick is an officially bilingual province. The board wished to offer French immersion programs to francophone students in English schools, a measure that the Société des Acadiens considered contrary to the New Brunswick *Schools Act* because of concerns about the standard of French-language instruction in the immersion classes.[10] The Société brought an action in the New Brunswick Court of Queen's Bench for an injunction to prevent the board from offering the courses.

The Queen's Bench judge made a decision in favour of the Société, and the board decided not to appeal. However, a number of parents of the students affected banded together to form the Association of Parents for Fairness in Education, and this association filed an application with the New Brunswick Court of Appeal for leave (permission) to appeal the Queen's Bench decision. Arguments were presented in both English and French. The association's application for leave to appeal was granted by a three-judge panel, which included two bilingual judges and an anglophone judge who claimed that he understood enough French to be able to hear the case. The Société appealed the panel's decision to the Supreme Court of Canada, in part on the grounds that the hearing violated section 19(2) of the *Charter*, which stipulates that "[e]ither English or French may be used by any person in . . . any court . . . of New Brunswick." The Société claimed that section 19(2) guarantees the right to be understood in either official language in the courts of New Brunswick and that the anglophone judge, Mr. Justice Stratton, did not comprehend enough French to be able to understand the arguments presented in French.

The Société des Acadiens lost in the Supreme Court, and in the process it was decided that the right to use either English or French in a court does *not* include the right to be understood in the language of choice. (It should be pointed out, however, that litigants do have a right to be understood, but this right stems not from section 19(2), but from the common-law principles of natural justice that are affirmed in sections 7, 11(d), and 14 of the *Charter* and in section 2(e) of the *Canadian Bill of Rights*.) It is worth comparing the judgments of the majority and the minority, as they contain very different views about the purpose of the language rights sections of the *Charter*.

THE MAJORITY DECISION

The majority decision was written by Mr. Justice Beetz, with Estey, (Julien) Chouinard, Lamer, and Le Dain concurring. Beetz grounded his approach to the issue on the assumption that there is a fundamental difference between the language rights and the legal rights protected by the *Charter*.

> [L]egal rights tend to be seminal in nature because they are rooted in principle . . . Language rights, on the other hand, although some of them have been enlarged and incorporated into the Charter, remain nonetheless founded on political compromise.[11]

Because language rights are the result of political compromises made by two linguistic communities attempting to coexist, Beetz considered that any broadening of these rights should be effected by the political process rather than by the courts. He noted that the language rights part of the *Charter* was clearly designed so that provinces in addition to New Brunswick could opt into it. All that would be required would be the consent of the legislature of the province involved and of the Senate and House of Commons. He was afraid that if the Supreme Court took an approach to language rights that indicated the language rights would be continually broadened, other provinces would be discouraged from opting in.

Beetz gave two additional reasons for interpreting the *Charter*'s language rights narrowly. First, he compared section 19, which concerns language rights in courts, with section 17, which protects language rights in Parliament and the New Brunswick legislature. Section 17 states that "[e]veryone has the right to use English or French in any debates and other proceedings of Parliament . . . [and] the legislature of New Brunswick." The wording of section 17 is parallel to that of section 19 except that section 17 deals with the legislative process. Beetz reasoned that section 17 could not possibly contain the assumption that anyone speaking in the legislature had a right to be understood by all other legislators in whatever language was being spoken. Because section 17 merely protected the right to speak, not the right to be understood, section 19 should be interpreted in the same way.

Second, Beetz argued that if section 19 had been meant to include a right to be understood in the language of the litigant's choice, the drafters of the *Charter* could have clearly indicated this intention. For example, section 20 of the *Charter*, which concerns the right of Canadians to receive services in French or English, refers to the right to "communicate." To Beetz, the word "communicate" plainly indicates the right to be understood. Because the drafters chose not to word section 19 in such a fashion, Beetz deduced that the right to be understood had deliberately been left out of section 19.

Beetz therefore concluded that section 19 of the *Charter* simply protects the right to use either English or French in court, and not the right to be understood in that language. He noted that litigants have a right to be heard by judges who "are capable by any reasonable means of understanding the proceedings . . . [but] this entitlement is derived from the principles of natural justice . . . and not from s. 19(2) of the *Charter*." On the question of whether Mr. Justice Stratton had sufficient knowledge of French to fulfill the natural justice requirements, Beetz wrote that "in the absence of any system of testing, it is for the judge to assess in good faith . . . his or her level of understanding of the language." It was not appropriate for the Supreme Court to question Stratton's judgment in this matter.

THE MINORITY VIEW

Justices Dickson and Wilson agreed with the majority that the Société des Acadiens must lose the appeal, but each issued a separate opinion. Both would have preferred a broader interpretation of section 19. But even given a more generous interpretation of the constitution, both Dickson and Wilson felt that the decision about whether Mr. Justice Stratton understood enough French to satisfy a beefed-up interpretation of section 19 should be left to the judge himself. Dickson and Wilson were concerned about the proper interpretation of section 19, not about the outcome of this particular case.

Chief Justice Dickson stressed the importance of language rights in the Confederation bargain.

Linguistic duality has been a long-standing concern in our nation. Canada is a country with both French and English solidly embedded in its history. The constitutional language protections reflect continued and renewed efforts in the direction of bilingualism . . . In the words of André Tremblay, "a broad, liberal, and dynamic interpretation of the language provisions of the constitution would be in line with the exceptional importance of their function."

Dickson would have preferred that the court had given such a broad and liberal interpretation to the *Charter*'s s. 19 by finding that it implied a right to be understood in the preferred language. He asked, "What good is a right to use one's language if those to whom one speaks cannot understand?"

Madame Justice Wilson's opinion was similar to Dickson's in its broad and liberal thrust, but she went further. For her, the language rights in the *Charter* imply that bilingualism is a goal Canadians are steadily moving toward but have not yet achieved. The courts must take this reality into account, she wrote, so that "[w]hat may be adequate today in terms of protection for the litigant's right under s. 19(2) may not be adequate tomorrow. . . .We are looking at a process which will call for a progressively expansive interpretation of the litigant's right under s. 19(2) to meet gradually increasing social expectations."[12] Wilson's approach is an excellent example of the theory that the constitution is a "living tree," capable of growth and development, as noted in chapter 1.

For Wilson, section 19(2) implies a right for litigants to be understood in the official language of their choice, and the appropriate level of understanding at the present time is "receptive bilingualism." This means that the listener can understand the full flavour of the argument in the litigant's language of choice, but may not necessarily speak that language fluently. Judges could legitimately use a translator to make comments to litigants in the language that they were not fluent in. Ultimately, however, the goal should be that judges understand and speak both languages equally well.

THE CONTRASTING APPROACHES ADOPTED BY THE JUDGES

It would be difficult to find a better illustration of judges differing over how the broad and general phrases in the *Charter* should be interpreted or of judges allowing their political views to influence their conclusions than the *Société des Acadiens* case. Beetz opted for a narrow interpretation of language rights so that the judges would not upset the delicate political compromise that had been worked out and so as to encourage politicians, not judges, to continue the process of developing more appropriate compromises on the language issue. In contrast, Dickson chose a broad interpretation of language rights because he perceived them to be central to Canada's existence. Wilson, too, supported a broad interpretation but also suggested that the judges themselves should gradually expand the scope of the language rights sections of the *Charter* as social expectations about bilingualism, and the practical means of satisfying them, increased.

One could speculate that two competing images of Canada were contending for the loyalty of the judicial mind. One is the notion that Canada should eventually reach such a high state of bilingualism that both francophones and anglophones can feel at home in any province. This perception has been associated with the views of Pierre Trudeau. The other image is of a Canada in which two separate linguistic communities find ways of coexisting as "two solitudes" without many in either community becoming bilingual. From this perspective, Quebec will become more unilingual as a francophone society and the other nine provinces will remain (or become more) unilingual as anglophone societies. This view has been associated with the Parti Québécois, some of the premiers in the anglophone provinces, and some conservative politicians.

Clearly, the opinions of Justices Dickson and Wilson were consistent with Trudeau's vision. It is tempting to think that the majority decision was based on the two solitudes notion. This may well be the case, although an alternative explanation is that some judges favouring the Trudeau ideal feared that judicially enforced bilingualism might lead to a backlash that would actually retard the dawning of the Trudeau vision. In any case, it is noteworthy that the three Quebec judges, as well as a bilingual Ontario judge (Le Dain), all preferred the narrow approach.

THE MANITOBA LANGUAGE RIGHTS REFERENCE[13]

In 1985 the Supreme Court of Canada declared that Manitoba statutes would not be valid unless enacted in both French and English and that all English-only statutes that had been created since 1890 were invalid. To understand this historic decision, some background is necessary.

BACKGROUND

Manitoba became a province of Canada under the *Manitoba Act*, which was entrenched in the *British North America Act, 1871*. The *Manitoba Act* is part of the formal constitution of Canada as defined by section 52 of the *Constitution Act, 1982*.

Section 23 of the *Manitoba Act* was for Manitoba what section 133 of the *Constitution Act, 1867* was for Quebec. It declared, among other things, that the acts of the Manitoba legislature shall be printed and published in both English and French. Up to 1890 the francophones and anglophones in Manitoba were roughly equal in number, but in that year a clear majority of anglophones gained control of the government in a provincial election. In 1890 the Manitoba legislature enacted the *Official Language Act*, which proclaimed English as the only official language of the province and declared that henceforth statutes would be printed and published only in English.

In 1892 a francophone litigant[14] challenged the constitutionality of the

Official Language Act in a county court and won. The *Act* was obviously *ultra vires*, and the judge declared this to be the case. The government simply ignored the decision and carried on enacting legislation only in English. Although the decision was technically binding on the government, the government decided not to appeal to a higher court. Thus, there were no precedents in a superior court to indicate that the *Official Language Act* was *ultra vires*, and county court decisions, according to the doctrine of *stare decisis*, are not binding on superior courts (see chapter 2). The litigant who won in the county court could not appeal because of the fact that he had won — appeals are available only to those who lose. Litigants successfully challenged the *Official Language Act* again in 1909 and 1976 with the same results: they won in the county court but the decisions were ignored by the government. In 1976 the Manitoba Attorney General simply announced that the government did not accept the ruling of the lower court, but the decision was not appealed because of the fear that the government would lose. These events should provide a good antidote to the belief that constitutional rights can always be successfully enforced by the courts.

The francophone litigant who won the 1976 case adopted a new strategy in 1978. He brought an application in the Manitoba Court of Queen's Bench that the *Official Language Act* was invalid. This time, in Peter Hogg's words, he was "fortunate enough to lose"[15] and so was able to appeal to the Manitoba Court of Appeal, where he won. This was a decision that the Manitoba government could not ignore, and it appealed to the Supreme Court of Canada in order to settle the issue. In 1979, in the *Forest* decision,[16] the Supreme Court declared the *Official Language Act* to be unconstitutional. The court did not discuss the broader consequences of this declaration regarding the validity of Manitoba statutes enacted since 1890 only in English.

At the same time as it rendered judgment in *Forest*, the court released its decision on the constitutionality of the sections of Quebec's Bill 101 that declared that statutes would be enacted only in French. The court had no difficulty in finding that these provisions were unconstitutional, as they violated section 133 of the *Constitution Act, 1867*. The case became known as *Blaikie No. 1*.[17] (Later, in *Blaikie No. 2*,[18] the Supreme Court further clarified the scope of section 133 by proclaiming that, in addition to the requirement that statutes must be enacted in English and French, regulations that were subject to the approval of the cabinet, the rules of practice in courts, and the rules of quasi-judicial tribunals had to be produced in both official languages.)

The Attorneys General of Manitoba and Quebec, during the hearings for *Forest* and *Blaikie No. 1*, had argued that a provincial government was entitled to amend its own internal constitution under section 92(1) of the *Constitution Act, 1867*, which gave the provinces the power to amend the "Constitution of the province, except as regards the Office of Lieutenant Governor." The court rejected this view. It proclaimed that the language rights in the constitution were an essential part of the Confederation bargain and were designed to prevent provincial legislatures from destroying minority language rights.

Within twenty-four hours of the Supreme Court's decisions in *Blaikie No. 1* and *Forest*, the Quebec legislature had re-enacted in both official languages all of the statutes that had been passed only in French since 1977. This task was made easier by the fact that the government had continued to produce unofficial English versions of the statutes. The Manitoba legislature was not so quick. It began to enact some statutes in both official languages, but many statutes continued to be enacted only in English. Francophones in Manitoba became impatient. Roger Bilodeau, a francophone who had been charged with a traffic offence, developed a strategy designed to spur the legislature along. He pleaded not guilty on the grounds that his summons had been issued only in English and that the *Highway Traffic Act* and *Summary Convictions Act* themselves were unconstitutional, having been enacted only in English. The results of the *Bilodeau* case are discussed in the next section.

Before the *Bilodeau* case could be heard by the Supreme Court, the federal government decided to send a reference question to the court about the status of Manitoba laws. This was because of the fear that the *Bilodeau* decision might address only the narrow issue of the status of the *Highway Traffic Act* and the *Summary Convictions Act*. The reference asked, among other things, whether all the Manitoba statutes published only in English since 1890 were invalid, and if so, under what circumstances they might have some legal force and effect. The Supreme Court heard arguments on both the *Bilodeau* case and the *Manitoba Language Rights Reference* at the same time in 1984. The judgment on the *Manitoba Language Rights Reference* was released in 1985, and on the *Bilodeau* case in 1986.

THE DECISION

One opinion was presented for the entire panel, which consisted of Justices Dickson, Beetz, Estey, McIntyre, Lamer, Wilson, and Le Dain. By following the precedents established by the *Blaikie* No. 2 and *Forest* decisions, the court had no difficulty in declaring that all of Manitoba's statutes enacted in English only after 1890 were invalid.

This conclusion presented a dilemma around the question about how Manitoba statutes could regain legal force. Because all statutes from 1890 were invalid, the current Manitoba legislature had no legal standing, having been elected under an invalid electoral law. For the same reason, Manitoba had no legal courts, public service, or police force. What existed in the province was a legal vacuum, and there was no obvious way to remedy the situation because a legal government did not exist and could not be created. In a strictly legal sense, Manitoba was under the control of an unconstitutional regime.

For guidance, the Supreme Court looked to the decisions of other common-law courts that had had to contend with the effects of governments acting unconstitutionally. For example, for several years after Pakistan's independence in 1947, laws were enacted without royal assent, and all of them were eventually deemed to be invalid. In 1963 in Cyprus, normal legislative procedures proved impossible because an insurrection physically prevented most Turkish Cypriots from participating in the government. In 1965 Ian Smith, representing Southern Rhodesia's white minority, illegally declared the country independent. In legal matters arising out of each of these cases, courts found the "doctrine of necessity" helpful.

According to the doctrine of necessity, civilization cannot exist without the rule of law. Therefore, the courts cannot tolerate a legal vacuum. The doctrine of necessity holds that the laws of an illegal government must be deemed to be effective to the extent that they do not violate the constitution. That particular interpretation of the doctrine of necessity was only partly helpful to the Canadian Supreme Court, because all of Manitoba's laws from 1890 onward definitely violated the constitution by being enacted only in English. Therefore, the Supreme Court developed its own version of the doctrine of necessity:

"the constitution will not suffer a province without laws. Thus the constitution requires that temporary validity and force and effect be given to the current acts of the Manitoba legislature from the date of this judgment, and that rights, obligations, and other effects which have arisen under these laws . . . are deemed temporarily to have been and continue to be effective and beyond challenge. It is only in this way that legal chaos can be avoided and the rule of law preserved"[19]

After hearing more evidence, the court decided to give the Manitoba legislature until December 31, 1988, to re-enact in French and English the then current statutes, regulations, and rules of court.

THE IMPLICATIONS OF THE MANITOBA LANGUAGE RIGHTS REFERENCE

This fascinating case and its predecessors — *Forest* and the two *Blaikie* cases — illustrate the close connection between section 133 of the *Constitution Act, 1867* and the *Charter*, as well as some aspects of the ongoing politics of language in Canada. It is clear that sections 16–23 of the *Charter* are really extensions of the language rights contained in section 133 of Canada's first "little bill of rights,"[20] the *Constitution Act, 1867*. For the sake of simplicity, it is perhaps unfortunate that section 133 and section 23 of the *Manitoba Act* were not moved into the *Charter*.

The fate of section 23 of the *Manitoba Act*, as it stood from 1890 to 1985, illustrates both the limits and potential of constitutionally entrenched language rights. Section 23 was no help at all to Franco-Manitobans during that time period. Their political influence was simply not great enough to ensure that their constitutional rights would be respected, and judicial remedies are often ineffective in the face of overpowering political forces. As well, the fact that language rights were *not* enforced in Manitoba for almost a century probably goes a long way toward explaining why so many Franco-Manitobans assimilated into the anglophone community, and why most francophone Quebeckers stopped emigrating to Manitoba. If some way had been found in the 1890s to protect the constitutional rights of

Franco-Manitobans, the vision of Canada in which both Anglophones and Francophones feel at home in any part of the country might well be closer to reality today.

THE *MACDONALD*[21] AND *BILODEAU*[22] CASES AND BILINGUAL SUMMONSES

In 1980 Roger J. A. Bilodeau received a summons for speeding contrary to Manitoba's *Highway Traffic Act*. The summons was issued in English only. In 1981 Duncan Cross MacDonald received a summons for speeding contrary to a Montreal city bylaw. His summons was in French only. Both pleaded not guilty in their respective provinces on the grounds that the summonses were ineffective unless issued either in both official languages or in the language of choice of the recipient. In addition, Bilodeau argued that the Manitoba *Highway Traffic Act* and *Summary Convictions Act* were *ultra vires* because they had been enacted only in English. Both Bilodeau and MacDonald were convicted. They appealed and lost in their respective provincial Courts of Appeal. The Supreme Court of Canada granted both litigants leave to appeal because of the importance of the constitutional issues they raised. The judgments were released on the same day in 1986.

MacDonald based his claim on section 133 of the *Constitution Act, 1867*, which states that "either English or French . . . may be used by any Person or in any Pleading or Process in or issuing from any Court of Canada established under this *Act*, and in or from all or any of the Courts of Quebec." Bilodeau's case was founded on section 23 of the *Manitoba Act*, which is almost identical to section 133 except that "Manitoba" is substituted for "Quebec." Both argued that because they have the right to plead in their official language of choice, the state has a correlative duty to respect that right by issuing a summons in the language of choice or by issuing a bilingual summons. The appellants also drew on the *Blaikie No. 2* decision, which settled that the rules of practice for the courts of Quebec must be issued in both languages. If the rules of practice had to be in both official languages, then other official court documents, such as summonses, logically had to be in both languages as well.

The majority on the Supreme Court did not accept this argument. In *MacDonald*, the opinion was written by Mr. Justice Beetz, with Estey,

McIntyre, Lamer, and Le Dain concurring entirely, and Dickson concurring in the constitutional question. In *Bilodeau*, Chief Justice Dickson wrote the majority opinion, with Beetz, Estey, McIntyre, Lamer, and Le Dain concurring. Madame Justice Wilson wrote a dissenting opinion in both cases.

THE MAJORITY OPINIONS

The majority looked closely at the wording of sections 133 and 23 and determined that there were two kinds of language rules in the constitution: those that impose a duty to use both official languages and those that permit the use of one or both languages at the discretion of the speaker. They concluded that sections 133 and 23 *require* the use of both official languages only for the enactment and publication of statutes and the creation and publication of regulations (including the rules of practice in court). The permissive parts of sections 133 and 23 concern the debates in Parliament and in the Quebec or Manitoba legislatures, and pleadings and processes in the courts of Canada, Quebec, or Manitoba. The permissive sections allow people to use either language at their discretion, but *do not require* the use of both languages. According to the majority, the authorities responsible for establishing the courts in the provinces — that is, the provincial legislatures — are permitted to decide whether English or French or both should be used in court processes such as summonses, just as litigants have the discretion to speak English or French or both in court.

In the *MacDonald* decision, the majority noted that MacDonald had based his entire submission on section 133. He had not argued that the right to a fair hearing (as protected by the common-law principles of natural justice in sections 7, 11(d), and 14 of the *Charter* and section 2 of the *Canadian Bill of Rights*) required that he receive a translation of the summons. Therefore, the majority did not decide this issue. In *obiter*, however, the majority hinted that if MacDonald had requested a translation of the summons, the court would be obliged to provide it, not because of section 133, but pursuant to fair hearing rights.

> *It is axiomatic that everyone has a common law right to a fair*
> *hearing, including the right to be informed of the case one has*
> *to meet and the right to make full answer and defence. Where*

> *the defendant cannot understand the proceedings because he*
> *is unable to understand the language in which they are being*
> *conducted, or because he is deaf, the effective exercise of these*
> *rights may well impose a consequential duty upon the court to*
> *provide adequate translation.*[23]

MacDonald had not requested a translation of the summons from the court, but had obtained his own translation. In court he had presented his case in English and had been understood in that language. Therefore, his right to a fair hearing was not in question. His conviction stood.

In the *Bilodeau* case, the majority held that pursuant to the doctrine of necessity (discussed above under the *Manitoba Language Rights Reference*) the *Highway Traffic Act* and *Summary Convictions Act* remained temporarily valid. Therefore, Bilodeau's conviction also stood.

THE DISSENT

Madame Justice Wilson anchored her dissent in both cases on an analysis of the relation between rights and duties (see chapter 1). She stressed that in legal theory, when a person is granted a right in law, then another person or body has a correlative duty to respect or meet that right. For example, section 10 of the *Charter* states that anyone detained by the police has a right to be informed of the right to counsel. This means that the police have a duty to inform anyone they detain of that right. Wilson's opinion is a scholarly analysis of the legal theory; she refers to leading theorists, including H. L. A. Hart, Wesley Newcomb Hohfeld, John Austin, G. W. H. Hegel, John W. Salmond, and, in the Canadian context, William Lederman and James McRuer.

Wilson noted that the courts could fulfill their section 133 and 23 duties in this situation in at least two ways: by issuing bilingual summonses or by issuing unilingual summonses that also state, in the other official language, that the court will provide a translation at the request of the summons recipient. After reviewing the history of section 133, she concluded that the latter method would fulfill the court's obligation.

Because neither the court in Quebec nor the court in Manitoba had proceeded against the appellants by issuing proper summonses, Wilson concluded that these courts had no jurisdiction to convict.

THE SIGNIFICANCE OF THE *MACDONALD* AND *BILODEAU* DECISIONS

The decisions of the majority in these two cases are in the same vein as in the *Société des Acadiens* decision. They present a narrow interpretation of the language rights in the constitution so as to avoid antagonizing linguistic majorities in Manitoba and Quebec and to allow politicians to work out compromises that will expand language rights, if they are to be expanded.

It is noteworthy that even Chief Justice Dickson sided with the majority view in these cases, whereas in the *Société des Acadiens* decision he took the broader view. Consistent with his position to interpret language rights as narrowly as reasonably possible, in the *Société des Acadiens* case it may have seemed unreasonable that a right to speak in the language of choice in court would not include the right to be understood. In *MacDonald* and *Bilodeau*, however, he may have felt that a narrower interpretation of language rights was possible without seeming to stretch credulity.

THE *MERCURE* CASE[24] AND LANGUAGE RIGHTS IN SASKATCHEWAN AND ALBERTA

Father André Mercure, a francophone priest in Saskatchewan, was charged with speeding in 1981. When he appeared in court, he applied for permission to proceed with his trial in French. He claimed he had a right to enter a plea and to proceed in French pursuant to section 110 of the *North-West Territories Act*, which became part of the law of Saskatchewan pursuant to section 16 of the *Saskatchewan Act* (1905). Section 110 provides for the protection of French and English language rights parallel to those provided for Quebeckers in section 133 of the *Constitution Act, 1867* and for Manitobans in section 23 of the *Manitoba Act*. (The *Saskatchewan Act* brought Saskatchewan into Confederation, and it is now part of the formal constitution of Canada defined by section 52 of the *Constitution Act, 1982*.) Section 16 of the *Act* provides for the continuance of the laws of the old Northwestern Territory in Saskatchewan until they are amended or repealed by the new legislature of Saskatchewan. Section 110 of the *North-West Territories Act* had never been amended or repealed. (The legislature of the Northwestern Territory had made an attempt to repeal section 110 in 1891, but the effort failed because the correct procedures were not followed.)

Father Mercure was denied permission to enter a plea and to proceed in French, and he appealed this decision all the way to the Supreme Court of Canada. The court rendered a decision in his favour in 1988, but by then he had died. (Although the issue of the speeding ticket was moot because of Father Mercure's death, the court decided to hear the case anyway because the judges felt it would be in the public interest to settle the constitutional issue.)

All nine judges heard the appeal, which indicated the importance of the case. The decision of the majority was written by Mr. Justice Gerard La Forest and concurred with by Dickson, Beetz, Lamer, Wilson, and Le Dain. Mr. Justice Estey wrote a dissenting opinion, with which McIntyre concurred.[25]

THE MAJORITY OPINION

The majority held that section 110 of the *North-West Territories Act* still applied in Saskatchewan. Therefore, Saskatchewan was in a similar position to Manitoba after the *Manitoba Language Rights Reference*: none of its laws were valid, as none had been enacted in both languages. As in Manitoba, Saskatchewan laws were declared temporarily valid pursuant to the doctrine of necessity, and the province was given a reasonable time to make amends.

Section 110 of the *North-West Territories Act*, however, differed in one important respect from section 133 of the *Constitution Act, 1867* and section 23 of the *Manitoba Act*. In 1890 some anglophone members of Parliament had pressed for amendments to the *North-West Territories Act* that would make the territories unilingual. These members had a vision of Canada in which the French language would be eliminated throughout the country. The majority in Parliament, however, felt that the language issue should be resolved by the legislature of the territories, not by Parliament. As a result, section 110 was amended to allow the territorial legislature to abolish the bilingual provisions if it chose to do so. La Forest reasoned that because section 110 contained this provision for its own amendment, the Saskatchewan legislature could, if it chose, simply repeal section 110.

> *Accordingly, the legislature may resort to the obvious, if*
> *ironic, expedient of enacting a bilingual statute removing the*

restrictions imposed on it by s. 110 and then declaring all
existing provincial statutes valid notwithstanding that they
were enacted, printed, and published in English only.[26]

The court had been invited by Mercure to declare that the language rights in section 110 were entrenched in the constitution and could only be changed pursuant to the amending formula described in section 43 of the *Constitution Act, 1982* — the agreement of Parliament and the provincial legislature concerned. Section 43 covers "any amendment to any provision that relates to the use of the English or the French language within a province." The majority rejected this suggestion, however, because the *Saskatchewan Act* stated that laws inherited from the North-West Territories could be amended by the new provincial government.

It remained for the majority to determine "the reasonable means necessary to ensure that the [judges] understand the proceedings [if they do not speak the preferred official language of the litigants]." This was an issue that had not been determined in the *MacDonald, Bilodeau,* or *Société des Acadiens* cases, since in each of these cases the judge or judges involved were deemed to have comprehended the language used by the litigant. La Forest noted that regardless of section 110, witnesses may address the court in the language they are most comfortable with, and the court has a duty (presumably under common law and sections 7, 11(h), and 14 of the *Charter*) to provide a translator. In addition he concluded that litigants at least deserve to have proceedings recorded in the official language they use in court. He pointed out that "the proceedings, for example, may continue in the Court of Appeal where the judges may quite properly wish to refer to the exact words used by a person at trial, words that person has a right to use." Because Father Mercure had not been allowed to enter a plea in French, the majority held that the conviction should be quashed.

THE MINORITY OPINION

Justices Estey and McIntyre considered that section 110 of the *North-West Territories Act* was of even less assistance to francophones in Saskatchewan than the majority thought. Their approach seemed to be to let sleeping dogs lie. They concluded that section 110 of the *North-West Territories Act* was inapplicable after 1905. Estey claimed that the *Saskatchewan Act* created a new legislature and new courts; this meant that section 110, which referred to the old legislature and the old courts, was not relevant. Even if it were assumed that section 110 had been incorporated into the laws of Saskatchewan, section 110 would have become spent with the termination of the old legislature of the Northwestern Territory and the old courts of the territories. From this perspective, Father Mercure had no right to plead in French at his trial.

THE POLITICAL CONSEQUENCES OF THE *MERCURE* DECISION

Until 1885, the majority of settlers in what is now Saskatchewan and Alberta were francophone. That proportion has now dropped to about 3 per cent. One reason for this was that government policies encouraged the settlement of the west by non-francophones. In addition, since 1890, the territorial and then the provincial governments have supported policies that have encouraged the assimilation of francophones, such as the refusal to establish francophone schools. The *Mercure* decision merely restored to prairie francophones a few of the rights they should have enjoyed all along.

Those restored rights, as might be expected, were short-lived. Two months after the February 1988 Supreme Court decision, the Saskatchewan legislature repealed section 110 of the *North-West Territories Act*. However, the government announced that some statutes would be translated into French and that French could be used in both the legislature and the courts. In June the federal government agreed to pay for most of the cost of translating statutes into French and for most of the other costs incurred in the provision of additional translators and francophone court reporters. As well, the federal government agreed to help fund a prairie language institute. The institute would help train provincial public servants to develop a capacity in French, and in addition it would provide instruction in nineteen other minority languages spoken on the prairies. By including the other minority languages in the language institute, the package of reforms became politically more palatable in a province where francophones constitute one of the smaller ethnic minorities.

The *Mercure* decision also had implications for Alberta, which was in exactly the same position as Saskatchewan regarding section 110 of the

North-West Territories Act. In June Alberta premier Don Getty announced that Alberta would take measures similar to those in Saskatchewan by repealing section 110 but providing limited services to Alberta's sixty-three thousand francophones.

Although most francophone associations in Alberta and Saskatchewan were critical of the provincial governments for not restoring francophone rights to the same level as existed in Manitoba after the *Manitoba Language Rights Reference,* Quebec's premier, Robert Bourassa, praised the two prairie governments for at least providing a small improvement to services for francophones. He said that he recognized it was impractical to provide a greater range of rights to such a small proportion of the population. Once again, Bourassa was promoting the two solitudes concept of Canada. Moreover, some suggested that Bourassa's comments might be intended to help justify future provincial government action in Quebec to limit the rights of Quebec anglophones. The Supreme Court was soon to render judgment in the *Ford*[27] and *Devine*[28] cases, concerning the English-only signs provisions of Bill 101. If Saskatchewan and Alberta reduced the rights of their francophone minorities by repealing section 110 of the *North-West Territory Act,* Quebec would be equally justified in using the *Charter's* override clause, section 33, to limit the rights of the anglophone minority in Quebec. As we saw in chapter 3, this is precisely what happened in December 1988.

LANGUAGE RIGHTS CASES, 1990–2013

Leading language rights cases beginning in 1990 have all engaged the language rights in the *Charter* relevant to primary and secondary schools.

MAHE V. ALBERTA, 1990[29]

The inclusion of s. 23 — minority-language education rights — in the *Charter of Rights* provided an opportunity for francophones outside of Quebec and New Brunswick to ensure that their children received their primary and secondary education in French, if that is what the families desired.

In 1982, a group of francophone parents in Edmonton considered that there was a sufficient number of francophone families in the city to justify a French-language elementary and secondary school in the city that would have its own school board elected by the francophone parents. After Confederation, in the late nineteenth century, a number of Quebecois families settled in what is now Alberta, mostly in the northern parts of the province that were still in need of homesteaders. The immigration likely would have continued except that, as noted earlier, the educational school rights which they thought they had under s. 93 were denied by the anglophone majority, and the corrective mechanism available to the federal government in s. 93 was not employed. Some of these immigrants had moved to Edmonton, and were joined by francophones from Quebec and other parts of Canada, but it was a challenge for them to maintain their French language and heritage until 1982, when s. 23 of the *Charter* provided new hope.

In 1982, there were nearly three thousand adult francophone citizens living in Edmonton, and amongst them they had nearly four thousand school-aged children.[30] Shortly after the *Charter* came into effect in 1982, a number of the francophone parents petitioned the Alberta government for "a new French-language public elementary school in Edmonton, which would have the following features: (1) it would instruct Francophone children exclusively in the French language and in a totally 'French' environment; (2) it would be administered by a Committee of Parents under the structure of an autonomous French School Board; and (3) it would have a programme reflecting the French linguistic culture."[31] Provincial policy was that no separate French-language school districts would be created, and the francophone parents were advised to approach Edmonton's public school board, and also the city's Roman Catholic school board. Both boards rejected the proposal as presented, and so Jean-Claude Mahe, two other francophone parents, and a francophone association began the litigation that led to this particular Supreme Court of Canada case. French was the first language learned and still understood by Mahe and two of the other parents, and so all three were qualified under s. 23(1) to have their children educated in French anywhere in Canada.

In spite of its refusal to meet all the demands of the francophone parents, the Roman Catholic school board agreed to convert a French-immersion school, École Maurice Lavallée, into a pure French-language school, and to provide parents with input through an advisory board. The school opened in 1984. Nevertheless, this development, while helpful, did not provide the parents with the control they desired over the French-language school through having their own school board, so their litigation continued. The parents had little success at trial and the Alberta Court of Appeal, and so the case reached the hearing stage at the Supreme Court of Canada in 1989.

The case was heard by a seven-judge panel. Mostly because of judicial retirements and new appointments, only two of the judges on the panel had sat on the panel that heard the *Société des Acadiens* case in 1986: Chief Justice Brian Dickson and Bertha Wilson. Both Dickson and Wilson had taken a more generous approach toward language rights than the other five judges in that case. In the *Mahe* case, Dickson wrote the decision for a unanimous court. The *Mahe* decision was the first in which the Supreme Court of Canada considered the meaning of s. 23 of the *Charter*. Because of the importance of this case, there were a number of intervenors, including the Attorneys General of Alberta, Saskatchewan, Manitoba, Ontario, Quebec, and Canada, and the Commissioner of Official Languages for Canada.

Mahe and the other parents considered that s. 23(3) gave them the right to management and control over the French language school in Edmonton. The wording of s. 23 (3) is:

> 23 (3) The right of citizens of Canada under subsections (1) and (2) to have their children receive primary and secondary school instruction in the language of the English or French linguistic minority population of a province
>
> (a) applies wherever in the province the number of children of citizens who have such a right is sufficient to warrant the provision to them out of public funds of minority language instruction; and
>
> (b) includes, where the number of those children so warrants, the right to have them receive that instruction in minority language educational facilities provided out of public funds.

Dickson began the opinion by defining the purpose of s. 23: "to preserve and promote the two official languages of Canada, and their respective cultures, by ensuring that each language flourishes, as far as possible, in provinces where it is not spoken by the majority of the population." He argued that s. 23(3) provided provincial governments with a mandate to provide minority-language education on a "sliding scale," with 23(a) marking the minimum requirement of minority-language educational "instruction," and (b) marking the maximum obligatory requirement of "minority-language educational facilities." He was skeptical about providing a "magic number" that indicated the meaning of "where the number . . . warrants," because any cut-off would be unfair to a group that had fallen just short. In terms of how many students would be required for governments to provide the minimum instruction under 3(a), Dickson refused to provide a number, because the minimum requirement was not the issue in the *Mahe* case; however, he hinted that the minimum number would be the number required for quality instruction.

With regard to whether s. 23(3)(b) refers to the physical school facilities used for instruction, or some degree of management and control over teaching facilities, Dickson concluded that 23(3)(b) means that "minority language parents possess a measure of management and control over the educational facilities in which their children are taught." This is because the French text for 23(3)(b) is clearer than the English text, and the Ontario Court of Appeal had come to the same conclusion in a case that did not advance to the Supreme Court.[32] As well, providing minority-language parents with some degree of management and control is consistent with the purpose of s. 23, which is not only to preserve and promote the two official languages, but also their respective cultures.

In determining what degree of management and control francophone parents must have in order to ensure that the purpose of s. 23 is fulfilled, Dickson reviewed the recommendations of the Royal Commission on Bilingualism and Biculturalism (1968). As well, he indicated that a separate francophone school board, in some small jurisdictions, might place such a heavy administrative burden on a small school board that the quality of education might suffer, thus discouraging students from enrolling. He concluded that

> [w]hat is essential . . . is that the minority language group
> have control over those aspects of education which pertain

*to or have an effect upon their language and culture. This
degree of control can be achieved to a substantial extent by
guaranteeing representation of the minority on a shared school
board and by giving these representatives exclusive control
over all of the aspects of minority education which pertain to
linguistic and cultural concerns.*[33]

In terms of deciding what degree of management and control francophone parents should have, Dickson declared that this constituted a policy decision best left to local authorities. It is the role of the courts to outline general obligations, and the role of the appropriate governing bodies to decide how to meet their obligations.

*At this stage of early development of s. 23 jurisprudence, the
appropriate response for the courts is to describe in general terms
the requirements mandated. It is up to the public authorities to
satisfy these general requirements. Where there are alternative
ways of satisfying the requirements, the public authorities may
choose the means of fulfilling their duties. In some instances this
approach may result in further litigation to determine whether
the general requirements mandated by the court have been
implemented. I see no way to avoid this result, as the alternative
of a uniform detailed order runs the real risk of imposing
impractical solutions. Section 23 is a new type of legal right in
Canada and thus requires new responses from the courts.*[34]

The general obligations of the appropriate authorities further to s. 23(3) were described by Dickson as follows:

*(1) The representation of the linguistic minority on local
boards or other public authorities which administer minority
language instruction or facilities should be guaranteed;*

*(2) The number of minority language representatives
on the board should be, at a minimum, proportional to the*

number of minority language students in the school district,
i.e., the number of minority language students for whom the
board is responsible;

(3) The minority language representatives should have
exclusive authority to make decisions relating to the minority
language instruction and facilities, including:

(a) expenditures of funds provided for such instruction
and facilities;

(b) appointment and direction of those responsible for the
administration of such instruction and facilities;

(c) establishment of programs of instruction;

(d) recruitment and assignment of teachers and other
personnel; and

(e) making of agreements for education and services for
minority language pupils.[35]

Another issue that the court had to determine was whether s. 23 rights were affected by s. 29 of the *Charter* ("Nothing in this *Charter* abrogates or derogates from any rights or privileges guaranteed by or under the Constitution of Canada in respect of denominational, separate, or dissentient schools") or s. 93 of the *Constitution Act, 1867* (allocation of the responsibility of education to the provinces, and protection of denominational school rights at the time the province entered Confederation). The court concluded that s. 29 and s. 93 had no impact on the implementation of s. 23 in the Roman Catholic school board in Edmonton, as denominational and non-denominational issues could operate so as to not interfere with each other.[36]

With regard to the meaning of "where the number . . . warrants," Dickson made the following general observations:

The numbers warrant provision requires, in general, that
two factors be taken into account in determining what s. 23
demands: (1) the services appropriate, in pedagogical terms,
for the numbers of students involved; and (2) the cost of the
contemplated services. The first, pedagogical requirements,

*recognizes that a threshold number of students is required
before certain programmes or facilities can operate effectively.
There is no point, for example, in having a school for only ten
students in an urban centre. The students would be deprived
of the numerous benefits which can only be achieved through
studying and interacting with larger numbers of students . . .*

*Cost, the second factor, is not usually explicitly taken
into account in determining whether or not an individual
is to be accorded a right under the* Charter. *In the case of
s. 23, however, such a consideration is mandated. Section 23
does not, like some other provisions, create an absolute right.
Rather, it grants a right which must be subject to financial
constraints, for it is financially impractical to accord to every
group of minority language students, no matter how small,
the same services which a large group of s. 23 students are
accorded . . .*[37]

In applying these principles to Edmonton, Dickson noted that although nearly 4,000 francophone students were eligible to attend L'École Maurice Lavallée, the enrolment only stood at 242, which was too small for the province or the city to be required to provide a separate francophone school board under s. 23. However, he wrote that if the enrolment increased significantly, a separate francophone board might be appropriate.

Finally, the court had to decide the question of whether the *Alberta School Act* violated s. 23 of the *Charter*. Dickson concluded that in general the *Act* complied with s. 23 so long as the general obligations specified in the *Mahe* decision were met. However, one of the *Act*'s regulations required that 20 per cent of the instruction in any Alberta school be provided in English. Dickson wrote that while some English instruction was clearly needed, the Alberta government had not fulfilled its s. 1 obligation to demonstrate why 20 per cent English instruction was necessary, and so that particular regulation was declared unconstitutional.

Therefore, in many respects, Mahe and the other francophone parents won their case. Although they did not achieve a separate francophone school board at that time, they were provided with a guarantee that they would have representation on the Roman Catholic district school board in Edmonton at least in proportion to the number of francophone children attending the French-language school, and that these representatives would be provided with "exclusive authority to make decisions relating to the minority language instruction and facilities."

Given the court's tepid approach toward language rights in the *Société des Acadiens* case, many were surprised that the court went as far as it did in *Mahe* to defend minority-language education rights. However, given the change in the court's personnel prior to 1990, and given that Chief Justice Dickson authored the opinion, the court's unanimous judgment supporting a generous but policy-sensitive reading of s. 23 is understandable.

DOUCET-BOUDREAU V. NOVA SCOTIA (2003)[38]

Doucet-Boudreau is another case dealing with the implementation of s. 23, which shows the judiciary's power when formulating an innovative remedy in order to force school boards to move more quickly when implementing s. 23 guarantees.

On behalf of all francophone families who have rights under s. 23 of the *Charter*, Glenda Doucet-Boudreau and four other francophone parents in Nova Scotia, together with a non-profit organization that advocated for francophone education in Nova Scotia, sued the Nova Scotia government for negligence in failing to implement the terms of s. 23 in a timely fashion.

It was not until 1996 that the Nova Scotia legislature took some action further to s. 23 and the *Mahe* guidelines by creating a French-language school district to cover all of Nova Scotia. However, the French-language school district relied on the discretion of the minister of education and the cabinet to "construct, furnish, and equip schools,"[39] and it was only in 1998 that promises were made to construct French-language schools in different parts of the province. But even after this announcement, nothing happened, and so Doucet-Boudreau and the other parents began their litigation. Their case went to trial in 1999, and the trial judge considered the plight of Nova Scotia francophones, the decades-long discrimination against them in the Nova Scotia education system, the lack of real action by the government since 1982, and the increasing rate of assimilation. The

Nova Scotia government had conceded that it had an obligation to provide French-language facilities further to s. 23. Therefore, the only issue in this case was the length of time the government was taking to honour its constitutional obligations.

The trial judge, Justice Arthur LeBlanc, found that the unreasonable length of time the government was taking to honour its s. 23 obligations constituted a violation of s. 23, and he was not content simply to order the government to provide facilities. LeBlanc found that the Mahe test justified the provision of French-language schools in five Nova Scotia locations. He ordered them to be opened by September 2000, although three of them would be allowed to operate in temporary facilities for between six months and a year. In order to enforce this order, LeBlanc interpreted s. 24(1), the remedies section of the *Charter*, broadly. Section 24(1) states that "Anyone whose rights or freedoms, as guaranteed by this *Charter*, have been infringed or denied may apply to a court of competent jurisdiction to obtain such remedy as the court considers appropriate and just in the circumstances." The controversial part of his decision was that he ordered representatives of the Attorney General to report back to him on March 23, 2000, and several other dates, regarding progress made on the provision of the facilities.[40]

The Attorney General was of the opinion that the trial judge had exceeded his jurisdiction under s. 24(1) because of the reporting requirement, and appealed. The Nova Scotia Court of Appeal overturned the trial judge's order for the Attorney General to report back to him. The francophone parents then appealed to the Supreme Court of Canada. The Supreme Court decided in favour of the francophone parents, upholding the trial judge's novel remedy in a five to four decision.

The decision of the majority was written by Justices Iacobucci and (Louise) Arbour. They first had to consider an argument from the Attorney General that by the time of the Supreme Court hearing, the French-language facilities had been provided, and so the issue was moot. However, the court decided that there was still an important live legal controversy about the appropriateness of the trial judge's order to report back, and invoking the *Borowski* decision on mootness (see chapter 6), the court proceeded with the hearing.

The Attorney General argued that in the common-law tradition, once a court has given an order, it ceases to have jurisdiction, and so the order to report back was outside of a trial court's jurisdiction. However, the majority noted that the *Charter* is to be given a broad and liberal interpretation, and being a constitutional document, an interpretation based on technicalities is unacceptable. As well, the government's rationale for the long delay in providing French-language facilities was not persuasive, and it was reasonable for the trial judge to doubt whether the facilities would be provided as quickly as possible without the extraordinary remedy he applied.

The Supreme Court minority was opposed to departing from the common-law tradition of ending a trial court's jurisdiction over a matter, even an important constitutional matter relating to s. 23. The minority was also critical of the remedy as being excessively activist and violating the doctrine of the separation of powers between the judicial and political branches of government.

Given the legitimate frustration of francophone Nova Scotians about the delays in implementing s. 23 in their province, the Supreme Court's majority decision was a signal about the importance of s. 23 in Canada's constitutional makeup. The decision has left the court vulnerable to new charges of excessive activism, but no doubt the majority accepted this situation as the penalty for making what they considered the constitutionally correct choice in a novel area of law.

OTHER S. 23 CASES

Following *Doucet-Boudreau*, two cases indicate the Supreme Court may have adopted a more restrained approach to s. 23. The first was *Gosselin (Tutor of) v. Quebec*, decided by the Supreme Court in 2005.[41] The issue here was whether the Canada clause in the constitution permitted francophone parents to send their children to publicly-funded English-language schools in order to ensure that their children would be proficient in English as well as French. Some francophone parents had tried to circumvent the restrictions of the Canada clause and Quebec's *Charter of the French Language* by sending their children to a private English-language school for a short period and then claiming that because their children had attended school in English, the children subsequently were entitled to attend publicly-funded English schools. The trial court, the Quebec Court of Appeal, and the Supreme Court of Canada all agreed that francophone parents did not have a constitutional right to send their children to publicly-funded English-language schools in Quebec in such situations because this would "read out of the Constitution the compromise contained in s. 23."[42]

The second case was *Conseil scolaire francophone de la Colombie-Britannique v. British Columbia*, decided in 2013.[43] The issue in this case was whether a francophone school board in BC, along with a francophone parents association, could introduce affidavits into a court proceeding dealing with s. 23 of the *Charter* in French only. When it became a colony in 1858, BC had "received" into its body of laws a 1731 English statute, which required court proceedings to be in English. The province of BC had left that statute untouched. The majority concluded that exhibits were part of proceedings, and so must be accompanied by an English translation. The minority, however, concluded that the francophone school board operates in French, that exhibits are not within the definition of "court proceedings," and that giving trial judges the discretion to accept exhibits in French, especially when all involved could read the documents, was another way of acknowledging the importance of s. 23 in Canada's constitutional scheme.

JUDICIAL INTERPRETATION OF LANGUAGE RIGHTS

From the perspective of the cases discussed in this chapter, it is clear that the Supreme Court has decided to uphold language rights where their existence is unquestionable in the *Charter* or other parts of the constitution — an approach particularly evident in the *Quebec Protestant School Board* case, the *Manitoba Language Rights Reference*, the *Mahe* case, and the *Doucet-Boudreau* decision. However, early on the court also decided to interpret language rights narrowly so as to signal that if basic language rights are to be extended, this should come about as a result of political solutions, not judicial ones.

The decisions in *Société des Acadiens*, *Bilodeau*, *MacDonald*, and *Mercure* illustrate the restrained approach toward language rights that the court took to begin with. In the first case, it was decided that the right to speak the minority language in court does not include the right to be understood in that language. The second and third cases settled that summonses need only be issued in one of the official languages in the provinces with bilingual guarantees emanating from section 133 of the *Constitution Act, 1867*, the *Charter*, or another part of the constitution (Quebec, New Brunswick, and Manitoba). Although the *Mercure* decision did extend section 133–like guarantees to Alberta and Saskatchewan for a few months, the majority decision in a sense invited the provinces to repeal the minority-language rights.

However, beginning with the *Mahe* decision, and continuing through *Doucet-Boudreau*, the court took a broader, more comprehensive approach to language rights, or at least to the minority-language education rights contained in s. 23. Although the narrowness of the earlier decisions would have disappointed the proponents of the Pierre Trudeau vision of Canada, *Mahe* and *Doucet-Boudreau* would have given them new hope. Nevertheless, it often appears that once the Supreme Court has taken a bold step that some would label activist, it then takes either a pause or a small step back, which may have been the case with *Gosselin (Tutor of) v. Quebec* and *Conseil scolaire francophone de la Colombie-Britannique v. BC*.

CHAPTER 8

ABORIGINAL RIGHTS: OUTSIDE THE *CHARTER* BUT INSIDE THE RIGHTS REGIME

When Canada's *Charter of Rights and Freedoms* was drafted beginning in 1980, Aboriginal rights were not part of the original plan. The original conception of the *Charter* was that it would include beefed-up versions of the traditional human rights developed over centuries through the common law, an enhanced version of language rights and language education rights, and mobility rights to counteract restrictive provincial residency regulations. Various Aboriginal groups expressed outrage that the rights they once thought had been guaranteed by the Royal Proclamation of 1763 and by treaties signed either with the British Crown or the Canadian government, and which had often been ignored, were not even mentioned in the *Charter*. Their opposition to the Trudeau government's *Charter* and patriation project gathered a good deal of support from many non-Aboriginal Canadians, and eventually led to a widespread consensus that if the constitutional impasse of 1981 were ever to be resolved, recognition of Aboriginal rights would have to be part of the solution.[1]

Aboriginal rights did not seem to fit within the *Charter* itself, as these rights applied to a particular group of Canadians, although these rights would need to be recognized by Canadians as a whole. The resolution worked out was to place Aboriginal rights into s. 35 of the *Constitution Act, 1982*, the first section of that act after the *Charter*. The reason why this book contains a chapter on Aboriginal rights is because since 1982, the Supreme Court's jurisprudence on s. 35 has applied similar principles and approaches to the interpretation of Aboriginal rights as it has applied to the *Charter*. Thus, a comprehensive understanding of judicial interpretation of rights in Canada must include Aboriginal rights.

Section 35 originally read as follows:

> **35.** *(1) The existing aboriginal and treaty rights of the Aboriginal peoples of Canada are hereby recognized and affirmed.*
>
> *(2) In this Act, "aboriginal peoples of Canada" includes the Indian, Inuit, and Métis peoples of Canada.*

Subsection (1) refers to existing Aboriginal and treaty rights. Federal and provincial politicians recognized that some Aboriginal treaty rights had been ignored over the years or overridden by federal or provincial legislation. Governments were able to get away with this because Canadian courts had often interpreted the treaties as they would international agreements. According to common-law principles of judicial interpretation, the courts recognize and apply only "domestic" legislation — i.e., primary legislation that has been duly enacted by Parliament or provincial legislature, or secondary legislation that is authorized by the primary legislation, such as municipal bylaws or the laws of territorial legislatures. International treaties may be helpful when interpreting legislation, but unless the treaties have been enacted into domestic legislation, the courts do not recognize them. Thus, what the courts had recognized up to 1982 was the content of treaties as reflected in domestic legislation, which did not necessarily include all of the rights actually contained in the treaties. Full implementation of the original content of the treaties might prove extremely costly to the federal and provincial governments.

Most Aboriginal groups, for a number of reasons, did not think that s. 35 went nearly far enough to guarantee their rights. First, there was strong opposition to the word "existing" in s. 35(1) because that word might imply what was left of Aboriginal rights after government encroachment on them. Second, in 1982 there were vast expanses of Canada where no treaties or land claim agreements had ever been signed. These areas included most of British Columbia, parts of Yukon and the Northwest Territories (which at the time included all of Nunavut), parts of northern Ontario and Quebec, and all of Newfoundland and Labrador. Aboriginal peoples wanted assurance that future treaties or land claims agreements would have constitutional protection. Third, Aboriginal peoples generally wanted to govern themselves. They wanted the inherent right to self-government recognized. Fourth, as readers will recall from chapter 1, the *Lavell* and *Bédard* decisions of the Supreme Court in 1974 left Aboriginal women with fewer rights than Aboriginal men because treaty rights could be passed on only through patrilineal lines. This decision ignited a movement amongst some female Aboriginal leaders to demand equal rights for Aboriginal women. This debate was focused within the reserves themselves, where some Aboriginal men were reluctant to give up the patrilineal system. By 1982, it was generally conceded that Aboriginal women had prevailed in the equality debate, but there was concern that s. 15 of the *Charter*, the equality section, might not apply to the federal government's constitutional jurisdiction over Aboriginal peoples. Aboriginal women demanded an additional guarantee of gender equality. Fifth, Aboriginal peoples wanted assurance that the parts of the constitution that affected them most would not be amended in the future without their consent.

These were complex issues that could not be settled in the time frame set by the federal government and nine provinces for patriation in early 1982. There are hundreds of Aboriginal bands in Canada with very different histories and traditions. They do not speak with a unified voice any more than do the various ethnicities of Europe or Asia. It was decided that the best way forward would be to proceed with including s. 35 in the 1982 constitutional amendment package, but also to include a constitutional commitment to convene a constitutional conference within one year, attended by the prime minister, the provincial premiers, and representatives of Aboriginal peoples, who would consider a resolution to this important issue.

The constitutional conference was duly held in 1983, and it resulted in the first, and to 2014 the only, amendment to the Canadian constitution under the 1982 "seven-fifty" amending formula.[2] This formula states that most parts of the constitution can be amended with the agreement of Parliament and the legislatures of at least seven provinces that together represent at least fifty per cent of Canada's population.[3] The amendment added the following two sections to s. 35:

> *(3) For greater certainty, in subsection (1) "treaty rights" includes rights that now exist by way of land claims agreements or may be so acquired.*
>
> *(4) Notwithstanding any other provision of this Act, the Aboriginal and treaty rights referred to in subsection (1) are guaranteed equally to male and female persons.*

After the addition of s. 35(4) was that the federal *Indian Act* was amended to provide somewhat more equal treatment to Aboriginal women with regard to the inheritance of treaty rights.[4]

The amendment also resulted in the insertion of s. 35.1 immediately following s. 35.

> *35.1 The government of Canada and the provincial governments are committed to the principle that, before any amendment is made to Class 24 of section 91 of the "Constitution Act, 1867", to section 25 of this Act or to this Part,*
>
> *(a) a constitutional conference that includes in its agenda an item relating to the proposed amendment, composed of the Prime Minister of Canada and the first ministers of the provinces, will be convened by the Prime Minister of Canada; and*
>
> *(b) the Prime Minister of Canada will invite representatives of the Aboriginal peoples of Canada to participate in the discussions on that item.*

Section 91(24) is the section of the *Constitution Act, 1867* that gives the federal Parliament jurisdiction over "Indians and lands reserved to

Indians." Section 25 refers to section 25 of the *Charter of Rights*, which states that the *Charter* shall "not be construed so as to abrogate or derogate from any Aboriginal, treaty or other rights or freedoms that pertain to the Aboriginal peoples of Canada including any rights or freedoms that have been recognized by the Royal Proclamation of October 7, 1763; and any rights or freedoms that now exist by way of land claims agreements or may be so acquired." "This Part" refers to s. 35.

Although there was an agreement amongst the first ministers to proceed with the 1983 amendments, there was no consensus amongst the Aboriginal representatives that their concerns had been resolved. For example, Aboriginal women wanted assurance that they would be represented at future constitutional conferences that dealt with Aboriginal rights; Aboriginal representatives in general wanted a guarantee that future constitutional changes affecting them could not occur without their explicit consent; and many Aboriginal groups insisted on a constitutional recognition of a right to Aboriginal self-government. Three more constitutional conferences were held to address these issues — in 1984, 1985, and 1987 — but all ended in failure. The result was that Aboriginal peoples came to rely on litigation rather than political negotiation to address their rights claims.

It is important to note the importance to Aboriginal peoples of the Royal Proclamation of 1763, which reads in part as follows:

> . . . [T]he several Nations or Tribes of Indians with whom We
> are connected, and who live under our Protection, should not
> be molested or disturbed in the Possession of such Parts of Our
> Dominions and Territories as, not having been ceded to or
> purchased by Us, are reserved to them, or any of them, as their
> Hunting Grounds.[5]

The Proclamation was issued by King George III as an attempt to settle the grievances of Aboriginal peoples in the British colonies of North America (which at the time included what is now the United States) and conflicts between the native peoples and the colonies that were determined to expand to the west, taking over control of traditional Aboriginal lands in the process. The king, who had as much say over colonial policy as the British cabinet or Parliament at that time, hoped to assure Aboriginal peoples that their land rights would be recognized, and they would be fairly compensated for lands taken over by settlers. In general the Aboriginal peoples at the time therefore viewed the British Crown as their champion and protector in the face of some colonists who viewed that Aboriginal population as a nuisance, a conquered people, or worse, somehow less than human — as some considered the black slaves they had imported or purchased. In fact, the opposition to the Royal Proclamation amongst a large swath of the colonists in what is now the United States was one of the key factors that ignited the American Revolution. It is no wonder that the Aboriginal peoples tended to remain loyal to the British Crown during the War of Independence and during the War of 1812. In fact, there is a good argument that the United States could well have captured what is now Canada during either the War of Independence or the War of 1812 had it not been for the military resistance of the Aboriginal peoples to the designs of the United States.

The trust that the Aboriginal peoples of Canada placed in the Royal Proclamation and the Treaty of Niagara was never fully realized either in Canada's colonial period or after 1867. That is why many Aboriginal leaders continued to look to the British Crown for protection against the erosion of their rights, arguing that the British Crown could not delegate its 1763 commitments to the Canadian Parliament. In the cases reviewed in this chapter, note the frequent reference to the obligations stemming from the Royal Proclamation and the obligation of the Canadian government to honour these obligations.

The most important pre-Charter case regarding Aboriginal rights was the *Calder* case, decided by the Supreme Court in 1973.[6] Prior to *Calder*, courts in Canada generally rejected the recognition of Aboriginal rights and Aboriginal treaty claims, for two reasons. First, the Aboriginal understanding of the treaties was not considered because Aboriginals were not thought to have cultures with a concept of law that allowed them to participate in the Crown's legal system. Second, the only law recognized by the courts was domestic law; there was no law generated by treaties. *Calder* was the first case in which this outdated approach, which was clearly racist and Eurocentric, began to show signs of weakening.

The issue in the Calder case was whether the Nishga band had any say about government decisions to make use of the Nishga's traditional lands in the Nass Valley of British Columbia. No treaties had been signed with the Nishga. A panel of seven judges heard this land claims case. Six of the seven judges conceded that Aboriginal peoples had title to the lands they occupied prior to European settlement. Three judges, Wilfred Judson, Ronald Martland, and Roland Ritchie, adopted a restrained interpretation of how title could be extinguished. They argued that government regulation had implicitly extinguished Aboriginal title in the case of the Nishga. They relied heavily on early nineteenth-century United States Supreme Court precedents that had been adopted by Canadian courts. They also held that the Royal Proclamation of 1763 did not apply west of the Rockies because in 1763, much of British Columbia west of the Rockies was unexplored by Europeans. However, three judges, Emmett Hall, Wishart Spence, and Bora Laskin, wrote that this restrained position was outdated and wrong. The United States precedents relied on by Judson, Martland, and Ritchie were written at a time when racism held sway, and it was time for Canadian courts to adopt the more enlightened approach of the current era. As for the Royal Proclamation of 1763, Hall, Spence, and Laskin provided persuasive evidence that the Royal Proclamation was intended to apply to all North American lands claimed by the United Kingdom, including unexplored lands. They referred to the Royal Proclamation as the "Indian Bill of Rights," with the same force of law throughout the British Empire as the Magna Carta.[7] They concluded that under common law, the Aboriginal peoples had a general right to sue the Crown, and the fact that British Columbia had not enacted a specific statute enabling the Crown to be sued simply meant that traditional common-law procedures would need to be used to bring the suit, as they had been in this case. As a result, the Nishga people possessed the "right to enjoy the fruits of the soil, of the forest, and of the rivers and streams within the boundaries" of their traditional lands, and that this right had not been extinguished through a treaty.[8]

The seventh judge, Louis-Philippe Pigeon, decided the case on a technicality. He ruled that the Nishga did not have the right to sue the Crown unless the Crown had provided explicit permission for the suit.

Although the Nishga lost the case, the decision of Hall, concurred in by Spence and Laskin, opened the door to the possibility that the courts would one day recognize Aboriginal rights more broadly. Section 35 of the *Constitution Act, 1982* provided that opportunity.

SPARROW (1990)[9]

Section 91 of the *Constitution Act, 1867* grants the federal Parliament the power to regulate fisheries and oceans. By the early 1980s, the federal *Fisheries Act* allowed for special fishing licences for Aboriginal bands in order to try to accommodate their traditional fishing activities that provided food for the bands. The special licence granted to the Musqueam band, which resides in the vicinity of Vancouver in the Fraser River estuary, allowed the use of drift nets not longer than fifty fathoms, although longer nets had previously been permitted. Ronald Edward Sparrow, a member of the Musqueam band, was convicted of fishing with a net longer than the *Act* allowed. Sparrow appealed the conviction based on the claim that the *Act*'s length restriction was a violation of s. 35(1). The litigation reached the Supreme Court of Canada, which decided the case more or less in favour of Sparrow in 1990.

The decision for "The Court"[10] was penned jointly by Chief Justice Dickson and Justice La Forest. These judges noted that "[f]or many years, the rights of the Indians to their Aboriginal lands — certainly as legal rights — were virtually ignored . . . By the late 1960s, Aboriginal claims were not even recognized by the federal government as having any legal status."[11] However, the *Calder* decision forced the government to re-evaluate its position on Aboriginal rights, and in 1973 the government declared that it was "now ready" to negotiate with Aboriginal peoples, and "where their traditional interest in the lands concerned can be established, an agreed form of compensation or benefit will be provided to native peoples in return for their interest,"[12] even without formal supporting documents.

The court went on to characterize the inclusion of s. 35(1) in the *Constitution Act, 1982* as "the culmination of a long and difficult struggle in both the political forum and the courts for the constitutional recognition of Aboriginal rights."[13] It was noted that because s. 35(1) is not part of the *Charter*, it is not subject to the s. 1 limitations clause or the s. 33 override clause. This indicates the important place of Aboriginal rights in the constitution. "When the purposes of the affirmation of Aboriginal rights are considered, it is clear that a generous, liberal interpretation of the words in the constitutional provision is demanded."[14]

The Crown had argued that "existing" Aboriginal rights in s. 35(1) meant what was left over after the federal and provincial governments had restricted Aboriginal rights, such as fishing rights, through legislation. The court found that such a narrow interpretation of s. 35(1) would be inconsistent with the importance of s. 35(1) in the constitution and a "generous, liberal" interpretation. As well, freezing what Aboriginal rights were left over as of April 1982 would result in a "patchwork"[15] of Aboriginal rights, as provincial encroachment on Aboriginal rights would vary from province to province. As a result, the only sensible approach would be to consider existing Aboriginal rights as any Aboriginal rights recognized by treaties or the Royal Proclamation that had not been clearly extinguished by a treaty or government legislation. The argument that regulations had been enacted that limited Aboriginal rights could be treated as an implied extinction of these rights was rejected.

At the same time, the court rejected the notion that governments could not regulate Aboriginal rights. For example, the Aboriginal right to fish might become meaningless without regulations meant to conserve the fish stock for future generations of Aboriginal peoples. However, any government regulation affecting Aboriginal rights would need to be for the benefit of the Aboriginal peoples themselves and would need to reflect the results of negotiations with the Aboriginal peoples affected.

Based on this approach, did the regulations under the federal *Fisheries Act* that prohibited Sparrow from using a net longer than fifty fathoms violate s. 35(1)? The court recognized that answering this question was the role of a trial judge, not an appeal court, and so this question was returned to the trial court for determination, but with guidelines from the Supreme Court. The trial court would need to ask and then answer a number of questions based on the evidence before it.

First, does the drift-net length restriction have "the effect of interfering with an existing Aboriginal right"[16] so that a *prima facie* interference of the right is demonstrable? To answer that question, several additional questions need to be posed.

> *First, is the limitation unreasonable? Second, does the regulation*
> *impose undue hardship? Third, does the regulation deny to*
> *the holders of the right their preferred means of exercising that*
> *right? The onus of proving a prima facie infringement lies on the*
> *individual or group challenging the legislation.*[17]

If the trial court finds that there is a *prima facie* interference with an Aboriginal right, is this interference justified? To answer that question, another set of questions must be posed.

> *First, is there a valid legislative objective? . . . If a valid*
> *legislative objective is found, the analysis proceeds to*
> *the second part of the justification issue . . . That is, the*
> *honour of the Crown is at stake in dealings with Aboriginal*
> *peoples. The special trust relationship and the responsibility*
> *of the government vis-à-vis Aboriginals must be the first*
> *consideration in determining whether the legislation or action*
> *in question can be justified.*[18]

Two more justification questions arise: "whether there has been as little infringement as possible in order to effect the desired result . . .; and, whether the Aboriginal group in question has been consulted with respect to the conservation measures being implemented."[19]

The *Sparrow* decision was a landmark for the recognition of Aboriginal rights. The Supreme Court declared that s. 35(1) should be interpreted in a purposive and liberal way. Aboriginal rights still exist either under treaty or the Royal Proclamation unless clearly extinguished by the federal government. However, Aboriginal rights can be regulated by government as long as the government exercises its fiduciary duties in a way that can be demonstrated in court to be responsible. Readers have likely noted that the test for permissible government regulation of Aboriginal rights bears some resemblance to the Oakes test for the application of s. 1 of the *Charter*. This is not surprising, given that the court had become used to thinking about limitations to rights from the Oakes perspective, and that the court tries to interpret constitutional documents in a consistent manner.

VAN DER PEET (1996)[20]

In 1987, Dorothy Van der Peet sold ten salmon that had been caught by her spouse, an Aboriginal man who was operating under an Indian food fish licence that was issued under the authority of Canada's *Fisheries Act*. The licence was meant to provide Aboriginal peoples with the ability to catch fish for their own use, and prohibited the sale or barter of fish caught pursuant to the licence. Ms. Van der Peet admitted to selling the fish but claimed that the selling of fish was part of the tradition of her band, the Sto:lo of the lower Fraser River area of British Columbia, and that therefore this activity was protected under s. 35(1) of the *Constitution Act, 1867*.

Ms. Van der Peet was convicted at trial, won at summary appeal, lost again in the British Columbia Court of Appeal, and lost again in the Supreme Court of Canada. Critical to the outcome of this case was the interpretation of evidence about whether the selling or bartering of fish was part of the traditional activity of the Sto:lo people and therefore protected by s. 35(1).

The court split seven to two on this decision, with Chief Justice Lamer writing the decision for the majority. He began his analysis by observing that although Aboriginal rights refer only to Aboriginal people, there are nevertheless a number of principles developed in the interpretation of the *Charter* that apply to the interpretation of Aboriginal rights. These include applying a purposive approach, which means interpreting the constitution in the light of changing circumstances and always keeping in mind the interests the provision was meant to protect.[21] The *Sparrow* decision was also cited, with emphasis on the need for a "generous and liberal interpretation" of Aboriginal rights, and the government's fiduciary responsibilities.[22] Although *Sparrow* recited the need for a purposive approach, the actual purpose of Aboriginal rights was not articulated there. In setting the stage for defining the purpose of Aboriginal rights, Lamer quoted Professor Brian Slattery. According to Slattery, the law surrounding Aboriginal rights is neither English nor aboriginal in origin: it is a form of intersocietal law that evolved from long-standing practices linking the various communities."[23] Lamer concluded that "the aboriginal rights recognized and affirmed by s. 35(1) are best understood as, first, the means by which the Constitution recognizes the fact that prior to the arrival of Europeans in North America the land was already occupied by distinctive aboriginal societies, and as, second, the means by which that prior occupation is reconciled with the assertion of Crown sovereignty over Canadian territory."[24] Therefore, in order for an activity to qualify as an aboriginal right, "an activity must be an element of a practice, custom, or tradition integral to the distinctive culture of the aboriginal group claiming the right."[25]

In determining an Aboriginal rights claim, Lamer stated that it is "crucial to be sensitive to the aboriginal perspective itself on the meaning of the rights at stake." It must also be recognized, however, that that perspective must be framed in terms cognizable to the Canadian legal and constitutional structure."[26] He asserted that when determining practices integral to the Aboriginal culture — those that are protected by s. 35(1) — the critical time period is that *prior* to contact with Europeans. In order for a practice to receive protection through s. 35(1), it must have been an activity integral to the Aboriginal culture prior to European contact, and continued, at least intermittently, up to the time of the litigation. Of course, practices evolve over time, and the courts must accept the legitimacy of this evolution in order to provide a "generous and liberal interpretation" of rights that is not "frozen in time." Nevertheless, the practice must be anchored in pre-contact practices. Again, evidence of these practices need not conform to common-law tort standards; Aboriginal evidence must not be "undervalued."[27]

Lamer examined the trial court record for this case, which included anthropological evidence and evidence from Aboriginal oral tradition. He concluded that although there may have been some bartering involving fish prior to European contact, that practice did not become commonplace until after European contact. As a result, he concluded that the bartering of fish by the Sto:lo (which for constitutional purposes could legitimately transform into the selling of fish) was not an integral part of the pre-contact culture of the Sto:lo and therefore not protected by s. 35(1).

Although Lamer's analysis emphasized the importance of considering evidence that seriously takes into account the Aboriginal perspective on rights and allows for the evolution of Aboriginal practices that can be protected by s. 35(1), his conclusion does seem to freeze Aboriginal rights into essentially pre-contact practices. This approach places a very high burden on Aboriginal peoples to demonstrate that current Aboriginal practices, in order to receive constitutional protection, are grounded on pre-contact practices that have evolved in a way that is acceptable to the courts.

The two dissenting judges were L'Heureux-Dubé and McLachlin. L'Heureux-Dubé claimed that s. 35(1) should not be limited to pre-contact times. Otherwise, why were Métis rights also included in s. 35(1)? Second, Aboriginal rights should be interpreted according to the general nature of Aboriginal culture — not just specific activities. There was ample evidence that salmon fishing had been part of the Sto:lo culture for a very long time and that bartering of salmon with other tribes took place. L'Heureux-Dubé would have decided the case in favour of Van der Peet with regard to the existence of the right to barter or sell fish but would have sent the case back to trial on the question of whether the right had been extinguished, as insufficient evidence had been submitted.

McLachlin argued that the right of the Sto:lo to sell fish was protected by s. 35(1) as part of their tradition and that the regulations that prohibited Van der Peet from selling fish had not met the fiduciary requirements of the *Sparrow* decision. She also argued that this right had not been extinguished.

The Supreme Court's decision in *Van der Peet* demonstrates that although the court is unanimous in its determination to interpret s. 35(1) in a way that corrects the pre-*Calder* denial of Aboriginal rights, the majority of judges are hesitant at this stage to interpret s. 35(1) as generously and liberally as they claim to do because of fear of unknown consequences. However, by recognizing both the importance of Aboriginal perspectives about their rights and evidence from oral tradition and anthropologists, the court also sent a signal to Aboriginal rights claimants that with persuasive enough evidence, they might win future rights cases.

DELGAMUUKW (1997)[28]

The *Delgamuukw* decision was the first land rights decision of the Supreme Court after the 1973 *Calder* decision and after the insertion of s. 35(1) into the constitution in 1982. The decision recognized the scope of Aboriginal title to Canadian lands where title had not been extinguished by a treaty. However, rather than granting title, the court set out a number of guidelines that it hoped would result in negotiations between Aboriginal peoples and governments to settle title claims through the political process rather than through litigation.

After British Columbia entered Canada in 1871, there was political resistance to negotiating treaties with Aboriginal peoples. The Canadian constitution gives control of "public lands"[29] to provincial governments, and the provincial government took the position that "common-law native title did not apply in British Columbia."[30] Even after the *Calder* decision, the province resisted serious negotiation. A number of hereditary chiefs of the Gitkscan and Wet'suwet'en peoples in British Columbia brought suit to the BC Superior Court in 1984 for ownership and jurisdiction over 58,000 square kilometres of land in the northwest interior of the province — an area about the size of New Brunswick. (Although the federal government had declared that it was ready to negotiate land claims with the Gitkscan and Wet'suwet'en peoples in 1977, the negotiations had not gone well, in part because of provincial resistance, and so the hereditary chiefs went to court instead.) At the trial, the Gitkscan and Wet'suwet'en introduced a great deal of evidence about the traditional occupancy and use of their homeland, which included 133 territories and 71 "Houses."[31] Evidence was presented over 374 days, resulting in a 400-page decision by Superior Court Chief Justice Allan McEachern in 1991.[32] The Gitkscan and Wet'suwet'en lost with regard to their land claim, but McEachern declared that they had "usufructuary" rights, i.e., the legal right to continue using their traditional lands as they had prior to European contact. However, this area was smaller than the area designated by the Aboriginals. The Gitkscan and Wet'suwet'en appealed to the BC Court of Appeal, where they won on some issues in 1993. The BC Court of Appeal decision set the stage for further negotiations involving Gitkscan and Wet'suwet'en representatives and the governments of Canada and BC. These negotiations broke down, however, resulting in numerous Aboriginal protests.[33] In 1996, the BC Attorney General appealed the 1993 Court of Appeal decision to the Supreme Court of Canada.

The Supreme Court appeal was heard by a panel of seven, but because of the death of Justice Sopinka, the judgment was from a panel of six. The main decision was written by Chief Justice Lamer and concurred in by McLachlin, Cory, and Major. Justices LaForest and L'Heureux-Dubé wrote separate decisions that differed from the majority on some points.

To help make sense of the many complex issues raised by this case, it is useful to consider it in sections.

THE ADMISSIBILITY OF EVIDENCE FROM ABORIGINAL TRADITIONAL SOURCES

The trial judge had dismissed much of the evidence submitted by the Gitkscan and Wet'suwet'en because it did not meet the common-law standard for evidence. However, building on the *Van der Peet* decision, Lamer stated that the courts must "adapt the laws of evidence so that the aboriginal perspective on their practices, customs, and traditions and on their relationship with the land, are given due weight by the courts."[34] He referred to a special tradition of oral history for the Gitkscan and Wet'suwet'en people respectively known as the "adaawk and kungax". These oral histories were repeated at ceremonial events and represented on "totem poles, crests, and blankets,"[35] as well as in song. Dissenters were given an opportunity to dispute the "official" understanding of the recitations. Lamer noted that the trial judge had not had the benefit of reading the court's 1996 decision in *Van der Peet* and therefore had not given the Aboriginal oral evidence suffi-cient weight. Thus, the trial judge's findings of fact were in error, and a higher court could legitimately substitute its own findings of fact. However, rather than substitute its own findings of fact, the Supreme Court ordered a new trial.

> The trial judge's treatment of the various kinds of oral histories
> did not satisfy the principles I laid down in Van der Peet.
> These errors are particularly worrisome because oral histories
> were of critical importance to the appellants' case. They used
> those histories in an attempt to establish their occupation
> and use of the disputed territory, an essential requirement
> for aboriginal title . . . Had the trial judge assessed the oral
> histories correctly, his conclusions on these issues of fact might
> have been very different.
>
> In the circumstances, the factual findings cannot stand.
> However, given the enormous complexity of the factual issues
> at hand, it would be impossible for the court to do justice to
> the parties by sifting through the record itself and making
> new factual findings. A new trial is warranted, at which the

> *evidence may be considered in light of the principles laid down*
> *in* Van der Peet *and elaborated upon here.*[36]

PRINCIPLES GUIDING LAND CLAIMS SETTLEMENTS

Lamer wrote that settling Aboriginal land claims is best accomplished through negotiation rather than litigation.[37] The remainder of Lamer's decision set out the principles that must guide land claims negotiations, as well as litigation, should negotiations prove unsuccessful.

Lamer wrote that Aboriginal title "can be summarized by two propositions: first, that aboriginal title encompasses the right to exclusive use and occupation of the land held pursuant to that title for a variety of purposes, which need not be aspects of those aboriginal practices, customs, and traditions which are integral to distinctive aboriginal cultures; and second, that those protected uses must not be irreconcilable with the nature of the group's attachment to that land."[38] As well, Aboriginal title means communal title: Aboriginal title can be held only by the Aboriginal community, not by individuals. In order to facilitate individual ownership, the community would first need to cede or sell the land to the Crown.[39] The use of Aboriginal title lands cannot be frozen in time so as to prevent Aboriginals from benefitting from the land, as some bands have benefitted from the use of Indian reserve land in a variety of ways. However, the land may not be used in a way that would destroy the traditional bond that Aboriginals have with their land — for example, by developing a strip mine or creating a parking lot.[40]

Aboriginal title rights, as described above, are not absolute. The Crown can encroach on Aboriginal title in order to fulfill its fiduciary duties toward the Aboriginals, or for the greater public good, so long as the "honour of the Crown" (the duties and obligations of the government) is upheld. In elaborating the limits to infringement, Lamer built on the principles enunciated in the *Sparrow* decision.

> *First, the infringement of the aboriginal right must be in*
> *furtherance of a legislative objective that is compelling and*
> *substantial . . . The second part of the test of justification*
> *requires an assessment of whether the infringement is consistent*

with the special fiduciary relationship between the Crown and
aboriginal peoples . . . Three aspects of aboriginal title are
relevant here. First, aboriginal title encompasses the right to
exclusive use and occupation of land; second, aboriginal title
encompasses the right to choose to what uses land can be put,
subject to the ultimate limit that those uses cannot destroy the
ability of the land to sustain future generations of aboriginal
peoples; and third, that lands held pursuant to aboriginal title
have an inescapable economic component.[41]

What kinds of legislative objectives would meet the "compelling and substantial" text? Lamer answers that ". . . the development of agriculture, forestry, mining, and hydroelectric power, the general economic development of the interior of British Columbia, protection of the environment or endangered species, the building of infrastructure and the settlement of foreign populations to support those aims, are the kinds of objectives that are consistent with this purpose and, in principle, can justify the infringement of aboriginal title. . . ."[42] With regard to the government's fiduciary duties, Lamer emphasized the importance of consultation with Aboriginal peoples, the importance of fair compensation for encroachments on their land, and where there is a conflict between Aboriginal interests and the general public, showing greater deference to Aboriginal interests.

Two other points are important. First, the Gitkscan and Wet'suwet'en claims had also included a claim of some form of self-government. Lamer wrote that this was an issue that would also need to be decided through negotiation or another trial, although the evidence showed that the Gitkscan and Wet'suwet'en did have evidence that might back up such a claim.[43] Finally, only the federal Parliament can extinguish Aboriginal title under s. 91(24) of the *Constitution Act, 1867*.[44] The provinces have no such role. However, because British Columbia has jurisdiction over the lands claimed by the Gitkscan and Wet'suwet'en, the province must work with the federal government to negotiate the settlement of land claims by the Gitkscan and Wet'suwet'en.

The Gitkscan and Wet'suwet'en, as well as other Aboriginal groups in Canada, interpreted the Supreme Court decision in *Delgamuukw* as a victory, even though they did not get everything they had hoped for from the decision. The court ruled that where there were no land claims settlements, Aboriginal groups could still claim title. Aboriginal oral evidence was given greater weight, and governments had a duty to negotiate.

In 1999, the Nishga finally succeeded in negotiating a treaty with BC and Canada — the culmination of the litigation that led to the Supreme Court's decision in *Calder* in 1973. An independent Treaty Commission was set up in British Columbia to help facilitate land claims settlements. A treaty has been in effect with the Tsawwassen First Nation since 2009 and with the Maa-nulth First Nations since 2011. Three other draft treaties are pending final approval either by one of the Aboriginal bands or the federal government. As of 2014, negotiations were in various stages with fifty-six other bands.[45] As Peter Russell and others observed, "while the Supreme Court can clarify the constitutional principles that underlie the First Nations' relations with Canada, it cannot settle the concrete issues involved in each case. Settlement involves an ongoing mixture of litigation in the courts and political negotiations."[46]

MARSHALL (1999)[47]

Donald Marshall Jr. was the son of a Mi'kmaq hereditary grand chief in Nova Scotia. In 1971, when he was seventeen, he was wrongfully convicted of murder. He was released after spending eleven years in jail.[48]

In 1993, Marshall was caught fishing for eels without a licence, out of season, and with illegal nets. Wary of the justice system, he phoned a Mi'kmaq chief to request advice. The chief told him that according to treaties the Mi'kmaq had signed with the British, he had a right to fish and should keep doing so.[49] He eventually caught 210 kilograms of eels and sold them for nearly $800. At that point he was charged with violating federal fishing regulations. Having been through the justice system once and having won, he may have felt better prepared for a new legal battle than other Mi'kmaq fishers.

Marshall was convicted for violating the regulations at trial, and his conviction was upheld by the Nova Scotia Court of Appeal. However, Marshall was acquitted by the Supreme Court of Canada in a five to two decision. His acquittal was a major victory for Aboriginal rights as it signalled that thanks to s. 35(1), Aboriginals still possessed the hunting and fishing rights they had been granted by treaties with the British in the late 1700s.

The decision for the majority was written by Justice Binnie and concurred in by Lamer, Cory, McLachlin, and Iacobucci. The treaties Marshall relied on were the Treaty of Peace and Friendship between the British government and the Maliseet that was signed in Halifax in 1760, and other Treaties of Peace and Friendship between the British government and several Mi'kmaq bands signed in 1760 and 1761. The British had defeated the French in 1958 at Louisbourg, and in 1959 at Quebec, and were anxious to win the friendship and support of the Aboriginals of the region, who had been allies of the French. The 1760 and 1761 treaties secured for the Mi'kmaq and other Aboriginal peoples, amongst other things, the right to trade the products of their hunting, fishing, and gathering, but required them to trade exclusively at British "truck houses," or trading posts.[50]

Key to the interpretation of the treaty by the majority and minority was their interpretation of the evidence about the Mi'kmaq understanding of the meaning of the treaty in preliterate times. Some of the evidence on behalf of the Mi'kmaq was presented at trial by William Wicken, a professor of history at York University,[51] and some of the evidence on behalf of the Crown was presented by Stephen Patterson, a professor of history at the University of New Brunswick.[52] At trial, the judge was persuaded more by the evidence of Professor Patterson, whereas in the Supreme Court of Canada, Binnie and the judges who signed on to his decision were persuaded more by the evidence of Professor Wicken. Professor Patterson argued that it was the Maliseet who had demanded a special right to trade with the British for "necessaries," not the Mi'kmaq; what the Mi'kmaq were promised was simply to be treated equally under the law like any other British subject. The evidence emphasized by Marshall's experts was that the British made identical promises in the treaties to the Mi'kmaq as to the Maliseet, and therefore the evidence about the importance of the promise of trade made to the Maliseet in 1760 applied equally to the Mi'kmaq.

The British abandoned the truck-house system in 1762 in favour of a system of licensed traders, which itself was abandoned in 1780. The Crown argued that the promise of the right to trade lapsed with the end of the truck-house system. Binnie disagreed. He wrote, "My view is that the surviving substance of the treaty is not the literal promise of a truck-house, but a treaty right to continue to obtain necessaries through hunting and fishing by trading the products of those traditional activities subject to restrictions that can be justified under the Badger test."[53] For Binnie, the present day interpretation of "necessaries" is the right to a "moderate livelihood."[54]

In concluding his judgment, Binnie stated that

> [t]he appellant caught and sold the eels to support himself and his wife. Accordingly, the close season and the imposition of a discretionary licensing system would, if enforced, interfere with the appellant's treaty right to fish for trading purposes, and the ban on sales would, if enforced, infringe his right to trade for sustenance. In the absence of any justification of the regulatory prohibitions, the appellant is entitled to an acquittal.[55]

Clearly, the federal Department of Fisheries had not taken into account the Aboriginal treaties of the 1700s because departmental officials did not think they applied, or more likely, were unaware of them. However, this decision also stated that the government had the right to regulate Aboriginal fishing rights so long as the regulations took into account the "honour of the Crown," the fiduciary responsibility of the Crown, infringed Aboriginal rights as little as necessary to achieve legitimate policy objectives, and were enacted only after consultation with the Aboriginal peoples affected.

The Supreme Court's decision was released on September 18, 1999. Of course, consultations had not occurred with the Aboriginal people, and regulations tailored to Aboriginal needs, the honour of the Crown, the Crown's fiduciary responsibility, and general conservation imperatives had not been drafted. In the absence of such regulations, some Aboriginal fishers in the Maritimes concluded that they were now unregulated and could fish without regard to any Department of Fisheries regulations with impunity. Their violation of the fishing regulations angered non-Aboriginal fishers, which led to civil unrest and violence, especially at the fishing port of Burnt Church, New Brunswick, in early October.[56] The federal minister of fisheries personally intervened to persuade the Aboriginal fishers to accept a voluntary moratorium on fishing out of season, and promised consultation on new regulations that would apply to them. A group of non-Aboriginal fishers, the West Nova Fishermen's Coalition, applied to the Supreme Court for a rehearing of the *Marshall* decision.

A "rehearing" of a court decision was unprecedented at the time because judicial decisions are final unless appealed, and there is no appeal of a Supreme Court decision. However, in an effort to quell the violence and unrest after the September 18 decision, the Supreme Court released a decision about the request for a rehearing on November 17, 1999. Not surprisingly, the court rejected the application for a rehearing, but in its reasons, restated its reasoning in its September 18 decision.[57]

The September 18 decision stated that Aboriginal treaty fishing rights protected by s. 35(1) were nevertheless subject to regulation in the best interests of the Aboriginal people. However, in the September 18 decision, the court emphasized the importance of respecting treaty rights more than the government's power to regulate treaty rights under certain conditions.

It was not likely that representatives of the Maritime Aboriginals and non-Aboriginal fishers took the time to carefully read the September 18 decision in the light of the Supreme Court's previous jurisprudence, in order to understand that a new set of regulations that respected both Aboriginal and non-Aboriginal rights needed to be worked out very soon. Cooler heads did not prevail.

In hindsight, if the Supreme Court could have anticipated the impact of a decision that acquitted Marshall but did not suspend the inapplicability of the fishing regulations to Aboriginal people while the federal government considered alternatives, a differently worded decision would likely have been released. The decision could still have acquitted Marshall but maintained the status quo while time was provided to draft new regulations in consultation with both Aboriginal and non-Aboriginal fishers.

In many decisions, the Supreme Court is cognizant both of local conditions and of the impact of its decisions on these local conditions. These are taken into account because the court is representative of all Canadian regions. The local-conditions factor is not relevant to the legal reasoning that goes into the outcome of the decision, but it is relevant with regard to how the decision is written. However, in the *Marshall* decisions, there was no Supreme Court judge from the Maritimes participating, and perhaps that is why the potential impact of the first Marshall decision was not taken into account in the court's judgement.

The second *Marshall* decision did not immediately quell the civil unrest that resulted from the September 18 decision. However, cooler heads did eventually prevail, and new fisheries regulations were created, after proper consultation with Aboriginal and non-Aboriginal fishers, that have more or less been tolerated by both sides.

It should be noted that the first *Marshall* decision encouraged a group of thirty-five Mi'kmaq to start logging operations on Crown land in New Brunswick without a licence. They assumed that the treaties of 1760 and 1761 gave them the right to cut timber on what they considered to be traditional Mi'kmaq territory and to sell it commercially. It is ironic that amongst this group of thirty-five were two Marshalls: Stephen Frederick Marshall and Kenneth M. Marshall. Stephen Frederick Marshall's name appeared first on the list of men charged with violating the New Brunswick timber-cutting regulations, and so the case became known as *R. v. Marshall* [2005]. The Marshalls who litigated before the Supreme Court in 2005 did not fare nearly well as Donald Marshall Jr. in 1999. The convictions of Stephen Frederick Marshall and the others charged with him were upheld. The Supreme Court found that the 1760 and 1761 treaties referred only to products being traded at that time, and timber was not amongst these products. As well, the court found that there was insufficient evidence to show that the timber was being cut on traditional Mi'kmaq territory.[58]

HAIDA NATION (2004)[59]

The *Calder* and *Delgamuukw* decisions led to years or decades of land claims negotiations, interspersed with litigation when negotiations broke down. Is non-Aboriginal development allowed to proceed on lands claimed by Aboriginal communities during this long process? That is the question addressed by the *Haida Nation* decision of 2004.

For centuries, the Haida Nation has called the Haida Gwaii islands[60] home. The island archipelago is situated off the west coast of BC and has an area of more than 10,000 square kilometres, twice that of Prince Edward Island. The Haida have claimed title to the islands since about 1900, but their claim had not been legally recognized in the 1990s when the BC government granted new permits to a lumber company to cut trees on the islands. The Haida had not been consulted. In 2000, the Haida launched a lawsuit challenging the legality of the permits. The BC government had been issuing logging permits on the Haida Gwaii for nearly a century, but it was not until the advent of s. 35(1) of the *Constitution Act, 1867* and the *Delgamuukw* decision pursuant to it, that they thought they might have the legal means of objecting to the permits.

When the case reached the Supreme Court of Canada in 2004, it was heard by a seven-judge panel, which decided unanimously that the Crown is obligated to consult with Aboriginal peoples before approving permits or developments on land on which Aboriginal peoples have a legitimate claim. This is an important decision because it sets out the responsibilities of the provincial governments in consulting with Aboriginal peoples prior to approving non-Aboriginal commercial activities on lands claimed by Aboriginals. It sets the stage for two far-reaching 2014 Supreme Court decisions which found that the governments of British Columbia and Ontario had failed to meet their obligations as set out in the *Haida Nation* decision.

The court's decision was written by Chief Justice McLachlin. She began her opinion by emphasizing the importance of the case to both the Haida Nation and the government.

> *The government holds legal title to the land. Exercising that legal title, it has granted Weyerhaeuser [a timber company] the right to harvest the forests in Block 6 of the land. But the Haida people also claim title to the land — title which they are in the process of trying to prove — and object to the harvesting of the forests on Block 6 . . . In this situation, what duty if any does the government owe the Haida people? More concretely, is the government required to <u>consult</u> with them about decisions to harvest the forests and to <u>accommodate</u> their concerns about what if any forest in Block 6 should be harvested before they have proven their title to land and their Aboriginal rights?*

> *The stakes are huge. The Haida argue that absent*
> *consultation and accommodation, they will win their title*
> *but find themselves deprived of forests that are vital to their*
> *economy and their culture. Forests take generations to mature,*
> *they point out, and old-growth forests can never be replaced.*
> *The Haida's claim to title to Haida Gwaii is strong, as found*
> *by the chambers judge. But it is also complex and will take*
> *many years to prove. In the meantime, the Haida argue, their*
> *heritage will be irretrievably despoiled.*[61]

McLachlin then moved directly to the court's holding.

> *I conclude that the government has a legal duty to consult with*
> *the Haida people about the harvest of timber from Block 6,*
> *including decisions to transfer or replace Tree Farm Licences.*
> *Good faith consultation may in turn lead to an obligation to*
> *accommodate Haida concerns in the harvesting of timber,*
> *although what accommodation if any may be required cannot*
> *at this time be ascertained. Consultation must be meaningful.*
> *There is no duty to reach agreement. The duty to consult*
> *and, if appropriate, accommodate cannot be discharged by*
> *delegation to Weyerhaeuser. Nor does Weyerhaeuser owe any*
> *independent duty to consult with or accommodate the Haida*
> *people's concerns, although the possibility remains that it could*
> *become liable for assumed obligations. . . .*[62]

The term "good faith consultation" is not an empty generalization. It has a long history in the common law, particularly in labour law. It implies giving serious consideration to the points of view of others and making an honest effort to accommodate legitimate concerns. It implies integrity of process, and it is closely connected with the honour of the Crown. This good faith consultation must occur where an Aboriginal group has a strong *prima facie*[63] case for a land claim, even though the claim may be far from settlement. McLachlin notes that

*[w]here a strong prima facie case exists for the claim, and
the consequences of the government's proposed decision
may adversely affect it in a significant way, addressing
the Aboriginal concerns may require taking steps to avoid
irreparable harm or to minimize the effects of infringement,
pending final resolution of the underlying claim.
Accommodation is achieved through consultation, as this
Court recognized in R. v. Marshall, [1999] 3 SCR 533, at
para. 22: ". . . the process of accommodation of the treaty
right may best be resolved by consultation and negotiation."
This process does not give Aboriginal groups a veto over what
can be done with land pending final proof of the claim. The
Aboriginal "consent" spoken of in* Delgamuukw *is appropriate
only in cases of established rights, and then by no means in
every case. Rather, what is required is a process of balancing
interests, of give and take.*[64]

The judgment emphasized that the government has both a moral and a
legal duty to consult.[65] However, the extent of the consultation is proportionate to the strength of the *prima facie* case for a land claim.

*The content of the duty to consult and accommodate varies
with the circumstances. Precisely what duties arise in different
situations will be defined as the case law in this emerging
area develops. In general terms, however, it may be asserted
that the scope of the duty is proportionate to a preliminary
assessment of the strength of the case supporting the existence
of the right or title, and to the seriousness of the potentially
adverse effect upon the right or title claimed.*[66]

The emphasis in the *Haida Nation* decision on proportionality in determining the extent of the consultation required by government representatives is very general. In the case at hand, the Haida had demonstrated a very
strong case for a claim, and so the consultation should have been extensive
and there should have been clearly demonstrable attempts to accommodate

the Haida demands. The Haida example is at the high end of accommo-dating the Aboriginal perspective.[67] Other situations may not be as clear. However, the *Haida Nation* decision seems to advise governments to err on the side of caution lest they and the companies they provide permits to are liable for damages after successful Aboriginal land claims settlements.

One's first impression of the *Haida Nation* decision is that from a theor-etical perspective, it is eminently sensible. There must be some reasonable accommodation by governments with regard to decisions that will affect lands that are likely to be recognized in the future as subject to Aboriginal title. However, human beings do not always behave reasonably, and nego-tiations are often difficult when the political and cultural stakes are high. What happens when the process of "balancing interests, of give and take" breaks down? That question is addressed in two 2014 decisions of the Supreme Court.

TSILHQOT'IN NATION (2014)[68]

The Tsilhqot'in Nation consists of several thousand Aboriginals in six bands that have lived for centuries in central British Columbia on land they have always considered theirs. There was no treaty or land claims agree-ment that applied to their traditional territory. In 1983, the BC government granted a permit to a logging company to cut trees in an area claimed by the Tsilhqot'in. The Tsilhqot'in objected. Civil unrest resulted in blockades of logging roads by Aboriginal protesters and their supporters. The Tsilhqot'in began land claims litigation for part of their territory where several hundred Tsilhquot'in resided. Negotiations and litigation proceeded until 2012, when the BC Court of Appeal decided that the Tsilhqot'in claim had not yet been established but might be in the future. As a result, the Tsilhqot'in appealed that decision to the Supreme Court of Canada, along with a request that the Supreme Court grant Aboriginal title.

The Tsilhqot'in won their appeal, and the Supreme Court recognized title. The unanimous decision of the eight-judge panel[69] was written by Chief Justice McLachlin. It relied heavily on the *Haida Nation* decision.

McLachlin pointed out that the British Columbia government had made no attempt to consult the Tsilhqot'in or to accommodate their concerns about logging in their territory. The position of the BC government was that logging was necessary to battle a pine-beetle infestation, and that this concern along with the economic benefits to the people of British Columbia from the logging constituted a legislative objective substantial and compelling enough to infringe Aboriginal interests without consultation. However, it turned out there was no compelling evidence either for a pine-beetle infestation or economic benefits to the province, and even if such evidence existed, there would still be need for consultation with the Tsilhqot'in because of substantial evidence for a land claim.

To illustrate the complexity of the land claim and duty to consult on issues before the court, McLachlin outlined the trial process.

> In 2002, the trial commenced before Vickers J. of the British Columbia Supreme Court, and continued for 339 days over a span of five years. The trial judge spent time in the claim area and heard extensive evidence from elders, historians, and other experts. He found that the Tsilhqot'in people were in principle entitled to a declaration of Aboriginal title to a portion of the claim area as well as to a small area outside the claim area.[70]

She noted that "[t]he dual perspectives of the common law and of the Aboriginal group bear equal weight in evaluating a claim for Aboriginal title"[71] and that the trial judge had achieved the correct balance. In order to prove a land claim, the Aboriginal occupation "must be *sufficient*; it must be *continuous* (where present occupation is relied on); and it must be *exclusive*."[72] She noted that with regard to a "semi-nomadic indigenous group" like the Tsilhqot'in, determining whether the standard had been met would be challenging. The BC Court of Appeal focused on the villages in the claim area the Tsilhqot'in had occupied and would have restricted the land claim to these areas. However, McLachlin objected that such an approach would lead to a patchwork of land claims settlements that would be unfair to the Aboriginal peoples. She concluded there was enough evidence to demonstrate the Tsilhqot'in had continuously occupied the claimed area for centuries and that their occupation was "exclusive" in the sense that other Aboriginal groups would require permission to pass through territory the Tsilhqot'in considered to be their own. In terms of setting boundaries for such claims, McLachlin conceded that there was conflicting evidence. However, the trial judge had done his best by giving careful consideration to all the evidence, actually visiting the area and talking to elders, and that the final disposition of the trial judge was the only way to bring closure and set the boundaries.

With regard to the government's duty to consult prior to authorizing commercial activity in areas claimed by Aboriginal groups, McLachlin wrote:

> *The degree of consultation and accommodation required lies on a spectrum as discussed in* Haida. *In general, the level of consultation and accommodation required is proportionate to the strength of the claim and to the seriousness of the adverse impact the contemplated governmental action would have on the claimed right. "A dubious or peripheral claim may attract a mere duty of notice, while a stronger claim may attract more stringent duties."*[73] *The required level of consultation and accommodation is greatest where title has been established. Where consultation or accommodation is found to be inadequate, the government decision can be suspended or quashed.*
>
> *Where Aboriginal title is unproven, the Crown owes a procedural duty imposed by the honour of the Crown to consult and, if appropriate, accommodate the unproven Aboriginal interest. By contrast, where title has been established, the Crown must not only comply with its procedural duties, but must also ensure that the proposed government action is substantively consistent with the requirements of s. 35 of the* Constitution Act, 1982. *This requires both a compelling and substantial governmental objective and that the government action is consistent with the fiduciary duty owed by the Crown to the Aboriginal group.*[74]

This part of the *Tsilhqot'in Nation* decision is perhaps the most important with regard to Aboriginal groups in other parts of Canada with pending land claims and to provincial governments considering approving commercial operations on such lands. Clearly, the Supreme Court will not tolerate avoidance of the duty to consult in good faith. In order to emphasize that there are serious consequences for ignoring this duty, McLachlin wrote:

> *I add this. Governments and individuals proposing to use or exploit land, whether before or after a declaration of Aboriginal title, can avoid a charge of infringement or failure to adequately consult by obtaining the consent of the interested Aboriginal group.*[75]

The remainder of the court's decision considers whether the BC *Forest Act* applies to areas with pending land claims and to Aboriginal land where there is a settled land claim. The *Forest Act* regulates the cutting of timber on Crown land but not on private land. The purpose of the regulation is to allow the harvesting of timber for economic benefit and, at the same time, to ensure conservation, safety, the prevention of forest fires, and to promote the health of the forests. The court decided that areas claimed by Aboriginal groups are Crown lands subject to the *Forest Act* but also subject to the duty to consult as outlined above. Once Aboriginal groups have gained title, however, their lands are no longer Crown lands and therefore not subject to the *Forest Act*. However, the provincial government may still enact regulations with regard to forestry on Aboriginal title land, so long as the fiduciary duty of the Crown toward the Aboriginals is maintained and there is sufficient consultation with the Aboriginal groups affected. The court also confirmed that provincial government has jurisdiction to regulate the cutting of timber on Aboriginal title lands in spite of federal jurisdiction over "Indians" in s. 91(24) of the *Constitution Act, 1867*.[76]

The *Tsilhqot'in Nation* decision, released on June 26, 2014, had an immediate impact on First Nations communities that held Aboriginal title or were claiming Aboriginal title, but which had not been consulted — or felt they had not been consulted in good faith — about commercial developments on their traditional lands. Several initiated court action to stop the commercial activities pending consultation.[77]

GRASSY NARROWS FIRST NATION (2014)[78]

In 1873, the government of Canada signed Treaty 3 with the Ojibway Nation in what is now northwestern Ontario and eastern Manitoba, north of Kenora, Ontario. The government was anxious to conclude this treaty in order to ensure the building of the Canadian Pacific Railway through this territory to complete the transcontinental railway promised to British Columbia by Prime Minister Macdonald.[79]

The Ojibway lived in the Keewatin area, which was then under the control of the Canadian government as part of the Northwest Territories. The treaty established a reserve of about forty square kilometres, plus "annuity payments, goods, and the right to harvest the non-reserve lands surrendered by them until such time as they were 'taken up' for settlement, mining, lumbering, or other purposes by the Government of the Dominion of Canada."[80] In 1912, the non-reserve lands were ceded by the federal government to Ontario. The major issue in dispute in this case was whether only the federal government could "take up" (i.e., authorize commercial use of) the non-reserve lands, or whether Ontario could take up the lands with or without federal involvement.

In 1997, the Ontario government authorized a pulp and paper company to clear-cut a large area of non-reserve lands that the Grassy Narrows band, descendants of the Ojibway who signed Treaty 3, still held harvesting rights for under Treaty 3. In 2005, following the *Haida Nation* decision, the Grassy Narrows First Nation initiated litigation in the Ontario Superior Court to set aside the forestry company's licence as a violation of Treaty 3.

In 2006, the trial judge divided the trial into two phases. The first phase was to determine which order of government, federal or provincial, had the authority to take up the Keewatin lands where the Ojibway had harvesting rights. The trial judge concluded that the Canadian government must be involved, and the Ontario government appealed. The Ontario Court of Appeal held in 2013 that only the Ontario government could take up the lands in question, and the Grassy Narrows First Nation appealed to the Supreme Court of Canada. Four provinces intervened in support of Ontario, and sixteen First Nations groups intervened either singly or jointly, indicating the importance of the outcome of this litigation both to the provinces and the Aboriginal peoples of Canada.

The unanimous decision of a seven-judge panel of the court was written by Chief Justice McLachlin. Her decision was facilitated to some extent by the *Tsilhqot'in Nation* decision released just two weeks earlier. She concluded that under s. 109 and s. 92(5) of the *Constitution Act, 1867*, the provinces owned and controlled Crown lands, including the lands where the Grassy Narrows First Nation had harvesting rights. However, under the doctrine of the honour of the Crown, the Ontario government had a fiduciary responsibility to the Grassy Narrows First Nation to manage these lands only after meaningful, good-faith consultation with representatives of the Grassy Narrows peoples, so that any commercial development would not unnecessarily interfere with the harvesting rights of the Grassy Narrows peoples.[81]

The result of this decision was a minor win for provincial interests — only the provinces (excluding the Territories) have the right to take up lands that Aboriginal peoples have some claim over — but perhaps a more important win for the Aboriginal peoples. Their right to be consulted meaningfully and their interests taken into account, over all lands to which they have some claim — whether or not title exists or is being claimed — was resoundingly confirmed.

For example, since the *Delgamuukw* decision in 1997, the Algonquin of Ontario have been negotiating with the federal and Ontario governments for title over more than 47,000 hectares of land in eastern Ontario between Ottawa and North Bay. This is an area in which the Ontario government has been granting timber-cutting permits.[82] As a result of the Grassy Narrows decision, the Algonquin of Ontario now have the ammunition to apply for court injunctions to stop commercial operations about which they have not been consulted and the right to be consulted prior to the granting of future permits. Similarly, Aboriginal groups across Canada could demand meaningful consultation about the use of any lands over which they have some type of claim.

Section 35(1) of the *Constitution Act, 1867* has had a profound impact on Aboriginal rights in Canada with regard to land claims, the interpretation of treaties, and the use of traditional lands. The jurisprudence has grown slowly but steadily as the courts digest both the enormous complexity of the issues and the history of Aboriginal peoples in Canada. We are clearly not at the end of the jurisprudential process regarding s. 35(1), and perhaps still closer to the beginning than the middle, given the hundreds of unsettled land claims across Canada.

The Aboriginal rights decisions of the Supreme Court demonstrate similarities with the court's decisions about the *Charter of Rights*. For example, the approach taken toward reasonable limits in s. 1 of the *Charter* is close to the test the court has developed for infringement of Aboriginal rights, and the court has tried to give both the *Charter* and s. 35(1) a purposive, broad, and liberal interpretation. The major difference is that when determining Charter rights, the court declares what these rights are and then enforces them. With regard to s. 35(1), the court clearly prefers negotiated settlements and a resort to litigation only when negotiations break down. However, in the *Haida, Tsilhqot'in Nation,* and *Grassy Narrows First Nation* decisions, the court is showing signs of losing patience with the slow pace of some negotiations and the seeming resistance of some governments to negotiate in good faith.[83] As well, the court will continue to struggle with the tension between its insistence that Aboriginals continue to maintain the traditional uses of Aboriginal lands in a communal form in order to keep title and the desire of some Aboriginal groups to use their traditional lands for modern purposes, some of them non-communal.[84]

It will take decades to settle many of the current Aboriginal rights issues. Until then, lawyers may benefit as much as First Nations from the ensuing litigation unless the federal and provincial governments show leadership and negotiate in good faith in order to recognize legitimate Aboriginal land claims expeditiously for the good of the whole Canadian society.

CHAPTER 9

THE *CHARTER* AND HUMAN RIGHTS

In the Introduction, I quoted Donald Smiley's assertion that "the degree to which human rights are safeguarded is the final test by which any polity should be judged." Have the *Charter* and s. 35 on Aboriginal rights improved Canada's prospects for a favourable judgment? I will provide a framework that may be useful in answering this question. First, I will summarize my approach to human rights. Next, I will present my impressions about how the *Charter* and s. 35 have affected thinking about human rights in Canada. Finally, I will suggest some ways in which the positive effects of the *Charter* can be enhanced and its direct or indirect negative influences minimized.

HUMAN RIGHTS

At the most basic level, human rights can be thought of as considerations which are owed to every human being and which every person owes to others, in recognition that all persons are equally deserving of respect, a sense of self-worth, and fair treatment. Liberal democracies such as Canada, the United States, and the countries of Western Europe have pursued this goal by endeavouring to maximize individual liberty, and through providing procedural safeguards, promoting a degree of social equality and encouraging political participation.

The concept of interpersonal respect implies that everyone both is owed respect and owes respect to others. If there is a conflict between the two in a specific instance, it is necessary to make a value judgment about which is to be given preference. For example, are human rights promoted most effectively by respecting the desires of Ernst Zundel and James Keegstra to disseminate their beliefs freely or by promoting the self-worth of the Canadian Jewish community by banning the publication of materials that suggest stereotypes and advocate hatred? Does fair treatment mean that procedural safeguards in the criminal justice system should be rigorously enforced so that there is almost no chance that an innocent person will be mistreated? Or should less emphasis be placed on procedural safeguards so that the police might be able to prevent crime more effectively?

These kinds of value conflicts are often presented as a tension between the promotion of individual human rights and a commitment to the larger community. My own view is that it is not very useful to think of human rights in terms of individual claims devoid of corresponding responsibilities. The concept of civil rights makes no sense except in respect to *relations* among people. A hermit has no use for civil rights until he or she interacts with others.

From this perspective, I suggest that a commitment to human rights, or rights-consciousness, is supported by the belief that the consideration one owes to others is as important as the consideration owed to oneself. Such an attitude will not automatically yield "correct" decisions about how to act, but it is likely to lead to certain tendencies regarding both beliefs and actions.

For example, a person committed to human rights is likely to be more tolerant of the diversity of beliefs in the community (except sometimes with regard to others who are intolerant) than someone not so committed. As Paul Sniderman has noted, such tolerance is associated with higher levels of education. The more people know about different cultures, religions and ideologies, the less their inclination to accept false stereotypes and the greater their willingness to tolerate the existence of beliefs and life-styles outside their own culture and that they do not necessarily agree with.[1]

A "mixed" attitude to authority is probably also conducive to a commitment to human rights. Persons who are tolerant are unlikely to acquiesce unquestioningly to authority figures simply because of a belief that submission to authority is the right thing to do. In their eyes, legitimate authority figures must earn esteem, for example, by respecting human rights.[2] Finally, a commitment to human rights means being as interested in promoting the self-fulfilment of others as in developing one's own creative potentials.[3]

There are some who would consider the *Charter* simply as a means of protecting individuals from unreasonable encroachments on their rights and liberties by governments. While this is one function of the *Charter*, it could also serve a more fundamental objective — to promote higher levels of rights-consciousness in society. This is certainly not a goal that the *Charter* can be expected to achieve on its own, but it can be hoped that the *Charter* will at least make a contribution to this end. From this perspective on civil rights, I will speculate about the impact the *Canadian Charter of Rights and Freedoms* may have had on the beliefs and actions of Canadians. My comments will be organized around four dimensions affected by the *Charter*: national unity, liberal-democratic values, the political process and the legal system.

THE *CHARTER*'S IMPACT ON THINKING ABOUT HUMAN RIGHTS
NATIONAL UNITY

According to the strategy of the government of Pierre Trudeau for nation-building, the *Charter*'s primary purpose was to promote national unity. It was hoped that the *Charter* would encourage national debates about important issues, and that these debates would cut across regional and ethnic cleavages. It was also hoped that the *Charter* would cultivate national rather than regional loyalties through providing a common base of language and mobility rights.

The Promotion of National Debates

As a vehicle for fostering national debates and diverting attention away from ethnic and regional divisions, the *Charter* has had mixed results. For example, the Supreme Court's decisions on abortion, the right to strike, anti-terrorism legislation, and prostitution have all generated controversies that have produced more of a liberal-conservative split than divisions along regional or ethnic lines. This result may have drawn our attention away from a preoccupation with regional and ethnic issues, at least temporarily. On the other hand, the Supreme Court's decisions about the commercial signs provisions of Quebec's Bill 101 and minority language education rights in Quebec have generated disputes that have divided Canadians according to both language and region.

At a more basic level, the central question is whether the public debates the *Charter* has given rise to have encouraged more interpersonal respect and understanding. Amongst those who take the time to read the key *Charter* decisions and consider carefully the evidence discussed, the result may be a better and deeper understanding of the complex issues involved, and as a result, a higher level of rights-consciousness. This is because for the most part, Supreme Court decisions on the Charter and Aboriginal rights have been clearly written and insightful, both on the majority and minority sides whenever the court is split. As well, the Supreme Court decisions on language rights may have contributed to a greater public acceptance of Canada's bilingual nature. However, amongst those who already have hardened and somewhat intolerant attitudes, I suspect that the *Charter* and the court decisions emanating from it have not had much impact. For example, members of the pro-life and pro-choice movements seem no closer to tolerating the views of their opponents than they were before. And those who are opposed in principle to the safe injection site in Vancouver's lower east side are not likely to change their views because of the evidence summarized in the Supreme Court's decision on *Insite* that the program saves lives and successfully tackles drug addiction.

If the *Charter* has not engendered much more interpersonal respect and tolerance through the debates it has generated, this result is not by and large the fault of the judges. In contrast to the narrow, legalistic approach to the interpretation of the *Canadian Bill of Rights* the Supreme Court adopted during the 1960s and 1970s — which was unlikely to give rise to a society more respectful of civil liberties — a number of the Charter decisions of the Supreme Court could be considered as at least having the potential to encourage a greater overall commitment to human rights among those who read them. However, if enlightened judicial decisions about human rights are to have an impact on society as a whole, ways must be found to disseminate more effectively the judges' reasoning, and not just the "bottom line" of who wins or loses court decisions. My impression is that the quality of journalism about human rights issues has improved in the quality media outlets since 1982. However, fewer Canadians seem to be relying on quality journalism, turning instead to social media news summaries of questionable value.

Language and Mobility Rights

The policy of extending bilingual services has continued in the federal public service and in New Brunswick. However, most of the progress that has occurred was not required by the bilingual rights parts of the *Charter*, sections 16 to 22. It occurred largely because of the policy priorities of the governments in power. In Ontario, since 1982 the provincial government has probably made as much progress as the federal government or New Brunswick in providing government services in French, although Ontario has not opted into the language rights section of the *Charter*.

Until 1990, the Supreme Court interpreted the bilingual rights sections of the *Charter* in a restrained fashion, as illustrated by the *Société des Acadiens* case (1986). The strategy of the Court has been to leave the extension of language rights to future political compromises. Sections 16-22 of the *Charter* have had little impact on the state of language rights in Canada, and therefore little bearing on the rights-consciousness of Canadians.

In contrast, section 23 of the *Charter*, which has created new minority language education rights for both francophones and anglophones, has had repercussions in several ways even prior to Supreme Court decisions about section 23. After 1982, provincial governments in the anglophone provinces established more extensive French-language school facilities. Judicial decisions in the lower courts began to promote the advancement of these facilities in Ontario, Alberta, and Saskatchewan. Then the Supreme Court of Canada, in *Mahe* (1990) *Doucet-Boudreau* (2003), enunciated a generous, though policy-sensitive interpretation of s. 23, which supported the expansion of French-language school facilities in the Anglophone provinces. The French-language school reforms in the anglophone provinces may help to counteract the pressures towards assimilation experienced by the franco-phone minorities outside Quebec. In fact, the number of people whose first official language is French, and who speak French at home, has increased significantly in Alberta, British Columbia, and Ontario, although their pro-portion of the general population has remained stable or decreased because of immigration from non-francophone countries.[4] It appears that section 23 is fostering a general atmosphere of bilingualism across Canada, so that francophones as well as anglophones are feeling freer to move to any prov-ince without fear of losing their linguistic heritage. If section 23 is having this effect, it will certainly augment the sense of self-worth of francophone Canadians and thus will contribute to the advancement of human rights.

With regard to Quebec, the Supreme Court has struck down the sec-tion of Bill 101 that denied English-language education to children of anglophones from other provinces. Although this decision created some resentment among Quebec nationalists, the additional English-language school privileges thus established has not created a threat to the survival of the French language.[5] As well, in 2005 the Supreme Court upheld the Quebec government's measures to prevent some parents from attempting to circumvent French language education rules.[6] Section 23 has contributed towards the sense of self-worth of anglophone Canadians who move to Quebec — thus enhancing human rights — without preventing the Quebec government from preserving the French language in Quebec.

Section 6 of the *Charter* — mobility rights — has had some limited impact. In 1989, the Supreme Court ruled that the restrictions that law societies placed on interprovincial partnerships were too restrictive under section 6. This decision encouraged the creation and expansion of inter-provincial law firms,[7] which has made the legal culture in Canada more pan-Canadian. In 2009, the Federal Court decided that a Canadian citizen visiting family abroad had a right to return to Canada pursuant to section 6, even though Canadian authorities tried to block his return arbitrarily.[8] Over time, section 6 could possibly foster a greater sense of self-worth and opportunity among Canadians who wish to work in an inter-provincial context, as well as among Canadians arbitrarily pre-vented from returning home.

LIBERAL-DEMOCRATIC GOALS

The liberal-democratic goals consist of the three traditional liberal values of optimum freedom, social equality, and procedural fairness, plus the more recent democratic goal of facilitating more meaningful public participation in the political process. In three decades, the *Charter* has contributed to several important changes in how our society promotes these values. However, the changes, though significant, are more evolutionary than revolutionary. This is partly because of Canada's "excellent historical record on human rights and freedoms compared to other nations."[9] That record, though not perfect, did provide a platform which has been built upon by Charter decisions and other forces in Canadian society.

Optimum Freedom

The *Charter* has resulted in little change in the amount of freedom enjoyed by Canadians, though Canadians who have benefitted from these changes have witnessed important advancements. The federal *Lord's Day Act* is gone, but the provinces have been left with a fairly wide mandate to enact secular Sunday-closing legislation. Nevertheless, I was moved by a comment made to me by one of my graduate students not long after the *Lord's Day Act* was struck down in the *Big M* decision of 1985. Her parents had immigrated to Canada from India, and she and her family had experienced discrimination. She told me that the Supreme Court's decision to strike down the *Lord's Day Act* had made her feel proud to be a Canadian for the first time because she now felt included. Similarly, in the Supreme Court's decision in *Multani* in 2006 about whether Sikh children may wear the kirpan at school, the Court expanded the scope of freedom of religion, while ensuring sensible safety procedures are adopted.

Unions initially failed to persuade the Supreme Court that the *Charter* implies the right to strike or bargain collectively. However, in the *Health Services Bargaining Association v. BC* decision of 2007, the Supreme Court backtracked to some degree to curtail a clear abuse of power by the provincial government.

The Supreme Court declared that the *Charter* provides merchants in Quebec with the right to post bilingual outdoor signs — as long as French predominates — but the Quebec government initially avoided the effects of this decision through the use of a section 33 override. In the end, however, cooler heads prevailed, and both sovereignist and federalist governments in Quebec have decided to abide by the Supreme Court's balanced approach.

In the *RJR-MacDonald* decision of 1995, the Supreme Court curtailed what it considered overbroad legislation limiting tobacco advertising, but subsequently deferred to evidence-based legislation that in some respects curtailed tobacco advertising even further.

With regard to the issue of hate speech, although the Supreme Court struck down the dated legislation used to convict Ernst Zundel, it upheld the more recent, evidence-based anti-hate speech legislation that resulted in the conviction of James Keegstra. And in the two best-known pornography cases, *Butler* and *Sharpe*, the Supreme Court simply fine-tuned restrictive government legislation.

In the *Chaoulli* decision of 2005, the Supreme Court nudged the Quebec government to allow medical doctors to operate private clinics in Quebec for a limited number of procedures, but that decision did not affect the rest of Canada. In the *Insite* (2011) and *Bedford* (2013) decisions, the Supreme Court emphasized the fact that liberty includes security, which means not being subjected to unnecessary insecurities resulting from deficiencies in government policies.

Overall, the Supreme Court has curtailed some overbroad legislation that unnecessarily restricts freedom, but these decisions have not resulted in a seismic shift in government policies.

Social Equality

The Supreme Court's *Andrews* decision of 1989 was a refreshing departure from the narrow approach to equality the Supreme Court took under the *Bill of Rights*. It opened the door to the possibility of a broader considera-tion of social equality issues under the Charter. However, as Chief Justice McLachlin has noted, the resolution of equality issues is one of the most difficult that the Court has had to deal with. As a result, it has generally pursued a cautious approach.

The group that has benefitted the most from social equality litigation is the gay and lesbian community. Slowly, between the cautious *Egan* deci-sion of 1995, and the *Reference re Same-Sex Marriage* in 2004, Canadian courts, and eventually the Supreme Court of Canada, recognized gay equality rights. Three reasons come to mind for this gradual change. First, it is difficult, if not impossible, to present evidence that meets legal standards that proves that gay relationships result in harm to society. Second, the AIDS crisis of the 1970s to 1990s affected a great many Canadian families. In response, many gay individuals came "out of the closet," and numerous Canadians became more cognizant of same-sex issues. Some became more understanding and tolerant than they had been previously.[10] Third, social culture changed in Canada to become more tolerant of gay relationships. The courts adapted to this societal change.

Another group that benefitted from Charter jurisprudence on equality was birth fathers, who won the equal right to parental leave in *Schachter* in 1992. The physically challenged were also victorious in the *Eldridge* decision of 1997, in which the Supreme Court held that the deaf had a right to interpreters in order to obtain equal access to health care in hospitals. Aboriginal Canadians benefitted when affirmative action programs for Aboriginal groups were upheld in the *Kapp* decision of 2008.

In most other respects, the equality rights decisions of the Supreme Court maintained the status quo. In the *Roman Catholic High School Funding* case of 1986, the Supreme Court ruled that the special educational rights granted to Roman Catholics in the constitution cannot be negated by the *Charter*. The Supreme Court refused to interfere with government policy that did not provide equal rights to the fetus in the *Borowski* and *Daigle* decisions of 1989. In the 1990 *McKinney* decision, the Supreme Court upheld the right of governments to impose compulsory retirement. In the *Symes* decision of 1993, and the *Thibaudeau* decision of 1995, the male majority on the court upheld government legislation that women's groups had claimed resulted in systemic discrimination against women. In *Law* (1999) and *Gosselin* (2002), the Supreme Court declined to extend the concept of equality in pension and social welfare legislation respectively beyond what was in the legislation. Government policy in BC regarding the funding of treatment for autism was upheld in *Auton* in 2004, and the policy of a provincial government to delay equal pay for equal work to women was upheld by the Court in 2004 in *Newfoundland v. NAPE* because of the depressed state of the provincial economy.

In sum, the Supreme Court has demonstrated a willingness to rule in favour of the expansion of equality rights where there is clear and compelling evidence to do so, and where the evidence is less persuasive, the Court has upheld existing government policy.

Procedural Fairness

"Arguably, the impact of the *Canadian Charter of Rights and Freedoms* is most visible in the field of criminal law."[11] Up to 1997, two-thirds of the issues brought to the Supreme Court in 352 cases dealing with the *Charter* and some other rights issues concerned legal rights. As well, twenty of the thirty federal statutes struck down by the Supreme Court up to 1997 involved legal rights.[12]

One way of looking at the court's legal rights decisions is to view them from the perspective of a crime control approach, a due process approach, or a victim's rights approach.[13] A crime control approach attempts to expedite criminal investigations and prosecutions so as to increase the rate of convictions. The due process emphasizes procedural safeguards to minimize wrongful convictions, and ensure that accused persons are treated as innocent until proven guilty, and receive a fair trial. Both these approaches sometimes overlook the impact of crimes and the criminal justice system on the victims of crime. Victims' rights can be acknowledged either by ensuring that criminals are punished, or by adopting a restorative justice approach that places more emphasis on the healing of victims and the rehabilitation of criminals. There is no doubt that judges wrestle with these perspectives when deciding hard cases, consciously or unconsciously.[14]

In a number of important decisions, the Supreme Court has emphasized the due process model. The *Therens* decision (1985) resulted in the exclusion of breathalyzer evidence whenever the police had not informed recipients of the breathalyzer tests of their prior right to counsel. The *BC Motor Vehicle Act (1985)* and *Burns* (2001) decisions demonstrated that the Supreme Court would not necessarily interpret the *Charter* as merely procedural, but might on some occasions provide new substantive rights to accused persons. The *Southam* (1984), *Morgentaler* (1988) and *Singh* (1985) decisions all sent signals to governments and public officials that closer attention must be paid to due process safeguards. In *Seaboyer* (1991) and *Mills* (1999), the Supreme Court had to consider not only crime control vs. the right to a fair trial in sexual assault cases, but also the right of sexual assault victims to privacy. The court emphasized the right to a fair trial, but in *Mills* it demonstrated that it could be persuaded by evidence from Parliamentary research about new approaches to protecting privacy, while at the same time ensuring the right to a fair trial for accused persons. In the *Charkaoui* (2007 and 2008) and *Khadr* (2008 and 2010) decisions, the court demonstrated the importance of observing due process even when dealing with the threat of terrorism — otherwise we undermine the democratic values on which our country is founded. In *Insite* (2011) and *Bedford* (2013), the Supreme Court extended the *Charter's* protection of security of the person to two vulnerable groups — drug addicts and sex workers — thus demonstrating the potential of section 7 of the *Charter* to protect groups that have little political clout.

The Supreme Court's interpretation of legal rights has resulted in the legal system treating accused persons and the vulnerable with more respect. On the other hand, it is possible that the publicity surrounding judicial decisions on procedure may have reinforced the view that rights consist more of considerations owed to individuals than of considerations individuals owe to others. To the extent that this has happened, the new procedural safeguards may not have had an entirely positive effect on rights-consciousness.

Democratic Rights

The Supreme Court has adopted a principled approach to Canadian democracy based on Chief Justice Brian Dickson's analysis in the *Oakes* case of 1986. Dickson stated that a free and democratic society is based on "respect for the inherent dignity of the human person, commitment to social justice and equality, accommodation of a wide variety of beliefs, respect for cultural and group identity, and faith in social and political institutions which enhance the participation of individuals and groups in society."[15]

This approach was applied to the test that governments would need to meet in attempting to justify "reasonable" limits to the *Charter's* rights and freedoms that can be "demonstrably justified in a free and democratic society" — further to section 1 of the *Charter*. The *Oakes* test for the application of reasonable limits creates an obligation on the part of governments that wish to limit a right. They must produce evidence that the limit to a right or freedom is an important legitimate government objective, that the means used is rationally connected to the objective, that rights are limited as little as necessary, and that the limit does more good than harm in a democratic context. This evidence-based obligation helps to ensure that governments take seriously their commitment to human rights, and that policy-makers think carefully about whether limiting rights is really necessary to achieve a policy objective. In the *Saskatchewan Electoral Boundaries* case of 1991, the Saskatchewan government was able to demonstrate that its variations from the principle of the equal right to vote were likely to enhance the broader objectives of democracy. However, in the *Sauvé* cases of 1993 and 2002, the federal government was not able to produce compelling evidence that taking the right to vote away from citizens serving time as prisoners would promote rehabilitation, or serve the broader objectives of democracy. In *Harper v. Canada* (2004), the court was convinced by government evidence that restrictions on electoral spending by third-party groups were justified in order to promote more fair election results. And in *Opitz v. Wrzesnewskyi* (2012), the court's majority stressed the importance of not erecting unnecessary barriers to voting.

The court has adopted a consistent approach to the analysis of democracy in non-Charter cases related to democratic rights, such as the *Quebec Secession Reference* of 1998, and the *Senate Reference* of 2014. The emphasis has always been on the broader goals of democracy as enunciated in the *Oakes* decision of 1986 in the context of Canadian history. This focus on principles such as the dignity of the human person, social justice, equality, tolerance, the enhancement of democratic institutions, and the promotion of participation is clearly meant to promote rights-consciousness.

Political participation in democracies, according to political theorists like John Stuart Mill and Jean Jacques Rousseau, requires far more than voting.[16] For them, citizen participation in policy-making can have an educative value that can promote a more tolerant society. Patrick Monahan has urged the judiciary to interpret the entire *Charter* from the perspective of promoting democracy and community. Wherever possible, he suggests, judges should decide cases in a way that would encourage more public participation in the resolution of policy issues.[17] Whether the *Charter* has or can have this kind of impact on public participation in democracy is difficult to answer. To the extent that the *Charter* and judicial decisions surrounding it have led to pride in Canadian citizenship, perhaps it has facilitated more participation. As noted in the Preface, the *Charter of Rights* is supported by the vast majority of Canadians, and according to a 2014 survey, it was the top choice of Canadians when choosing items that keep Canadians united.

Public Officials

It is useful to think of the *Charter* not only as a guide to judges conducting judicial review, but also as a set of instructions to legislators, cabinet ministers, and public servants, as Brian Slattery has suggested.[18] Therefore, members of these groups could be expected to take an active role in considering the implications of the principles behind the *Charter* by attempting to ensure that these principles are reflected in legislation, policies, and actions.

Politicians

There are no obvious examples of how the *Charter* may have had a direct impact on politicians' thinking about human rights in their policy-making roles. The *Charter*, however, has had a fairly important indirect impact on their behaviour in two respects. First, politicians must develop strategies for reacting to politically sensitive judicial decisions about the *Charter*, such as those on abortion or the commercial signs provisions of Quebec's Bill 101. To date, these reactions often appear to have been calculated more to minimize potential damage in terms of public support than to promote greater respect for human rights. Second, there are indications that some politicians are using the *Charter* as a means of avoiding troublesome political issues.

For example, in 1982 Premier William Davis of Ontario evaded taking a clear position about the extension of French-language schools by referring his province's *Education Act* to the Court of Appeal for an opinion about whether it conformed to section 23 of the *Charter*. In 1985 the Conservative government of Premier Grant Devine in Saskatchewan avoided the abortion issue by referring controversial anti-abortion legislation to the Court of Appeal. Also in 1985, Ontario's new premier, David Peterson, was able to deflect criticism about his support for the expansion of funding to Roman Catholic high schools by referring the legislation to the Court of Appeal. During the 1988 election campaign, Prime Minister Brian Mulroney said that he would announce his government's strategy on the abortion issue only after the Supreme Court announced its decision in the *Borowski* case. The government ensured that this decision would not occur until after the election by refusing to bring a motion before the Supreme Court to quash the appeal.

According to the *Department of Justice Act*, the Attorney General of Canada is required to vet every government-sponsored bill introduced into the House of Commons, and every new regulation, and report to the House of Commons whether any bill or regulation is not compliant with the *Charter of Rights*.[19] The strengths and weaknesses of this vetting system up to the early 2000s have been analyzed by James Kelly. Department of Justice lawyers conduct an extensive analysis of bills and regulations, as required by law, and this information provided the federal cabinet with detailed information about possible Charter violations, and advice about how Charter requirements could be met.[20] After the election of the Harper government in 2006, however, the Conservative cabinet was often resistant to conclusions by Department of Justice officials that some of its proposed legislation would not likely withstand Charter scrutiny in the courts. The government proceeded with many of its "tough on crime" bills in spite of having been advised that the legislation would almost certainly be struck down. A new strategy adopted by the government after 2013 was to encourage the implementation of its crime agenda into the House of Commons though private members' bills, which are not legally required to be vetted by the Department of Justice.[21] The result of the Harper government's resistance to the *Charter* is that the Supreme Court has indeed struck down a number of Conservative statutes, and this has occurred even after Harper-appointed judges became a majority on the Supreme Court.

It appears that the *Charter* has done little to encourage some politicians to take a more deliberate and active role in promoting higher levels of interpersonal respect in society than they otherwise would have. On the contrary, some politicians have used the *Charter* to avoid taking a stand on sensitive human rights issues.

Public Servants

James Kelly found that 53 per cent of Charter issues considered by the Supreme Court of Canada up to 1997 involved claims that public officials violated the *Charter*, rather than challenges to the constitutional validity of a law.[22] Such cases would include, for example, a claim that a police officer had failed to inform a detainee of the right to counsel, that a customs official used unreasonable search methods, or that a social worker did not observe procedural safeguards when apprehending a neglected child.

The higher procedural standards the courts have discovered in the *Charter* may promote greater respect for individuals among public officials, as well as a higher sense of self-worth among those who have dealings with government officials. On the other hand, the new procedural safeguards may place burdensome and time-consuming demands on law-enforcement officials and public servants, with the consequence that victims of crime are less well protected and persons dealing with government officials are subjected to longer waits and poorer service in some respects. However, the new stress on procedure is not necessarily detrimental, on balance. For example, it does not seem unreasonable for a police officer to inform a detainee of the right to counsel before a breathalyzer test at a police station or to accommodate that right. The task of creating new rules governing abortions that would respect procedural safeguards ought to be well within the capacity of competent policy-makers. And according to the Canadian Bar Association and various refugee support groups, it should be possible to create refugee-determination procedures that would respect the new standards of procedural fairness *and* allow for the expeditious processing of refugee claims.

If there is resistance to the new procedural safeguards among public servants, it may be a result of the lack of appreciation of their central importance to our political system.

The Policy Process

When I worked for the Alberta government from 1982 to 1985, my impression was that rather than trying to understand the implications of the *Charter of Rights*, and implement the principles contained within it, some public servants regarded the *Charter* as an obstacle that needed to be avoided. The tendency of many in the policy-making process to try to avoid Charter considerations is illustrated by the reaction of the federal Department of Employment and Immigration to the *Singh* decision of 1985. Rather than trying to develop expeditious and fair methods of handling refugee claimants in Canada, policy-makers focused on developing strategies for keeping refugee claimants from coming to Canada in the first place so that fewer Charter claims would arise.

However, based on my experience since 1985 in liaising with many federal, provincial and municipal public servants, my sense is that after three decades of experience with the *Charter*, public servants are not only more aware of the rights and freedoms the *Charter* purports to protect and advance, but they are more supportive of human rights as a pillar of democracy.

THE LEGAL SYSTEM
Judges

The Canadian judiciary has adopted a dramatically different approach to the interpretation of human rights legislation since 1982. Prior to that year, judges at all levels were reluctant to give a broad interpretation to the *Canadian Bill of Rights* and other human rights legislation because of the fear of interfering with legislative supremacy. The 1982 constitutional changes gave the judiciary a clear mandate to interpret the *Charter* liberally and to apply these interpretations even if it meant striking down statutes. Although the courts have accepted this responsibility, the new role has not turned the judges into ardent social reformers. The Supreme Court of Canada, which sets the tone for the entire judicial system, was described as only "moderately activist" by Peter Russell.[23]

One measure of the degree to which judges might be considered social reformers is the proportion of human rights cases in which the judges uphold the right claimed by an individual litigant. From 1960 to 1982, of a total of thirty-five Bill of Rights cases that came before the Supreme Court, there were only five "individual wins" of this sort (fourteen per cent). According to James Kelly, from 1982 to 1997 individual litigants won nearly thirty-one per cent of their Charter claims.[24]

It is useful to keep in mind the nature of judicial policy-making under the *Charter*. The courts make human rights policies in two ways. The first is to define the specific content of general phrases: whether "freedom of association" contains a right to strike; whether the "right to life" covers a fetus; whether the "right to security of the person" includes the right of women to make decisions about abortions; and so on. The second is to decide whether a government objective that violates a right (once it is defined) can be considered a "reasonable limit" under section 1.

The legal reasoning skills judges have learned are of limited value in making these second-level kinds of decisions. A master's degree in public administration might be far more helpful. Take, for example, the *Edwards* case regarding Ontario's secular Sunday-closing legislation.[25] The Court had practically no empirical data about the importance to the people of Ontario of a common pause day. The judges had been presented with outdated information on which to base their decision about whether the method of implementing Sunday closing was rationally connected with the objective of a common pause day. When it came to considering whether other approaches might infringe the rights of non-Sabbatarians less, the Court had to work with limited information from counsel about different approaches that had been tried elsewhere. The Court might have benefited from a more comprehensive list of alternatives that professional public policy specialists could have produced.

In short, judges have reluctantly accepted the policy-making role that they were presented with by the 1982 decision to amend the constitution to include the *Charter of Rights and Freedoms*. To begin with, judges were making human rights policy decisions more or less in a vacuum. However, during the past three decades, my research indicates that the quantity and quality of evidence presented to judges by counsel has improved.[26]

Lawyers

Good lawyers will do their best to ensure that they prepare high-quality evidence in Charter cases. In my experience, lawyers with a background in public policy and administration, either through their university education or their career experience, are more likely to be successful in hiring credible expert witnesses, and ensuring that evidence is presented in a way that is understandable to judges.

The responsibility of the legal profession to ensure that judges have the best evidence available to them in deciding Charter cases is very high. It is not simply a matter of winning cases. In order to promote right-consciousness, lawyers need to puzzle through the implications of the Charter cases they take on for Canadian society as a whole. They need to find the highest-quality experts with regard to the issues at hand, and they need to ensure that the evidence is presented in court as accurately as possible.

During my career, I have had the experience of working with lawyers as an expert witness in four cases, one of which was decided by the Supreme Court of Canada.[27] In each of the cases, I was able to build on my professional research up to the time of the case. In each case, not all of the research I had conducted supported the client's position unequivocally. The lawyers I worked with had integrity and felt that because my evidence was collected impartially, it was more likely to be credible to the judges who read it.

However, my experience as an expert witness brought to my attention the fact that the adversary system, in which judges rely on counsel for all of the evidence they consider, is an imperfect support for advancing rights-consciousness through the *Charter*. In a perfect system, judges would have access to complete and impartial information with regard to all of the Charter cases they are seized with. Whether they do have adequate evidence depends on the quality and integrity of legal counsel, expert witnesses, and the funds available for litigation.

WAS IT WORTH IT?

In chapter 2, I noted that Charter skeptics had four major apprehensions: that the *Charter* would erode the democratic skills of ordinary Canadians and legislators alike; that the *Charter* would favour the powerful in society who can afford litigation; that the *Charter* would divert attention away from more serious threats to social well-being; and that, because the courts are inappropriate institutions for policy-making, their interpretations of human rights would likely be disappointing. On the other hand, supporters of the *Charter* cheerfully assumed that an entrenched *Charter* is bound to protect human rights better than the pre-1982 system had.

It is up to readers to decide for themselves whether all of the effort that Canadians have put into Charter litigation has helped to make Canada a better country. Apart from that question, the conclusion of some international legal academics is that the *Canadian Charter of Rights and Freedoms*, and the decisions of the Supreme Court about the *Charter*, have set an international standard that is being followed in many other courts around the world, from New Zealand to Israel to South Africa. In these countries, Canadian human rights precedents are cited more frequently than those from the United States Supreme Court.[28]

THE CHARTER AND RIGHTS-CONSCIOUSNESS

In asking whether the *Charter* will have a positive effect on rights-consciousness, one should keep two points in mind. First, the job of promoting and protecting human rights belongs to everybody — politicians, public servants, members of interest groups, and the general public — in addition to judges and the legal profession. Second, in the final analysis, the measure of our commitment to human rights is the degree to which we believe in and practise interpersonal respect, the extent to which we are all able to achieve a sense of self-worth and encourage it in others, and the success we have in treating each other fairly.

The ultimate effect of the *Charter* will depend primarily on the integrity of those who are involved in its application, secondly on the procedures through which it is interpreted and applied, and lastly on the nature of the instrument itself.

ACKNOWLEDGEMENTS

I am grateful to so many people for their help and support in the preparation of this book that it is hard to know where to begin. I built on the content from *The Charter of Rights*, published by James Lorimer & Co. in 1989, and so I first want to reiterate my appreciation to the key people who helped me then. Donald Smiley, Peter Russell, Timothy Endicott, and Curtis Fahey, my editor at Lorimer, read through the entire draft of the 1989 book, and provided me with helpful comments. The following people read parts of the 1989 manuscript, and I am indebted to them for their suggestions: Eilonwy Morgan, Doris and Monty Annear, Richard Cullen, Fred Fletcher, Marc Gold, Chief Judge C. A. Kosowan, Chief Justice J. H. Laycraft, Peter McCormick, Stephen Newman, Leo Panitch, Rob Shropshire, Christine Sypnowich, George Szablowski, Martin Thomas, Ellen Turley, and Reg Whitaker.

I began working on this book in the 2000s, but my work was delayed by new family and administrative responsibilities. The Supreme Court has released some of its most important decisions since 2000, and as a result of the delay, I have been able to refer to these in this book. I am thankful to Jim Lorimer for his exceptional patience.

I am grateful for Peter Russell's advice about Aboriginal rights issues. I am also grateful to my graduate and undergraduate students at York University, who have heard and commented on the cases I presented in class, and thus have had an impact on how the cases are summarized. Answering their questions has helped me to make this book more readable. Several people have given me sage advice about drafts of this book, including Morgan Tunzelmann, Nicole Habib, and Diane Young, all editors at Lorimer, and Kristopher Crawford-Dickinson, the conscientious Teaching Assistant for several years in my undergraduate course on the *Charter*. Prubjoth Sidhu assisted both in earlier and later stages of my research. I am also thankful to those who wrote reviews for the 1989 book, especially the most critical reviews, which I hope this book has benefitted from.

I would also like to thank colleagues from whom I have learned much about human rights through informal discussions over the past three decades. They include Carl Baar, Peter Hogg, Lorne Sossin, Patrick Monahan, John Evans, Robert Drummond, Ray Bazowski, Byron Sheldrick, Susan Dimock, Dagmar Soennecken, Soren Frederiksen, Peter Constantinou, James Simeon, Gregory Levine, Gregory Tardi, Rainer Knopff, Samuel LaSelva, Ted Morton, Sidney Peck, David Shugarman, Brian Slattery, Trevor Farrow, Lesley Jacobs, Michael Tulloch, Andy Knight, Terry Conlin, and Irvin Studin. I am especially grateful for having had the opportunity to participate in the Constitutional Law Group at Osgoode Hall Law School which was organized first by Professor Peter Hogg in the 1980s, and afterwards by Professor Marc Gold and others. Subsequently, I have learned a great deal from the annual Osgoode Hall Law School Constitutional Cases Conferences.

All of the above have contributed towards improving the manuscript, but I take full responsibility for its shortcomings.

I have received helpful comments from graduate and undergraduate students too numerous to mention. I am especially thankful to Tina Motavelli, David Brand, Kandace Bond, Chuck Smith, Sandra Han, Volga Sorikova, Paulo A. Ruiz Garcia, and Reese Simpkins. There are many others who have provided assistance in various forms either for the 1989 book or this one, including Lilian Polsinelli, Margo Barreto, Jasmattie Jewan, Margaret Bertram, Peter Gabor, Munyonzwe Hamalengwa, Betty Knapp, Susan Dimock, Linda Kuttis, Robert MacDermid, Diane McCallum, Helen Morgan, Joanna Morgan, John Morgan, Angie Swartz, Anne Stretch, Judy Wolever, and Pat Vadacchino.

Most importantly, I am indebted to my wife, Eilonwy Morgan, without whose good cheer, editorial advice and tolerance for my unusual working hours neither the 1989 nor this book would ever have been completed. As well, I am grateful to our three children — Christina, Philip and Girum — who engaged me in intense discussions about human rights issues. These discussions helped me to clarify essential points.

It is impossible for me to thank them all enough, not only for the benefit of their insights, but for their good humour and encouragement.

SELECT BIBLIOGRAPHY

Clement, Dominique. *Canada's Rights Revolution: Social Movements and Social Change, 1937–82*. Vancouver: UBC Press, 2008.

Dworkin, Ronald M. *Justice for Hedgehogs*. Cambridge, Mass: Harvard UP, 2011.

———. *Is Democracy Possible Here?* Princeton, NJ: Princeton UP, 2006.

———. *Law's Empire*. London: Fontana, 1986.

———. *A Matter of Principle*. Cambridge, Mass: Harvard UP, 1985.

———. *Taking Rights Seriously*. Cambridge: Harvard UP, 1978.

Greene, Ian. *The Courts. Canadian Democratic Audit*. Vancouver: UBC Press, 2006.

Greene, Ian, with Carl Baar, Peter McCormick, George Szablowski, and Martin Thomas. *Final Appeal: Decision-making in Canadian Courts of Appeal*. Toronto: Lorimer, 1998.

Greene, Ian, and David Shugarman. *Honest Politics: Seeking Integrity in Canadian Public Life*. Toronto: Lorimer, 1997.

Foster, Hamar, Heather Raven, and Jeremy Webber. *Let Right Be Done*. Vancouver: UBC Press, 2007.

Hausegger, Lori, Mattthew Nennigar, and Troy Riddell. *Canadian Courts: Law, Politics and Process*. Toronto: Oxford UP, 2009.

Hiebert, Janet. *Charter Conflicts: What is Parliament's role?* Montreal and Kingston: McGill-Queen's University Press, 2002.

Hirschl, Ran. *Towards Juristocracy*. Cambridge, MA: Harvard University Press, 2004.

Hogg, Peter. *Constitutional Law of Canada*, 5th ed. Supplemental, Volume 2, Carswell 2007; or alternatively, the most recent Student Edition of *Constitutional Law of Canada*.

Howe, Paul, and Peter H. Russell, editors. *Judicial Power and Canadian Democracy*. Montreal & Kingston: McGill Queen's, 2001.

Humphrey, John P. *Human Rights and the United Nations: A Great Adventure*. New York: Transnational Publishers, 1984

Ignatieff, Michael. *The Rights Revolution*, 2nd Edition. Toronto: House of Anansi, 2007.

James, Patrick. *Constitutional Politics in Canada after the Charter: Liberalism, Communitarianism, and Systemism*. Vancouver: UBC Press, 2010.

Kelly, James B. *Governing with the Charter: Legislative and Judicial Activism and Framers' Intent*. Vancouver: UBC Press, 2005.

Kelly, James B., and Christopher P. Manfredi, *Contested Constitutionalism: Reflections on the Canadian Charter of Rights and Freedoms*. Vancouver: UBC Press, 2009.

Knopff, Rainer, and F. L. Morton. *Charter Politics*. Toronto: Nelson, 1992.

MacFarlane, Emmett. *Governing from the Bench: The Supreme Court of Canada and the Judicial Role*. Vancouver: UBC Press, 2013.

MacIvor, Heather. *Canadian Politics and Government in the Charter Era*. Toronto: Thomson Nelson, 2006.

Malcolmson, Patrick, and Richard Myers. *The Canadian Regime*. Toronto: U of T Press: 2014.

Mandel, Michael. *The Charter of Rights and the Legalization of Politics in Canada*. Toronto: Thompson Educational Publishing, 1992.

Manfredi, Christopher P. *Judicial Power and the Charter: Canada and the Paradox of Liberal Constitutionalism*, 2nd ed. Don Mills, ON: Oxford University Press, 2001.

McCormick, Peter. *Supreme at Last: The Evolution of the Supreme Court of Canada*. Toronto: Lorimer, 2000.

——. *Canada's Courts*. Toronto: Lorimer, 1994.

McMurtry, Roy. *Memories and Reflections*. Toronto: U of T Press, 2013.

McNeil, Kent. *Emerging Justice?: Essays on Indigenous Rights in Canada and Australia*. Saskatoon: Native Law Centre, University of Saskatchewan, 2001.

Monahan, Patrick, with Byron Shaw. *Constitutional Law*. Toronto: Irwin, 2013.

——. *Politics and the Constitution: The Charter, Federalism and the Supreme Court of Canada*. Toronto: Carswell, 1987.

Morton, F. L., and Rainer Knopff. *The Charter Revolution and the Court Party*. Peterborough: Broadview, 2000.

Petter, Andrew. *The Politics of the Charter: the Illusive Promise of Constitutional Rights*. Toronto: U of T Press, 2010.

Rawls, John. *Political Liberalism*. New York: Columbia UP, 2005.

——. *Justice as Fairness: A Restatement*, Erin Kelly, editor. Cambridge, MA: Harvard UP, 2001.

——. *A Theory of Justice*. Cambridge, MA: Harvard UP, 1999.

Roach, Kent. *The 9/11 Effect: Comparative Counter-terrorism*. New York: Cambridge UP, 2011.

——. *Due Process and Victims' Rights: The New Law and Politics of Criminal Justice*. Toronto: U of T Press, 1999.

Romanow, Roy, John Whyte, and Howard Leeson. *Canada ... Notwithstanding: The Making of the Constitution, 1976–1982*, 25th Anniversary Edition. Toronto: Carswell, 1984.

Russell, Peter H. *Recognizing Aboriginal Title: The Mabo Case and Indigenous Resistance to English-Settler Colonialism*. Toronto: U of T Press, 2006.

——. *Constitutional Odyssey: Can Canadians Become a Sovereign People?*, 3rd ed. Toronto: U of T Press, 2004.

——. *The Judiciary in Canada: The Third Branch of Government*. Toronto: McGraw-Hill Ryerson, 1987.

Russell, Peter H., Rainer Knopff, Thomas M. J. Bateman, and Janet L. Hiebert. *The Court and the Charter: Leading Cases*. Toronto: Emond Montgomery, 2008.

Slattery, Brian J. *Ancestral Lands, Alien Laws: Judicial Perspectives on Aboriginal Title*. Saskatoon: University of Saskatchewan Native Law Centre, 1983.

Smiley, Donald V. *The Canadian Charter of Rights and Freedoms*. Toronto: Ontario Economic Council, 1981.

——. "The Case against the Canadian Charter of Human Rights." *Canadian Journal of Political Science* 2 (1969): 277.

Sniderman, Paul M., Joseph F. Fletcher, Peter H. Russell, and Phillip E. Tetlock. *The Clash of Rights: Liberty, Equality, and Legitimacy in Pluralist Democracy*. New Haven, CT: Yale University Press, 1996.

Trudeau, Pierre Elliott. *Against the Current: Selected Writings 1939–1996*. Edited by Gérard Pelletier. Translated by George Tombs. Toronto: McClelland & Stewart, 1996.

ENDNOTES

PREFACE

1   Donald V. Smiley, "The Case Against the Canadian Charter of Human Rights," *Canadian Journal of Political Science* 2 (1969): 277.

2   For example, in a poll conducted in 2002, nearly 90 per cent of Canadians had heard of the *Charter*, and of these, more than 90 per cent across Canada (including Quebec) thought the *Charter* was a good thing for Canada. See Tracey Tyler, "Support for Charter Runs Strong: Survey; Approval Highest in Quebec on 20-Year-Old Rights Law," *Toronto Star*, April 12, 2002, p. A7. According to a 2014 survey, the *Charter of Rights* was the first choice of a plurality of Canadians who were asked to choose amongst eleven items that keep Canada united. See Benjamin Shingler, the Canadian Press, "Charter of Rights and Universal Health Care Unites Canadians: Poll," accessed August 20, 2014, http://www.ctvnews.ca/canada/charter-of-rights-and-universal-health-care-unites-canadians-poll-1.1892818.

3   See Ian Greene, Carl Baar, Peter McCormick, George Szablowski, and Martin Thomas, "Personality and the Appellate Judge," Ch. 2 in *Final Appeal: Decision-Making in Canadian Courts of Appeal* (Toronto: Lorimer, 1998), and Donald R. Songer, "The Changing Profile of Justices on the Supreme Court," Ch. 2 in *The Transformation of the Supreme Court of Canada, An Empirical Analysis* (Toronto: U of T Press 2008).

4   This approach is developed further in Ian Greene and David Shugarman, *Honest Politics: Seeking Integrity in Canadian Public Life* (Toronto: Lorimer, 1997), and Ian Greene et al., *Final Appeal*, op. cit.

5   The URL for the Supreme Court's website is http://www.scc-csc.gc.ca/.

CHAPTER 1

1   Ronald Dworkin, *Taking Rights Seriously* (London: Duckworth, 1978), 180–182.

2   Paul M. Sniderman, Joseph F. Fletcher, Peter H. Russell, and Phillip E. Tetlock, *The Clash of Rights: Liberty, Equality, and Legitimacy in Pluralist Democracy* (New Haven, CT: Yale University Press, 1996).

3   It can be argued that mutual respect is the foundational principle for both human rights and democracy. See Ian Greene and David Shugarman, *Honest Politics: Seeking Integrity in Canadian Public Life* (Toronto: Lorimer, 1997), and Ian Greene, Carl Baar, Peter McCormick, George Szablowski, and Martin Thomas, *Final Appeal: Decision-making in Canadian Courts of Appeal* (Toronto: Lorimer, 1998).

4   C. B. Macpherson, "Berlin's Division of Liberty," in *Democratic Theory: Essays in Retrieval* (Oxford: Clarendon, 1973), and *The Real World of Democracy* (Toronto: Oxford University Press, 1972).

5   See W. N. Hohfeld, *Fundamental Legal Conceptions as Applied in Judicial Reasoning*, 1919; W. R. Lederman, "The Nature and Problems of a Bill of Rights," *Canadian Bar Review* 4 (1959); and H. L. A. Hart, *Definition and Theory in Jurisprudence*, 1954.

6   Dworkin, op. cit., and John Rawls, *A Theory of Justice* (Cambridge, MA: Belknap Press of Harvard University Press, 1999).

7   Cynthia Williams, "The Changing Nature of Citizen Rights" in Alan Cairns and Cynthia Williams, *Constitutionalism, Citizenship and Society in Canada* (Toronto: University of Toronto Press, 1985), 99; and Thomas Pocklington, "Against Inflating Human Rights," *Windsor Yearbook of Access to Justice* 2 (1982): 77.

8   Wynberg v. Ontario, [2006] OJ 2732 (Ont. Ct. A.).

9   Donald V. Smiley, *The Federal Condition in Canada* (Toronto : McGraw-Hill Ryerson, 1987).

10   See Syndicat Northcrest v. Amselem, [2004] SCC 47, in which the Supreme Court of Canada decided that a condominium corporation must accommodate a Jewish ceremonial structure on a balcony because this accommodation did not cause undue hardship, and Bruker v.

Marcovitz, [2007] SCC 54, in which a majority of the court allowed a woman to sue her former husband because he refused to allow her to obtain a *get*, a divorce under Jewish law.

11 *Immigration and Refugee Protection Act*, SC 2001, c. 27.

12 Charkaoui v. Canada (Citizenship and Immigration), [2007] 1 S.C.R. 350.

13 Regina v. Morgentaler, [1988] 1 S.C.R. 30.

14 See A. C. Grayling, *Towards the Light: The Story of the Struggles for Liberty and Rights that Made the Modern West* (London: Bloomsbury, 2007).

15 Arar Inquiry, at http://en.wikipedia.org/wiki/Maher_Arar#Canadian_Commission_of_Inquiry, accessed June 19, 2014, and Canada (Prime Minister) v. Khadr, [2010] SCC 3.

16 See Sniderman et. al., *Clash of Rights*. The authors conducted a survey of the attitudes of Canadians toward human rights issues. Amongst other things, they discovered that most Canadians think that some inequality in wealth resulting from differences in ability or effort is justified, but too large a gap is not fair or acceptable.

17 R. v. Keegstra, [1990] 3 S.C.R. 697.

18 Chaoulli v. Quebec (Attorney General), [2005] SCC 35, [2005] 1 S.C.R. 791.

19 John Stuart Mill, *On Liberty*, c. 1859 (Oxford; New York: Oxford University Press, 2008).

20 John Locke, Second Treatise of Government, (c. 1690), ed. C.B. Macpherson (Indianapolis, IN, Hackett: 2011).

21 Entick v. Carrington, [1765] 19 St. Tr. 1030, 95 E.R. 807 (KB).

22 See Peter Hogg, *Constitutional Law of Canada*, 5th ed. supplemental, vol. 2, Ch. 34.2, s. 5(e).

23 "The Political Role of the Supreme Court of Canada in its First Century," *Canadian Bar Review* 53 (1975): 577, 592.

24 Ronald Dworkin, *Law's Empire* (Cambridge, MA: Belknap, 1986); *A Matter of Principle* (Cambridge, MA: Harvard Univ. Press, 1985); and *Taking Rights Seriously* (London: Duckworth, 1978).

25 Patrick Monahan, *Politics and the Constitution: The Charter, Federalism and the Supreme Court of Canada* (Agincourt, ON: Carswell, 1987).

26 C. B. Macpherson, *The Real World of Democracy* (Toronto: Canadian Broadcasting Corporation: 1965).

27 Adam Smith, *An Inquiry into the Nature and Causes of the Wealth of Nations* (London: Methuen & Co., Ltd., 1776).

28 Thomas Paine, *The Rights of Man*, c. 1791–92 (Harmondsworth: Penguin, 1969).

29 Grayling, *Towards the Light*, op. cit., Ch. 4–6.

30 See "Why We Have the Bill of Rights," Ch. 8 in Leonard W. Levy, *Original Intent and the Framer's Constitution* (New York: Macmillan, 1988), 137–173.

31 In the late 1800s, the Northwestern Territory included what is now Alberta, Saskatchewan, Yukon, Nunavut, the North-West Territories, much of northern Quebec, and northern and western Ontario and Manitoba.

32 Peter Hogg, *Constitutional Law of Canada*, 5th ed. supplemental (Toronto: Carswell, 2009), Ch. 28, s. 4(a).

33 The Canadian military's overall success during World War I convinced many Canadians that allowing the United Kingdom to continue determining Canada's external relations was no longer appropriate. The *Balfour Declaration* of 1926 recognized Canada's external independence, and the *Statute of Westminster* of 1931 put this into imperial law. See Hogg, *Constitutional Law of Canada*, 5th ed. supplemental, vol. 2, Ch. 3, s. 3.

34 A. V. Dicey, *Introduction to the Study of the Law of the Constitution*, c. 1885 (London: Macmillan, 1959).

35 Union Colliery Co. of B.C. Ltd. v. Bryden, [1899] AC 580 (PC).

36 Cunningham v. Tomey Homma, [1902] AC 151 (PC).

37 Johnson v. Sparrow, [1899] QSC 104.

38 Loew's Theatres v. Reynolds, [1921] Q.R. 30 B.R. 459.

39 Franklin v. Evans, [1924] 55 OLR 349.

40 Christie v. York Corporation, [1940] S.C.R. 139.

41 Quong-Wing v. Regina, [1914] 49 S.C.R. 440.

42 W. S. Tarnopolsky, *The Canadian Bill of Rights*, 2nd ed. (Toronto: McClelland and Stewart, 1975), and *Discrimination and the Law in Canada* (Toronto: R. DeBoo, 1982).

43 Edwards v. A.-G. Can., [1930] AC 124, on appeal from [1928] S.C.R. 276.

44 1937 Third Session Alberta Legislature, Bill 9, "*An Act to Ensure the Publication of Accurate News and Information*," cited as the *Accurate News and Information Act*.

45   Reference re Alberta Statutes, [1938] 1 S.C.R. 100.

46   Co-op Committee on Japanese Canadians v. A.-G. Can., [1947] AC 87 (PC).

47   See Walter S. Tarnopolsky, *The Canadian Bill of Rights*, 2nd ed. (Toronto: McClelland and Stewart, 1975)

48   CanadaArchives.ca, *Royal Commission to Investigate the Facts Relating to and the Circumstances Surrounding the Communication, by Public Officials and Other Persons in Positions of Trust of Secret and Confidential Information to Agents of a Foreign Power*, retrieved on July 27, 2014 at http://www.archivescanada.ca/english/search/ItemDisplay.asp?sessionKey=1143412449030_2 06_191_57_196&l=0&lvl=2&v=0&coll=1&itm=257663&rt=1&bill=1

49   Cynthia Williams, "The Changing Nature of Citizen Rights," in Alan Cairns and Cynthia Williams, *Constitutionalism, Citizenship and Society in Canada* (Toronto: University of Toronto Press, 1985), 99. See also Dominique Clément, *Canada's Rights Revolution: Social Movements and Social Change, 1937–82* (Vancouver: UBC Press, 2008), 42–45.

50   Dominique Clément, "Canada's Rights Movement — A History," at http://www. historyofrights.com/introduction.html, accessed June 19, 2014.

51   Saumur v. Quebec and A.-G. Que., [1953] 2 S.C.R. 299.

52   Switzman v. Elbling and A.-G. Que., [1957] S.C.R. 285.

53   Roncarelli v. Duplessis, [1959] S.C.R. 121.

54   See Walter Stewart, *The Life and Political Times of Tommy Douglas* (Toronto: McArthur & Company, 2003).

55   The United Nations *Charter*, adopted in 1945, states in its preamble that the people of the United Nations are determined "to regain faith in fundamental human rights, in the dignity and worth of the human person, in the equal rights of men and women and of nations large and small . . ." This was considered not sufficiently clear and prescriptive, and so the UN's secretary-general asked John Humphrey to move to New York from Montreal to draft an international bill of rights. It proved difficult to secure agreement on how such a bill could be enforced, so the project was pursued in several stages. First, the *Universal Declaration of Human Rights* was approved by the General Assembly in 1948. Next, the *International Covenant on Economic, Social and Cultural Rights*, and the *International Covenant on Civil and Political Rights* were drafted and approved by the General Assembly in 1966; both became operative in 1976 with Canada as a signatory to both. The two instruments have specific requirements for compliance. See Robert F. Gorman and Edward S. Mihalkanin, *Historical Dictionary of Human Rights and Humanitarian Organizations*, 2nd ed. (Lanham, MD: Scarecrow, 2007).

56   John P. Humphrey, *Human Rights and the United Nations: A Great Adventure* (New York: Transnational Publishers, 1984). (This book is an autobiography.)

57   Personal interview by author with a member of John Humphrey's family, April 2002.

58   W. H. McConnell, *Commentary on the British North America Act* (Toronto: Macmillan, 1977).

59   Regina v. Therens et al., [1985] 1 S.C.R. 613.

60   Robertson and Rosetanni v. The Queen, [1963] S.C.R. 651.

61   Regina v. Big M. Drug Mart Ltd. et al., [1985] 1 S.C.R. 295.

62   Regina v. Drybones, [1970] S.C.R. 282.

63   A.-G. Can. v. Lavell and Isaac v. Bédard, [1974] S.C.R. 1349.

64   Bliss v. A.-G. Can., [1979] 1 S.C.R. 183.

65   Oil, Chemical and Atomic Workers International Union v. Imperial Oil Ltd. and A.-G. BC, [1963] S.C.R. 584. This decision forced the NDP to work hard to collect individual donations through personal contacts. The result was renewed NDP support, which led to subsequent election victories for the party.

66   Re Lavigne and Ontario Public Service Employees Union et al., (1986), 55 OR (2d), 449, and R. v. Lavigne, [1989] 1 S.C.R. 1591.

67   Walter v. A.-G. Alta., [1969] S.C.R. 383.

68   Nova Scotia Board of Censors v. McNeil, [1978] 2 S.C.R. 662.

69   A.-G. Can. and Dupond v. Montreal, [1978] 2 S.C.R. 770.

70   Peter Russell, *Leading Constitutional Decisions*, 4th ed. (Ottawa: Carleton University Press, 1987).

71   OPSEU v. A.-G. Ontario, [1987] 2 S.C.R. 2.

72   Ivor Jennings, *The Law and the Constitution*, 5th ed. (London: University of London Press, 1961); Geoffrey Marshall, *Constitutional Theory* (Oxford: Clarendon Press, 1980); See also Hogg, *Constitutional Law of Canada*, 5th ed. supplemental, vol. 2, Ch. 35.3(c).

CHAPTER 2

1   Rainer Knopff and F. L. Morton, "Nation-Building and the Canadian Charter of Rights and Freedoms," in A. Cairns and C. Williams, *Constitutionalism, Citizenship and Society in Canada*, vol. 33 of research studies commissioned by the Royal Commission on the Economic Union and Development Prospects for Canada (Toronto: University of Toronto Press, 1985), 133.

2   Alan Cairns and Cynthia Williams, "Constitutionalism, Citizenship and Society in Canada: An Overview," in A. Cairns and C. Williams, op. cit., 1–50.

3   See Pierre Elliott Trudeau, *Approaches to Politics*, 2nd ed., trans. Ivon Owen, Preface by Jacques Hébert, Foreword and Introduction by Ramsay Cook (Toronto: Oxford University Press, 2010).

4   Ibid.

5   Cynthia Williams, "The Changing Nature of Citizen Rights," in Alan Cairns and Cynthia Williams, *Constitutionalism, Citizenship and Society in Canada* (Toronto: University of Toronto Press, 1985), 99.

6   The Victoria Charter stipulated that provinces with more than 25 per cent of the population (then Ontario and Quebec) would have a veto. As well, two out of four western provinces representing at least 50 per cent of the population of the west would need to approve an amendment, and because of the west's population distribution at the time, BC would effectively have a veto. As well, two out of four Atlantic provinces representing 50 per cent of the Atlantic region's population would need to approve a constitutional amendment.

7   See Peter Hogg, *Constitutional Law of Canada*, 5th ed. supplemental, vol. 2, Ch. 4.1(a).

8   I learned this in an interview that I conducted in 1986 with one of the former premiers who opposed unilateral patriation.

9   Re: Resolution to Amend the Constitution, [1981] 1 S.C.R. 753.

10 For a first-hand account of these negotiations, see Roy McMurtry, *Memoirs and Reflections* (Toronto: U of T Press, 2013). McMurtry, a key figure in the compromise, was Ontario's Attorney General at the time.

11 Reference re: Amendment to the Canadian Constitution, [1982] 2 S.C.R. 791.

12 Peter Hogg, *Meech Lake Constitutional Accord Annotated* (Toronto: Carswell, 1988).

13 Ian Greene, "A Constitutional Amendment in Canada and the United States," Ch. 8 in Stephen L. Newman, ed., *Constitutional Politics in Canada and the United States* (Albany, NY: State University of New York Press, 2004, 249–271).

14 Donald V. Smiley, "The Case against the Canadian Charter of Human Rights," *Canadian Journal of Political Science* 2 (1969): 277.

15 Abdelrazik v. Canada, [2009] FC 580 (F.C.) (Zinn, J.).

16 Hogg, *Constitutional Law of Canada*, 5th ed. supplemental, vol.2, Ch. 46.1(b).

17 Paul Koring, "Abdelrazik Sues Ottawa for $27 Million," *Globe and Mail*, September 24, 2009, accessed June 19, 2014, http://www.theglobeandmail.com/news/politics/abdelrazik-sues-ottawa-for-27-million/article1299382/.

18 United States v. Burns, [2001] 1 S.C.R. 283. The court held that if an assurance that the death penalty will not be imposed by the foreign jurisdiction is not obtained, then the section 7 rights of the person being extradited would be violated.

19 Black v. Law Society of Alberta, [1989] 1 S.C.R., on appeal from [1986] 3 W.W.R. 590.

20 Taylor v. Institute of Chartered Accountants, [1989] 59 DLR (4th) 656 (SK. CA).

21 Re *Mia* [1985] 17 DLR (4th) 385 (BCSC).

22 Canada v. Kamel, [2009] FCA 21.

23 Law Society of Upper Canada v. Skapinker, [1984] 1 S.C.R. 357.

24 For example, see Hunter et al. v. Southam Inc., [1984] 2 S.C.R. 145, and Regina v. Big M Drug Mart Ltd. et al., [1985] 1 S.C.R. 295.

25 In 2000, the Canadian Parliament enacted the *Crimes Against Humanity and War Times Act*, which provided for the prosecution of war criminals in Canadian courts, regardless of where the offence had been committed. (See *Crimes Against Humanity and War Crimes Act*, CANLII, accessed June 19, 2014, http://www.canlii.org/en/ca/laws/stat/sc-2000-c-24/latest/sc-2000-c-24.html.) In 2009, Desire Munyaneza was convicted of war crimes committed in Rwanda in 1994 and sentenced to life imprisonment without parole for twenty-five years. (Sidhartha Banerjee, "Life Sentence for Rwandan Convicted of War Crimes,"

Toronto Star, October 29, 2009, accessed June 19, 2014, http://www.thestar.com/news/ canada/2009/10/29/life_sentence_for_rwandan_convicted_of_war_crimes.html .)

26   Corporation professionnelle des médecins du Québec v. Thibault, [1988] 1 S.C.R. 1033, and Krug v. The Queen, [1985] 2 S.C.R. 255.

27   *Regina v. Lyons*, [1987] 2 S.C.R. 309, and Regina v. Milne, [1987] 2 S.C.R. 512.

28   Regina v. Beare; Regina v. Higgins, [1988] 2 S.C.R. 387.

29   Mills v. The Queen, [1986] 1 S.C.R. 863.

30   Dubois v. The Queen, [1985] 2 S.C.R. 350, and Regina v. Manninen, [1987] 1 S.C.R. 1233.

31   A.-G. Can. v. Lavell and Isaac v. Bédard, [1974] S.C.R. 1349.

32   Laurence A.Tribe, ed., *American Constitutional Law*, 3rd ed. (Mineola, NY: Foundation Press, 1988). See, for example, Regents of the University of California v. Bakke, [1978], 438 US 265, 98 S. Ct. 2733.

33   Hogg, *Constitutional Law of Canada*, 5th ed. supplemental, vol. 2, Ch. 56.6(a).

34   Some parents — both anglophone and francophone — who wanted their children educated in French but who did not qualify under s. 23, would send one child to an English-language private school for a short time and then apply to have that child transferred to a publicly-funded English-language school along with the child's siblings. Legislation passed by the Quebec government in 2004 (Bill 104) stated that attendance at an unsubsidized private school could not be considered when determining whether children qualified to attend an English-language school. In 2009, the Supreme Court declared that Bill 104 violated s. 23 because it did not limit the sibling clauses as little as necessary. The court gave the Quebec government one year to amend it in order to comply with s. 23. (Nguyen v. Quebec (Education, Recreation and Sports), [2009] 3 S.C.R. 208.)

35   A.-G. Que. v. Association of Quebec Protestant School Boards et al., [1984] 2 S.C.R. 66.

36   RWDSU v. Dolphin Delivery Ltd., [1986] 2 S.C.R. 573.

37   Re Blainey v. Ontario Hockey Association, [1986] 54 OR (2d) 513.

38   Vriend v. Alberta, [1998] 1 S.C.R. 493.

39   Hunter et al. v. Southam Inc., [1984] 2 S.C.R. 145.

40   Regina v. Therens et al., [1985] 1 S.C.R. 613.

41   Re Ontario Film and Video Appreciation Society and Ontario Board of Censors, [1984] 45 OR (2d) 80, on appeal from [1983] 41 OR (2d) 583.

42   See the web page for the Ontario Film Review Board at http://www.ofrb.gov.on.ca/. According to the Board, "Film boards are responsible for applying community standards to regulate the boundary between films that cause harm and films that are suitable for public display and consumption. The Ontario Film Review Board has the discretion — and the responsibility — to refuse to approve films that contain depictions of explicit sexual assault, degrading and dehumanizing activities, sexual activities with minors, and so on.") (http://www.ofrb.gov.on.ca/english/faq_page4.htm)

43   Regina v. Hufsky, [1988] 1 S.C.R. 621; Regina v. Thomsen, [1988] 1 S.C.R. 640; and R. v. Ladouceur, [1990] 1 S.C.R. 1257. See Hogg, *Constitutional Law of Canada*, 5th ed. supplemental, vol. 2, Ch. 38.7(b).

44   The Queen v. Oakes, [1986] 1 S.C.R. 103.

45   When these overrides expired, the Parti Québécois government of Quebec decided not to re-enact them, likely due in part to the popularity of the *Charter* in Quebec, and possibly due to international criticism of Quebec for using the override in this way.

46   In Reference re Public Service Employee Relations Act (AB), [1987] 1 S.C.R. 313, the majority on the Supreme Court reasoned that freedom of association in the *Charter* does not imply a right to strike. This decision was overruled by the Court in 2007 in Health Services and Support–Facilities Subsector Bargaining Assn. v. British Columbia, [2007] 2 S.C.R. 391.

47   Ford v. A.-G. Quebec, [1988] 2 S.C.R. 712.

48   In 2004, the Supreme Court declared that the definition of marriage is a federal responsibility, and therefore Alberta's attempt to prohibit same-sex marriages was unconstitutional. Reference re Same-Sex Marriage, [2004] 3 S.C.R. 698, 2004 SCC 79.

49   See Hogg, *Constitutional Law of Canada*, 5th ed. supplemental, vol. 2, Ch. 39.2.

50   Ibid., Ch. 40.2(d), 40.2(e).

51   Doucet-Boudreau v. Nova Scotia (Minister of Education), [2003] 3 S.C.R. 3, 2003 SCC 62.

52   Abdelrazik v. Canada, [2009] FC 580 (F.C.)

53   Parliament of Canada, Minutes of Subcommittee on International Human Rights of the

Standing Committee on Foreign Affairs and International Development, Evidence, April 29, 2008, 39th Parliament, 2nd Session, accessed June 19, 2014, http://www.parl.gc.ca/HousePublications/Publication.aspx?DocId=3449878&Language=E&Mode=1&Parl=39&Ses=2.

54 Hamdan v. Rumsfeld, 548 U.S. 557 (2006).

55 Richard J. Wilson, "Omar Khadr: Domestic and International Litigation Strategies for a Child in Armed Conflict Held at Guantanamo," 11 *Santa Clara J. Int'l L.* (2012), p. 29. Accessed Semptember 30, 2014. http://digitalcommons.wcl.american.edu/cgi/viewcontent.cgi?article=1236&context=facsch_lawrev.

56 Canada (Prime Minister) v. Khadr, Neutral citation: 2010 SCC 3. The court held that Canada's foreign affairs are administered under the Crown's prerogative powers — powers not at this time controlled by Parliament — and therefore beyond the purview of the courts to impose a remedy.

57 Khadr was the only foreign national left at the Guantanamo detention centre after the British and Australian governments repatriated their nationals.

58 F. L. Morton, and M. J. Withey, "Charting the Charter, 1982–1985: A Statistical Analysis," Research Unit for Socio-Legal Studies, University of Calgary, Occasional Papers Series, Research Study.

59 Regina v. Big M Drug Mart Ltd. et al., [1985] 1 S.C.R. 295.

60 Peter H. Russell, "The Political Purposes of the Canadian Charter of Rights and Freedoms," *Canadian Bar Review* (Charter ed.) 61 (1983): 30.

61 Cynthia Williams, "The Changing Nature of Citizen Rights," in Alan Cairns and Cynthia Williams, *Constitutionalism, Citizenship and Society in Canada* (Toronto: University of Toronto Press, 1985), 99.

62 Rainer Knopff and F. L. Morton, "Nation-Building and the Canadian Charter of Rights and Freedoms," in Alan Cairns and Cynthia Williams, *Constitutionalism, Citizenship and Society in Canada*, 133.

63 Benjamin Shingler, "What unites Canada? Charter of Rights and universal health care: poll respondents," The Canadian Press. http://www.cp24.com/news/what-unites-canada-charter-of-rights-and-universal-health-care-poll-respondents-1.1892837.

64 Ian Greene, *The Courts*, Canadian Democratic Audit series (Vancouver: UBC Press, 2006), 149.

65 Ibid.

66 For example, see Paul M. Sniderman, Joseph F. Fletcher, Peter H. Russell, and Philip E. Tetlock, *The Clash of Rights: Liberty, Equality, and Legitimacy in Pluralistic Democracy* (New Haven: Yale University Press, 1996), and Maureen Mancuso, Michael M. Atkinson, André Blais, Ian Greene, and Neil Nevitte, *A Question of Ethics: Canadians Speak Out* (Toronto: Oxford University Press, 1998).

67 John Stuart Mill, *On Liberty and Other Essays*, c. 1859; edited with an introduction and notes by John Gray (Oxford; New York: Oxford University Press, 2008).

68 Leonard W. Levy, ed., *Judicial Review and the Supreme Court* (New York: Harper & Row, 1967).

69 Christopher P. Manfredi, *Judicial power and the Charter: Canada and the Paradox of Liberal Constitutionalism*, 2nd ed. (Don Mills, ON: Oxford University Press, 2001). Also, Rainer Knopff and F. L. Morton, *Charter Politics* (Toronto: Nelson, 1992), and Andrew Petter, *The Politics of the Charter: The Illusive Promise of Constitutional Rights* (Toronto: University of Toronto Press, 2010).

70 Lorne Slotnick, "Use of union dues for political causes does not violate Charter, court rules," *Globe and Mail*, 31 January 31, 1989, A1.

71 Ibid., and *R. v. Lavigne* [1989] 1 S.C.R. 1591. See also Michael Mandel, *The Charter of Rights and the Legalization of Politics in Canada* (Toronto: Thompson Educational Publishing, 1994); Allan Hutchison, *Waiting for Coraf: A Critique of Laws and Rights* (Toronto: U of T Press, 1995).

72 F. L. Morton and Rainer Knopff, *The Charter Revolution and the Court Party* (Peterborough, ON:Broadview Press, 2000), and Knopff and Morton, *Charter Politics*, op. cit.

73 Michael Mandel, op. cit., and Allan C. Hutchinson, *Waiting for Coraf: A Critique of Law and Rights* (Toronto: University of Toronto Press, 1995).

74 Re BC Motor Vehicle Act, [1985] 2 S.C.R. 486.

75 For a list of the cases in which the Supreme Court has overruled itself, see Hogg,

Constitutional Law of Canada, 5th ed. supplemental, vol. 2, Ch. 8.7.

76   The Supreme Court of Canada has a superb library with staff who can provide judges with supplemental information upon request. As well, each judge has three clerks (recently graduated law students) who assist with research. Clerkship positions also exist in provincial appellate courts and the Federal Court of Appeal, as well as in some superior courts.

77   See James B. Kelly, *Governing with the Charter: Legislative and Judicial Activism and Framers' Intent* (Vancouver: UBC Press, 2005).

78   Peter W. Hogg and Allison A. Bushell, "The Charter Dialogue Between Courts and Legislatures," *Osgoode Hall Law Journal* 35 (1997): 75.

79   Singh et al. v. Minister of Employment and Immigration, [1985] 1 S.C.R. 177.

80   For other examples, see L. A. Pal and F. L. Morton, "Impact of the Charter of Rights on Public Administration," *Canadian Public Administration* 221 (1985); Morton and Knopff, op. cit.; Knopff and Morton, op. cit.; Janet Hiebert, *Charter Conflicts: What is Parliament's Role?* (Montreal and Kingston: McGill-Queen's University Press), 2002; Christopher P. Manfredi, *Judicial Power and the Charter: Canada and the Paradox of Liberal Constitutionalism,* 2nd ed. (Don Mills, ON: Oxford University Press, 2001); Ran Hirschl, *Towards Juristocracy* (Cambridge, MA: Harvard University Press, 2004); James Kelly, *Governing With the Charter,* op. cit., and James Kelly and Christopher Manfredi, *Contested Constitutionalism,* op. cit.

81   The results of these interviews are presented in Ian Greene, Carl Baar, Peter McCormick, George Szablowski, and Martin Thomas, *Final Appeal: Decision-making in Canadian Courts of Appeal* (Toronto: Lorimer, 1998), and Peter McCormick and Ian Greene, *Judges and Judging: Inside the Canadian Judicial System* (Toronto: Lorimer, 1990).

82   For a detailed description of judicial appointment systems in Canada, see Greene, *The Courts,* op. cit., Ch. 2.; op. cit., 36.

83   Katie Snowball, "Courts Personnel and Expenditures, 2000/01," Report 85-403-XIE (Ottawa: Canadian Centre for Justice Statistics, Statistics Canada).

84   Ibid.

85   Office of the Commissioner of Federal Judicial Affairs for Canada, and "Disclosure for 2005 under the Public Sector Salary Disclosure Act, 1996: Government of Ontario — Judiciary," accessed June 19, 2014, http://www.fin.gov.on.ca/en/publications/salarydisclosure/2006/judiciary06.pdf.

86   Greene, *The Courts,* 60–62. In 1990, fewer than 6 per cent of Canadian judges were women. In 2009, 22 per cent of those elected to the Canadian Parliament were women, according to a study published by the Public Policy Forum ("A Statistical Breakdown of Canada's 40th Parliament, with Comparisons to the 39th Parliament," (Ottawa: Public Policy Forum, April 2009), accessed June 19, 2014, http://www.ppforum.ca/publications/lessmale-even-less-educated-even-less-experienced-%0Beven-more-white.

87   Greene, *The Courts,* 62–63. Prior to the 1980s, there were few, if any, Aboriginal judges in Canada.

88   McCormick and Greene, *Judges and Judging,* 64–65.

89   Ibid.

90   Ibid.

91   Dennis Olsen, *The State Elite* (Toronto: McClelland and Stewart: 1980).

92   Peter H. Russell, *The Judiciary in Canada: The Third Branch of Government* (McGraw-Hill Ryerson, 1987).

93   The proportion of judges who had been strong supporters of a political party prior to their appointment has likely declined from more than 80 per cent in the 1970s to perhaps 60 per cent in the 1990s (Greene et al., *Final Appeal,* 36).

94   Statistics Canada, "Education, Training and Learning," analysis of 2006 census, accessed June 19, 2014, http://www41.statcan.gc.ca/2009/1821/cybac1821_000-eng.htm.

95   Paul M. Sniderman, *Personality and Democratic Politics* (Berkeley: University of California Press, 1975).

96   Richard Sigurdson, "Left- and Right-wing Charterphobia in Canada: A Critique of the Critics," *International Journal of Canadian Studies* 7–8: 95–115.

97   Peter H. Russell, "The Political Purposes of the Canadian Charter of Rights and Freedoms," *Canadian Bar Review* 61 (1983): 52.

98   Peter H. Russell, "The Charter and Canadian Democracy," in Kelly and Manfredi, eds., *Contested Constitutionalism,* op. cit., 287, at p. 302.

99   Ibid., p. 304.

CHAPTER 3

1   Regina v. Big M Drug Mart Ltd. et al., [1985] 1 S.C.R. 295.
2   Ibid., para. 115.
3   Hunter et al. v. Southam Inc., [1984] 2 S.C.R. 145, 156 ff.
4   Big M, op. cit., para. 94.
5   Hunter, op. cit., p. 155.
6   Big M, op. cit., para. 121.
7   Ibid., para. 120.
8   Ibid., para. 96.
9   Ibid., para. 120.
10   Dickson pointed out that in 1903 the Judicial Committee awarded the federal government
     jurisdiction over legislation like the *Lord's Day Act* because it constituted a criminal
     prohibition based on a religious purpose. But with the *Charter*, that kind of criminal legis-
     lation became unconstitutional. *Big M*, para. 54.
11   Regina v. Edwards Books and Art Ltd., [1986] 2 S.C.R. 713.
12   Multani v. Commission scolaire Marguerite-Bourgeoys, [2006] 1 S.C.R. 256.
13   Gurinder Singh Mann, *Sikhism*, Religions of the World Series (Upper Saddle River, NJ:
     Prentice Hall, 2004), 40–62, and W. H. McLeod, *Historical Dictionary of Sikhism* (Toronto:
     Scarecrow Press, 2005), 33.
14   Multani, op. cit., para. 4.
15   Ibid., para. 3.
16   Although Justice Major took part in the hearing, he retired prior to the judgment-writing
     stage of the case.
17   Multani, op. cit., para. 25. In Trinity Western University v. British Columbia College of
     Teachers, [2001] 1 S.C.R. 722, the Supreme Court upheld the right of a private evangelical
     Christian university to maintain a code of conduct that prohibited homosexual activity by
     defining the limits of rights in question. Similarly, in Syndicat Northcrest v. Amselem, [2004]
     2 S.C.R. 551, the court interpreted the right to "peaceful enjoyment of their property and
     to personal security" in the Quebec *Charter of Rights* narrowly and found no conflict with
     freedom of religion, which enabled Orthodox Jews to set up a *succah,* or ceremonial hut, on
     their balconies in a co-owned property in spite of the rules of the co-owned property.
18   Although LeBel generally agreed with the reasoning of Charron, he wrote that it was quite
     legitimate to decide some freedom of religion cases by narrowing the scope of freedom of
     religion. Multani, paras. 140–155.
19   Multani, para. 34.
20   Ibid., para. 35. In *Amselem*, the court refused to inquire into whether the Jewish religion
     actually requires the setting up of a *succah* in the way it was being done with regard to this
     case. The key was that the litigants sincerely believed that their religion required them to set
     up a particular structure out of doors.
21   Ibid., para. 40.
22   Ibid., para. 48.
23   Ibid., para. 53.
24   Ibid., para. 37.
25   Ibid., paras. 71, 78.
26   Ibid., para. 60.
27   Ibid., para. 75.
28   Ibid., para. 74.
29   Ibid., para. 56 ff.
30   Ibid., para. 65, quoting from the decision of a board of inquiry established by the Ontario
     Human Rights Commission in 1990 to investigate a complaint that the Peel Board of
     Education discriminated against Sikhs by prohibiting the wearing of kirpans in Peel district
     schools. See Pandori v. Peel Bd. of Education, [1990] 12 C.H.R.R. D/364.
31   Ibid., para. 78.
32   Ibid., para. 79.
33   Regina v. Jones, [1986] 2 S.C.R. 284.
34   Alberta v. Hutterian Brethren of Wilson Colony, [2009] SCC 37, [2009] 2 S.C.R. 567. It
     should be noted that only a minority of Hutterites in Alberta objected to having their photos
     on their drivers licenses.

35   Health Services and Support Facilities Subsector Bargaining Assn. v. British Columbia, [2007] SCC 27, para. 22.
36   RWDSU v. Dolphin Delivery Ltd., [1986] 2 S.C.R. 573.
37   Ibid., para. 25.
38   Law Society of Upper Canada v. Skapinker, [1984] 1 S.C.R. 357.
39   RWDSU, para. 20.
40   A.-G. Can. and Dupond v. Montreal, [1978] 2 S.C.R. 770.
41   RWDSU, para. 23.
42   British Columbia Government Employees Union v. A.-G. of BC, [1988] 2 S.C.R. 214.
43   Ibid., para. 68.
44   Ibid., para. 70.
45   Ibid., para. 71.
46   Reference re Public Service Employee Relations Act (Alta.), [1987] 1 S.C.R. 313.
47   Leo Panitch and Donald Swartz, *The Assault on Trade Union Freedoms: From Consent to Coercion Revisited.* Toronto: Garamond, (1988).
48   Health Services and Support Facilities (2007) case, op. cit.
49   Dunmore v. Ontario (Attorney General), [2001] 3 SCR 1016.
50   Ibid., paras. 14–16.
51   Health Services and Support Facilities (2007) case, op. cit., para. 4.
52   SBC 2002, C. 2.
53   Health Services and Support Facilities (2007) case, op. cit., paras. 7, 11.
54   Ibid., para. 19.
55   Ibid., para. 20. My research indicates that when faced with conflicting difficult decisions, appellate judges are motivated by a sense of what seems to be the most just course of action. It appears that the majority was appalled at the injustice of the arbitrary limits on collective bargaining imposed by the impugned legislation and, building on *Dunmore*, felt compelled to correct the injustice. A judge I interviewed on the Ontario Court of Appeal in the 1990s went so far as to admit that the judge would sometimes ignore an "unjust" precedent of the Supreme Court of Canada. See Ian Greene, Carl Baar, Peter McCormick, George Szablowski, and Martin Thomas, *Final Appeal: Decision-making in Canadian Courts of Appeal* (Toronto: Lorimer, 1998), Ch. 10.
56   Ibid., paras. 27, 28.
57   Ibid., para. 30.
58   Ibid.
59   Ibid., paras. 25, 38–68.
60   Ibid.
61   68 U.N.T.S. 17 ("Convention No. 87").
62   BC Health Services, para. 79.
63   Ibid.
64   Ibid., para. 81.
65   Ibid., paras. 82–86.
66   Ibid., para. 91.
67   Ibid., para. 89.
68   Ibid., para. 90.
69   Ibid., para. 130. McLachlin and LeBel also found that provisions of the *Act* dealing with the reassignment of employees constitute relatively minor interference with collective bargaining, and so are not covered by s.2(d). para. 131.
70   Ibid., paras. 143–144.
71   Ibid., paras. 148–161. Madame Justice Deschamps agreed with much of the reasoning of McLachlin and LeBel but would have struck down only one section of the *Act* by applying a different analysis of s. 1.
72   Devine v. A.-G. Quebec, [1988] 2 S.C.R. 790.
73   Ford v. A.-G. Quebec, [1988] 2 S.C.R. 712.
74   Ibid., para. 33.
75   Ibid.
76   Ibid., para. 43.
77   Ibid., para. 42.
78   Ibid.

79   Ibid., para. 40.

80   Virginia State Board of Pharmacy v. Virginia Citizens Consumer Council Inc., [1986] 425 US
      748.

81   Ford, para. 59.

82   Ibid, para. 73.

83   Ibid., para. 82.

84   Devine v. A.-G. Quebec, [1988] 2 S.C.R. 790.

85   Ibid., para. 18.

86   Ibid., para. 31.

87   Ibid., para. 30.

88   Human Rights Committee of the United Nations, opinion of the committee regarding
      submission of complaint by John Ballantyne, Elizabeth Davidson, and Gordon McIntyre,
      May 5, 1993, accessed July 29, 2014, http://www1.umn.edu/humanrts/undocs/html/
      v359385.htm.

89   Act to Amend the Charter of the French Language, S.Q. 1993, c. 40 (Bill 86).

90   The 1993 legislation was challenged at the Quebec Court of Appeal in R. v. Entreprises W.
      F. H. [2001] R.J.Q. 2557 (C.A.), and found to be constitutional. An application for leave to
      appeal to the Supreme Court of Canada was denied.

91   RJR-MacDonald Inc. v. Canada, (Attorney General) [1995] 3 S.C.R. 199.

92   Canada (Attorney General) v. JTI-Macdonald Corp., [2007] 2 S.C.R.. 610, para. 7. The new
      legislation also increased the amount of space taken up by health warnings on packaging,
      from 33 per cent to 50 per cent. Janet Hiebert was critical of Parliament for implementing
      the majority's prescription for creating legislation relating to tobacco advertising that would
      comply with the Charter. She would have preferred the approach that Parliament took in
      Charter Conflicts: What is Parliament's Role? (McGill-Queen's University Press, 2002).

93   JTI-Macdonald, op. cit. Chief Justice McLachlin wrote the decision for a unanimous nine-
      judge panel. In this decision, the court referred to the dialogue theory developed by Peter
      Hogg and Allison Bushell, stating that even if Parliament attempts to follow the advice of a
      previous decision of the court about how to avoid a Charter violation, the government still
      needs to fully justify the revised legislation (para. 11).

94   RJR-MacDonald, op. cit., para. 144.

95   Ibid.

96   Ibid., paras. 153–159.

97   Ibid., para. 160.

98   Ibid., para. 162.

99   Ibid., para. 170.

100   Ibid., para. 191.

101   Ibid., para. 67.

102   Ibid., para. 72.

103   Ibid., para. 73. He listed hate speech, pornography, and prostitution as examples of issues
      that are "further from" the core values of freedom of expression.

104   Ibid., para. 74. In her decision, McLachlin was critical of La Forest's argument. She agreed
      that in cases where the freedom of expression issue is at some distance from the core values
      of freedom of expression, there needs to be greater deference shown to government, but "[d]
      eference must not be carried to the point of relieving the government of the burden which
      the Charter places upon it" to justify a breach of Charter rights" (para. 136).

105   Ibid., para. 82.

106   Ibid., para. 94.

107   Ibid., paras. 95–109. La Forest noted that tobacco companies had developed "ingenious
      tactics to circumvent [lower levels of] restrictions" (para. 103).

108   Ibid., para. 112.

109   R. v. Keegstra, [1990] 3 S.C.R. 197.

110   Philip Rosen, "Hate Speech," Depository Services Program, Government of Canada, accessed
      June 19, 2014, http://dsp-psd.pwgsc.gc.ca/Collection-R/LoPBdP/CIR/856-e.htm.

111   Robert Mason Lee, "Keegstra's Children: Jewish Conspiracy as High School Social Studies
      Class," Saturday Night, May 1985.

112   R. v. Keegstra, op. cit., 22 (opinion of Chief Justice Dickson).

113   Lee, "Keegstra's Children," op. cit.

114 R. v. Keegstra, op. cit., p. 21.
115 Ibid.
116 Ibid., pp. 69–70.
117 Ibid., pp. 70--71.
118 Ibid., p. 71.
119 Ibid., p. 74.
120 Ibid., pp. 65–66.
121 Ibid., p. 74.
122 Ibid., pp. 74–76.
123 Ibid., p. 76.
124 Ibid., pp. 77–78.
125 Ibid., p. 83.
126 Ibid., p. 84.
127 Ibid., p. 86.
128 Ibid.
129 Ibid., p. 92.
130 Ibid., p. 93.
131 Ibid., p. 129.
132 Ibid., p. 165.
133 Ibid., p. 167. Dickson countered by stating that the fact that public officials have occasionally misinterpreted s. 319(2) does not in itself provide evidence that the law itself is unconstitutional.
134 Ibid., p. 169.
135 Ibid., p. 171. For thoughtful academic support of McLachlin's position, see Stephan Braun, *Democracy Off Balance: Freedom of Expression and Hate Propaganda Law in Canada* (Toronto: University of Toronto Press, 2004).
136 R. v. Zundel, [1992] 2 S.C.R. 731.
137 Ibid., p. 20.
138 Ibid., quoting Sir William Holdsworth, *A History of English Law* (5th ed., 1942), vol. III, at p. 409.
139 Ibid., p. 46.
140 Ibid., p. 47.
141 Ibid., p. 48.
142 Ibid., p. 56.
143 Ibid.
144 Ibid., p. 91.
145 Anti-Defamation League, "Ernst Zundel," accessed July 29, 2014, archive.adl.org/holocaust/zundel.html, and CBC News, "Zundel Released from German Prison," March 1, 2010, accessed June 19, 2014, http://www.cbc.ca/news/world/story/2010/03/01/zundel-release.html.
146 Ross v. New Brunswick School District No. 15, [1996] 1 S.C.R. 825.
147 Ibid., para. 3.
148 Ibid., para. 2.
149 Ibid., para. 6.
150 Ibid., para. 7.
151 Ibid., para. 40.
152 Ibid., para. 43.
153 Ibid., para. 57 ff.
154 Ibid., para. 96.
155 Ibid., para. 98.
156 Ibid., para. 107.
157 Communications New Brunswick, News Release, "UN Human Rights Committee Rejects Malcolm Ross Claim (00/12/06)", accessed June 19, 2014, http://www.gnb.ca/cnb/news/hrc/2000e1029hr.htm.
158 R. v. Butler, [1992] 1 S.C.R. 452.
159 Criminal Code of Canada, Revised Statutes of Canada 1985, c. C-46, s. 163(8).
160 Ibid., p. 31, quoting from the opinion of Chief Justice Dickson in Towne Cinema Theatres Ltd. v. The Queen, [1985] 1 S.C.R. 494, at pp. 508–9.

161   Ibid., p. 34.

162   Butler, op. cit., p. 38.

163   *Duhaime Legal Dictionary*, accessed June 19, 2014, http://www.duhaime.org/
      LegalDictionary/P/Pornography.aspx.

164   Ibid.

165   Butler, op. cit., p. 38.

166   Ibid., p. 40.

167   Ibid., p. 54.

168   Ibid., p. 51.

169   Ibid., p. 61.

170   Ibid., pp. 66–67.

171   R. v. Sharpe, [2001] 1 S.C.R. 45.

172   Thomas Bateman, Janet Hiebert, Rainer Knopff, and Peter H. Russell, *The Court and the
      Charter: Leading Cases* (Toronto: Emond Montgomery, 2008), 95.

173   For example, see Tonda MacCharles, "Top Court to Rule on Child Porn Case Today," *Toronto
      Star*, January 26, 2001, A6.

174   See Bateman et. al, *The Court and the Charter*, op. cit., pp. 95–96.

175   Sharpe, op. cit., paras. 25–26.

176   Ibid., para. 28.

177   Ibid., para. 34, quoting from House of Commons Debates, 3rd Session, 34th Parliament, vol.
      XVI, June 3, 1993, at p. 20328.

178   Ibid., para. 82.

179   Ibid., para. 94.

180   Ibid., para. 99.

181   Ibid., para. 129. Following the Supreme Court decision, much of the media commentary
      was critical of the reading down of s. 163.1 and supportive of the minority position on
      the Supreme Court. See, for example, Luiza Chwialkowska, "Minority View: Freedom
      of Expression Not Absolute: Three Judges," *National Post*, January 27, 2001, A8. Other
      commentary praised the Supreme Court for making a balanced decision without yielding to
      pressure from either side. See Rod Mickleburgh and Colin Freeze, "Both Sides Claim Victory,"
      Globe and Mail, January 27, 2001, A4.

182   Ibid., para. 103.

183   Ibid., paras. 131–243.

184   Ibid., para. 13.

185   Other similar cases include Little Sister Book and Art Emporium v. Canada, [2000] 2. S.C.R.
      1120, in which the Supreme Court considered whether obscenity included sado-masochistic
      literature that some gays and lesbians argued was part of their unique culture and should
      be treated differently from heterosexual pornography (the Supreme Court rejected that
      argument), and Reference re *ss. 193 and 195.1(1)(c) of the Criminal Code* (Man.), [1990] 1
      S.C.R. 1123, in which the Supreme Court upheld the constitutionality of the *Criminal Code*
      provision outlawing communicating for the purpose of prostitution.

CHAPTER 4

1   Dixon v. BC (Attorney General), [1986] 7 BCLR (2d) 174.

2   Dixon v. British Columbia (Attorney General), [1989] 248 (BC SC).

3   Reference re Provincial Electoral Boundaries (Sask.), [1991] 2 S.C.R. 158.

4   For example, see Baker v. Carr, 369 US 186 [1962], and Reynolds v. Simms, 377 US 533
      [1964].

5   Reference re Prov. Electoral Boundaries (Sask.), 44.

6   Edwards v. Attorney General for Canada, [1930] AC 124, at p. 136.

7   Reference re Prov. Electoral Boundaries (Sask.), p. 30.

8   Ibid., quoting from R. v. Oakes, [1986] 1 S.C.R. 103, at p. 136.

9   Reference re Prov. Electoral Boundaries (Sask.), p. 34.

10   Ibid., p. 43.

11   Figueroa v. Canada (Attorney General), [2003] SCC 37.

12   See Ian Greene and David Shugarman, *Honest Politics: Seeking Integrity in Canadian Public Life*
      (Toronto: Lorimer, 1997), Ch. 1.

13 Reference re Secession of Quebec, [1998] 2 S.C.R. 217.
14 Another factor that led to the reference question on the secession of Quebec was the fact that Guy Bertrand, a former *indépendantiste* politician turned federalist, began litigation to seek a declaration from the Quebec Superior Court that the separation of Quebec from Canada would violate the rights of Quebeckers to enjoy the benefits of the *Canadian Charter of Rights and Freedoms*. Bertrand's litigation was eventually absorbed into the reference question.
15 Reference re Secession of Quebec, para. 2
16 Over the objections of the *amicus curiae*, the court affirmed that Parliament has jurisdiction to assign the Supreme Court with the responsibility to answer reference questions, and that the questions in this case are justiciable, i.e., amenable to a legal analysis. As well, the court rejected the notion that the questions are political, and therefore not appropriate for it to address. The court affirmed its conclusion in the Reference re Objection by Quebec to a Resolution to Amend the Constitution, [1982] 2 S.C.R. 793 that the *Canada Act, 1982* is valid law, even though it was enacted by the British Parliament over objections by the *indépendantiste* government of Quebec.
17 Reference re Secession of Quebec, para. 34.
18 Ibid., para. 42.
19 Ibid., para. 49.
20 Ibid., para. 54.
21 Ibid., para. 58.
22 Ibid., para. 63, quoting from Reference re Provincial Electoral Boundaries (Sask.), [1991] 2 S.C.R. 158, at p. 186.
23 Ibid., para. 64.
24 Ibid., para. 68.
25 Ibid.
26 Ibid., para. 70.
27 Ibid., para. 71, quoting from Reference re Manitoba Language Rights, [1985] 1 S.C.R. 721, at p. 749. See also chapter 7, on language rights.
28 Ibid., para. 76.
29 Ibid., paras. 79–82.
30 Ibid., para. 87.
31 Ibid., para. 154.
32 Bill 99 (RSQ, c. E-20.2), enacted in 2000. An English language-rights group challenged the constitutionality of the Quebec legislation, but it was only in 2014 that the litigation reached the Quebec Superior Court.
33 Reference re *Supreme Court Act*, ss. 5 and 6, 2014 SCC 21.
34 Ibid., para. 49, quoting from (Peter H. Russell, *The Supreme Court of Canada as a Bilingual and Bicultural Institution* (1969), at p. 8).
35 Reference re Senate Reform, 2014 SCC 32.
36 Rachel Mendleson, "Giving non-citizens the right to vote in city elections: Your questions answered," *Toronto Star*, June 12, 2013, accessed August 1, 2014. http://www.thestar.com/news/city_hall/2013/06/12/giving_noncitizens_the_right_to_vote_in_city_elections_your_questions_answered.html
37 Although provincial legislation gave Quebec prisoners the right to vote, federal penitentiaries in Quebec, blaming administrative inconvenience, refused to set up procedures for inmates to vote in provincial elections. In Lévesque v. A.-G. Can., [1986] 2 F.C. 287, the Federal Court rejected that rationale and ordered the penitentiaries to set up the necessary procedures.
38 Re Clifford Maltby et al., [1983] 2 CRD 300-01 (Saskatchewan Queen's Bench).
39 Reynolds v. A.-G. of BC, [1984] 4 CRD 325.30-01 (BC Court of Appeal), on appeal from [1983] 2 CRD 325.30-01 (Supreme Court of BC).
40 Jolivet et al. v. The Queen, [1983] 3 CRD 325.30-01 (Supreme Court of BC).
41 For example, A.-G. Can. v. Gould, [1984] 1 F.C. 1133 (Federal Court of Appeal), on appeal from [1984] 1 F.C. 1119 (Federal Court, trial div.); Badger et al v. A.-G. Man., [1986] 8 CRD 325.20-01 (Manitoba Queen's Bench); Lukes et al. v. Chief Electoral Officer, [1986] 8 CRD 325.30-01.
42 Thomas Claridge, "Ontario's Judge Restores Prisoners' Voting Rights after Charter Challenge," *Globe and Mail*, July 20, 1988, A1.

43 Arthur Schafer, "Ballots Behind Bars: the struggle for prisoners' right to vote," Centre for Practical and Applied Ethics, University of Manitoba. Accessed August 1 2014. http://umanitoba.ca/faculties/arts/departments/philosophy/ethics/media/Ballots_Behind_Bars.pdf

44 Telephone interview with Richard Sauvé, June, 2014.

45 Sauvé v. Canada (Attorney General) (1988), 66 O.R. (2d) 234. However, in the same year, prisoners in Manitoba won the right to vote at trial: Badger v. Canada (1988), 55 Man. R. (2d) 198 (Q.B.).

46 Arthur Schafer, "Inmate Voting Rights: Two Recent Cases," Centre for Ethics, University of Manitoba. http://umanitoba.ca/faculties/arts/departments/philosophy/ethics/media/Inmate_voting_rights.pdf. Accessed August 1, 2014.

47 Sauvé v. Canada (Attorney General), [1993] 2 S.C.R. 438, affirming (1992), 7 OR (3d) 481.

48 Sauvé v. Canada (Chief Electoral Officer), [2002] 3 S.C.R. 519, 2002 SCC 68, para. 21.

49 Ibid., para. 23.

50 Seymour Martin Lipset was at the time Hazel Professor of Public Policy, George Mason University. See Debra Parkes, *Temple Political & Civil Rights Law Review*, "Ballot Boxes Behind Bars: Toward the Repeal of Prisoner Disenfranchisement Laws," 13 Temp. Pol. & Civ. Rts. L. Rev. 71.

51 See summary of evidence of Christopher Manfredi and Rainer Knopff in Arthur Schafer, "Inmate Voting Rights: Two Recent Cases," Centre for Ethics, University of Manitoba, http://umanitoba.ca/faculties/arts/departments/philosophy/ethics/media/Inmate_voting_rights.pdf, accessed August 1, 2014, and Christopher Manfredi, "The Day the Dialogue Died: A Comment on Sauvé V. Canada," (2007) 45 *Osgoode Hall Law Journal*, 105.

52 Thomas Pangle was at the time Professor of Political Science, University of Toronto. See commentaries in Schafer and Manfredi, Ibid.

53 Evidence presented by Sauve's experts including Dr. Grant Amyot, Dr. Arthur Schafer, Professor Neil Boyd, Professor Michael Jackson, and Mr. Eric Andersen (who had been employed in the Danish prison system for twenty-five years).

54 Report of Dr. Grant Amyot of Queen's University.

55 Sauvé v. Canada [2002], Opinion of Justice Gonthier, para. 182 ff.

56 *CBC News*, "12,500 prisoners get to vote on June 28," June 3, 2004. Retrieved August 3, 2014: http://www.cbc.ca/news/canada/12-500-prisoners-get-to-vote-on-june-28-1.485086

57 AC Grayling, *Towards the Light: The Story of the Struggles for Liberty and Rights that Made the Modern West* (London: Bloomsbury, 2007), p. 4.

58 Interview with Richard Sauvé, op. cit.

59 Ibid.

60 Parkes, op. cit., note 68.

61 Elections Canada, "Report of the Chief Electoral Officer of Canada on the 38th General Election Held on June 28, 2004". Retrieved August 1, 2015. http://www.elections.ca/content.aspx?dir=rep/off/sta2004&document=part2_div8&lang=e&section=res

62 Hoogbruin v. British Columbia (Attorney General) (1985), 24 D.L.R. (4th) 718 (BCCA).

63 Muldoon v. Canada, [1988] 3 F.C. 628 (T.D.).

64 Canada Disability Rights Council v. Canda, [1988] e F.C. 622 (T.D.).

65 D. Lipovenko, "Problems Plague Vote by Retarded," *Globe and Mail*, October 22, 1988, A1.

66 Report of the Chief Electoral Officer to Parliament, 1983, as quoted in National Citizens' Coalition v. A.-G. Can., [1984] 5 W.W.R. 436, para. 27.

67 National Citizens' Coalition v. A.-G. Can., op. cit.

68 Hiebert, Janet. "Fair Elections and Freedom of Expression under the Charter: Should Interest Groups' Election Expenditures be Limited?" *Journal of Canadian Studies* 23 (1989).

69 See Thomas M. J. Bateman, Janet L. Hiebert, Rainer Knopff, and Peter H. Russell, *The Court and the Charter: Leading Cases* (Toronto: Emond Montgomery, 2008), 183.

70 Harper v. Canada (Attorney General), [2004] 1 SC. 827.

71 Libman v. Quebec (Attorney General), [1997] 3 S.C.R. 569.

72 Harper v. Canada, op. cit., para. 67 ff.

73 Ibid., para. 92.

74 Ibid., paras. 77, 93 ff.

75 Ibid., para. 110.

76 Ibid., para. 110 ff.

77 Ibid., paras. 1–44.

78   Ibid., para. 128.
79   Ibid., para. 132.
80   Ibid., paras. 131–135.
81   Ibid., para. 79.
82   Bill C-23, the *Fair Elections Act*, introduced into the House of Commons on February 4, 2014, accessed June 23, 2014, http://www.parl.gc.ca/HousePublications/Publication.aspx?DocId=64 04810&Language=E&Mode=1&File=33#3.
83   Opitz v. Wrzesnewskyj, 2012 SCC 55, [2012] 3 S.C.R..
84   Ibid., para. 4.
85   Ibid., para. 10.
86   Ibid., para. 28, quoting from Figueroa v. Canada (Attorney General), 2003 SCC 37, [2003] 1 S.C.R. 912, para. 30.
87   Ibid., para. 30.
88   "Vouching" is a procedure whereby a registered voter can vouch for the identity of another person residing in the same polling district whose name does not appear on the official registered list of voters.
89   Section 524(1)(b) of the *Canada Elections Act*, as quoted in Opitz v. Wrzesnewskyj, para. 19.
90   Ibid., paras. 1–2.
91   Ibid., paras. 147–148.
92   Ibid., paras. 163–164.
93   Storey v. Zazelenchuk, [1983] 2 CRD 325.20-01 (Saskatchewan Queen's Bench).
94   Hedstrom v. Commissioner of Yukon Territory, [1986] 8 CRD 325.20-02 (Yukon Court of Appeal), on appeal from [1985] 6 CRD 325.30-02 (Yukon Supreme Court).
95   MacLean v. A.-G. Nova Scotia, [1987] 35 D.L.R. (4th) 306.
96   Harvey v. New Brunswick (Attorney General), [1996] 2 S.C.R. 876.
97   Jonson v. County of Ponoka, [1988] 12 CRD 400.10-01.
98   Fraser v. A.-G. Nova Scotia, [1986] 9 CRD 400.30-01 (Supreme Court of Nova Scotia).
99   Osborne v. The Queen, [1986] 9 CRD 400.30-02 (Federal Court, trial div.).
100   Osborne v. Canada (Treasury Board), [1991] 2 S.C.R. 69.
101   OPSEU v. A.-G. Ontario, [1987] 2 S.C.R. 2.
102   Patrick Monahan, *Politics and the Constitution: The Charter, Federalism and the Supreme Court of Canada* (Toronto: Carswell, 1987).
103   R. v. Oakes, [1986] 1 S.C.R. 103, at p. 136.

CHAPTER 5

1   F. L. Morton and M. J. Withey, "Charting the Charter, 1982–1985: A Statistical Analysis," Research Unit for Socio-Legal Studies, University of Calgary, Occasional Papers Series, Research Study 2.1.
2   Thomas M.J. Bateman, Janet L. Hiebert, Rainer Knopff, and Peter H. Russell, *The Court and the Charter: Leading Cases* (Toronto: Emond Montgomery, 2008), 14.
3   Peter H. Russell, "The First Three Years in Charterland," *Canadian Public Administration* 28 (1985): 367.
4   Hunter et al. v. Southam Inc., [1984] 2 S.C.R. 145.
5   See Frederick J. Fletcher and Daphne F. Gottlieb, "The Mass Media and the Politics: An Overview," in Michael Whittington and Glen Williams, eds., *Canadian Politics in the 1980's*, 2nd ed., 1984, 193.
6   Entick v. Carrington [1765], 19 St. Tr. 1030, 95 E.R. 807 (K.B.).
7   Peter H. Russell, "The First Three Years in Charterland," op. cit.
8   Regina v. Hufsky, [1988] 1 S.C.R. 621.
9   Ibid., para. 23.
10   Regina v. Hamill, [1987] 1 S.C.R. 301 and Regina v. Sieben, [1987] 1 S.C.R. 295. See also R. v. Ladouceur, [1990] 1 S.C.R. 1257, where the court found a random vehicle stop by the police to constitute an arbitrary detention, and R. v. Mellenthin, [1992] 3 S.C.R. 615, dealing with a unreasonable search at a traffic stop.
11   Regina v. Dyment, [1988] 2 S.C.R. 417.
12   Regina v. Simmons, [1988] 2 S.C.R. 495.
13   Singh et al. v. Minister of Employment and Immigration, [1985] 1 S.C.R. 177.

14   Duke v. The Queen, [1972] S.C.R. 917.

15   The Queen v. Drybones, [1970] S.C.R. 282.

16   The CRDD has offices in Toronto, Montreal, Vancouver, and Calgary, and as of 2011 had about 200 members. Under the Mulroney government, many appointments were based on political patronage, but under the Chrétien and Martin governments the quality of appointees gradually improved until in 2005, appointments were merit-based. The CRDD was replaced in 2012 by the Refugee Protection Division of the Immigration and Refugee Board.

17   Operation Dismantle Inc. et al. v. The Queen et al., [1985] 1 S.C.R. 441, on appeal from [1983] 1 F.C. 745.

18   Operation Dismantle v. The Queen, [1985] 1 S.C.R. 441. para. 63.

19   Regina v. Therens et al., [1985] 1 S.C.R. 613.

20   Chromiak v. The Queen, [1980] 1 S.C.R. 471.

21   Ronald Dworkin, *Taking Rights Seriously* (Cambridge, Mass: Harvard University Press, 1978).

22   Regina v. Therens et al., [1985] 1 S.C.R. 613. para. 57.

23   Regina v. Thomsen, [1988] 1 S.C.R. 640.

24   Ibid., para. 22.

25   Regina v. Hufsky, [1988] 1 S.C.R. 621.

26   Regina v. Collins, [1987] 1 S.C.R. 265.

27   Clarkson v. The Queen, [1986] 1 S.C.R. 383; Regina v. Manninen, [1987] 1 S.C.R. 1233; Regina v. Ross, [1989] 1 S.C.R. 3.

28   Regina v. Strachan, [1988] 2 S.C.R. 980; Regina v. Tremblay, [1987] 2 S.C.R. 435.

29   Regina v. Hamill, [1987] 1 S.C.R. 301; Regina v. Jacoy, [1988] 2 S.C.R. 548; Regina v. Sieben, [1987] 1 S.C.R. 295; Regina v. Simmons, [1988] 2 S.C.R. 495.

30   Regina v. Dyment, [1988] 2 S.C.R. 417; Regina v. Genest, [1989] 1 S.C.R. 59.

31   Re BC Motor Vehicle Act, [1985] 2 S.C.R. 486.

32   Roe v. Wade (1973), 410 US 113.

33   Duke v. The Queen, [1972] S.C.R. 917.

34   Reference re Anti-inflation Act, [1976] 2 S.C.R. 37. In two subsequent cases prior to the *BC Motor Vehicle* case, the Supreme Court accepted social science evidence: A.-G. Can. v. Canadian National Transportation Ltd., [1983] 2 S.C.R. 206; and Re Authority of Parliament in relation to the Upper House Reference, [1980] 1 S.C.R. 54.

35   Re BC Motor Vehicle Act, [1985] 2 S.C.R. 486. para. 53.

36   Ibid., para. 31.

37   Ibid., para. 63.

38   Ibid., para. 63.

39   Ibid., para. 105.

40   Valente v. The Queen et al., [1985] 2 S.C.R. 673.

41   For a fuller analysis of these events, see Ian Greene, "The Doctrine of Judicial Independence Developed by the Supreme Court of Canada," *Osgoode Hall Law Journal* 26 (1988): 177.

42   "Provincial court" refers here to courts with judges appointed by the province. It goes by this name in most provinces, but is known as the Ontario Court of Justice in Ontario and the Court of Quebec in Quebec.

43   Valente v. The Queen et al., [1985] 2 S.C.R. 673. para. 50.

44   Reference re Remuneration of Judges of the Provincial Court (PEI), [1997] 3 S.C.R. 3.

45   See Peter McCormick, "New Questions about an Old Concept: The Supreme Court of Canada's Judicial Independence Jurisprudence," *Canadian Journal of Political Science* 37 (2004), 839–862.

46   Reference re Remuneration of Judges, op. cit., para. 118.

47   Ibid. 99.

48   Ibid., para. 121.

49   Ibid., para. 131(emphasis in original text).

50   Ibid., para. 147 ff.

51   Ian Greene, *The Courts*, Canadian Democratic Audit series (Vancouver: UBC Press, 2006), 91.

52   Provincial Court Judges' Assn. of New Brunswick v. New Brunswick (Minister of Justice); Ontario Judges' Assn. v. Ontario (Management Board); Bodner v. Alberta; Conférence des juges du Québec v. Quebec (Attorney General); Minc v. Quebec (Attorney General), [2005] 2 S.C.R. 286, 2005 SCC 44.

53   The Queen v. Oakes, [1986] 1 S.C.R. 103.
54   Ibid., para. 73.
55   Ibid., paras. 78–79.
56   Regina v. Vaillancourt, [1987] 2 S.C.R. 6.
57   Regina v. Whyte, [1988] 2 S.C.R. 3. See also R. v. Swain, [1991] 1 S.C.R.. 933.; R. v. Daviault, [1994] 3 S.C.R. 63 (self-induced intoxication as a defence to a criminal charge); R. v. Stone, [1999] 2 S.C.R. 290 (defence of automatism must be established by the accused on the balance of probabilities); Makin v. New Brunswick, [2002] 1 S.C.R. 405 (the court refused to apply the Oakes test in a case dealing with judicial independence specifically looking at section 11(d)); and Hill v. Church of Scientology, [1995] 2 S.C.R. 63 (the court allowed for the application of the *Charter* to determine whether the common law is consistent with Charter values, but otherwise the *Charter* does not apply to the common law.)
58   Regina v. Morgentaler, [1988] 1 S.C.R. 30.
59   Regina v. Morgentaler, [1988] 1 S.C.R. 30, p. 32 and p. 56.
60   Ibid., pp. 68–69.
61   Ibid., pp.120–121.
62   Ibid. p. 173.
63   Roe v. Wade (1973), 410 U.S. 113.
64   Regina v. Morgentaler, op. cit., pp. 166, 172
65   Ibid. p. 182.
66   Ibid. pp. 39, 139, 141.
67   Ibid. p. 152.
68   R. v. Seaboyer; R. v. Gayme, [1991] 2 S.C.R. 577.
69   Kwong-leung Tang, "Rape Law Reform in Canada: The Success and Limits of Legislation," *International Journal of Offender Therapy and Comparative Criminology*, 42(3) (1998): 258.
70   Criminal Code of Canada, sections 246.6 and 246.7, later renamed sections 276 and 277, RSC, 1985, c. C-46
71   R. v. Seaboyer; R. v. Gayme, op. cit., p. 30.
72   Ibid., p. 42.
73   Ibid., p. 61.
74   Ibid., p. 52.
75   Ibid., p. 69.
76   Ibid., pp. 74–76.
77   L'Heureux-Dubé and Gonthier dissented in part. They found that s. 276 did not "overshoot the mark," and although it violated both s. 7 and s. 11(d) of the *Charter*, it could be upheld unders. 1.
78   Bateman, Hiebert, Knopff, and Russell, *The Court and the Charter*, op. cit., 237–238.
79   R. v. Darrrach, [2000] 2 S.C.R. 443.
80   R. v. O'Connor, [1995] 4 S.C.R. 411.
81   R.V. Mills, [1999] 3 S.C.R. 668.
82   Bateman, Hiebert, Knopff, and Russell, *The Court and the Charter*, op. cit., 266–67.
83   R. v. Mills, op. cit., para. 57.
84   United States v. Burns, [2001] 1 SCC 283.
85   In 1966, Parliament abolished the death penalty for all offences except for killing on-duty prison guards and police officers, and for some offences decided under military tribunals.
86   Burns, op. cit., para. 76.
87   After being apprehended in Canada the first time, Kindler escaped again, and was eventually recaptured.
88   Kindler v. Canada, [1991] 2 S.C.R. 779, p. 71 ff. The assumption that the conscience of Canadians would not be shocked was based on the reasonable-person test, not public opinion polls.
89   William A. Schabas, "Kindler and Death Row," *PhD Studies in Human Rights*, May 2011, accessed June 28, 2014, http://humanrightsdoctorate.blogspot.ca/2011/05/kindler-and-death-row.html.
90   Burns, op. cit., para. 8 ff. The court declined to define "exceptional cases," leaving that for future courts to decide in appropriate cases.
91   The court listed the following Canadian cases: Donald Marshall Jr., David Milgaard, Guy Paul Morin, Thomas Sophonow, and Gregory Parsons. Burns, op. cit., paras. 97–101.

92   Burns, op. cit., para. 102.

93   Burns, op. cit., paras. 82–93.

94   Ibid., para. 94 ff.

95   Ibid., para. 84.

96   Chaoulli v.Quebec (Attorney General) [2005] 1 SCR 79.

97   Bateman, Hiebert, Knopff and Russell, *The Court and the Charter*, op. cit., 325.

98   Chaoulli, op. cit., para. 16.

99   These are Quebec, Alberta, British Columbia, Manitoba, Ontario and Prince Edward Island. See Bateman et al., op. cit. 325.

100 See Janice Gross Stein, *The Cult of Efficiency* (Toronto: Anansi, 2002). Stein provides empirical evidence supporting this reasoning.

101 The *Quebec Charter* . . . right to personal inviolability . . . is a very broad right. The meaning of "inviolability" is broader than the meaning of the word "security" used in s. 7 of the *Canadian Charter*. In civil liability cases, it has long been recognized in Quebec that personal inviolability includes both physical inviolability and mental or psychological inviolability . . . ." Chaoulli, op. cit., para. 41.

102 Chaoulli, para. 138 ff.

103 Ibid., para. 112.

104 Ibid., para. 129 ff.

105 Ibid., para. 154-158.

106 Ibid., para. 166 and 210 ff.

107 Ibid., para. 209.

108 Bateman et al., p. 327.

109 Charkaoui v. Canada (Citizenship and Immigration), [2007] 1 S.C.R. 350; Charkaoui v. Canada (Citizenship and Immigration), [2008] 2 S.C.R. 326.

110 CBC News, "Security Certificates and Secret Evidence," December 14, 2009, accessed June 28, 2014, http://www.cbc.ca/news/canada/story/2009/08/21/f-security-certificates.html.

111 CBC News, "Charkaoui to Sue Ottawa for $24 Million," March 12, 2010, accessed June 28, 2014, http://www.cbc.ca/news/canada/ottawa/story/2010/03/12/mtl-cp-charkaoui-lawsuit.html.

112 Ibid.

113 Charkaoui v. Canada, [2007], op. cit., para. 11.

114 Ibid., para. 53.

115 Ibid., para 1.

116 "A New Review Mechanism for the RCMP's National Security Activities," Ottawa: Commission of Inquiry into the Actions of Canadian Officials in Relation to Maher Arar, 2006.

117 Charkaoui, 2007, op. cit., para. 26.

118 Ibid., para. 79.

119 Ibid., para. 86.

120 Charkaoui v. Canada (Citizenship and Immigration), [2008] 2 S.C.R. 326.

121 CBC News and The Canadian Press, "Charkaoui Declared a Free Man," October 14, 2009, accessed June 28, 2014, http://www.cbc.ca/news/canada/montreal/story/2009/10/14/charkaoui-certificate-lifted.html.

122 Canada (Justice) v. Khadr, 2 S.C.R. 125, 2008 SCC 28; and Canada (Prime Minister) v. Khadr, 2010 SCC 3, [2010] 1 S.C.R. 44.

123 Khadr 2010, op. cit., para. 24.

124 Khadr 2008, op. cit. This unanimous decision included Harper's first appointment to the Supreme Court, Mr. Justice Marshall Rothstein.

125 The subcommittee is part of the Standing Committee on Foreign Affairs and International Development.

126 Report of the Standing Committee on Foreign Affairs and International Development, Kevin Sorenson, MP Chair, Subcommittee on International Human Rights, Scott Reid, MP Chair, June 2008, 39th Parliament, 2nd Session.

127 Khadr, 2010, op. cit., at para. 25. This unanimous decision included two justices appointed by Steven Harper: Justice Rothstein and Justice Cromwell.

128 Gerald Chan, "Remedial Minimalism under Section 24(1) of the Charter: Bjelland, Khadr and Nasogaluak," op. cit., 360 ff., and Audrey Macklin, "Comment on Canada (Prime

Minister) v. Khadr (2010)," *Supreme Court Law Review* 51 (2010): (2d), 295, at p. 329.

129 Gerald Chan, "Remedial Minimalism" at p. 366, op. cit. and Audrey Macklin, "Comment on Canada v. Khadr," op. cit., at pp. 237–331. The reason given by the court in not ordering the federal government to request Khadr's repatriation was that foreign relations is a prerogative power of the federal cabinet, and the court does not have the evidence or expertise to decide an appropriate remedy.

130 As Macklin has pointed out, this reasoning is difficult to understand, given that the Obama administration clearly wanted Khadr repatriated to Canada. Audrey Macklin, "Comment on Canada v. Khadr", op. cit., at pp. 326–27.

131 Amnesty International, Omar Khadr: "Trial and Transfer Timeline," May 9, 2013, accessed July 20, 2014. http://www.amnesty.ca/our-work/updates/omar-khadr-trial-and-transfer-timeline

132 Sean Fine, "Khadr should be serving youth sentence, court rules," The Globe and Mail, June 9, 2014, A1.

133 Michelle Shephard, "Feds denying media access to Khadr," Toronto Star, Jjly 22, 2014, A2.

134 Terry Milewski, "Canada Accused of 'Complicity' in Torture in UN Report," June 1, 2012, accessed June 28, 2014, http://www.cbc.ca/news/politics/story/2012/06/01/pol-un-report-torture-canada-milewski.html. The Khadr case is amongst several mentioned in this report.

135 Canada (Attorney General) v. PHS Community Services Society, [2011] SCC 44.

136 Ibid., para. 4. In 1993, annual deaths from overdoses reached two hundred. Nearly 90 per cent of intravenous drug users are infected with Hepatitis C and nearly 20 percent are HIV positive (para. 9).

137 Ibid., headnotes.

138 Ibid. para. 138.

139 Ibid., para. 139.

140 Ibid., para. 127.

141 Ibid., para. 150.

142 Canada (Attorney General) *v.* Bedford 2013 SCC 72.

143 Frances M. Shaver and Julia Skikavich, "Prostitution," The Canadian Encyclopedia, published 2011 and edited 2014. Retrieved May 28 2014 at: http://www.thecanadianencyclopedia.ca/en/article/prostitution/

144 Ibid.

145 Bedford, op cit., para. 15.

146 *Reference re ss. 193 and 195.1(1)(c) of the Criminal Code (Man.)*, [1990] 1 S.C.R. 1123.

147 Neal Hall, "Life sentence without parole for 25 years," *Vancouver Sun*, December 11, 2007, accessed on June 30 2014 at http://www2.canada.com/vancouversun/features/pickton/story.html?id=94d2f590-2b4c-4eca-b1a5-501ec2f6f996

148 These are Criminal Code Section 210, as it relates to prostitution, and ss. 212(1)(j) and 213(1)(c).

149 Bedford, op. cit., para. 15.

150 Ibid. 43 ff.

151 Ibid., paras. 60–64.

152 Ibid., para. 127.

153 Ibid., para. 90.

154 Ibid., para. 165–169.

CHAPTER 6

1 Ployvios G. Polyviou, *The Equal Protection of the Laws* (London: Duckworth, 1980).

2 A-.G. Can. v. Lavell and Isaac v. Bédard, [1974] S.C.R. 1349.

3 Paul M. Sniderman, Joseph F. Fletcher, Peter H. Russell, and Phillip E. Tetlock, *The Clash of Rights: Liberty, Equality, and Legitimacy in Pluralist Democracy* (New Haven, CT: Yale University Press, 1996).

4 M. Patricia Marchak, *Ideological Perspectives on Canada* (Montreal; Ithaca [N.Y.]: McGill-Queen's University Press, 2011).

5 See Dominique Clément, Will Silver, and Daniel Trottier, "The Evolution of Human Rights in Canada," (Ottawa: Canadian Human Rights Commission and Minister of Public Works and Government Services, 2012). Accessed August 10, 2014. http://www.chrc-ccdp.ca/sites/

default/files/ehrc_edpc-eng.pdf, and Michael Ignatieff, *The Rights Revolution* (Toronto: House of Anansi Press, 2000).

6   Anne F. Bayefsky and Mary Eberts, *Equality Rights and the Canadian Charter of Rights and Freedoms* (Toronto: Carswell,1985).

7   Rt. Hon. Beverley McLachlin, PC, "Equality: The Most Difficult Right," *Supreme Court Law Review* 14 (2001): 17. Accessed August 10, 2014. http://pi.library.yorku.ca/ojs/index.php/sclr/article/view/34758/31590.

8   Andrews v. Law Society of British Columbia, [1989]1 S.C.R. 143, on appeal from [1986] 4 W.W.R. 242.

9   Law Society of Upper Canada v. Skapinker, [1984] 1 S.C.R. 357.

10   A.-.G. Can. v. Lavell and Isaac v. Bédard, [1974] S.C.R. 1349.

11   Bliss v. A.-G. Can., [1979] 1 S.C.R. 183.

12   Plessy v. Ferguson (1896), 163 US 537.

13   Brown v. Board of Education (1954), 347 US 483.

14   Law Society of British Columbia v. Andrews, [1989] 1 S.C.R. 143, para. 28.

15   Ibid., para. 34.

16   Ibid.

17   Regina v. Turpin, [1989] 1 S.C.R. 1296

18   Ibid., p. 1329.

19   Ibid., p. 1333.

20   Reference re Bill 30, An Act to Amend the Education Act (Ont.), [1987] 1 S.C.R. 1148, on appeal from(1986), 53 OR (2d) SB.

21   Tiny R. D. Sep. Sch. Trustees v. Regina, [1928] AC 363.

22   Reference re Bill 30, An Act to Amend the Education Act (Ont.), [1987] 1 S.C.R. 1148, para. 62 and 63.

23   Borowski v. A.-G. Can, [1989] 1 S.C.R., on appeal from [1987], 4 W.W.R 385 (Saskatchewan Court of Appeal).

24   Minister of Justice (Can.) v. Borowski, [1981] 2 S.C.R. 575.

25   Kirk Makin, "Murder of aged could be next, anti-abortion lawyer tells court," *Globe and Mail*, Oct. 5, 1988, A1.

26   Factum of the Women's Legal Education and Action Fund (LEAF) submitted to the Supreme Court of Canada in the case of Minister of Justice (Can.) v. Borowski, para. 49 ff. Accessed August 11, 2014. http://leaf.ca/wordpress/wp-content/uploads/2013/02/1989-borowski.pdf.

27   Minister of Justice (Can.) v. Borowski, op. cit., p. 31.

28   Kirk Makin, "Supreme Court refuses to rule on fetus rights," *Globe and Mail*, March 10, 1989, p. A1.

29   Tremblay v. Daigle, [1989] 2 S.C.R. 530.

30   The Canadian Civil Liberties Association, the Canadian Abortion Rights Action League, the Women's Legal Education and Action Fund, and the Attorney General of Canada argued on behalf of Daigle. REAL Women of Canada, the Campaign Life Coalition, the Canadian Physicians for Life, and the Association des médecins du Québec pour le respect de la vie supported Tremblay.

31   McKinney v. University of Guelph, (1987) 63 OR (2d) 1, 46 D.L.R. (4th) 193, 37 C.C.R. 44.

32   Ibid., p. 87.

33   McKinney v. University of Guelph, [1990] 3 S.C.R. 229.

34   The majority consisted of La Forest, Dickson, and Gonthier, with concurrence by Sopinka and Cory. The dissenters were Wilson and L'Heureux-Dubé.

35   Bhinder v. CN, [1985] 2 S.C.R. 561.

36   Ont. Human Rights Comm. v. Simpsons-Sears, [1985] 2 S.C.R. 536.

37   Bliss v. A.-G. Can., [1979] 1 S.C.R. 183.

38   Brooks v. Canada Safeway Ltd., [1989] 1 S.C.R..

39   Schachter v. Canada, [1992] 2 SCR 679.

40   Symes v. Canada, [1993] 4. S.C.R. 695.

41   Thibadeau v. Canada, [1995] 2 S.C.R. 627.

42   Ibid., p. 665.

43   Ibid., p. 628.

44   See "Thibaudeau v. Canada — 1995," Women's Legal Education and Action Fund website, accessed June 30, 2014, leaf.ca/cases/the-queen-v.-suzanne-thibaudeau/.

45 Eldridge v. British Columbia (Attorney General), [1997] 3 S.C.R. 624

46 Ibid., 625.

47 Canadian Association of the Deaf, "Health Care." Accessed August 14, 2014. www.cad.ca/health_care.php.

48 Law v. Canada (Minister of Employment and Immigration), [1999] 1 S.C.R. 497.

49 See Denise G. Reaume, "Law V. Canada (Minister of Employment and Immigration)," *Canadian Journal of Women and the Law* 18 (2006): 143. Accessed August 12, 2014, http://ssrn.com/abstract=1182627.

50 Law v. Canada, para. 9.

51 R. v. Kapp, [2008] 2 S.C.R. 483.

52 Miriam Smith, *Lesbian and Gay Rights in Canada* (Toronto: University of Toronto Press, 1999), and *Political Institutions and Lesbian and Gay Rights in the United States and Canada* (New York: Routledge, 2008).

53 Egan v. Canada, [1995] 2 S.C.R. 513.

54 Vriend v. Alberta, [1998] 1 S.C.R. 493.

55 M. v. H., [1999] 2 S.C.R. 3.

56 In the legal sense, "conjugal" refers to being in an intimate relationship, but the relationship does not necessarily have to involve sexual intercourse.

57 M. v. H., paras. 69, 70.

58 Ibid., paras. 145–147.

59 Ibid., para. 154 ff.

60 Reference re Same-Sex Marriage, [2004] 3 S.C.R. 698.

61 Ibid, para. 21.

62 Ibid., para 1.

63 Hendricks v. Québec (Procureur général), [2002] RJQ 2506; EGALE Canada Inc. v. Canada (Attorney General) [2003], 225 DLR (4th) 472, 2003 BCCA 251; Halpern v. Canada (Attorney General) [2003], 65 OR (3d) 161; Dunbar v. Yukon, [2004] YJ No. 61 (QL), 2004 YKS.C. 54; Vogel v. Canada (Attorney General), [2004] MJ No. 418 (QL) (QB); Boutilier v. Nova Scotia (Attorney General), [2004] NSJ No. 357 (QL) (SC); and N.W. v. Canada (Attorney General), [2004] SJ No. 669 (QL), 2004 SKQB 434.

64 In paragraph 68 of the Supreme Court same-sex marriage reference, op. cit., the court reviews other similar reference questions and notes that the circumstances were different enough that they could be distinguished.

65 Ibid., para. 71.

66 Ibid., para. 37 ff.

67 Ibid., paras. 56–58.

68 *CBC News*, "MPs defeat bid to reopen same-sex marriage debate," December 7, 2006. Accessed August 12, 2014. http://www.cbc.ca/news/canada/mps-defeat-bid-to-reopen-same-sex-marriage-debate-1.599856.

69 Gosselin v. Quebec (Attorney General), [2002] 4 S.C.R. 429.

70 Gosselin also claimed that the 1984 social welfare legislation violated the Quebec *Charter of Human Rights and Freedoms*, which was not affected by the Charter override. The analysis here focuses on the Canadian Charter of Rights claims.

71 Gosselin, op. cit., paras. 28–29.

72 Ibid., paras. 30–36.

73 Ibid., paras. 38, 39; emphasis in original text.

74 Ibid., paras. 37–58.

75 Ibid., paras. 59–62.

76 Ibid, paras. 63–66.

77 Ibid., para. 74.

78 Ibid., paras. 75–84. As well, McLachlin concluded that for reasons similar to those in the s. 15 analysis, there had been no violation of the Quebec *Charter of Human Rights and Freedoms* (paras. 85–96).

79 Ibid., para. 130. L'Heureux-Dubé and the other three dissenters also found that the breach of s. 15 could not be saved through a section 1 analysis.

80 Auton (Guardian *ad litem* of) v. British Columbia (Attorney General), [2004] 3 S.C.R. 657, 2004 SCC 78.

81 Ibid., para. 6.

82 Ibid., para. 11.
83 Ibid., paras. 34–38.
84 Ibid., para. 42.
85 Newfoundland (Treasury Board) v. NAPE, [2004] 3 S.C.R. 381.
86 See Ian Greene, *The Courts*, Canadian Democratic Audit series (Vancouver: UBC Press, 2006), p. 98–99 and March 12, 2003, letter from Richard Scott, Chair, Canadian Judicial Council, to Clyde Wells. Accessed August 12, 2014. https://www.cjc-ccm.gc.ca/english/news_en.asp?selMenu=news_2003_0619_c_en.asp
87 Newfoundland v. NAPE, op. cit., para. 41.
88 Ibid., para. 84.
89 Ibid., para. 105.
90 R. v. Kapp, [2008] 2 S.C.R. 483.
91 R. v. Sparrow, [1990] 1 S.C.R. 1075.
92 R. v. Kapp, op. cit., para. 11.
93 Ibid., para. 27 ff. As well, Justice Bastarache issued a separate concurring opinion in which he claimed that the pilot sales program was also constitutional pursuant to s. 25 of the *Charter*, a claim that was rejected by the other eight judges.
94 Ibid., para. 15.
95 Ibid.
96 Ibid., para. 16.
97 Ibid.
98 Ibid., para. 17.
99 Ibid., para. 19.
100 Ibid., para. 22. In footnotes, more than a dozen academic critiques of the Law test are listed, including Hogg, *Constitutional Law of Canada*, 5th ed. supplemental, vol. 2, Ch. 55.9(b).
101 Kapp, op. cit., para. 24.
102 Ibid., para. 41.
103 The court emphasized purpose over effect, because affirmative action programs might be new and therefore in need of refinement. But to ensure that governments do not try to save a deliberately discriminatory program under the guise of affirmative action, a judiciary examining an ameliorative program is urged to ask, "Was it rational for the state to conclude that the means chosen to reach its ameliorative goal would contribute to that purpose? For the distinction to be rational, there must be a correlation between the program and the disadvantage suffered by the target group." Ibid., para. 49.
104 Governments can not claim that a program intended to punish or restrict is ameliorative, and they must be able to demonstrate that the program has a reasonable chance of success. Ibid., paras. 53–54.
105 "'Disadvantage' under s. 15 connotes vulnerability, prejudice, and negative social characterization. Section 15(2)'s purpose is to protect government programs targeting the conditions of a specific and identifiable disadvantaged group, as contrasted with broad societal legislation, such as social assistance programs." Ibid., para. 55.

CHAPTER 7

1 A.-G. Que. v. Association of Quebec Protestant School Boards et al., [1984] 2 S.C.R. 66.
2 Société des Acadiens du Nouveau-Brunswick Inc. et al. v. Association of Parents for Fairness in Education et al., [1986] 1 S.C.R. 549.
3 Reference re Manitoba Language Rights (Order), [1985] 2 S.C.R. 347.
4 MacDonald v. City of Montreal et al., [1986] 1 S.C.R. 460.
5 Bilodeau v. A.-G. Man. et al., [1986] 1 S.C.R. 449.
6 Regina v. Mercure, [1988]1 S.C.R. 234.
7 A.-G. Que. v. Association of Quebec Protestant School Boards et al., [1984] 2 S.C.R. 66.
8 The Quiet Revolution began with the defeat of the ultra-conservative Union Nationale (UN) government in 1960 and its replacement by the Liberals under Jean Lesage. In 1966, the UN took power again, but was replaced by the Liberals under Robert Bourassa in 1970. In 1976, the independentist Parti Québécois gained power, and was replaced by the Liberals again in 1985.
9 Société des Acadiens du Nouveau-Brunswick Inc. et al. v. Association of Parents for Fairness in Education et al., [1986] 1 S.C.R. 549.

10   The Société des Acadiens considered that francophone students deserved their own separate classes in French according to the *Schools Act*. French immersion classes are intended to teach French to non-francophones, and so the Société considered that the quality of French instruction might be inferior to the level of French in classes intended specifically for francophones.

11   Société des Acadiens du Nouveau-Brunswick , op. cit., p. 6.

12   Ibid., p. 99.

13   Re Manitoba Language Rights, [1985] 1 S.C.R. 721.

14   Pellant v. Hebert (1981), 12 RGP 242.

15   Peter Hogg, *Constitutional Law of Canada*, 5th ed. supplemental, vol. 2, Ch. 56.4(c) and Peter Hogg, *Meech Lake Constitutional Accord Annotated* (Toronto: Carswell, 1988).

16   A.-G. Man. v. Forest, [1979] 2 S.C.R. 1032.

17   A.-G. Que. v. Blaikie (No. 1), [1979] 2 S.C.R. 1016.

18   A.-G. Que. v. Blaikie (No. 2), [1981] 1 S.C.R. 312.

19   Re: Manitoba Language Rights, op. cit., para. 107.

20   The term "little bill of rights," referring to s. 133 of the *Constitution Act, 1867*, was coined by Peter Hogg in his *Constitutional Law of Canada*, 5th ed. supplemental, vol. 2, Ch. 34.4(b).

21   MacDonald v. City of Montreal et al., [1986] 1 S.C.R. 460.

22   Bilodeau v. A.-G. Man. et al., [1986] 1 S.C.R. 449.

23   MacDonald v. City of Montreal, op cit., para. 114.

24   R. v. Mercure, [1988] 1 S.C.R. 234.

25   Mr. Justice Julien Chouinard sat on the appeal but became ill and resigned before the decision was prepared.

26   Mecure, op. cit., p. 280.

27   Ford v. A.-G. Quebec, [1988] 2 S.C.R. 712.

28   Devine v. A.-G. Quebec, [1988] 2 S.C.R. 790.

29   Mahe v. Alberta, [1990] 1 S.C.R. 342.

30   Ibid., p. 3.

31   Ibid., p. 14.

32   Ibid., pp. 34–35.

33   Ibid., pp. 39–40.

34   Ibid., p. 40.

35   Ibid., pp. 41–42.

36   Ibid., pp. 44–48.

37   Ibid., pp. 49–50.

38   Doucet-Boudreau v. Nova Scotia (Minister of Education), [2003] 3 S.C.R. 3.

39   Ibid., para. 4.

40   Ibid., para. 7.

41   Gosselin (Tutor of) v. Quebec (Attorney General), [2005] 1 S.C.R. 238.

42   Ibid., p. 3.

43   Conseil scolaire francophone de la Colombie-Britannique v. British Columbia, 2013 SCC 42.

CHAPTER 8

1   For more detailed accounts of these complex events, see Peter H. Russell, *Constitutional Odyssey: Can Canadians Become a Sovereign People?*, 3rd Edition (Toronto: University of Toronto Press, 2004), and Peter H. Russell, Rainer Knopff, Thomas M. J. Bateman, and Janet L. Hiebert, *The Court and the Constitution, Leading Cases* (Toronto: Emond Montgomery, 2008), 411.

2   These changes were accomplished through the *Constitutional Amendment Proclamation, 1983*.

3   In addition to the "seven-fifty" formula, there are four other amending formulae that apply to specific parts of the constitution. These formulae are described in Part V of the *Constitution Act, 1982*.

4   The *Indian Act* was amended in 1985 and again in 2010. See Canada, Indian and Northern Affairs Canada, René Dussault, and Georges Erasmus, Royal Commission of Aboriginal Peoples, vol. 1, "Indian Act: Indian Women," 300–302 (Ottawa: The Commission, 1996), and see Indian Affairs and Northern Development Canada, "Gender Equality in Indian Registration Act," accessed August 14, 2014, https://www.aadnc-aandc.gc.ca/eng/1308068336 912/1308068535844.

5   Calder v. Attorney-General for British Columbia [1973] S.C.R. 313, at 398.
6   Calder v. Attorney-General for British Columbia [1973] S.C.R. 313.
7   Ibid., p. 395.
8   Ibid., p. 422.
9   R. v. Sparrow, [1990] 1 S.C.R. 1075.
10 The case was heard by a panel of seven, though one member, McIntyre, retired prior to the writing of the judgment.
11 Sparrow, op. cit., p. 1103.
12 Ibid., p. 1104.
13 Ibid., p. 1105.
14 Ibid., p. 1106.
15 Ibid., p. 1093.
16 Ibid., p. 1111.
17 Ibid., p. 1112.
18 Ibid., p. 1113–1114.
19 Ibid., p. 1119.
20 R. v. Van der Peet, [1996] 2 S.C.R. 507. Also in 1996, the Supreme Court released two other decisions dealing with claims that s. 35 provided Aboriginals with rights to engage in what they claimed were traditional activities. See R. v. Gladstone, [1996] 2 S.C.R. 723, and R. v. Pamajewon, [1996] 2 W.C.R. 821.
21 Van der Peet, op. cit., para. 21, Hunter v. Southam and Big M Drug Mart specifically cited.
22 Ibid., para. 23–25.
23 Ibid., para. 42, quoting Brian Slattery, "The Legal Basis of Aboriginal Title," in Frank Cassidy, ed., Aboriginal Title in British Columbia: Delgamuukw v. The Queen (1992), at pp. 120–21.
24 Ibid., para. 43.
25 Ibid., para. 46.
26 Ibid., para. 49, quoting in part from Sparrow, p. 1112.
27 Ibid., para. 68.
28 Delgamuukw. v. British Columbia, [1997] 3 S.C.R. 1010.
29 Section 92(5) of the Constitution Act, 1867 gives the provinces jurisdiction over "The Management and Sale of the Public Lands belonging to the Province and of the Timber and Wood thereon," and s. 109 states that "All Lands, Mines, Minerals and Royalties belonging to the several Provinces of Canada . . . at the Union . . . shall belong to the several Provinces . . . subject to . . . any Interest other than that of the Province in the same." In the provinces, all "Crown lands" are therefore provincial property.
30 Russell et al., 2008, p. 424.
31 A House is a group of clans united under a chief.
32 Delgamuukw, paras. 5–6.
33 Gitxsan Treaty Office, "Delgamuukw — A Community Struggle for Aboriginal Title," accessed July 21, 2014, http://www.upperskeena.ca/vmc/english/index.htm.
34 Delgamuukw, para. 84.
35 Ibid., para. 93.
36 Ibid., paras. 106–107.
37 Ibid., para. 186.
38 Ibid., para. 117.
39 Ibid., para. 115.
40 Ibid., para. 128. On this point, La Forest and L'Heureux-Dubé would have restricted the use of title lands to "part of the aboriginal society's traditional way of life" (para. 190 ff.).
41 Ibid., paras. 161–166. Emphasis was in the original text of the decision.
42 Ibid., para. 165.
43 Ibid., paras. 170–171
44 Ibid., para.172 ff.
45 Updates on the progress of negotiations are published by the British Columbia Treaty Commission at http://www.bctreaty.net/index.php.
46 Russell et al., The Court and the Constitution (2008), p. 424.
47 R. v. Marshall, [1999] 3 S.C.R. 456, and R. v. Marshall, [1999] 3 S.C.R. 533.
48 Sandra Martin, "The Life and Death of Donald Marshall Jr.," Globe and Mail, Aug. 6, 2009, accessed July 21, 2014, http://www.theglobeandmail.com/news/national/the-life-and-death-

of-donald-marshall-jr/article4283981/?page=2. The circumstances of Marshall's wrongful conviction led to a Commission of Inquiry, which made a number of recommendations to improve Nova Scotia's justice system.

49 Ibid.

50 See Russell et al., *The Court and the Constitution (2008)*, p. 440.

51 See William C. Wicken, *Mi'kmaq Treaties on Trial: History, Land and Donald Marshall Junior* (Toronto: University of Toronto Press, 2002).

52 See Stephen Patterson, "The Marshall Decision as Seen by an 'Expert Witness,'" *Canada Watch* 8, no. 1–3 (Sept.–Oct. 2000): 57.

53 R. v. Marshall, [1999] 3 S.C.R. 456, para. 56. The Badger test is a more recent refinement of the Sparrow test regarding the conditions under which governments can legitimately regulate Aboriginal rights. See R. v. Badger, [1996] 1 S.C.R. 771.

54 Ibid., para. 59.

55 Ibid., para 66.

56 *CBC News Online*, "The Marshall Decision," May 9, 2004, accessed July 21, 2014, http://www.cbc.ca/news2/background/fishing/marshall.html.

57 R. v. Marshall, [1999] 3 S.C.R. 533.

58 R. v. Marshall; R. v. Bernard, [2005] 2 S.C.R. 220, 2005 SCC 43.

59 Haida Nation v. British Columbia (Minister of Forests), [2004] 3 S.C.R. 511, 2004.

60 Until 2010, these islands were officially known as the Queen Charlotte Islands. In 2010, the name was changed to Haida Gwaii as part of reconciliation agreement between the Haida and the BC government.

61 Haida Nation, op. cit., paras. 6–7.

62 Ibid., para. 10.

63 *Prima facie* is a term that refers to sufficient evidence to credibly support a claim, even though the claim has not been finally determined.

64 Haida Nation, op. cit., paras. 47–48.

65 Ibid., para. 9 ff.

66 Ibid., para. 39.

67 Ibid., para. 72 ff.

68 Tsilhqot'in Nation v. British Columbia, [2014] SCC 44.

69 The Supreme Court was short one judge because of litigation over the legitimacy of the federal government's appointment of Marc Nadon to the Supreme Court to fill a Quebec vacancy.

70 Tsilhqot'in Nation, op. cit., para. 7.

71 Ibid., para. 14.

72 Ibid., para. 25.

73 Haida Nation, op. cit., para. 37.

74 Tsilhqot'in Nation, op. cit., paras. 79–80.

75 Ibid., para. 97.

76 Ibid., para. 151.

77 "B.C. First Nations Take Action on Top Court's Land-Title Ruling," *Globe and Mail*, July 11, 2014, A4.

78 Grassy Narrows First Nation v. Ontario (Natural Resources), [2014] SCC 48.

79 Ibid., para. 1.

80 Ibid., para. 2.

81 Ibid., paras. 51–52.

82 Vincent Donovan, "High Court Rulings Could Cause Ripple Effects," *Toronto Star*, July 12, 2014, A9.

83 In British Columbia, there have been some successes in reconciling Aboriginal perspectives with government objectives. See Tony Penikett, *Reconciliation: First Nations Treaty Making in British Columbia* (Vancouver: Douglas & McIntyre, 2006).

84 Tom Flanagan and Ravina Bains, "Title's True Meaning: Billable hours," *Globe and Mail*, July 16, 2014, A 13.

CHAPTER 9

1 Paul M. Sniderman, *Personality and Democratic Politics* (Berkeley: University of California Press, 1975).

2   See Paul M. Sniderman, Joseph F. Fletcher, Peter H. Russell, and Phillip E. Tetlock, *The Clash of Rights: Liberty, Equality, and Legitimacy in Pluralist Democracy* (New Haven, CT: Yale University Press, 1996), Ch. 8, "Value Pluralism."

3   See, for example, C. B. Macpherson, *The Real World of Democracy* (Concord, Ont.: Anansi, 1992).

4   Statistics Canada, "French and the *francophonie* in Canada: Language, 2011 Census of Population," Catalogue no. 98-314-X2011003. Retrieved August 30, 2014. http://www12. statcan.gc.ca/census-recensement/2011/as-sa/98-314-x/98-314-x2011003_1-eng.cfm. In Alberta, the proportion of people reporting French as their mother tongue increased 18 percent between 2006 and 2011.

5   Ibid. The proportion of francophones in Quebec has remained relatively stable.

6   Gosselin (Tutor of) v. Quebec (Attorney General), [2005] 1 S.C.R. 238.

7   Black v. Law Society of Alberta, [1989] 1 S.C.R. 591.

8   Abdelrazik v. Canada, [2009] FC 580 (FC)

9   F. L. Morton, "The Political Impact of the Canadian Charter of Rights and Freedoms," *Canadian Journal of Political Science* 20, no. 1 (March 1987): 31–55, at p. 32.

10   See André Picard, "How the advent of AIDS advanced gay rights," *Globe and Mail*, Aug 15, 2014. Accessed August 31, 2014. http://www.theglobeandmail.com/life/health-and-fitness/ health/how-the-advent-of-aids-advanced-gay-rights/article20083869/?page=all.

11   Hon. Marc Rosenberg, "Twenty-Five Years Later: The Impact of the *Canadian Charter of Rights and Freedoms* on the Criminal Law," *Supreme Court Law Review* 45, 2nd Series (2009). Accessed September 1, 2014. http://www.ontariocourts.ca/coa/en/ps/publications/twenty- five_years_later.htm

12   James B. Kelly, "The *Charter of Rights and Freedoms* and the Rebalancing of Liberal Constitutionalism in Canada, 1982–1997," *Osgoode Hall Law Journal* 37, no. 3: 625–695, at p. 648 and 657. The cases analyzed by Kelly included all cases dealing with the *Charter of Rights*, Aboriginal rights in s. 35 of the *Constitution Act, 1982*, and language rights in sections 93 and 133 of the *Constitution Act, 1867*. Over time, the proportion of legal rights issues dealt with by the Supreme Court has been declining because of issues being settled.

13   See Kent Roach, "Four Models of the Criminal Process," *Journal of Criminal Law and Criminology* 89, no. 2 (1999): 671.

14   See Ian Greene, Carl Baar, Peter McCormick, George Szablowski and Martin Thomas, *Final Appeal: Decision-making in Canadian Courts of Appeal* (Toronto: Lorimer, 1998).

15   R. v. Oakes, [1986] 1 S.C.R. 103, at p. 136.

16   See Carole Pateman, *Participation and Democratic Theory* (Cambridge: Cambridge University Press, 1970).

17   Patrick Monahan, *Politics and the Constitution: The Charter, Federalism and the Supreme Court of Canada* (Toronto: Carswell, 1987).

18   Brian J. Slattery, "A Theory of the Charter," *Osgoode Hall Law Journal* 25 (1987): 701.

19   Section 4.1 (1) of the *Department of Justice Act* reads as follows: ". . . [T]he Minister shall, in accordance with such regulations as may be prescribed by the Governor in Council, examine every regulation transmitted to the Clerk of the Privy Council for registration pursuant to the *Statutory Instruments Act* and every Bill introduced in or presented to the House of Commons by a minister of the Crown, in order to ascertain whether any of the provisions thereof are inconsistent with the purposes and provisions of the *Canadian Charter of Rights and Freedoms* and the Minister shall report any such inconsistency to the House of Commons at the first convenient opportunity. *Department of Justice Act*, R.S.C., 1985, c. J-2.

20   James B. Kelly, *Governing with the Charter: Legislative and Judicial Activism and Framers' Intent* (Vancouver: UBC Press, 2005).

21   Sean Fine, "Tory crime bill endangered after Senate debates wrong version," *Globe and Mail*, August 28 2014, p. A1.

22   James Kelly, "The *Charter of Rights and Freedoms* and the Rebalancing of Liberal Constitutionalism," op. cit., p. 654.

23   Peter H. Russell, "Canada's Charter of Rights and Freedoms: A Political Report," *Public Law* (UK), 1988: 385.

24   James Kelly, "The *Charter of Rights and Freedoms* and the Rebalancing of Liberal Constitutionalism," op. cit., p. 648.

25   Regina v. Edwards Books and Art Ltd., [1986] 2 S.C.R. 713.

26   I have collected the complete supreme court records of more than thirty Supreme Court decisions on the Charter from 1984 to 2014. These complete records contain all of the evidence presented to judges beginning with the original trial, through to the provincial court of appeal, and finally at the Supreme Court.

27   Ell v. Alberta, [2003] 1 S.C.R. 857, 2003 SCC 35. I was an expert for the Alberta crown, which won in the Supreme Court.

28   Daniel Schwartz, "Charter of Rights turns Canada into a 'constitutional' trendsetter," *CBC News*, April 16, 2012. Accessed September 2, 2014. http://www.cbc.ca/news/canada/charter-of-rights-turns-canada-into-a-constitutional-trendsetter-1.1216350; and John Ibbitson, "The Charter proves to be Canada's gift to world," *Globe and Mail*, April 15, 2012. Accessed September 2, 2014. http://www.theglobeandmail.com/news/politics/the-charter-proves-to-be-canadas-gift-to-world/article4100561/.

INDEX